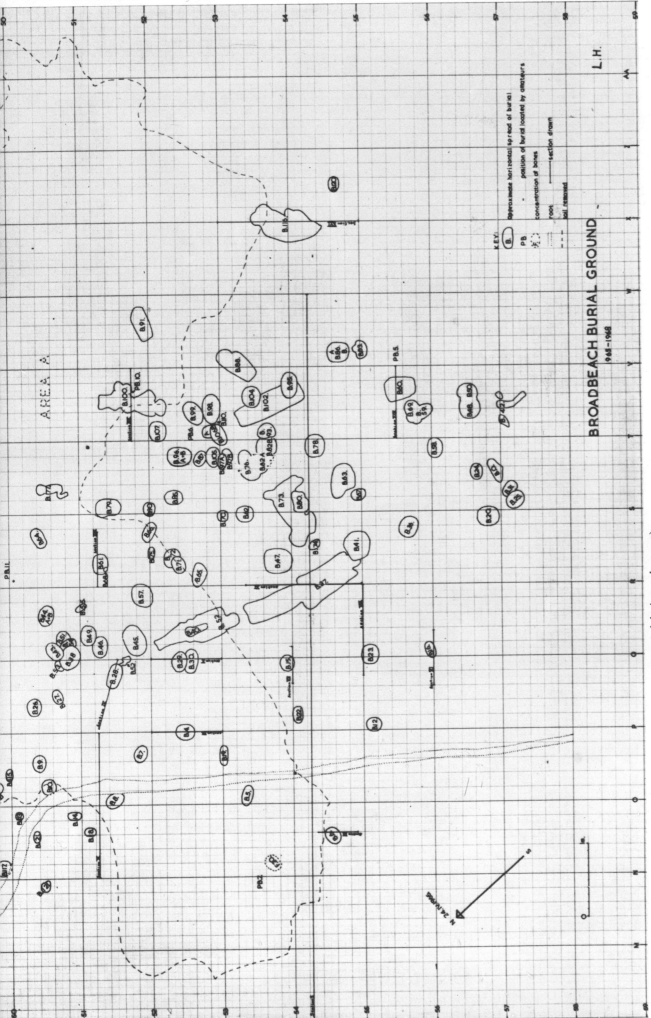

Map 12.   Broadbeach burial ground: distribution of burials (inset: areas excavated during each season).

An archaeological analysis
of the Broadbeach Aboriginal
burial ground

An archaeological analysis of the Broadbeach Aboriginal burial ground

Laila Haglund

University of Queensland Press

© University of Queensland Press, St. Lucia, Queensland, 1976

Printed and bound by Dai Nippon Printing Co. (HK) Ltd., Hong Kong

Distributed in the United Kingdom, Europe, the Middle East, Africa, and the Caribbean by Prentice-Hall International, International Book Distributors Ltd., 66 Wood Lane End, Hemel Hempstead, Herts., England

National Library of Australia
Cataloguing-in-publication data

Haglund, Laila
    An archaeological analysis of the Broadbeach
    Aboriginal burial gound.

    Bibliography.
    ISBN 0 7022 0860 4.

    1. Aborigines, Australian — Antiquities. 2. Burial.
    I. Title.

994.004991

"The state of man does change and vary,
now sound, now sick, now blyth, now sary,
now dansand mirry, now like to die:-
Timor Mortis conturbat me."

William Dunbar, "Lament for the Makers"

Contents

Illustrations and Tables

PLATES

Stone artifacts

TABLES

Preface

The excavation of Broadbeach Aboriginal Burial Ground described in this report was carried out over a period of three years between April 1965 and August 1968. We spent six seasons of two to three weeks each in the field. The material recovered consists of a large number of human skeletons and a considerable amount of associated artifacts and food debris. At the end of 1968 the results of the first four seasons were presented as an M.A. thesis to the University of Queensland. The emphasis in the thesis was on tracing patterns and details of burial rites, and the typology of the associated lithic material was discussed mainly in relation to these. Some aspects and lines of argument which were explored in great detail in the thesis and which have since been shown to be irrelevant or misleading have been left out or only briefly referred to in this report. The same applies to some lists and appendices which would be of interest only to somebody restudying the material. There are copies of the thesis available in the libraries of the University of Queensland and the Australian Institute of Aboriginal Studies in Canberra.

In this report I shall try to describe the whole volume of material recovered, from as many aspects as possible at present. The anatomical study has not, however, been completed. Dr. W. B. Wood, lecturer in anatomy at the University of Queensland, took part in the first seasons of excavation, visited us during later seasons, and has done a preliminary analysis of much of the skeletal material, mainly that of adults. He is now working on a detailed analysis of the whole corpus of material. It is likely that when this has been finished it will be possible to say more about burial rites and traditions. It seems foolish, however, to further postpone the publication of the main archaeological material and the preliminary anatomical analysis. The detailed anatomical analysis will probably be published as a series of journal articles. I hope to be able to follow these up with an article commenting on any new data of archaeological importance extracted from the skeletal material.

Other specialists have analyzed animal bones, shells, rocks, etc.; their reports are included as appendices.

There are several points about this excavation that I would like to emphasize in this Preface since they may have affected the quality of the work and hence of the results. Details will be given later in the report itself.

The work on the site started ten years ago. At that time there was no legislation to protect Aboriginal relics. The existence of an Aboriginal burial ground here was not known to local Aborigines nor was any record of it to be found. The bones of Aborigines along with the soil around them were spread over gardens on the Gold Coast to fertilize the soil. The soil contractors neither had nor asked permission from the landowner to remove soil from the ridge and there was no way of stopping them, bar placing a permanent guard on the site; and nobody would have paid the salary of a guard. The difficulties of guarding the site were made clear to us in quite drastic ways while we were working there.

It was a rescue excavation. We had no means of protecting the site once it was known. On the other hand, we could only work during university vacations when volunteers were available. This meant that we had to push on and excavate even when we would have preferred to first spend more time assessing the material already recovered to find problems and aspects that might be usefully concentrated on during another season. It meant that we had to work regardless of the weather which was often very wet and which certainly on occasion led to loss of information.

For most seasons I was the only person present with archaeological training or any experience of excavation work. This meant that during the earlier seasons, as I had to supervise all aspects of the work all the time, only a small work force could be employed. In later seasons when our student helpers had gained experience and we had some experienced helpers from the University of Sydney as well, it was possible to employ more people and work much faster. Inevitably the lack of experience of the work force during earlier seasons resulted in mistakes being made and some details of burials and stratigraphy not being noted.

As there was no tradition of organized archaeological fieldwork or associated studies in Queensland, we started with the bare rudiments of equipment. Although this had little effect on the quality of the work, it kept the rate of progress slow. The Australian bush tradition of ingenuity and the possibilities of fencing wire were most impressively displayed by Dr. Wood and some of the students. In time we built up a good store of equipment. More serious was the difficulty at that stage of finding specialists in other fields, especially the natural sciences, who could be persuaded, or who could find time, even if willing, to advise on and study such things as the environmental aspects of the burial ground.

We all did our best, however, and I would like to thank all those who helped to make it possible to recover this anatomical material and so much of its archaeological context.

First, I would like to thank all those students who so cheerfully and faithfully worked under what were often very difficult conditions. Dr. W.B. Wood handled the anatomical studies during the first seasons and worked out the method of recording such details for each burial. Any archaeologist who has worked on burials will know what it means to be able to turn to an anatomist in the field for advice. Dr. M.J.C. Calley patiently helped us with the problems of administration and practical organization as well as much constructive criticism.

I am also most grateful to the late Vice-Chancellor of the University of Queensland, Sir Fred Schonell, for his personal interest and support; to Dr. A. Bartholomai, director of the Queensland Museum, for his assistance in studying the animal remains from the site; to the Geological Survey of Queensland for analyzing soil samples and allowing me to reproduce a resulting graph; and to Professor P. Lawrence, Dr. I. McBryde, Dr. D.J. Mulvaney, Judith and John Clegg, and Ms. B. Meehan for constructive criticism of both form and content of my reports on the work.

The land on which the burial ground was found belongs to Mermaid Keys Development Pty. Ltd., a subsidiary of Alfred Grant Pty. Ltd. Mr. Grant has been most understanding and helpful, giving us immediate permission to excavate and allowing us to keep the site open for several years.

The Australian Institute of Aboriginal Studies in Canberra and the University of Queensland contributed to the excavation expenses and encouraged me, with research grants, to write up this material as soon as possible.

Finally I would like to mention that this report was accepted for publication in 1972. For some time, however, it seemed that a book like this might be offensive to members of the local Aboriginal community and publication was shelved. There has now been much more dialogue between Aborigines and archaeologists about such matters, and I hope this book will be accepted as an interesting document which throws light on some aspects of the complex culture of the Aborigines in the Brisbane area. I know from many discussions that their descendants have a keen interest in this.

Much has happened in the archaeological field in Australia since 1972. It has not been possible to incorporate more than brief references to the most important findings. A detailed revision would have meant another great delay in publication.

Sydney, August 1975   Laila Haglund

CHAPTER 1

The burial ground

This chapter deals with the recent history of the site and the theoretical and practical approach to the problems of its excavation. (The excavation techniques are described in detail, Appendix F.) As many statements have to remain hypothetical because of the unusual character of the site, I would like to make clear the kind of evidence on which they are based.

History of the site

The site at Broadbeach was accidentally discovered early in June 1963[1] by a group of local soil contractors who were removing soil for sale as lawn top-dressing without the consent or knowledge of the owner of the land. They were also digging up human bones. This fact became known and was eventually reported to the police. A group of local people interested in recording and preserving antiquities in the area suggested that the burials were Aboriginal and were allowed to be present at the subsequent police investigations. They recorded and photographed these proceedings, and after the police had satisfied themselves that the bones were Aboriginal, they located a few more burials by probing. We were able to use some of the information collected on this occasion; the details are given in Appendix D. Some burials that were found by probing, but not removed, we later excavated.

The anthropology section of the department of psychology at the University of Queensland was notified but at that time was unable to exploit the information. Unfortunately, the individual burials recovered by the police were jumbled during transport, but the remains of about eight burials were later delivered to the department of anatomy at the University of Queensland and have now been added to the corpus of burials.

In 1965, Dr. W.B. Wood, who was looking for Queensland Aboriginal skeletal material suitable for a comparative study, heard about the site from Mr. J. Clegg, then in the department of psychology. Dr. Wood applied to the Australian Institute of Aboriginal Studies in Canberra for funds to recover the remaining burials in the site. Mr. F.D. McCarthy, principal of the institute, who knew that I had just arrived in Brisbane, suggested that Dr. Wood should ask me to take charge of the excavation, pointing out that the site was likely to be of importance because of its archaeological as well as its anatomical material.

The site

The burial ground is located about 1.5 kilometres inland from the present-day coastline at Mermaid Beach, southeast Queensland (map 1).[1] The coastal stretch in this area consists of a sandy beach, 60 metres wide in places, running almost due north from rocky outcrops at South Nobby and Burleigh Heads, terminating in a spit, formed by the northward drift of sand, which keeps turning the mouth of the Nerang River to the north (map 1). Behind the foredune is a well-developed series of parallel dunes with seams of mineral sands. Still further inland is the lower part of the coastal plain, consisting of broad sandy flats and swamps, and narrow belts of swamp alternating with low sand ridges. The latter curve in the same way as the parallel beach dunes.[2]

The almost flat top of one of these narrow ridges became the burial ground. The highest point of this is about 4 metres above sea level and only about 1 − 1.5 metres above the surrounding low-lying, marshy area (map 1). The uppermost part of the western slope is fairly abrupt, the eastern seaward slope more gradual. The sand forming the ridge is pale yellow, very well sorted, and extremely fine-grained (Appendix A). Tests with an auger showed the same pattern down to at least 4 metres below the top of the ridge. The ground-water level was then, after a long dry spell, at 3.6 metres below the top of the ridge.

Soil development is poor, consisting of a weak podsol down to about 1.2 metres below the thin turf cover (fig. 5). Where the soil is not disturbed by burials, activities connected with burials, and/or modern interference, there is a steady decrease in acidity from the slightly acid turf-level to the neutral parent sand at the base (Appendix A).

There is a small brackish stream 500 metres to the east, another − now a canal − the same distance to the north; a loop of the main Nerang River comes within 1.5 kilometres of the site to the northwest. The marshland is still very extensive.

Modern vegetation is sparse, consisting mainly of grass and bracken with scattered *Eucalyptus, Banksia,* and *Melaleuca* trees. The trees are in several cases clearly ring-barked; some of these are very big (fig. 1). The area has been cleared for grazing but was once under rain forest.[3] The evidence from animal bones found in the site suggests that this may have been the case when the ridge was used as a burial ground although animals of many different environments are represented.

The faunal remains (Appendix B) consist mainly of marsupials, especially large bandicoots and pademelons. There are few remains of reptiles in the site, a kind of carpet snake being most common; fishbones are present but rare, and birds are absent. The animals represented are all still present in southeast Queensland. Only native animal remains were found in the site; one bullock tooth came from the upper part of the disturbed soil in area A and was probably due to recent grazing. Almost all bone fragments are clearly food remains and belong to the period of the burial ground. This is indicated by their usually intimate association with the burials. (It is unlikely that the site was ever used as a campsite, see pp. 34–38.)

There were no surface indications of the site. Since the stump of a very massive tree, identified as a Forest Red Gum *(Eucalyptus tereticornis,* fig. 1), dominates the western border of the burial ground (map 2), sending its roots through it, local enthusiasts

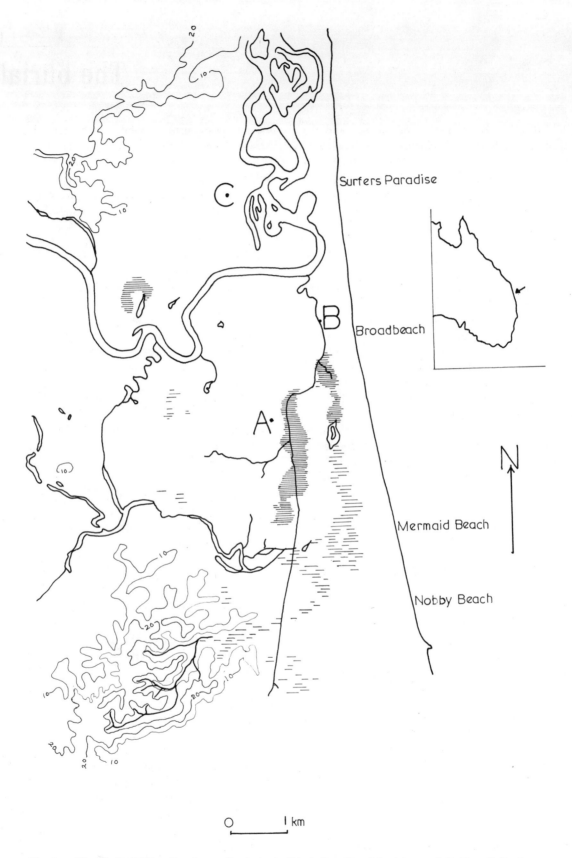

Surfers Paradise

Broadbeach

Mermaid Beach

Nobby Beach

N

O   1 km

Map 1.   The Southport-Broadbeach area (inset: Australia). **A**, Broadbeach burial ground; **B**, Cascade Gardens midden; **C**, Bundall burial ground.

Fig.1. Area C disturbance in foreground. Datum point on tall dead tree to the left. The large burnt stump to the right is the Forest Red Gum. Typical vegetation: grass and bracken, few trees. Camera facing southwest.

romantically suggested that this tree, obviously once very impressive, would be a possible reason for selecting this particular spot. This is impossible, however, for reasons discussed in chapter 3. The burial ground is very much older than the tree.

Approach to and scope of the excavation

It was clearly not only desirable to recover this skeletal material for study, but also urgent, if it were not to be lost forever. There were many reasons that prevented us from setting aside and preserving part of the burial ground for future excavation and study. The land is to be developed in the way typical of the area, that is, canals will be dug, and the sand removed used to build up the level of the adjacent land to make it suitable for building purposes. No legislation to protect Aboriginal antiquities existed until our work was almost completed, and even if it had, it would not have been very useful in this case. Since there are no surface indications of the presence of burials, it would have been difficult to suggest a reasonable area for resumption by the Crown without extensive test excavations.[4] Such excavations would certainly have accelerated the decay and erosion of the rest of the site. If an area had been resumed, it would still have been almost impossible at that stage to prevent vandalism. There are no houses nearby, the burials were close to the surface, the ground soft, and the area part of the belt of unofficial rubbish dumps encircling most Australian communities. Even had the Aboriginal Relics Preservation Act of 1967 been in

force when we started this excavation, it is doubtful whether the site would have been protected by it. It takes years before the general public becomes aware of legislation of this kind and of the severe penalties to which the vandal, if identified, is liable.[5]

As much of the burial ground as possible had to be excavated urgently. Much damage was done between our seasons in the field. Pauses were unavoidable, since neither the students nor the leaders of the excavation were available during term-time. The landowners put up a barbed-wire gate and a sign warning trespassers. The gate was cut and broken, the sign torn down. We erected a fence of steel posts and wire around the area being excavated. When we returned for another season, the wire had been cut and the posts stolen. We tried shoring up the sides of our trenches to reduce erosion damage between seasons but curious visitors removed the boards and scrabbled behind them, causing more damage than natural erosion would.

There was also, until the Aboriginal Relics Preservation Act came into force, a very real danger that some unqualified enthusiasts would start looting the site to get human bones for their private collections. We tried to keep the location of the site secret to avoid hordes of tourists, as it is close to the popular resorts on the Gold Coast. The secrecy, however, resulted in many local rumours about treasures to be found and there were even local opportunists seeking miners' rights over the area.

There was also the aspect of conservation. It seemed quite clear that the burials were deteriorating more rapidly each year. At least two factors could be identified. The road running just west of the ridge, only 12 to 13 metres away, is now being used by many trucks which thunder past at great speed. Every time this happens the whole ridge vibrates noticeably. Since many of the burials were very fragile and already cracking because of root penetration and chemical processes, the vibrations were gradually shaking them to powder. The volume of traffic has increased appreciably each season we have spent there.

A second factor was recognized when, during one of our seasons, we found many curl-grubs — larvae of Christmas Beetles (*Anaplognathus*) — feeding on the bony table of some burials.[6] Figures 2 and 24 show good examples of the result, the erosion of the bone at first sight suggesting an advanced stage of tertiary syphilis. It is possible that their presence, apparently recent, is the result of some slight change in the ecology of the site.

One possible advantage to be derived from a total excavation was that this might result in a large and perhaps fairly complete population sample. Any statistical inferences would thus be more soundly based. Since it was, to our knowledge, the first large Aboriginal burial ground to be scientifically excavated in Australia, a total excavation would indicate the range of differences one might expect to find in such a site and whether a partial excavation could be expected to give an accurate picture of a whole site.[7] The results from Broadbeach should be of relevance to neighbouring areas at least.

We found a large area (map 12, area C, and fig. 1) cleared down to pale sterile sand. A few dark stains with some fragments of bone and loose teeth, the last traces of former burial pits, suggested that as much as one-quarter of the burial ground might have been removed

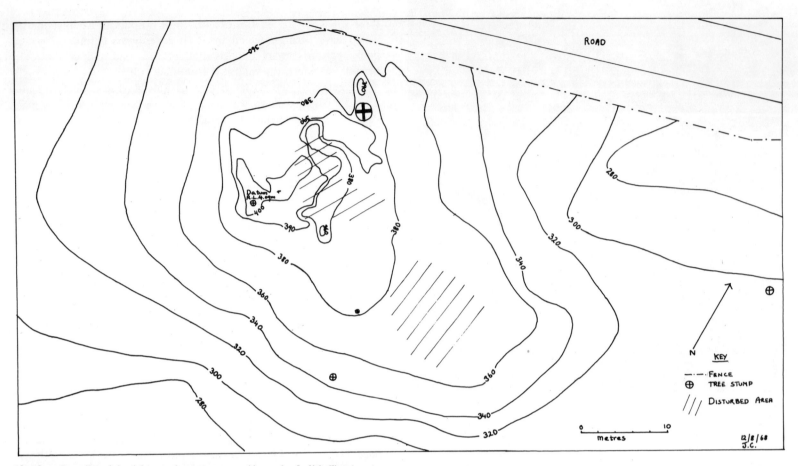

Map 2.   Broadbeach burial ground: contour map (drawn by Judith Clegg).

Fig.2. B.5 after lift 13. Note effect of larval attack on pelvis (B5/011). Camera facing south.

before our excavations started. Out of 228 square metres excavated, only 148 remained undisturbed by modern interference. The disturbance was concentrated to the burial area (the flat top of the ridge). In area A, however, it was more shallow and according to local information had taken place two or three years prior to our first season. Much or most of the topsoil above the shell horizon (pp. 34–39), and sometimes even the shell horizon itself, had been removed. Some disturbance below this level resulted from the removal of eight burials during the police investigation (figs. 3 and 4). There was, when we started, a good turf cover all over this area. Area B suffered a more drastic disturbance — and more tragic in that it took place within the ten days between my first seeing the site and the start of the excavations — for at least seven more burials were destroyed and probably others removed without leaving a trace. We met the culprit, a soil contractor running a one-man firm, but it was impossible to extract any useful information from him about the burials that he had dug into.

Excavation: plan and problems

The site was laid out in a grid; the sides of each square were 1 metre long and the diagonals of the grid ran approximately north, south, east, and west (map 12). Each square was named after the grid-lines forming its northwest and southwest borders. The squares were excavated in the order indicated on map 12, inset A. We started

Fig.3. Modern pit, dug with small entrenching tool during police investigations. Filled in by silting. Camera facing south.

Fig.4. B.131, slightly damaged vertical bundle. Note modern pit to the left. Camera facing west.

in two different parts of the burial ground, part of the team salvaging what remained of the disturbed burials protruding in area B, the rest starting at line J and working towards the southeast. The main section (fig. 5) was taken along the southwest face of the balk in squares J to W 55, i.e. 25 centimetres southwest of line 54. Erosion between seasons made it necessary to break the section after square V 55 but, fortunately, the section had already cut through a number of the stratigraphically most important burials.

Since we wanted stratigraphical and other archaeological evidence as well as burials, if at all possible, we turned first to the relatively undisturbed area just southwest of the very disturbed part from which burials had already come. Line J was selected as the starting point since this was the end of the abrupt part of the western and shorter slope. All burials already found had come from the top of the ridge and in such a low-lying area it seemed reasonable to expect them to be confined to the highest and driest spots. This turned out to be the case, not one burial so far having been found beyond the flat top of the ridge. (Compare maps 12 and 2; contour line 380 encloses almost all the burials found.) Time being short, we were gratified to find that this approach led straight into the densest part of the burial ground and that only a minimum of time had been spent on sterile squares.[8] Once this undisturbed area had been explored to its southwest border, we could turn to the northeast and tackle the disturbed part, making use of the knowledge of burial types, features, and stratigraphical relationships already gained.

Where there were burials, they were very close together, particularly in the central area (figs. 6 and 69). Two square metres

without any bones are probably a reliable indication that the border of the burial ground has been reached. A number of test pits were dug outside the estimated borders and none of these contained any burials.

Balks of 25 centimetres were left unless the position and angle of a burial demanded otherwise. Two levels were recognized in each square, level one containing all material from the turf to the base of the shell horizon, level two all material below this except for what was contained in a definite burial pit, which would be kept separate. Where possible, these levels were subdivided. The work progressed in spits 2 - 4 centimetres thick depending on and following minor horizons and lenses and taking into account the outlines of each pit. The major division was useful in comparing objects from a similar stratigraphic position over such a wide area. The ridge was almost undifferentiated, but the lower border of the shell horizon was always made the border of one spit.[9] The consistency of the sand made excavation difficult. As long as the sand was uniformly wet from the surface down into the sterile base, it was possible to think of leaving balks standing and of exposing fairly large vertical sections. It was usually dry, however, and then very loose, particularly below the topsoil, where it was no longer held together by roots, rootlets, and fine particles. It was often impossible to have a vertical face of more than 30 or 40 centimetres, or to leave this for more than a few hours, since beyond and after this the pressure from above and the increasing dryness would cause the sand at the base to trickle out, undermining the face and causing eventual collapse. The risk of this was increased when there had been a short shower in generally dry

KEY:

	turf		shells
	dark		bone
	sand		stone
	pale		find
	roots		burial
	charcoal		

SECTION I

L.H.

Fig.5. Section I (main section). Note how burial pits and general disturbance interfered with soil development southeast of line M.

weather. The rain would penetrate only the top layer of roots and humus and make this even heavier. Most sections were drawn piece by piece as they emerged, having been photographed first to ensure some pictorial record.

Most burials consisted of vertical bone bundles, sometimes 50 - 60 centimetres tall (chapter 2). As a result, the conflict between the requirements of the archaeologist and those of the anatomist was greater than usual. The former needed horizontal plans and vertical sections, big enough and clear enough to show the very subtle differences in colour and texture of the surrounding pit-fill and the original ridge (figs. 7, 8, 9, and 35). The latter needed the bones in the best possible state of preservation. As they were usually much intertwined, having been tightly packed before burial, the bundle had to be supported nearly all way round while they were freed. Fragile bones had to be hardened and left to dry (fig. 10). Lifting the bones was a serious game of Fiddlesticks, the possible repercussions of lifting any one bone having to be thought out well beforehand. A few very typical and very closely packed burials were hardened and lifted in toto for subsequent cleaning in the laboratory. The same was done to some clumps of very fragmentary bone, but the use of preservatives was avoided as much as possible since it would preclude the possibility of radiocarbon and some other tests later on.

These many unusual factors made it necessary to adapt some excavation techniques to our own requirements and to invent new ones to cope with our special problems. Though most of these are

Fig.6. Cluster of burials: B.103, B.108, B.109, all buried in separate pits. Note compactness of B.103 and serial vertebrae in B.109. Camera facing northeast.

Fig.7. B.28, a typical vertical bundle-burial. Note shell pocket on periphery of pit-surface, slight difference in colour between pit-fill and surrounding ridge, skull jammed between upper ends of long bones, mandible arched below skull. Camera facing east-north-east.

Fig.8. B.56, a vertical bundle-burial in section. Note thinness of vault, subtle differences in colour between pit-fill and surrounding matrix. Camera facing northeast.

Fig.9. B.123 showing in section. Note similar colouring of bone matrix and ridge. Camera facing north.

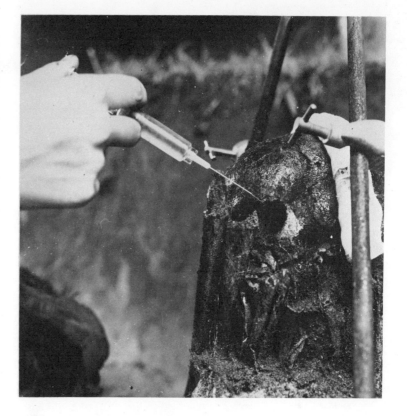

Fig.10. Use of syringe to apply PVA.

very simple, they will be described in full in Appendix F, as they may be useful to others confronted with this type of site. The description may also indicate to readers how much — or how little — reliance to place on the conclusions drawn.

With only one trained archaeologist present and a completely inexperienced work force, none of the recording of the work could be delegated, until, after the first seasons, some students had enough experience to undertake keeping complete and accurate lists of finds and photographs. Such a large number of burials entailed recording a large number of facts. To avoid chance forgetfulness, standard burial forms were prepared, listing the main and recurrent questions to be answered. The student learnt to look for and remember the answers for the burial on which he was working until they could be recorded. Unusual facts, general observations, and day to day progress I described in a field journal. Each burial was given a name by its finder. This proved safer than using numbers only, since one could be certain that instructions given were applied to the right burial, once this had individuality. Work on any one burial was as far as possible carried out by the same person from beginning to end. The attachment each worker formed to "his" burial produced marvels of patience and skill.

Drawing was largely but not completely replaced by photography, and was mainly used for recording sections rather than the position of bones in burials. The drawing of a section may take hours but does make it possible to emphasize features which are noticeable and recognizable to the eye but not to the camera. Usually the drawing was done by students once the important features to be shown had been pointed out to them. It would not have been safe for me to leave the progress of work unsupervised for the long periods needed for drawing. The decision to draw a burial in section seriously increased the risk of damage to the bones, especially in the case of vertical bundle-burials. The matrix of sand around the bone would dry and trickle out, leaving some bone unsupported. It also meant that one side of each bundle would have to be freed completely and left so for some time.

The decision not to draw every burial in the site was based on several considerations. Without experience and flair, it is very difficult to draw a recognizable bone. It is also very time-consuming. It would have been necessary to make multiple serial drawings in the case of a vertical or horizontal bundle-burial, although one detailed drawing can usually show all or most of the bones of an articulated horizontal burial. In the case of bundle-burials where the bones were tightly intertwined and not in anatomical relationship to each other, it was occasionally impossible for a layman to recognize and identify individual bones until they had been completely freed and lifted. (Dr. Wood could not take part in all our seasons of fieldwork.)

The method employed for recording the position of bones in each burial is described at the end of Appendix F.

CHAPTER 2

The burials

Burial types

Many different burial types and evidence of different ceremonies were found in this site. The most obvious differences were in the arrangement of bones. These differences form the basis for my categories of burial types, since many of the ceremonies discernible were applied to several of these types. The categories and subcategories are set out in table 1. I will describe them in turn.

Table 1. *Burial types*

Primary Burials	Secondary Burials

A. Extended	A. Bone bundle
	   a. vertical
	   b. horizontal

B. Partly dismantled	B. Bone parcel
C. Flexed	C. Cremation

The major distinction is between primary and secondary burials according to whether the articulated corpse or the bare bones were interred.[1] The corpse could be placed in any of several different positions and could be partly dismantled. Secondary burials have been subdivided according to how the bones were assembled and how the assemblage was placed. Further subtypes may emerge when all the bones in each burial have been studied and listed. It was noticed during the excavation that many burials lacked some bones, most frequently vertebrae and those of hands and feet. This could not have been due to decay as other bones were in a good state of preservation. We can only guess at the reason. Small bones may have been discarded or lost (if bones were carried around for a period before burial) or which bones were included in the bundle could have depended on the status of the deceased: young man, old man, woman, or child, or on the period in which the burial took place. It is possible that, when all burials have been studied in detail and the presence of particular bones subjected to statistical analysis, a pattern will emerge.

Primary burials

There were two main types of primary burials in this site, extended and flexed. The two *extended* burials, B.37 and B.52, were lying flat on their backs (figs. 11 and 12). The former had his arms parallel to the body and his legs straight, but the latter had his hands folded in over the pelvis, apparently because of B.40, a child, who was lying over his abdomen and pelvic girdle (fig. 13). B.37 was facing upwards, but his skull was tilted a little to the right; the skull of B.52 was lying on its left side. Both had most bones in the correct anatomical position so that at the time of burial ligaments, at least, must have held them together, but it is uncertain whether the bodies were fully covered with flesh. (Any displacement of bone noted could be due to shifting in loose sand or later disturbance.) The four *flexed* burials, B.73, B.77, B.100, and B.116, were lying

on one side with their knees drawn up (figs. 14, 15, and 16). The three adults all had their knees bent so acutely that the upper and lower parts of the limb were almost in contact, suggesting that they had been bound in that position after death, but the child was lying in a normal sleeping position. One hand was always close to the face, which was half resting on it, the other either near the face also, or near the pelvis. (The upper part of B.100 was somewhat twisted and her face inclined down, suggesting that she had been flung into the pit with her legs tied.)

One *unusual* primary burial, B.102, had been trussed up and butchered before burial.[3] The corpse was still articulated at that time. The upper part of the body was placed on its back (fig. 17) with the arms along the sides of the body. The skull and the upper cervical vertebrae had been cut off and placed within the thoracic cage. The pelvis and lower limbs had been separated from the upper trunk between the fourth and fifth lumbar vertebrae and the limbs then hyperflexed at the knees, so that the feet lay in front of the pelvis. The thoracic and abdominal viscera almost certainly had been removed before the burial.

Secondary burials

Most of these were bundle-burials. The corpse had, in most cases, been dismantled completely, the bones rearranged and then bound with some wrapping material, probably bark or skin, into a compact bundle. In all examples, the wrapping had disappeared but can be inferred from the shape of the burials. This would have been quite impossible to achieve in any other way (figs. 6 and 18).

Vertical bundle-burials were most common. There were just over eighty certain or probable examples.[4] The following paragraph is a description of the most frequent arrangement of the bones of adults and subadults.

The skull, usually upright, rested on top of, or just within, the top part of a bundle of postcranial bones (fig. 18). The mandible was just below the skull but had been separated from it and placed as an arch (figs. 7, 19, and 20). The long bones formed the vertical "walls" of the bundle, but were often massed in two groups at the front and back of the skull, giving the bundle an oval cross section (figs. 21, 22, 23, and 37).[5] The central core consisted of ribs, vertebrae, scapulae, clavicles, bones of hands and feet, and other smaller bones (fig. 24). The innominate bones were usually set beside each other at the base of the core (figs. 25, 26, and 39). Ribs had often been collected in two bundles, one containing those from the right, the other those from the left side of the rib cage. The bundles were sometimes on opposite sides of the bundle, sometimes on the same side and placed to form a near circle (figs. 6 and 27). The smaller bones and loose teeth had often collected at the base of the bundle (see figs. 61 and 70). Sometimes two or more vertebrae were found in such a position that they must have been held together by ligaments or other incompletely decomposed soft tissue (fig. 6).

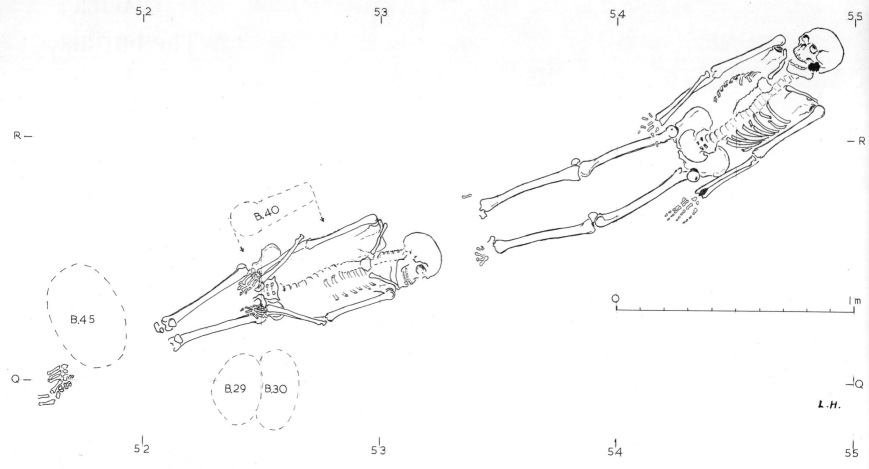

Fig.11. Plan showing B.37 and B.52, extended primary burials. Note that B.40 was found over the pelvic and abdominal regions of B.52. The dashed lines around B.29, B.30 and B.45 show the approximate outlines of these vertical bundle-burials. The feet of B.37 are not shown in detail since they were set with PVA and lifted as two blocks. Their bones were vertical and would certainly have slipped out of position if lifted one by one. All ribs on the right side of B.52 had been removed before the time of drawing the burial. Parts of the skeletons were still hidden by sand.

Fig.12. B.37, an extended primary burial. Note the stone on his left wrist, charcoal on his left cheek and foot, the toes pointing upwards, and the skull of B.52 to the far left. Camera facing east-south-east.

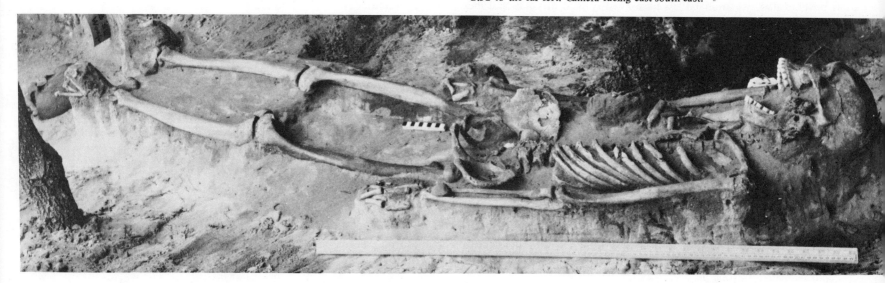

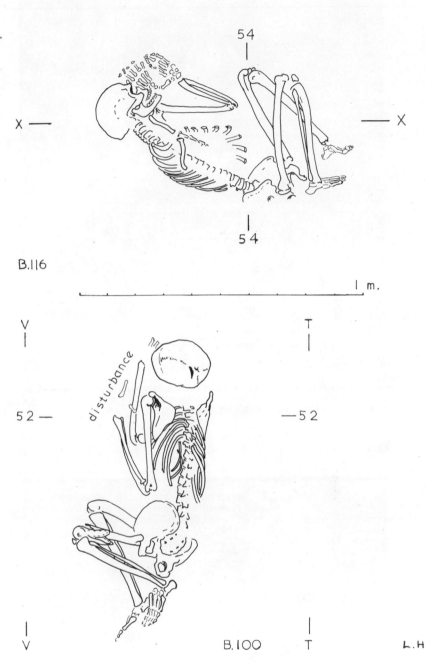

Fig.13. B.52 and B.40, an extended primary burial and a horizontal bundle-burial. Note the position of the left arm of B.52. Camera facing south-east.

Fig.14. B.100: skull, rib cage, and vertebrae. Note dark pit-fill in section across burial. Camera facing northwest.

Fig.15. Plans of B.100 and B.116, flexed primary burials. Note that the right scapula and arm of B.116 are missing but the hand was present and tucked under the face. Note also the gash in the skull of B.100 and the fractured left femur. (Parts of B.116 were still hidden in sand when the burial was drawn.)

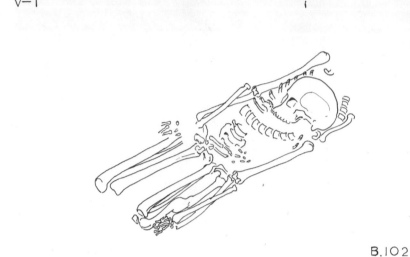

Fig.16. B.77, the flexed primary burial of a child. Note the skull splayed by pressure and the gently bent legs. Note also that the trench continued some distance beyond the skull end. Camera facing southeast.

Fig.17. Plan of B.102, dismembered primary burial.

Fig.18. B.16, a vertical bundle-burial. Note tight bundle, dark homogeneous matrix and numbering of skull fragments. Camera facing southeast.

Fig.19. B.7, a vertical bundle-burial. Note how a root growing through the skull had pushed the fragments apart, and the typical arrangement of bones with the mandible arched below the skull and a group of long bones at either end of the skull. Camera facing southeast.

Fig.20. B.125, a vertical bundle-burial. Note mandible arched below skull, major long bones massed at either end of skull. Camera facing north.

Fig.22. B.81, a typical vertical bundle-burial. Note the major long bones massed in two groups at either end of the skull and the homogeneous matrix around the bones. Camera facing north.

Fig.21. B.9, a vertical bundle-burial. Note thinness of vault fragments, held in situ mainly by rootlets, and poles of long bones. Camera facing east.

Fig.23. B.124, a vertical bundle-burial. Note oval cross section, major long bones grouped at either end of the skull, homogeneous pit-fill, little different in colour from surrounding ridge. Camera facing south.

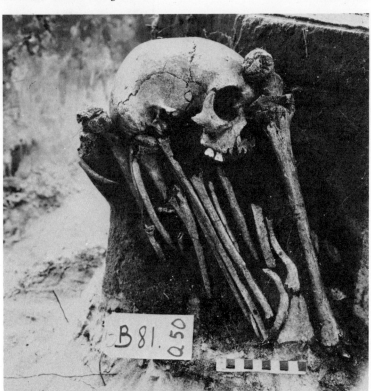

Fig.24. B.130, a vertical bundle-burial. Note ribs and smaller bones in core of bundle, and damage to bony table due to curl-grubs. Note also faint outline of pit where this cuts into C-horizon. Camera facing north.

Fig.25. B.17, a vertical bundle-burial. The base was in situ. Note oval cross section, paired pelvic bones and clean break of stout long bones. Camera facing south.

Fig.26. B.38 after lift 3. Note symmetrical arrangement of bones. Camera facing east.

Fig.27. B.131, a vertical bundle. Note ribs in two opposed bundles. Camera facing east.

Note that some *apparent bundle-burials* of children may, on the evidence of B.2, turn out to be of a rather different type. In this, the long bones retained their approximate anatomical relationship and the arrangement of all the other bones in the bundle could be explained, if a child's articulated body had been bound in the fully flexed foetal position and then firmly wrapped.[6] As the body decomposed, there would have been some separation of adjacent bone ends and the very small bones could have moved considerably. None of the adult bundles showed this pattern, but the children have not yet been studied in detail. This may well be related to the ease of carrying around the corpse of a child compared with the difficulty of carrying the corpse of an adult.

There were two distinct types of horizontal secondary burials. In the first type, the *horizontal bundle-burials,* of which we found six examples, the bones were arranged in very much the same way (fig. 28) as in the vertical ones, but the cross section tended to be more elongated, probably owing to the bones settling in the sand as the wrapping disintegrated.[7] The horizontal placement of the bundle in the beginning was clear from attendant funerary objects (to be described later) and from the fact that the top of the bundle would have protruded above ground, had it been placed on end.

The second type, the *horizontal parcel,* consisted of a bundle of long bones placed horizontally with the skull sitting on top somewhere near the centre.[8] There were only five certain cases of this. It was impossible to say whether skull and bones had been wrapped together — if at all — but this is not unlikely since these burials were all of very small children and skull and long bones therefore very small (figs. 29 and 30).

Fig.28. B.138, a horizontal bundle. Note compact arrangement of bones, dark pit-fill. Camera facing southwest.

Fig.30. B.70, a horizontal parcel. Some vault fragments have been removed, revealing a few teeth and fragments of skull base resting on horizontal long bones. Camera facing east.

Fig.29. B.25, a typical horizontal parcel. Note shell, part of a thin horizon, about to fall out of dry and cracking sand. Camera facing east-north-east.

Multiple burials. Many of these burials were multiple. It has already been suggested that this may have been the case for the extended burials. The full arguments for this will be given in the next chapter.

Some adult bundles contained the bones of small children and, in the case of B.61 and B.68, the juvenile bones had remained close together, caught between a clavicle and a scapula of the adult, so the child must have been deliberately wrapped inside the adult burial (fig. 31). This is also possible in other cases, however the small bones had assembled near the base and could derive from a disturbed burial as evidenced by B.53 in B.38.

A pit could contain several separate bundles deposited at the same time, as in the case of the burials B.38, B.51, and B.54 (fig. 93). It was clear from the slightly different base levels of the bundles that they were separate; but from their closely interwoven contours, they were obviously buried together (fig. 32).

It appears that the bones of two or more small children of similar age were sometimes wrapped together in the same bundle, as happened with B.44A and B.44B. In B.48 and B.50, the postcranial bones of two adults, a man and a woman, had been bundled together to form a vertical pillar and the skulls placed one on each side facing in opposite directions (fig. 32).

Cremations. There were also two cases of partial cremation, B.15 and B.39. The bones had been deliberately broken into fairly short pieces. Some were partly or completely charred, others not at all, and a few completely calcined (fig. 33).

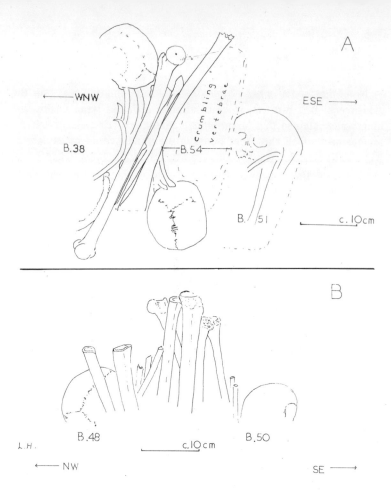

Fig.32. Multiple burials: B.38+51+54 and B.48+50. Note that we could not risk leaving these burials in position for detailed drawings to be completed. Further details are recorded on photographs.

Fig.31. B.61, adult vertical bundle-burial, and B.68, child buried in same bundle (arrow points to small bones near clavicle). Camera facing south.

Fig.33. B.15, a cremation. Note the outline of the densely packed clump of bones. Camera facing south.

Disturbed or incomplete burials

Many burials were badly decayed (figs. 34, 35, and 36) or disturbed; sometimes it was not possible to be sure of or even to suggest the original arrangement of the bones.[9] Some very fragile child burials were set with PVA and lifted as a block (fig. 37). Closer study in the laboratory may show to which type they belonged.

Some disturbance was recent and due to soil removal or to police investigations; some to the large size of the pits for the most recent burials; but some was clearly remote in time. This will be discussed later as relevant to the stratigraphy. Rarely, considering the density of burials, was one truncated by the pit for another (fig. 76).[10]

There could be a number of explanations for missing bones apart from disturbance. It could be due to disease, injury, or deliberate removal before death. No real evidence for this has been noticed so far except for cases of tooth avulsion.

There is also the possibility of loss or selection after death but before burial. The former will be discussed in the context of observed burial practices. Deliberate selection has been mentioned earlier and is undoubted in cases where the large size or regional limitation of the missing bones (e.g. skull or vertebral column) would make accidental loss unlikely and the good condition of the remaining bones would make decay equally unlikely as a cause.

Decay after burial has been due to pressure and movement of the matrix, root penetration, chemical processes connected with root activity, bacteria, rain water, and sometimes to the activities of

Fig.35. B.139, decayed burial, some teeth left in anatomical position. Note slight colour difference between pit-fill and ridge. Camera facing northwest.

Fig.34. B.121, a decayed burial. The bones of the skull, apart from the petrous bones, had disappeared. The teeth of the maxilla and mandible remained in their anatomical order. Camera facing east-south-east.

Fig.36. B.113, a decayed burial. The skull had disappeared but the teeth remained in their anatomical position. Note freshness of root from Forest Red Gum. Camera facing north.

Fig. 37. Vertical bundle-burial (B.125) lifted as a block. Note tight outline of bundle and its oval cross section.

insects and rodents. The degree of decay depended on the original size and consistency of the bone, on how long it had been in the ground, and on its position, horizontally and vertically, in the deposit. Being within or near the turf seemed to mean more rapid destruction, but attacks by curl-grubs seemed to take place mostly from about 40 to 70 centimetres below the surface.

There could also have been some loss during or after excavation. Possibly some small bones and teeth were not noticed during excavation, particularly when the sand was damp and clogging, but since we sieved every bit of sand excavated through a quarter-inch sieve and the finds include numerous small bone fragments and even unerupted milkteeth or teeth of small rodents, this is not likely to have happened very often. We know of at least one case of a bone having been secretly souvenired by a visitor during the excavations.[11] Bones which were much eroded and very fragmentary, especially those of juveniles, could sometimes not be identified and were recorded as "probably absent".

Burial practices

In discussing evidence for ritual and ceremonies in the interment of burials at Broadbeach, some patterns occur sufficiently frequently to be statistically relevant while others provide us with no more than a hint at what happened at the time of burial. But even these hints can be important for interpretation when considered against the unfortunately scant written records of traditional burial practices in this area. Written records are most relevant for the more recent

burials. Their relevance to those more remote in time is problematic but, as there is strong general evidence for continuity of tradition at this site, they should not be dismissed out of hand.

This section describes recurrent patterns in detail, making only passing reference to written records. The records, their reliability, and usefulness in interpretation will be discussed in chapter 6. The chronology of the burials will be discussed in the next chapter, but the reader may find it useful to refer to figure 74 and table 4, which show their position in the sequence. Appendix D lists the burials numerically in the order in which they were excavated and provides a tabulation of the kind of data used in this chapter. First, I will discuss pit-shape, then orientation of pits and orientation of the burials, evidence for wrapping of the bones before burial, the use of fire, the presence of shell, stone, and bone, red pigment, and finally evidence for continuity of tradition.

Burial pits

Where many burials were close together but in separate pits, the early pits had often been so cut into that it was impossible to reconstruct their original shape. The pattern given by undisturbed pits or those but little affected by disturbance, in all eighty-three, is consistent.

Sixty-seven of these held vertical burials of some kind, mostly the common bundle. There appeared to be three different types of pit (fig. 38), the section of each type probably reflecting a somewhat different method of digging. The outline of the pit-surface, however, appears related to the depth, tending more to oval the deeper the pit was dug. None of the types was restricted to any period of the burial ground.

A depth of 50 - 60 centimetres would seem the minimum for all but very small child bundles, and a depth of 70 - 80 centimetres the minimum for adult bundles. Child bundles usually ranged from 30 to 45 centimetres in length. An adult or adolescent bundle was from 45 to 55 centimetres long or even a little longer if the skull was set completely above the heads of the long bones. Adolescents above the age of twelve years have been grouped with adults in the figures quoted below, since long bones attain almost adult proportions in the early teens. The suggested minimum depth takes into account that the surface of the burial ground was raised at least some 10 centimetres during the period of use (p. 34) and probably some more thereafter.

Pit A was round in plan, usually with gentle slopes all round and a rounded or almost flat pit-floor. Twenty-one pits out of twenty-four were no more than 70 centimetres deep. This type seems mostly to have been dug to the exact depth needed for a particular burial. Nine out of fourteen children were in pits up to 60 centimetres deep and nine out of ten adults in pits up to 70 centimetres deep. This means that there may have been only a few centimetres of sand hiding a burial when it was left after the rites were completed.

The majority of pits were oval in plan, ranging from almost round through elliptic to egg-shaped.

Type B had one deep end, where the slopes were steep; other slopes were more gentle. Thirty-three pits of this type were noticed,

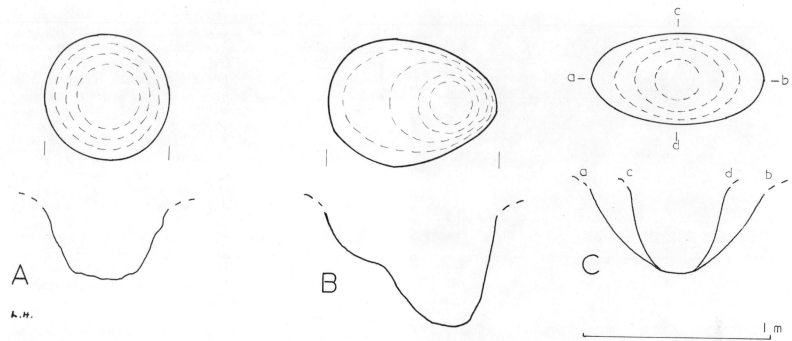

L.H.

Fig. 38. Pit-types: plan and section. Note that these are ideal types based on a number of excavated pits.

sixteen containing children, seventeen containing adults. None were less than 50 centimetres deep and one-third of both children and adults were in pits between 70 and 80 centimetres deep. Some pits were deeper still, for children going down to 90 and for adults to 100 centimetres. So, on the whole, pit B allows for a more generous cover of sand above the burial.

The same applies to pit C, of which there were only ten examples seen, five children in pits from 60 to 100 centimetres deep and five adults in pits from 70 to a little over 100 centimetres deep. This pit type has an elliptic plan with sections showing gentle slopes along two sides. The deepest part was midway between the two poles.

Taking the evidence of all three pit types together, we find that thirteen out of thirty-five children and twenty-four out of thirty-two adults were buried in pits only just deep enough to hold them; when extra depth was allowed, it was mostly a matter of only 5 - 10 centimetres. Only six pits were more than 90 centimetres deep. This state will be commented on in chapter 6 when discussing written records.

The shape of the pits holding the early extended burials and B.102 can only be inferred since all the sand above had been churned up by later pits. Even the lowest undisturbed parts of these trenches had blurred outlines, but they appear to have been roughly rectangular and moderately deep. The deepest, the trench for B.52, went down to 84 centimetres below the surface. Even considering that the surface has been raised some 10 centimetres since then, this makes for a considerable effort spent on digging these trenches compared to that normal for vertical burials. (The rise of 10 centimetres was calculated from the surface of pits for vertical burials.) Some sand may have been added to the ridge after the extended burials but before the vertical ones; this is not likely to have been much since the level of the ridge, as well as that of others in the area, appears to

be closely related to its mode of formation (cf. chapter 1, note 2).

Cremations and horizontal parcels were found in pits which, if undisturbed, could be seen to be of types A to C. The depth was less than 70 centimetres with one exception, B.55 in a pit of type C and 92 centimetres deep. This exception is worth noting since B.55 was a small baby, stillborn or dead soon after birth, and yet buried with some care at greater depth than usual (see p. 83).

The horizontal bundles were, as far as could be seen, always placed in oval pits with flat floors and fairly steep sides. The depth ranged from 50 to 73 centimetres and the pit-floor could mostly be seen to be no bigger than absolutely necessary.

Four pits which did not fit into any of these groups also held burials which were in other ways atypical – B.73, B.77, B.100, and B.116. These were all flexed primary burials and apparently the last to be buried in this site. Two pits were roughly oval, one subtriangular and one subrectangular in plan. The main differences lay in the much greater depth – except for B.77, a small child – and in the abrupt, almost vertical slopes in the lower part of the pits, meeting an almost flat pit-floor (figs. 82 and 87). There was also a difference in pit-fill. In the case of the three big pits (B.73, B.100, B.116), it was blotchy and the colour contrasts were sometimes sharp (fig. 87); the normal pit-fill was dark and homogeneous with no change in colour from top to bottom except for an occasional red stain, where pigment from the bones had been washed down (figs. 7, 17, 22, 23, 38, 39, and 60).

Orientation

The actual shape of the pits may have been the result of the digging techniques used; the long axis of the pit seems the result of deliberate choice. The sixty cases in which it could be established with some certainty have been tabulated in table 2. (The table shows the general direction of the axis. It was difficult to measure exactly

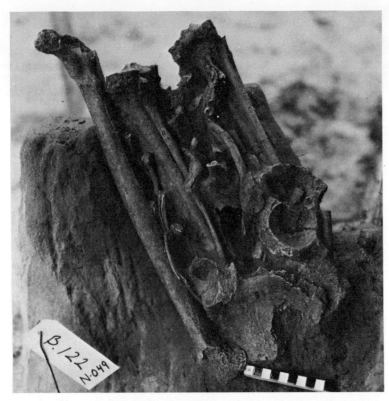

Fig.39. B.112, a typical vertical bundle-burial, tilted by push from the big root. Note symmetrical arrangement of bones with pelvic bones paired at the base of the bundle, and the homogeneous colour of the pit-fill. Camera facing west-north-west.

Table 2. *Long axis of burial pits*
(Figures in parenthesis indicate somewhat uncertain cases.)

Long Axis	A	B	C	D
N - S	8 + (2)			
NNW - SSE	4 + (1)			
NW - SE	8 + (1)			
WNW - ESE	2	(1)		
W - E	17 + (2)			
WSW - ENE	1	(2)		(1)
SW - NE	(2)			2
SSW - NNE		2 + (1)	3	
Total	48	6	3	3

the axis of these blurred pit-plans.) Vertical burials, horizontal parcels, and cremations have been grouped together in column A since it was clear that they followed the same rules of orientation as well as being placed in the same types of pit. The preferred axis was in forty-five cases out of forty-eight somewhere between west and north to east and south. (Two of the remaining three cases are somewhat doubtful due to disturbance.)

Burials in column A were then plotted according to their probable place within the sequence of burials. This sequence will be discussed further in the next chapter but it should be stressed here that many burials have been so placed on rather slender evidence.

The result for burials of stage O (or very early I?) was that one end of the pit was somewhere between west and north, the other somewhere between east and south with only two exceptions; in two-fifths of the cases, the axis was due west to east. The picture was the same for burials of stage I, with one-third of the pits being aligned due west to east, the rest (with one exception) somewhere between west and north running east or south. Stage II pits (or very late stage I?) followed a slightly different pattern. All but one were aligned with one end between north and northwest, the other between south and southeast. The sudden shift from a west-east emphasis could be more apparent than real, since the numbers involved are so small, particularly for the later burials. (Two-thirds of those tabulated here were placed in the earliest group.)

Horizontal bundles (mostly early) in column B, and extended burials (very early) in column C, seem to share a south-south-west to north-north-east axis; note that this applies also to the very late horizontal bundle, B.138.

The pits of the very late flexed burials, column D, were on a southwest to northeast axis or close to it.

The long axis of primary burials, horizontal bundles, and flexed burials coincided closely with that of their pits, as could be expected. Horizontal parcels and vertical bundles were not so consistent. Two-fifths of these were found to have their long axis at right angles or obliquely to that of their pit. (For vertical bundle-burials, this means the long axis of the usually oval transverse section.)

A more selective pattern emerged when the facial orientation of the skull — when present and in situ — was tabulated (see table 3). In a few cases, particularly those of vertical bundle-burials, the direction shown could be a little out, owing to some slight movement of the skull after burial. The latter was often, however, firmly jammed between the ends of the long bones in the upper part of the bundle (fig. 7). The columns in the table are, as in table 2, A for vertical burials and horizontal parcels, B for horizontal bundles, C for extended burials plus B.102, and D for flexed burials.

The four cardinal points but also the direction northwest were clearly of importance in selecting the final position of burials of group A. Some skulls facing in a direction somewhere between these points may, as suggested, have shifted somewhat since burial. Others may simply indicate lack of accuracy. The reason may have been a rather vague notion of the cardinal points or, more likely, a feeling that the matter was not important in a particular case. A direction somewhere between north and west was most favoured; this was the case also for horizontal bundles.

When the facial orientation of burials in column A was plotted according to relative age in the same way as the orientation of burial pits, the result was less informative.

Fifty per cent of burials of stage O (or very early I?) were facing somewhere between north and west, but the directions due north and northwest were favoured. Twenty-five per cent were facing east or close to east. The rest were equally divided between south, or some point between north and east or between east and south.

Table 3. *Orientation of skulls*

	N	NNW	NW	WNW	W	WSW	SW	SSW	S	SSE	SE	ESE	E	ENE	NE	NNE
A	10	3	6		9	2	1	2	5	1	2	2	11	3	2	2
B	2		2		1											
C			1											1		
D			1			1					2				1	

Fifty per cent of burials of stage I were also facing somewhere between north and west; the rest were scattered along the arc between north-north-east and west-south-west. Due south and due east appeared somewhat more important than intermediate points.

Stage II again appears to give a somewhat different picture. Half the skulls faced somewhere between northeast and east, a quarter faced due west and a quarter approximately south.

In primary burials the choice of direction was limited by the long axis of the burial. Here it is worth noting that where two burials (of any type) can be paired, they appear to have been placed to face in opposite directions. (Compare for example B.48 and B.50, two skulls set on either side of a common column of bones, one facing east and the other west.) So it may be no accident that, of the extended burials, B.37 was facing east and B.52 northwest, that is, in approximately opposite directions. It is tempting to pair also the flexed burials B.77 – a small child – and B.100 – a young woman – whose pits were very close together. One was facing northwest, the other southeast.

Wrapping

The relative position of the bones made it clear that at least bundle-burials must have been well and tightly wrapped before burial (fig. 18). This is supported by written records discussed in chapter 6. The outline of one cremated and broken up burial, B.15, suggests that the fragments were placed in something like a net bag before burial (cf. fig. 40). Other possible wrapping materials will be discussed in chapter 6. It was also in most cases clear that the skull must have been inside this bundle. If the orientation of the skull in the pit was a matter of tradition, this means that its orientation inside the bundle must have been known at the time of burial in at least a majority of cases. (But B.54, a typical vertical bundle-burial, buried with B.38 and B.51, was upside down. Since this is the only case of inversion found, it may well be accidental and due to the difficulties in handling three bundles at the same time, cf. fig. 32.) This could mean that the bundle was wrapped or rewrapped on the site or possibly that the wrapping did not completely cover the bundle. The presence of haematite crayons near the burial pits, discussed later in this chapter, may be relevant to the first suggestion. Loose teeth were found at the base of most vertical bundles and could have moved there after burial, but they were also found at the end away from the skull in horizontal bundle-burials (fig. 41). The latter must have been kept upright at some stage before burial in the ground to make this possible, and some time must have lapsed between the wrapping of the bundle and its burial to allow the teeth to work loose. The wrapping must also have been dense enough to prevent the loose teeth from being lost. It is possible that some of the bundles were originally packed and wrapped somewhere away from the burial site. There were, however, a great many loose teeth – particularly of juveniles – and small bones, as well as broken bits of human bone in level 1.[12] Not all of this could come from disturbed burials, since there were too few of these in level 2 to constitute sources of the loose fragments.[13] Many of these, especially the teeth, could have been overlooked if decayed corpses had been packed and wrapped just there; or bundles opened and repacked.

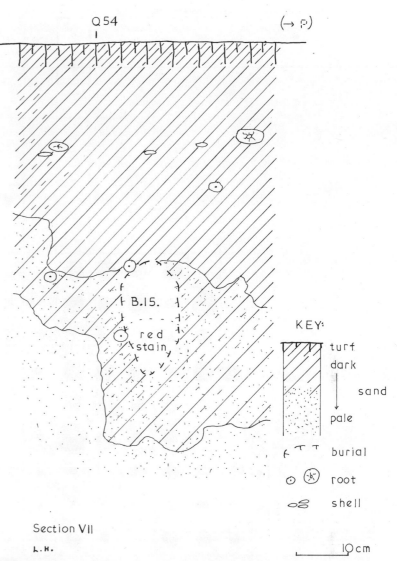

Section VII

L. H.

Fig. 40. Section VII through B.15, a cremation. Note the regular outline of the compact clump of bones.

Fig. 41. B.88, a horizontal bundle. Most of the bones already removed. Note tooth to the left (near rib) at opposite end of bundle from skull and mandible (far right). Camera facing north.

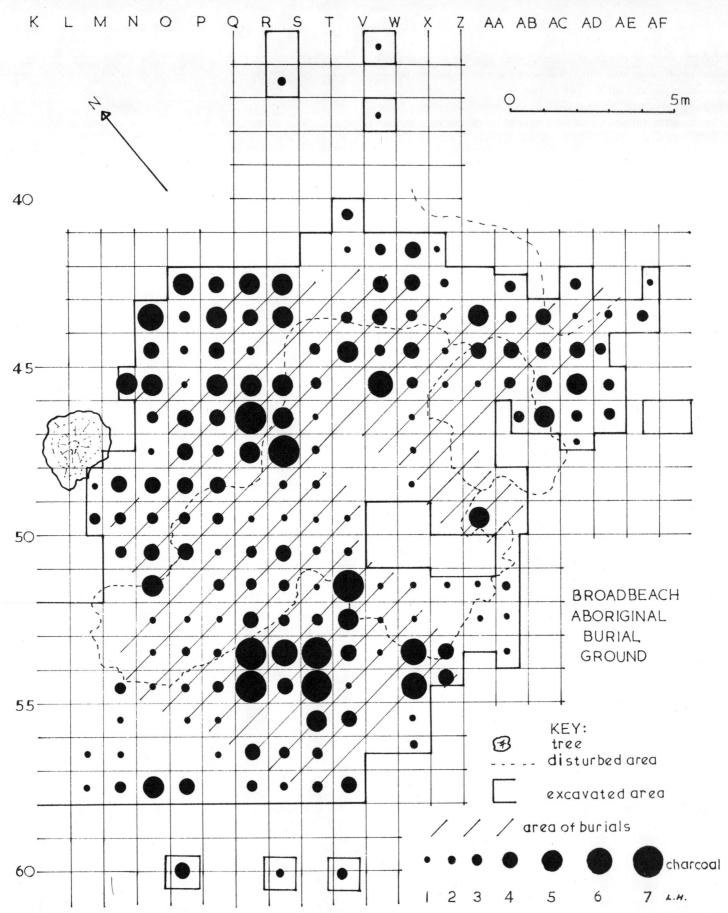

Map 5. Broadbeach burial ground: distribution of charcoal. Each circle indicates the total amount of charcoal present in levels 1 and 2 of each grid square. **1.** 1–5 grams; **2.** 5–10 grams; **3.** 10–25 grams; **4.** 25–50 grams; **5.** 50–100 grams; **6.** 100–200 grams; **7.** More than 200 grams.

Composite burial ceremonies

There are a number of other details that suggest that burial ceremonies at times – perhaps always – took place in several stages.[14] Apart from those just mentioned, there is, for example, the fact that very few bones showed signs of having been cut or scratched. Those we have found could either be shown to be the result of modern shovels (fig. 42) or of animal or root activity. This suggests that secondary burials were probably left to decompose and not artificially stripped of flesh and cut up. The cremations may be exceptions.

Little can be said about the extended primary burials in this respect. If B.37 and B.52 were not buried at the same time, then the pit for the earliest one may have been left open until the second had been buried (cf. chapter 3). The corpse may have been given a removable cover such as branches or leaves or a thin covering of sand.

Another suggestion that burial took place in stages comes from B.116, one of the flexed burials. This woman was found to lack one arm and scapula, the uppermost, that is the right ones. They had clearly been there when she was placed in the grave. The right clavicle was somewhat displaced as if tugged down at the shoulder end (fig. 15). The right hand was in its place, partly tucked underneath the face. It had been severed from the arm just above the wrist (fig. 43). A section through the pit-fill (fig. 44) shows that most of this could not have been disturbed after being put into place. The slopes from west, south, and southeast were steep almost up to the normal level of the shell horizon (see p. 34 and fig. 45). The northeast, north, and northwest slopes were less steep and the fill here patchy (fig. 46). A scatter of charcoal, mostly small fragments but also here and there in big lumps, covered the whole area of the pit. The following is a reconstruction of the probable series of events: When the woman was buried she was – on the evidence of her bent fingers and curled toes – still held together by tissues (fig. 47). The pit was filled in completely. Somebody who had taken part in this ceremony and who knew exactly where to dig and when, made (scraped?) a small pit down from the north, over the area of the arm, and removed it without disturbing the rest of the burial.[15] He then replaced the sand. Later a fire was lit over the pit, including the disturbed area. Note that this case and others mentioned below suggest that some ceremonies took place after filling the pit.

Fire

How much use was made of fire in the burial ceremonies is very difficult to establish. Some bones are darkened and detailed analysis may reveal some charring (figs. 48 and 49). In many instances, the colour could be due to leaching from a dark pit-fill above the burial. The two cremated burials are our only cases of human bone having been exposed to fire enough to be really calcined.

All over the site and in all levels, there were fragments of charcoal which could have come from disturbed burial fires but just as likely could be the result of occasional bush fires. All the charcoal was collected, however, and has been plotted according to weight on map 3. (The main feeder roots from the big stump can be seen dotted in

Fig.42. B.112, a vertical bundle-burial pushed over by soil contractors. Note cut marks – from spade? – at the top of the long bones just below the disturbed surface soil. Camera facing north.

Fig.43. B.116, a flexed primary burial. Note tightly flexed legs, right clavicle pulled out of position, right hand partly below the face. No right humerus, ulna, or radius found. Camera facing east.

X 53
soil
removed

X 54

X 55

KEY:

turf
dark

sand

pale

burial

shell

charcoal

root

stone

B.116.

Section XVI

L.H.

1 m

Fig.44. Section XVI through B.116, a flexed primary burial. Note the spread of charcoal all over the area of the pit-surface.

on map 12.) A large proportion of the charcoal in squares Q - R 48 came from a feeder root from the big stump; it was close to the surface here and fire had followed it some distance below the ground. The rest of this charcoal and the concentration in Q 47 were apparently mainly pieces fallen from the big stump which had been burning at some stage. Most of the other concentrations, that is, those in squares T 52, R - S /54 - 55 and W - X /54 - 55 came from the upper part or the surface of pits holding flexed burials.[16] Much of it was still in sheets as if from thick strips of bark or the side of a hollow log. The charcoal in Q 54 - 55 was mostly connected with B.37, an extended burial, and with B.15, a cremation. There was a small heap on the ankles and feet of B.37, another on his left cheek and just beside his left shoulder a big piece, probably the remains of a hollow log. This wood had clearly all burnt in situ, slightly discolouring the sand around the fires. They must have been fairly small. (Nothing similar was seen on or near B.52, the second extended burial, but there is a strong suggestion that a similar small

Fig.45. B.120, fragment of burial dumped on the lip of the pit for B.116 (bottom right corner). Note the steep slope and oval outline of the pit for the latter. Camera facing southwest.

Fig.46. B.116. Note steep slope of the pit to the right, a more gentle slope to the left, and patches of dark fill just above the skull. Camera facing southeast.

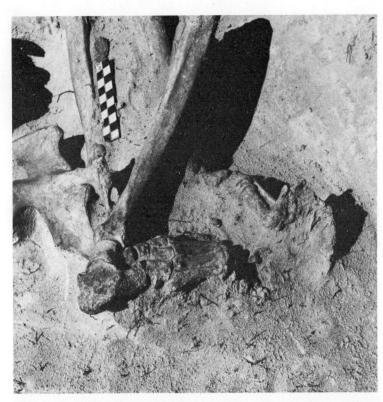

Fig.47. B.116 feet, clearly articulated at the time of burial. Camera facing east.

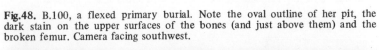

Fig.48. B.100, a flexed primary burial. Note the oval outline of her pit, the dark stain on the upper surfaces of the bones (and just above them) and the broken femur. Camera facing southwest.

Fig.49. B.88, a horizontal bundle. Part of the stone corona showing (a pale stone below the scale and a dark stone, F.1212, above the label). Note dark staining of bone and sand at skull end of bundle. Camera facing north.

fire was lit over the head end of B.88, a horizontal bundle, discolouring the bone and the surrounding sand — see fig. 49.) The charcoal found with B.15 (and with B.39, the second cremation) was all in fragments, probably scooped up with the bones. They could not have been burnt where they were found, as a fire large enough to produce so much calcination and charring would have left more charcoal and probably a considerable discolouration of the sand.

In at least one instance we found that a fire had been lit on the pit-surface over a bundle-burial, B.114 in P 49. The shell horizon had been dug through to make the pit, but was replaced over the latter by a thin band of charcoal (figs. 50 and 51). Charcoal scattered just below the shells on the pit-surface over B.126 and over part of the pit-surface above B.124 also may derive from such fires. They may have been fairly common, but only rarely has most, or all, of a pit-surface been left undisturbed.

Shell, stone, and bone in relation to burial pits

At the level of the shell horizon described early in chapter 3, there occurred tightly packed clumps of shell, mostly *Plebidonax deltoides*, some of them neatly stacked inside each other (fig. 28).[17] Amongst the shells were bits of animal bone, sometimes charred and often broken. The species and bones represented suggest that they were the remains of a meal (cf. Appendix B). Sometimes there were small flakes, thumbnail scrapers, and other small implements in or near the pockets, apparently used in connection with these and abandoned or lost. These implements will be described in more detail in chapter 5 and probable functions discussed. The pockets of shell were usually either close to the periphery of the pit[18] or near the centre.[19] Some typical examples, B.6, B.16, and B.136, have been shown in figures 52 and 53. On the southern half of the pit-surface over B.127, we found two concentric bands of shell roughly following the outline of the pit-periphery. (The bands may have been present over the northern half also but not noticed, since they were thin and obvious only when seen over a large horizontal section.)

In at least three cases, there were pockets of stone at this level. The pockets near B.12 and B.122 contained a jumble of waste flakes, fragments, and broken implements and were probably in the same category as the small scrapers, etc. just mentioned. But B.95 had two pockets of large, neat, well-made flakes on exactly opposite sides of the pit. All flakes in each pocket came from one piece of raw material (F.682a - e and F.706a - c). These should probably be considered as gravegoods, as should some very beautiful and well made implements found at this level, which will be described in chapter 5.

A little below this level there was, in two cases, B.36 and B.112, what could almost be called a cap of stones over the burial. They were mostly rough chunks and fragments. It is possible that these were meant to mark its position (but cf. p. 84).

Usually the pit-fill contained only a small quantity of stone. This was mostly small flakes, fragments, and implements. The latter were often broken. Clearly such stones were accidentally scraped into the pit with the fill. Some fine implements, or fragments of stone of unusual colours, found amongst the bones, seem to have been

Fig.50. B.114, a vertical bundle-burial. Note the shell horizon (top left third) stopping abruptly, replaced by thin line of small specks of charcoal at the same level. (Only the largest pieces show in the photograph.) Note subtle difference in colour between pit-fill and surrounding ridge. Camera facing northeast.

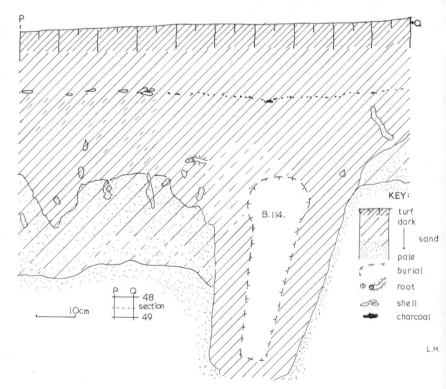

Fig.51. Section through B.114, a vertical bundle-burial (drawn from photographs and sketch in field notes). Note the charcoal replacing the shell horizon over the pit-surface.

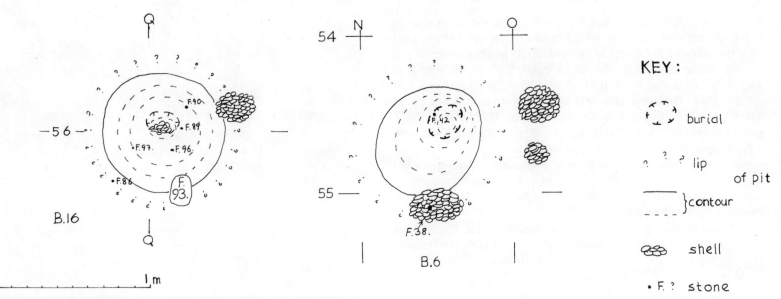

Fig.52. Pit-surfaces of B.6 and B.16, vertical bundle-burials. Note the axe (F.93) lying on the pit periphery. All stones shown on the drawing were lying on the pit-surface, i.e. at the level of the shell horizon. The outline of each burial shows its position in the pit some distance below the pit-surface.

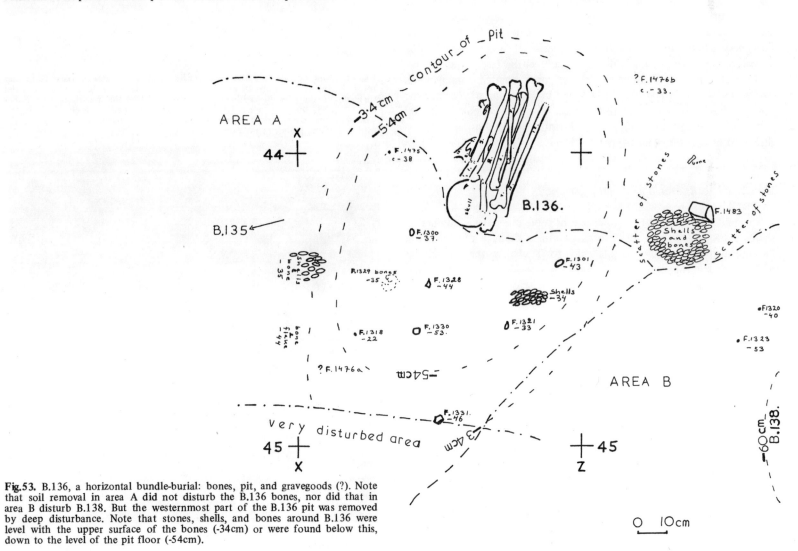

Fig.53. B.136, a horizontal bundle-burial: bones, pit, and gravegoods (?). Note that soil removal in area A did not disturb the B.136 bones, nor did that in area B disturb B.138. But the westernmost part of the B.136 pit was removed by deep disturbance. Note that stones, shells, and bones around B.136 were level with the upper surface of the bones (-34cm) or were found below this, down to the level of the pit floor (-54cm).

deliberately included in the bundle. In some cases, the bones were so closely packed that the stone could not have filtered in with the sand after the decay of the wrapping material. Some good examples of this are the pieces of polished axe found inside B.63 or the very neat scrapers found inside B.60, B.61, B.87, and B.28 (cf. plates 4 - 5: F.21, F.146). The latter also held some fine small oval and round flakes of translucent and white quartzite. In B.97A there was a geometric microlith as well as a long, plain, pointed flake. There were many other examples of this and many probable ones.[20]

Some plain flakes and some types of implement of oblong pointed shape which would normally be considered typologically different seem to be closely connected with burial rites. These will be discussed further in chapter 5.

Also, there were good complete implements in the fill of some pits, outside the bundle. One position (see p. 76) probably indicates that the implement had been placed there deliberately. Other pieces could be part of the fill by accident or could have fallen out of the bundle after the decay of the wrapping.

Many teeth and fragments of animal bones were found amongst the bones of the burials. This has been noted in forty-two burials so far, and the number will probably be greater when all burials have been examined in detail. In some cases, a few small fragments or teeth could have filtered in with the sand, but mostly the bones must have been present in the bundle before burial. It does not seem to be a case of burrowing animals dying inside a burial (see Appendix B).

In a few burials, there were one or more pointed animal bones (*Macropodid fibulae*) with polished tip. In B.28 this was within the core of the burial and close to the base. The two examples in B.109 were of different size (fig. 106). Possible interpretations will be discussed in chapter 6 and Appendix E.

Stones and shells in deliberate arrangements?

In eight cases described below, one or more stones or a number of shells appeared to have been arranged in a definite manner. The "arrangements" were so simple and so few that they could be accidental. On the other hand, they did not look accidental when seen in the field. I shall describe my perhaps subjective impressions here in case something similar is ever noticed in another burial ground.

Two of the horizontal bundles, B.40 and B.88, had a small semicircle of stones around the vault of the skull (fig. 54). The "corona" was made up of rough chunks as well as fragments and complete implements. (Neither appeared to be simply a scatter of pieces discarded after completed ritual.)

Two others had a stone placed across one arm. For B.37 this was a small pointed chunk of reddish stone (weathered basalt) placed on the left wrist (figs. 11 and 12). For B.73 it was a plain, rather thick flake, oblong and pointed, of red quartzite sitting across the upper, that is the left humerus (fig. 55).

A small piece of dark red jasper was lying on the skull of another horizontal bundle-burial, B.132. This may have ended up there, scraped in with the pit-fill, as the two examples just mentioned could have done. But it may be significant that they all share a red colour

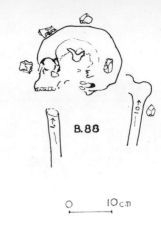

Fig.54. Stone coronas for B.40 and B.88, horizontal bundle-burials. Note that for B.40 the stones were all at exactly the same level, i.e. deposited on a flat surface, and that the pit had been partly filled before this was done. The stones around B.88, however, were lying level with the upper surface of the bones. The contour of the skull was not visible but has been drawn to show the position of the stones in relation to the skull.

Fig.55. B.73, a flexed primary burial. Note the tightly flexed legs and the oblong pointed flake, F.503, on the left humerus. Camera facing south.

and a pointed shape and, in the case of B.132, that the stone was lying on the highest part of the vault (fig. 56) and that the raw material was one used for some of the best-made implements found in the site. (These were of types apparently closely linked with the preparation of a burial for wrapping, see p. 76.)

A stone was lying on the centre of the skull of B.61 and B.79 which, linked with other features, seems to distinguish these burials along with B.72 from other vertical bundle-burials. In each of these, the skull was lying on its side and had apparently been placed so originally. (This was concluded from various anatomical details and the position of bone fragments. There were other cases of a skull lying on its side, but in B.64, part of the maxilla was still sitting on top of the bundle in a vertical position, see figure 57.) An oblong, pointed plain flake (F.490), identical in type with that on B.73, was lying on the skull of B.61, and a fragment of a polished axe (F.532) on that of B.79 (figs. 58 and 59). (If there was a similar arrangement for B.72, this had been disturbed when B.71, a skull and some bones, had been thrown on top of it during some late disturbance.) A semi-circle of spiral shell, identified as *Pyrazus ebeninus* and *Pyrazus australis,* reminiscent of the corona described earlier, was found some distance below the top of the burials at the level on which the skull rested (fig. 60). It was most distinctive for B.72 and B.79, less so for B.61, which had smaller shells in the corona and which had lost part of its pit-fill in a collapse after a rain storm, before it could be excavated. They were similar also with regard to pit-shape, which was of type B (see fig. 7). The fill in all three pits was very dark and full

Fig.57. B.64, a vertical bundle-burial. Note the vertical maxilla which shows that the skull was originally vertical and placed at the top of the bundle. Camera facing north.

Fig.58. B.61, a vertical bundle-burial with the skull placed on its side. Note the oblong pointed flake, F.490, lying over the left temporal region. Camera facing east.

Fig.56. B.132, a horizontal bundle. Note small stone on skull and shell horizon in section. (Some of the apparent colour differences in the section were due to rain which had penetrated the ground less where it was protected by tarpaulins.) Camera facing north.

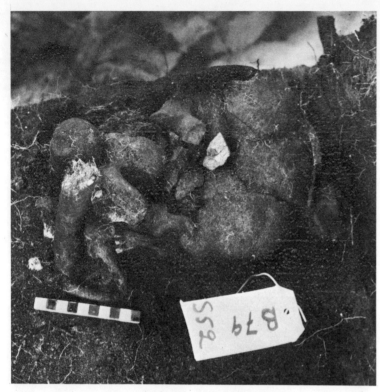

Fig.59. B.79, a vertical bundle-burial. Note the skull on its side, wedged between long bones, and a fragment of polished stone axe, F.532, resting on the right temporal region. Camera facing northwest.

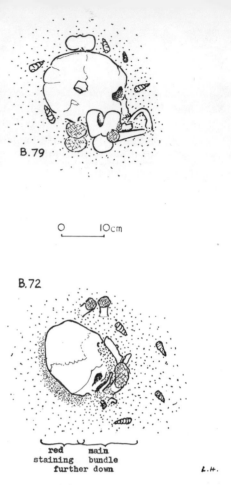

Fig.60. Shell coronas for B.72 and B.79, vertical bundle-burials. Note that the *Pyrazus* shells were lying at exactly the same depth and that other shells in the pit-fill were *Plebidonax deltoides.*

of shells – in fragments – of various kinds but predominantly *Plebidonax deltoides.* All three burials were of late adolescent or adult young males.[21] The burials were close together, placed in a triangle (see map 12). If they were not contemporary, they were certainly close in time and one of the few clear examples of a subgroup within the tradition of vertical bundle-burials.[22]

The use of spiral shells to form a pattern leads to the question of whether such shells always or often had some special ritual significance. They are striking in appearance, but it was noted once at an early stage of the excavations (for B.6) that such a shell had been found just before the vault of the burial appeared. We, therefore, kept a watch for any more instances of possible association. All shells of these two species were plotted and their possible relation to any particular burial investigated.[23] This led to the conclusion that there is little reason to regard them as having special significance except on the three occasions just described, but it is worth noting that in two instances, B.62 and B.87, there was one half of an oyster shell inside the bundle but no other shell in the pit-fill.[24]

Red pigment

Red pigment was present in the majority of burials, although the total number is not yet known. The pigment was noticed sometimes only as a red stain in the sand. This was often very faint and difficult to distinguish, particularly when the pit-fill was very dark. Doubtful cases were checked with a Munsell Soil Color Chart (see also

Appendix A). Occasionally the pigment could be seen on the bone itself and sometimes it was found in the form of small crumbs or specks of haematite, larger chunks or even big crayons near or in the pit (fig. 61).

There was no clear case of red pigment being associated with a primary burial, unless B.2 can be considered such. (The hyperflexed corpse could, however, have been dried and hard.) There were definitely crumbs of haematite in the undisturbed pit-fill surrounding this burial. In all other cases of primary burial, there was some haematite in the area of the burial (compare maps 12 and 4), but not very close to the bones, and just as likely to derive from some other burial there, for which pigment had been recorded.

Pigment was noticed in sixty-seven out of eighty-five vertical bundles. (This excludes the baby in B.61.)[25] The number is likely to increase when the bones of all burials have been studied closely. Eight bundles were set with PVA, lifted complete and have not yet been studied at all.[26] Of the remaining ten vertical bundles, five were very close to the surface, badly cut into in modern times and situated mainly within level 1, that is in dark soil with much rain water percolation. Four others were somewhat disturbed by later pits, so that pigment found nearby could not with certainty be attributed to them. This suggests that red pigment was used with few or no exceptions in the case of vertical bundle-burials.

Although, as a stain, it was usually only noticed towards the base of a burial, probably due to being washed down by rain-water, a few exceptions such as B.72 or B.89 suggest that it once covered all of it.

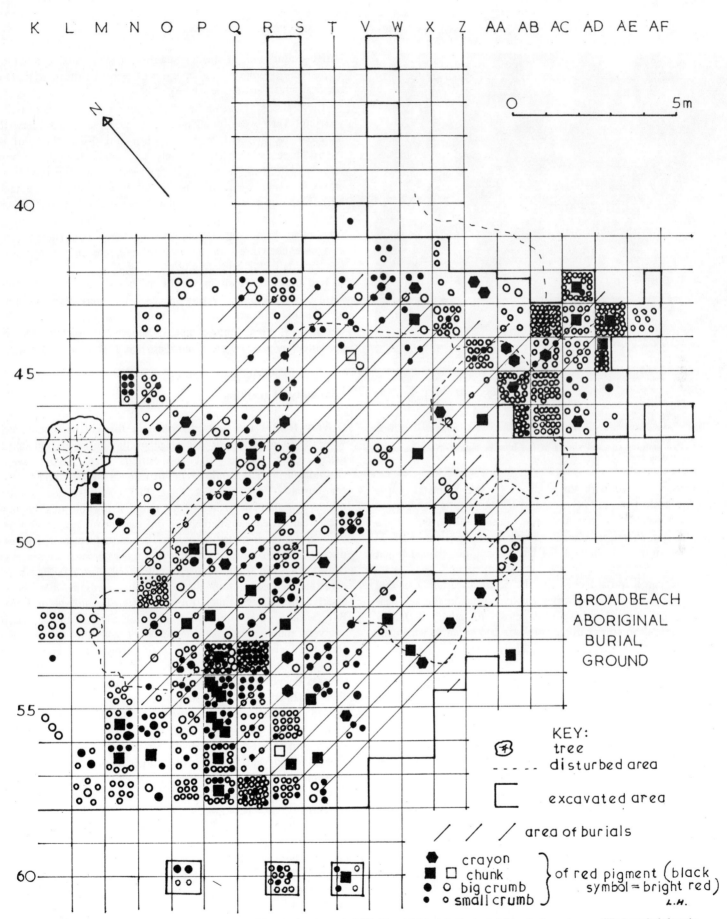

KEY:
tree
disturbed area

excavated area

area of burials

crayon
chunk
big crumb
small crumb
} of red pigment (black symbol = bright red)

L.H.

Map 4. Broadbeach burial ground: distribution of haematite. A symbol filled in with black indicates bright red pigment, an unfilled symbol that the pigment was a pale reddish brown.

Fig.61. B.7. Red staining of sand shows at the base of bundle. Note scatter of teeth. Camera facing east.

B.72, a vertical bundle with the skull on its side against a gentle pit-slope and away from the main core of the bundle, had a clear red stain descending vertically from the skull, outside the outline of the pit (fig. 60) and, therefore, clearly washed down from the skull. In B.89, the skull was at the top of the bundle and still stained bright red.

Of the five parcel burials, only one, B.55, could certainly be said to have been reddened. There was pigment present in the soil near the other four, but these were all close to other, definitely pigmented, burials. So it was not possible to be certain to which the crumbs of pigment belonged. It seemed likely, however, that they all had some.

Both the cremations were found to have many little crumbs of pigment amongst the bone fragments and there was a definite staining of some of these.[27]

Red pigment was present in the pits and as a stain on some bones of three of the horizontal bundles, B.40, B.91, and B.132. Some pigment was found in the pit of B.138 also but no stain noticed on the bones. These were, however, very dark and lying in very dark pit-fill.

Another 10 burials which could not be classified with certainty showed red staining of some bones or had fragments of pigment in their pit-fill. In all we found at least 85 certain or very probable instances of red pigment associated with secondary burials. (There were at least 139 of these, though some individuals were represented by a few bones only.)

The pigment in its various forms was found scattered all over the burial ground and, in smaller quantity, a little outside this (see map 4; the almost empty areas in the centre are the result of modern soil removal which cut deepest here).

The crayons of haematite, that is lumps with facets of polish, are puzzling. They were found mostly in level 1 and just below it, that is, close to the surface from which pits were dug. Out of the twenty-three examples found, only six were in the fill of a burial pit and four of these were clearly fragments only, the broken tips of crayons. Bones were, at least in some cases, wrapped long before burial and must have been reddened before wrapping. The crayons appear to have been used near the pits. The bone bundles may have been opened and the crayons used on the bones. The pigment may also have been used on the outside wrapping or for decorating the participants in the ceremony.

Red pigment found in the fill of burial pits was usually in the form of little crumbs or tiny specks. There were, however, a number of chunks without facets of polish and mostly about 2 to 3 centimetres long, approximately square or rectangular. Written accounts (see p. 83) suggest that these may have been gravegoods.

Continuity of tradition

Very few of the traits described in this chapter could be linked with one burial type or one stage of the burial ground only. (The next chapter shows that the various burial types overlapped chronologically.) It would seem then that a corpse could be prepared for burial in a variety of ways, that some treatments precluded others, but that, nevertheless, the range of possible treatments in any one burial varied considerably as did accompanying ceremonies. This picture is also suggested by written accounts from recent times to be discussed in chapter 6. As already suggested, such evidence can be considered valid for the most recent burials, since radiocarbon dates confirm the assumption made for other reasons that these were interred in modern times, probably after the arrival of Europeans. But, because other radiocarbon dates suggest that the earliest burials are very much older (see chapter 3), I will now discuss the traits considered above, together with their chronological implications. My impression is that, although the local population could ring the changes on quite a number of ritual details, the spectrum of possible rites remained much the same over the whole period of this burial ground. If this is so, it does suggest, coupled with the fact that this period was so surprisingly long, that traditions were changing very slowly and that evidence gathered from early European settlers may have some relevance to the early burials as well. But, as impressions are subjective, I shall now present evidence to support them.

Pit types A to C were formalized and used all through stages O to II. This may not be important; there are, after all, not many possible ways of digging a pit. The preference for certain directions in the alignment of pits and the burials within them seems a different matter. There may have been slight changes in emphasis from stage O to stage II; the selection of a certain direction seems more closely connected with burial types rather than with the relative age of the particular burial.

Also, there was apparently, through all stages, a great emphasis on symmetry. In the early extended burials, and perhaps also some late flexed ones, skulls face in opposite directions. Undisturbed and reasonably well preserved vertical bundles of all stages were almost invariably arranged strictly symmetrically (fig. 26).

The semicircle of stones around the skulls of the horizontal bundles B.40 and B.88 (both of stage O) differs little in idea from the semicircle of shells around the skulls of B.61, B.72, and B.79, all of stage II.

Bone points were found in B.102, from very early in stage O, but also in typical vertical bundles which were almost certainly considerably later in the sequence. (See Appendix E.)

The stone on the arm of B.37 and that on B.73 could be intentional; if so, they seem to reflect the same idea. The first was probably among the earliest, the other one of the very latest burials in the history of the burial ground.

The stone on the arm of B.73 is also a link with the subgroup of vertical bundle-burials mentioned earlier, being identical in shape and flaking technique to that resting on the skull of B.61. The presence of a polished axe, whether whole or broken, apparently links some typical vertical bundles (B.16, B.63, and B.113, all stage O or very early stage I) with the subgroup just mentioned (and possibly also with the horizontal bundles; a weathered polished axe found near

B.91 could have belonged to the latter).

Red pigment was common to all types of secondary burial, that is, was used through most stages of the burial ground. (Compare B.132 of stage O and B.72 of stage II as examples.)

The fires lit over the pits of late flexed burials were most noticeable, probably because the charcoal had not had so much time to be disturbed, but the same had been done over at least one late, typical, vertical bundle and probably over several other burials, not all late (p. 26). The small fires over the bones of B.37 (and possibly B.88), both very early, could not be clearly associated with food refuse and may be of a different character. But B.100, a late flexed burial, showed traces of fire well down in the pit as well as charcoal near the surface. And in the case of B.136, a horizontal bundle of stage I, the charcoal and debris normally associated with a pit-surface was found at the upper level of the bones instead.

It appears from some of the charcoal mentioned, and from shell pockets, animal bone, and discarded implements found in or on undisturbed pits, that a meal was part of the ritual in many cases, whether it was a matter of a vertical or horizontal bundle or a late flexed burial. It was not a matter of food deposited for the dead because, from the way shells were often stacked inside each other in the pocket, they must have been empty. The meal took place sometimes just before but mostly after finally filling the burial pit.

CHAPTER 3

Stratigraphy, relative and absolute dating

This chapter examines the stratigraphical relationships and offers a relative dating sequence. In addition, some absolute dates and related problems are discussed.

Evidence used in relative dating

The ridge

It was mentioned in chapter 1 that the sand ridge in which the burials occur is quite undifferentiated. Although it may have been built up in several stages, the parent materials are so uniform that borders between the stages cannot be distinguished. It is likely that the height of the ridge increased by some 10 centimetres during the period the burial ground was in use. Figure 62 shows the upper level of each vertical burial in the site. They are plotted in four groups according to relative age, stage O being the earliest. (The stages will be described later in this chapter.) I have already commented (p. 19) that the majority of burials were barely covered by sand when their pits were filled. Figure 62 suggests that they were buried from a surface that gradually increased in height. The picture outside the burial ground is of a continuous soil development in a sandy ridge stabilized by a turf cover (Appendix A).

Shell horizon

Where the surface over the burials was undisturbed, it was possible to distinguish a darker upper strip, level 1, some 25 - 30 centimetres thick, consisting of sand, humus, bits of bone — some human, some from other animals — charcoal, and some shells. In the lower part of this and above the lower, pale and pure sand (level 2), there was often a horizon of scattered horizontal shells and shell fragments (see fig. 5). Even when the horizon was thin, it was nevertheless definite, the shells usually being close to each other and rarely more than a few centimetres apart (figs. 7, 63, and 64). The pockets of shell found at this level have already been described. The presence of shell was clearly the result of human activity, apparently in connection with the burial rites, and the thin horizon a scatter from pockets of food debris. Nevertheless, quantities of shell and other food debris are minute compared with what is normally found in shell middens in this area and of this period[1] and much of what there was could be

Fig.62. Upper level of vertical burials arranged according to relative age. Numbers in the left margin show the depth below the modern surface of the uppermost bone surface in the burial. A T-sign indicates that this may be as left after burial, an arrow pointing upwards indicates that the bone was originally somewhat higher up or that some bone had been removed from the top of the burial before its excavation. The Roman numbers at the base of each division refer to the stage in the relative sequence of burials.

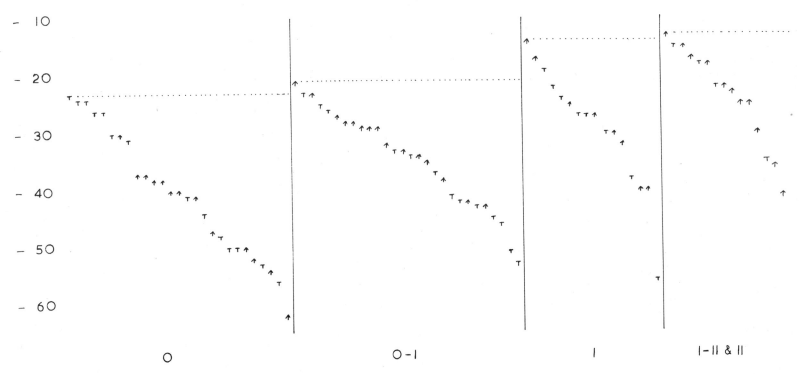

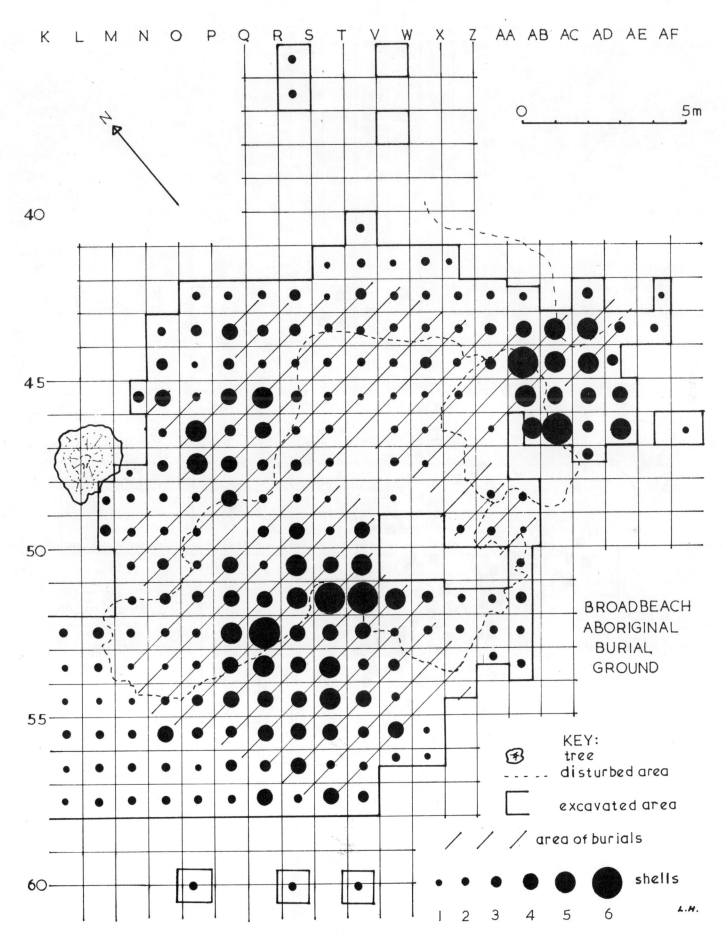

Map 5. Broadbeach burial ground: distribution of shell. Each circle indicates the total amount of shell present in levels 1 and 2 of the grid square.
1. 1–10 grams; **2.** 10–100 grams; **3.** 100–250 grams; **4.** 250–500 grams; **5.** 500–1,000 grams; **6.** More than 1,000 grams.

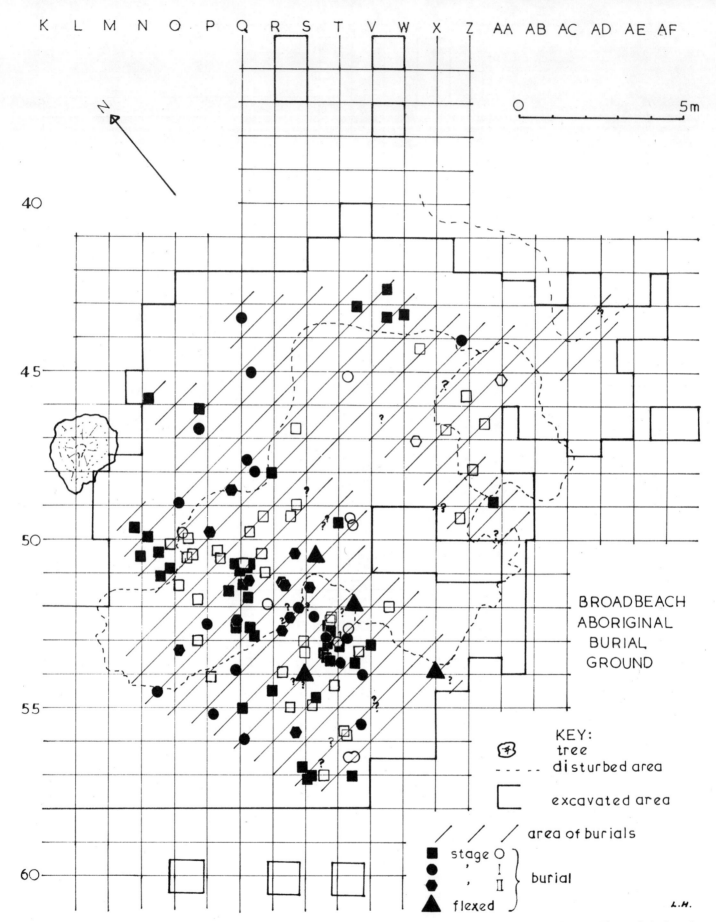

K L M N O P Q R S T V W X Z AA AB AC AD AE AF

N

0   5m

40

45

50

BROADBEACH
ABORIGINAL
BURIAL
GROUND

55

KEY:
🌲 tree
- - - disturbed area

☐ excavated area

/ / / area of burials

■ stage ○ }
● , ▯ } burial
⬢
▲ flexed }

60

L.H.

Map 6. Broadbeach burial ground: burials grouped according to relative age and the distribution of each group plotted. Note: The symbols show also the quality of the dating evidence. (Compare table 4.) Black symbols show burials of class A, unfilled symbols burials of class B, and question marks refer to burials of class C.

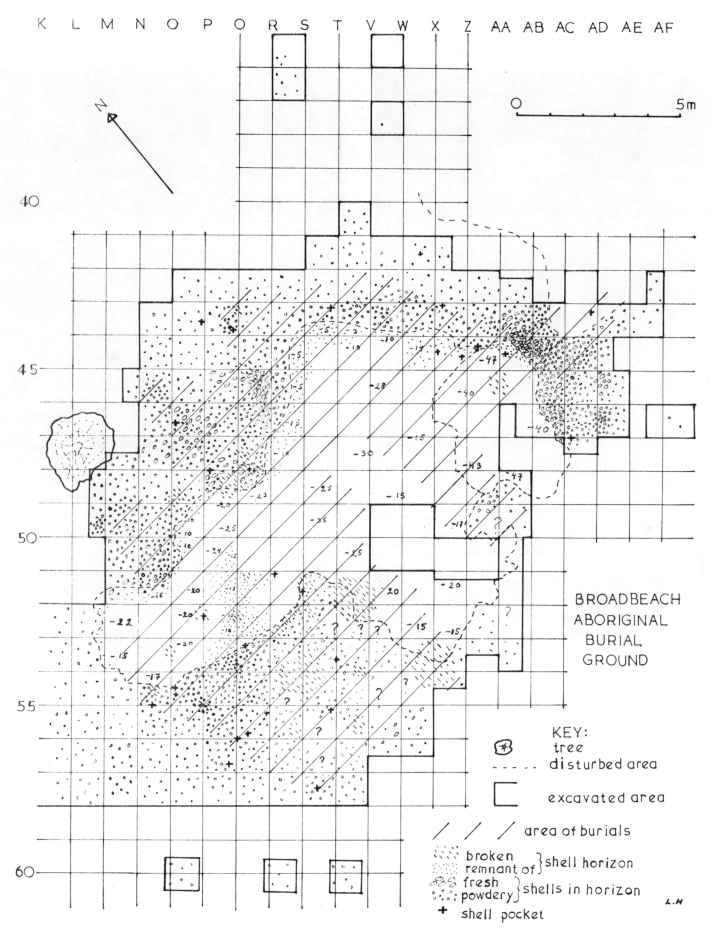

K L M N O P Q R S T V W X Z AA AB AC AD AE AF

5m

BROADBEACH
ABORIGINAL
BURIAL
GROUND

KEY:
tree
disturbed area
excavated area
area of burials
broken
remnant of } shell horizon
fresh
powdery } shells in horizon
shell pocket

L.H

Map 7.   Broadbeach burial ground: depth of soil removed by soil contractors indicated in centimetres below the modern surface. The physical state of the shell horizon has been shown as explained by the symbols on the map. This presentation was based on notes in the field journal and a visual inspection of the shells removed.

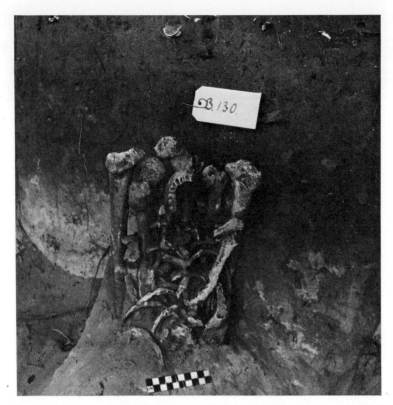

Fig.63. B.130, a vertical bundle-burial. The skull had been lifted; note arched mandible below this, ribs and smaller bones in core and damage to bony table due to curl-grubs. Camera facing north.

Fig.64. A thin but definite shell horizon over root crossing the B.117 pit (note skull just right of root). B.119 was in the same position on the opposite side of the balk. Note the continuation of the B.117 pit to the left of the root, visible as a darker patch. The bundle itself was below the root. Camera facing north-north-west.

seen to have been placed right on the surface of particular burial pits. This, together with written accounts (p. 84) and the long history of the site, suggests that it was never used as a campsite.

As a test of the connection between burials and shells, the latter have been weighed, square metre by square metre, and plotted on map 5.[2] The distribution coincided with the burials, the greatest amount of shell coming from the area with the greatest density of burials, as the maps show (compare maps 12 and 5). The shell debris decreased in quantity immediately outside the border of the burial ground.[3]

Once this horizon had formed in any part of the site, it would have been impossible to dig a pit through it and fill it again without some of the shell getting mixed with the fill of the pit. Where several burials were very close together, the presence of shell in the fill around some of them clearly indicated that these were later than the others. In these cases, the shell derived from the horizon which could be seen to be disturbed, or completely broken, over the pit (cf. fig. 51). The shells and the shell fragments were at all angles and in all parts of the pit-fill, and continued up into level 1 (cf. fig. 73). In a few cases there was shell in the pit-fill but also a weak horizon over the pit. There was then no real separation between pit-fill and horizon, the pit having been dug after the foundation of the horizon, but before the end of this stage which continued at least as long as the tradition of bundle-burials.

If the formation of this horizon was associated with the burials it was clearly a gradual thing, since nothing suggests that all or most of the burials were of the same date. Its value as a time-marker for the whole site depends very much on whether it began forming over the whole site within a fairly short time. This would not be the case if one part of the burial ground had been in use first and then another. The possibility of horizontal stratigraphy was tested by using the burials as well as the lithic evidence.

The burials were separated into four main stages based on their relative sequence and other stratigraphical evidence available. Such evidence will be given later in the chapter for some of them; details relevant to the others will be found in Appendix D. The flexed burials were separated from other late burials because they differed in kind and because they appeared to be later than most or all of these. Map 6 shows that burials of each stage were scattered over most of the burial ground. The later burials appear a little more restricted in area than the rest, but this restriction seems merely a tendency to cluster in the centre of the area.[4] This may perhaps be explained by the obvious preference for the highest parts of the ridge in conjunction with the gradual slight rise in level discussed.

The lithic evidence was used to confirm this picture, since much of the argument behind map 6 rested on the evidence from the shell horizon, the importance of which was still to be proven. Artifacts and stone waste were separated out as a group when it appeared certain that their raw material was one and the same nodule or a confined area on an outcrop. (The basis for such groupings will be discussed in detail in chapter 5 in connection with typology of artifacts. It was often, however, a matter of fragments fitting together or flakes fitting into flake scars.) Almost all of these groups show a wide scatter over all, or most, of the burial ground.[5] This pattern was so strong that one can probably disregard the fact that some mixing and redistribution must have taken place as the sand was shifted around during pit-digging. Since the site appears to have been used exclusively as a burial ground and without any noticeable break, it appears safe to assume that the stone was present because of the burials and its distribution closely related.[6] Parts of the same, usually small, nodule were used for burials in different parts of the burial ground, probably at the same time or nearly so (p. 62). There were a few cases of probable later re-use; this can be suspected, but not proven, in many more instances.

If all or most parts of the burial ground were in use at much the same time, if pockets of shell were associated with burial rites, and if a number of people took part in each ceremony, as tradition suggests (see chapter 6), then it probably would not take long to scatter shell all over such a small area, producing a valuable time-marker.

Thus, although it is possible that a burial with a little shell in its pit-fill was almost contemporary with one far from it in whose pit-fill there was no shell at all, it seems very likely that a burial with a great deal of shell in its fill from any part of the site was later than most burials from this site.

Tree roots

The big roots of the Forest Red Gum described in chapter 1 penetrated the site in all directions (see map 12). Although they caused extra difficulties and damaged the burials, they provided a certain amount of stratigraphical information. They formed a terminus ante quem for some burials and groups of burials. (The age of the tree and its root system will be discussed towards the end of this chapter in the context of absolute dating.)

A good example of this was B.117, a vertical bundle-burial. One of the main feeder roots from the stump had gone through the west-south-west upper part (ca. one-fifth) of its pit. As it expanded, it pushed the skull to northeast, away from the bundle underneath it, crushing and eroding the skull as well (figs. 65 and 66). The shell horizon which went over the burial pit and over the root was pushed upwards when the latter expanded and showed a distinct bulge (figs. 64 and 67).

In the case of B.122, another vertical bundle-burial, a root from the tree came just below the northeast part of its base. The swelling root lifted this and its thrust from northwest caused the bundle to tilt to the west (fig. 68). Another root, going between the vertical bundle-burials B.125 and B.123 (see map 12) pushed the base of the former to the north-north-east when expanding and caused B.123 to lean to the northwest (figs. 9 and 69). The same root reached another vertical bundle-burial, B.126, pushed the base of the skull and the mandible inside the vault and then eroded the bone itself. (Figure 70 shows how all bone within 4 centimetres of the periphery of the root has been "eaten" away.)

It is possible that expanding tree roots are one of the reasons why no burials later than stage I were found near the stump (see map 6).

Fig.65. B.117, a vertical bundle-burial damaged by swelling root from Forest Red Gum. The main bundle of bones stayed in the pit-fill below the root while skull was pushed to the right. Note developing soil horizons crossing the pit and the freshness of the wood in the root. Camera facing north.

Fig.66. Shell horizon and root over B.117 removed. The skull can be seen to have been pushed to the right of the column of long bones. Camera facing north-north-west.

Fig.67. A thin but definite shell horizon going over the root crossing the B.117 pit. (Part of skull is visible in lower right margin behind root.) Camera facing east.

Fig.68. Section XVIII through B.122 pit, a vertical bundle-burial. Note how the big root pushed the base of the bundle upwards.

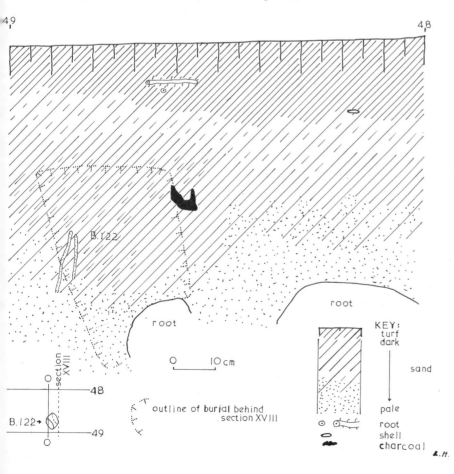

Fig.69. Section showing B.125, B.123, B.126, and empty pit to the far right (below modern disturbance). Note slight colour difference between fill and surrounding ridge for the three undisturbed burials. Camera facing northeast.

This area was extremely awkward to excavate (compare figs. 71 and 72). It would heave been just as awkward to dig pits for burials here, once the feeder roots had started forming and spreading.

Burial pits

Differences in colour, texture, and content of the fill in the burial pits gave some stratigraphical evidence. At times the fill of two or more pits intersected or covered the same area, but at different depths, e.g. the vertical bundle-burials B.29 and B.30 (fig. 73). Occasionally a pit cut through another burial; compare B.45, a vertical bundle-burial and B.52, an extended primary burial (see map

Fig.70. B.126 bundle (skull lifted) showing how the big root had eroded away all bone within 4 centimetres of its surface. Camera facing northwest.

Fig.71. B.125, a leaning vertical bundle-burial, supported with rods and clamps. Note that it was pushed out of position by the big root from the Forest Red Gum. Another root passed just beyond and above its skull.

Fig.72. Section close to the stump of the Forest Red Gum showing the size of the roots penetrating this area. Camera facing northwest.

12, fig. 11, and below). Examples of intersection (cf. chapter 2, note 10) enabled me to establish two major burial sequences proceeding from the early to the late stage of the burial ground. These plus a shorter sequence will be discussed next.

Sequence A

This section presents the facts and reasoning behind diagram A in figure 74.[7]

B.45: A vertical bundle burial (fig. 93). There was a distinct shell horizon over the surface of the burial pit well above the top of the bundle. Some small fragments of shell a little lower in the pit-fill were probably moved by roots. The pit itself cut through B.52 and to a lower level (map 12).

B.52: An extended primary burial. The bones below the knee were missing, but a talus was lying close to the right knee-joint (fig. 75). They were removed when the pit for B.45 was dug and the two

Fig.73. Section X through B.29 and B.30, vertical bundle-burials. Note the shells at the base of the B.29 pit.

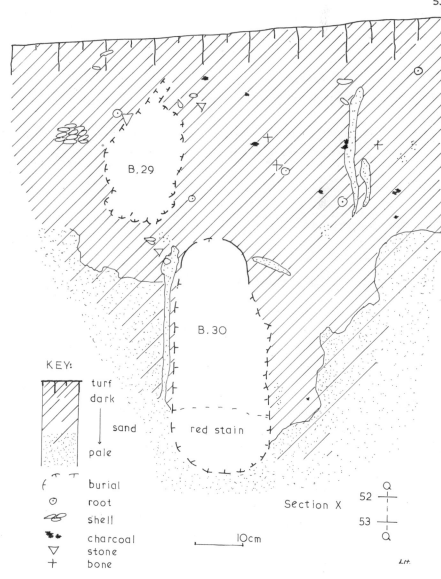

KEY:

turf
dark
↓
sand
pale

↑ ⊤ ⊤ burial
⊙ root
〰 shell
✦ charcoal
▽ stone
✝ bone

red stain

Section X

52
53

10cm

_Lh._

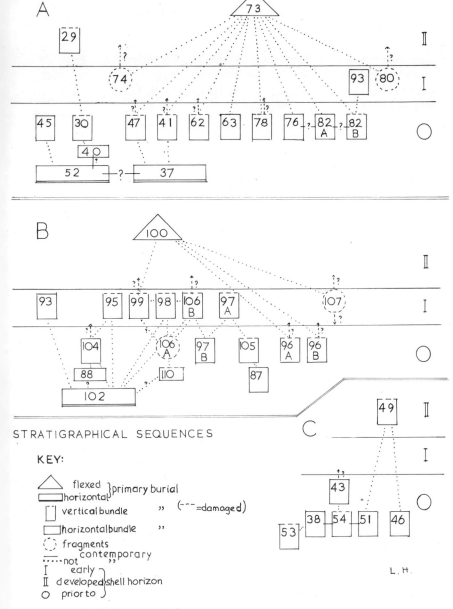

STRATIGRAPHICAL SEQUENCES

KEY:

△ flexed } primary burial
▭ horizontal
[ ] vertical bundle   "   (- - - = damaged)
▭ horizontal bundle   "
(⋅) fragments
⋯⋯ contemporary
⋯⋯ not   "
I   early ⎫
II developed ⎬ shell horizon
O   prior to ⎭

Fig.74. Stratigraphical sequences.

tibiae and fibulae were added to the B.45 bundle and reburied. To the north of B.45, and at the level of B.52, the remains of two slightly disturbed but apparently, at the time of burial, articulated feet were found just outside the pit for B.45 and clearly belonging to B.52 (fig. 11). (Note that one of the feet appears disturbed also by the pit for B.28.) Since B.52 was a primary burial, it must have decayed sufficiently for most bones to separate before the burial of B.45, otherwise the pulling away of the tibiae, etc. would have disturbed the other bones of the body. (The position of the talus suggests some bond with the tibiae.)

B.40: This bundle burial of a child was placed horizontally at interment since it was very neat and compact. It showed no signs of having shifted in the sand, and there was a neat horizontal semicircle of stones, a corona, around its skull (cf. fig. 54 and chapter 2). It was sitting over the midriff and pelvic basin of B.52, its long axis in line with that of B.52. The bundle was placed between the arms of the latter, the hands of which almost joined below the pelvis as if they were clasping the bundle (fig. 13 and 75). It seems quite impossible that B.40 could have been buried much later than B.52. If the latter had had time to decay at all, some of its bones would have been disturbed or damaged by the new burial, and this was not the case. It would also have been difficult to place B.40 in such symmetry with B.52 were not the latter in good condition and much of it visible. Everything suggests that the two burials were contemporary.

B.30: A vertical bundle-burial. Its upper part was splayed a little over B.40, but its base missed the latter, proceeding to a deeper level just missing B.52 also. The fill of its pit was very clean, containing only a few very small fragments of shell and charcoal, probably owing to the action of roots. The lower part of the burial was stained vivid red. A fracture in the top of the skull was probably the result of the digging of a pit for B.29, the bones of which were only about 5 centimetres away and a little higher up (figs. 73 and 76).

Fig.75. B.52, pelvis and hands after removal of B.40. Note stone and talus bone near right knee, no bones below the knees. Camera facing southeast.

Fig.76. B.29 and B.30 in section. Note a large stone near and shells below the base of B.29 (upper burial). Note also damage to B.30 skull vault. Camera facing east.

Fig.77. B.52 skull and B.37 feet. Note that the latter were at a higher level and pointing upwards. Note also dark stain from fire lit over the feet. Camera facing southeast.

B.29: A vertical bundle-burial. Part of level 1 had been removed by soil contractors whose shovels cut off the top part of the burial and scattered some of the pieces nearby. The fill of the burial pit below the level of disturbance was full of shells which suggests that the horizon was well developed at the time of burial (figs. 73 and 76).

B.37: This extended burial was lying in line with B.52, its feet only 15 - 20 centimetres away from the skull of the latter. They may have been buried simultaneously in the same trench. Although the feet of B.37 on the photographs appear to be slightly higher than the skull of B.52 (fig. 12) the whole of its trunk was lower and at much the same level as B.52 (fig. 77). The head and shoulders were slightly higher. (This suggests that the body was held by its feet and shoulders as it was lowered into a rough trench cut in loose dry sand, which was already pouring back below and around the body while it was being buried.) It is possible, however, that B.37 was buried a little later than B.52.[8] The position of the latter would then have had to be clearly marked or visible at the time, since the symmetry of orientation was too marked to be accidental. The shell horizon extended over the area of the burials, except where broken by pits for burials clearly later than B.37 and B.52 (fig. 78).

B.47: A vertical bundle-burial. Its pit splayed a little into the B.37 trench without disturbing this burial. The dark fill contained no shell except at the top. This could date from the time of burial or be the result of disturbance at the time B.73 was buried. The pit for B.73 cut into B.47 a little. Whether it also damaged the bones cannot be known until these have been analyzed. Some damage could be due to the fact that the burial tilted towards B.73 as the fill in the pit for this subsided.

B.41: A vertical bundle-burial. This was sitting above the skull of

Fig.78. Section above B.37. Note remnant of shell horizon (far left), B.47 pit (dark tinge in centre), and B.73 pit (right half). Camera facing east.

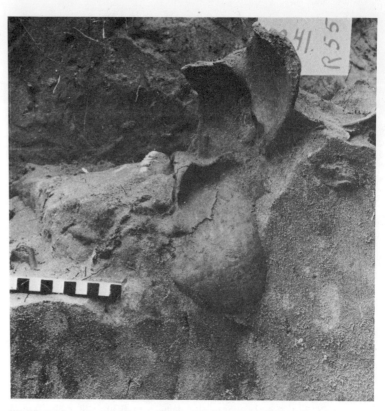

Fig.79. Pelvis of B.41 resting on skull of B.37. Camera facing east.

B.37 separated by a few centimetres of sand (fig. 79). Its location suggests that the position of B.37 was, by then, forgotten, but that the participants in the ceremony stopped digging when they struck the skull of the latter. Digging the pit for B.73 caused damage to the top part of the burial, particularly to the skull, and the part of B.41 which was not resting on B.37 slid down towards the B.73 pit when the fill in this settled (fig. 80). There was no shell in its pit-fill and no shell horizon above. It is possible that the latter was not well developed just here, but it is more likely that it was present, scraped off and thrown into the pit for B.73, the fill of which was full of lenses of dark soil with shells and fragments of human bone. It could, however, be later in the sequence than suggested on the diagram. It was certainly pre-B.73.

B.78: Once vertical, in a pit with dark fill without shells, this bundle-burial was pushed over and broken when the pit for B.73 was dug. A marked line of shells along the line of broken bones shows the lip of the pit for B.73 cutting the top of the burial and removing parts of it (figs. 5 and 81).

B.76: This bundle-burial was apparently once almost vertical. It was buried before B.73, but tilted towards the latter because the pit for this was dug very close to B.76 and its pit-fill would have provided less resistance before settling than the rest of the surrounding soil. Any pressure from above — possibly the weight of the pit-diggers — would have moved the burial in this direction, if it started off with a slight tilt which is likely if the bundle was not in the centre of a pit (cf. next paragraph). There was no shell in the fill around B.76, but an unusually marked shell horizon just above it dipped almost

Fig.80. B.41, collapsing vertical bundle-burial. Note teeth of B.37 near left margin, pit for B.73 in upper right corner. Part of B.41 rested on B.37, part had slid towards B.73. Camera facing northeast.

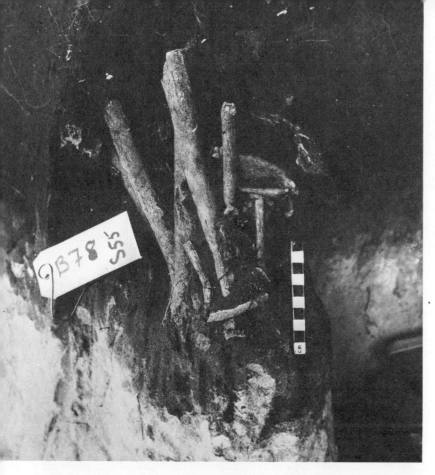

Fig.81. B.78, a vertical bundle-burial damaged in the process of digging the pit for B.73. Note the dipping line of shells and the breaks in the long bones at the same level, both showing the lip of the pit for B.73. Camera facing east.

Fig.82. B.76 and B.82A, vertical bundle-burials show below a shell horizon which dips sharply to the right of the burials, following the steep slope of the pit for B.73. Camera facing southeast.

vertically to the southwest into the pit for B.73 (cf. fig. 82 and comments on B.73).

Two other vertical bundle-burials, B.82A and B, were very close to it and the three could have formed a clutch buried at the same time (cf. B.38+54+51, sequence C). The outline of their pit was not clear, partly because both B.73 and B.93 cut into it and partly because some of the remainder collapsed into the pit for B.73 during our excavation.

B.82A: Closest to this pit, it came down in the collapse. It was apparent from observations and photographs that these bones were very close to and parallel with those of B.76, the dipping shell horizon going over both.

B.82B: A little further southeast and remaining in situ, it appeared to sit on the slope of a pit (this applied also to B.76), the centre of the pit apparently being in the area of B.82A. The southeast part of the top of the bundle had been damaged by the burial of B.93.

B.93: This bundle-burial was leaning over a part of B.82B. It was sealed by a shell horizon, which had started to form at the time of burial, bringing some fragments of shell into the fill. This burial cannot be directly related to B.73 in the stratigraphical diagram, since it was not associated with the disturbance caused by the latter, but the fairly small amount of shell in its pit suggests that it was earlier in time.

B.62: A vertical bundle-burial in a shallow pit without shells in the fill (but see p. 30) and probably once sealed by a shell horizon which was later disturbed by the pit for B.73. At the same time, the top of the burial was shifted to the northeast. This could not be the work

of the root going just above the burial, seen on figure 83, since this root grew from the northeast and the base of the burial was clearly in situ. A slightly sloping, then sharply dipping line of shells going over the southwest part of the burial and towards B.73 outlined the lip of the pit for the latter.

B.63: This originally vertical bundle-burial was sealed by a shell horizon and its fill contained no fragments of shell. It had tilted and splayed to the west, possibly because of pressure from a big root going through it and/or because it was very close to the pit for B.73, although apparently not directly damaged by it. The skull was badly smashed, but crushed rather than disturbed (fig. 84). In the lower part of level 1, above the burial, there was a scatter of shell and charcoal that appeared to be a continuation from the pit for B.73.

B.74: A few fragments of human bone embedded in a very dark lens with shells found deep down in the pit for B.73. These were probably once close to the surface and were perhaps originally buried after the shell horizon had begun to form (fig. 85).

B.80: Also fragments of a burial but not from the same person as B.74. It was found almost halfway down the pit in a dark lens with shells (fig. 86). Note its rectangular spread of 25 by 30 centimetres — one spadeful?

B.73: Although buried at a greater depth than any other burial found in the site, this was clearly one of the very latest burials. Its pit narrowly missed some burials, disturbed others, and must have destroyed a few. The body was flexed, fully articulated, and apparently not decayed at the time of burial (fig. 55). This contrasts sharply with the prevalence of secondary burials during the period

Fig.83. B.62, a damaged vertical bundle-burial. Note the root (cut off) which ran across lower half of skull and, near the right margin, a shell dipping along the slope of the B.73 pit. Camera facing southeast.

Fig.85. B.73 at the bottom of a very deep pit. Note B.74, a few fragments, in a dark lens. (Top right and centre show boards shoring up the sides of the pit and dry sand trickling down around them.) Camera facing south.

Fig.84. B.63 (left) and B.67 (right). Note shell between them at level of horizon. Camera facing south-south-west.

Fig.86. B.80, bone fragments in the B.73 pit-fill. Note the approximately rectangular spread of the fragments. Camera facing east.

between this and the earlier extended burials. The pit was much larger than those used for bundle-burials. It was subtriangular and steep-sided, particularly in the lower part where the sides were in places almost vertical, suggesting that it was dug with an efficient implement, perhaps a modern shovel or spade (cf. figs. 5, 82, and 87). The fill of the pit was also different from the usual homogeneous brown fill, almost indistinguishable from the surrounding sand. In this case, it consisted of lenses and pockets of often contrasting colour, particularly towards the bottom of the pit (fig. 87; cf. fig. 3, a modern pit, dug with a small shovel). The slight blurring of colour in the upper part suggests leaching since the time of burial. The lenses did not look as if they were the result of silting from the sides of the pit and the surrounding surface. They resembled a series of spadefuls of soil. (Compare B.80 and p. 62.) For the lenses of colour to be so clear and so differentiated, the fill must have been dug and replaced in large chunks, not scraped out a little at a time. To get such large chunks and clear outlines would have been difficult unless the sand in the lower part of the ridge was wet at the time. Higher up it was probably drier, since the shell horizon had started spilling into the pit as it was being filled (fig. 63). The pit must have been filled shortly after it was dug.[9]

Sequence B

This has one burial, B.93, in common with sequence A; most details relevant to this were described on p. 45. This section explains diagram B in figure 74.

B.88: This bundle-burial was horizontal. The bones formed a

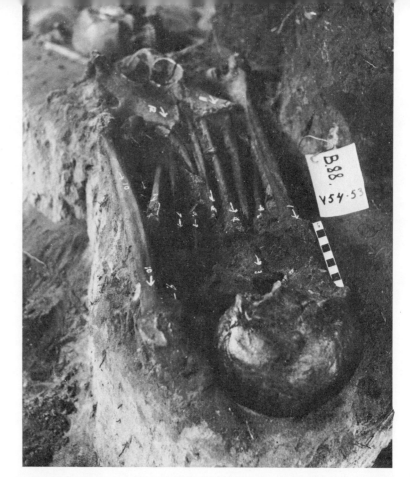

Fig.88. B.88, a horizontal bundle. Note its rectangular outline and the skull of B.102 in the background. Camera facing west.

rectangular shape (figs. 88 and 89). There was a well-developed shell horizon above it, but no shell further down (fig. 49).

Fig.89. B.88, a horizontal bundle. Note the vault of B.104 in the left margin. Camera facing down.

Fig.87. Part of section through pit for B.73. Note B.37 in bottom left corner, steep slope of pit past this burial and very dark lenses (containing shell) in pit-fill. Camera facing northeast.

B.104: A vertical bundle-burial just below the shell horizon, so close to this that pressure from above squashed the top of the skull and pressed shell fragments against it. There was no shell further down in its pit, which was dug deeper than B.88, the southeast side of the pit intruding a little over the latter. The floor of the pit was well above B.102.

B.95: The surface soil above this vertical bundle-burial was disturbed and the top part of the bundle damaged. The burial pit was dug through an established shell horizon and there were shells in its fill well below the level of disturbance and not as a result of this. The pits for B.104 and B.95 were clearly separate. The burial was sitting above the southern end of B.102 (its skull) and the latter must have been noted, but not disturbed, when the pit for B.95 was dug.

B.102: This atypical semiextended, semidisjointed burial was horizontal and buried at approximately the same level as burials B.37 and B.52, which were fully extended (fig. 17). The stain below the burial also suggested similarity in its colour and extent. But the burial was clearly disjointed before burial, not disturbed afterwards. The soil above it was cut into by pits for later burials, and there were no indications of the extent of the upper part of its trench, but the burial was clearly in situ before the development of any shell horizon.

B.93: Its burial pit splayed into the B.102 trench (see also sequence A).

B.110: A few long bones of a very small child found at much the same level as B.102 but a little in under the skull B.106A. They were probably horizontal in the ground, but were sitting in the dry humus-free pale sand, and started sliding out during the excavation of B.102. The pits dug for later burials in this area could account for the absence of some bones belonging to this individual.

B.98: A vertical bundle-burial whose top part was sitting just in the level of the shell horizon, which had started to form before the time of the burial. The burial pit narrowly missed B.102 and its upper part extended a little over the latter.

B.99: The burial pit seemed separate from that of B.98 and less deep, the general impression being that digging stopped when the latter was noticed. The whole burial was very disturbed and chopped up, apparently when the pit for B.100 was dug. Some broken long bones found above the skull may not belong to this burial (cf. B.107) and there were also some extra skull fragments. There were some shells in the fill, but these could be due to the disturbance.[10]

B.107: A few bits of bone, part of a burial disturbed by the pit for B.100 and not in situ. One of the fragments in B.99 fits a broken long bone in B.107. The fragments of shell around the bones could be due to the disturbance.

B.100: A flexed burial in a deep oval pit which interfered with several other burials, but which was itself undisturbed except at the southern end (figs. 14, 15, 48, and 91). The fill had marked lenses, some going right across the pit, of sharply contrasting colour and consistency: pale sand, greyish sand, very dark soil full of shells (and charcoal), the latter in large quantities near the top. The shell horizon must have been well developed at the time of burial.[11]

B.106A (skull only): This was sitting half-way between the skull of B.99 and the bundle of long bones called B.106B. The skull was first thought to have belonged to the latter but to have slipped away from

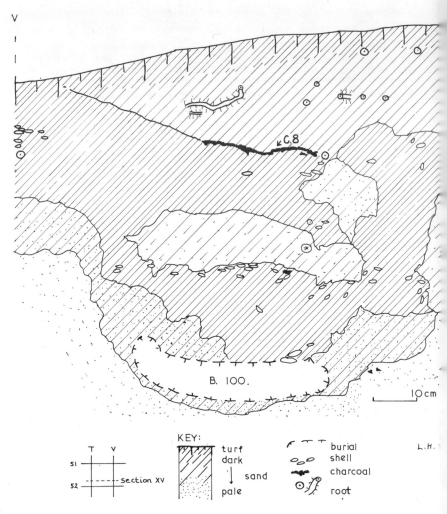

Fig.90. Section through B.100, a flexed primary burial. Note that there were lenses of shell and charcoal, more than shows in the section, in the pit-fill as well as near the pit-surface.

it. The bundle was leaning in that direction. The skull is more likely to be the remains of a burial disturbed by both B.98 and B.99. The top part of the B.98 bundle seemed to splay very slightly over the skull. There was no shell close to the skull itself.

B.106B: A tilted bundle whose top part penetrated well into level 1 above the shell horizon. This upper part was badly decayed and damaged.[12] There was some shell in the fill round the bones. The bottom of the pit was ca. 21 centimetres higher up than that for B.98 and the top of the burial would once have been considerably above that of the latter.

B.97B: A small, almost vertical, bundle buried just below the shell horizon. There was no shell in the pit-fill. The lip of the pit for B.106B splayed a little over the pit-surface.

B.97A: Once probably a vertical bundle but pushed over and decaying badly because so close to the surface. Its pit apparently caused some damage to that for B.105. The burial was wedged in between this and B.97B, the base of its pit higher up than those of the other two, and the pit-fill contained shells and shell fragments, all of which indicate that the shell horizon was well developed at the time of burial.

Fig.91. Cluster of burials: B.103, B.108, B.109, all buried in separate pits. Note compactness and oval cross section of B.103. Camera facing east.

Fig.92. B.87, a vertical bundle-burial. Fragmentary and fragile but undisturbed bones. Skull fragments have splayed to either side of the column of long bones below it. Camera facing east.

B.105: This was clearly in situ, but much of the top part was damaged by B.97A which brought shell into the uppermost part of the burial. The fill lower down was free from any fragments of shell. The size of the remaining vertical bundle indicated that it once reached just below the level of the shell horizon.

B. 87: The pit for B.105 did not cut into, but splayed a little over, the bones of this small vertical bundle-burial which was decayed but not disturbed (fig. 92). There was no shell in the fill apart from half an oyster shell inside the bundle itself (cf. p. 30).

B.96A and B: These were burials of two small children of the same age and close together. There was a faint suggestion of two pits at the base of the burials. There was no shell in the fill at that level. The upper parts of the burials had been badly damaged and scattered, probably when the pit for B.100 was dug. Many bone fragments were found in level 1 in this area, and even some not very close to the burials may be found to belong to them.

Sequence C

This section is an explanation of diagram C in figure 74.

B.53: The burial, apparently once a vertical bundle-burial, was set well down in a deep pit without any trace of shell in its fill. The pit for burials B.38, B.51, and B.54 cut into the burial from the southwest but not quite to the same depth, leaving some bones from the burial sitting below and some northeast of B.38 (fig. 93).

B.38: A clear undisturbed shell horizon went over this burial, and there was no shell in the pit-fill. The latter held burials B.51 and

B.54 as well (figs. 5, 32, and 93). The bundle was almost vertical, leaning a little to the east, some of its long bones lying parallel with, and against, some in B.54. It is unlikely that B.38 was inserted into this pit after the burial of B.54, since they were so close and the base of B.38 was at a lower level. If a pit had been dug past B.54 so near it, this would certainly have slipped into the new pit with the loose sand on which it was resting.[13]

B.54: This bundle was upside down but the arrangement of bones was otherwise typical of vertical bundle-burials (fig. 94). Although the base of the burial was a little higher up than those of B.38 and B.51, it could not have been inserted between them, since B.38 was leaning over it and the outlines of B.54 and B.51 where they met formed a distinct S-line (fig. 32). Although there was much shell above the burial there was none in the fill around it. (Both B.38 and B.51 showed a marked red staining of the bone in the lowest part of the bundle and of the sand nearby, but no such stain was seen on B.54; it could, however, have washed down beyond the base level of this.)

B.51: A typical bundle-burial, almost vertical. This was sitting on the gentle southeast slope of a big pit. It was close to B.54, its skull partly over that of the latter (fig. 32). There was no shell in the fill, but the shell horizon above was disturbed, probably by B.49 (fig. 93).

B.38, B.51, and B.54: Their pit had a steep side to the northwest and west where it was also deepest, sloping more gently upwards to the northeast and southeast, suggesting that it was scooped out from west-north-west to east-south-east. The three burials were part of a

Fig.93. Burials crowded in small area. B.43 (far left) was leaning over B.38 + B.54 (not showing) + B.51. B.49 was partly above B.46. The dark stain in the foreground between B.46 and B.45 shows the pit for B.28. The feet of B.52, just left of B.45, have been removed. Camera facing east-south-east.

Fig.94. B.54, a typical vertical bundle but upside down. Camera facing east.

clutch, the long axis of this going from northwest to southeast, the whole clutch leaning a little to the northeast, and the tops of the burials leaning towards the centre of the clutch.

B.43: All the topsoil, including the shell horizon above the burial, was here removed by soil contractors, leaving only a thin layer of disturbed sand just above the burial, a vertical bundle. A little further south, in the undisturbed area, a clear shell horizon could be seen at a level above that of the burial. The horizon probably covered the burial; it was present in patches nearby wherever only a shallow depth of soil had been removed. There was no shell in the pit-fill. The vault of the skull was badly crushed in spite of its thick bone, probably because of pressure from above, during, or after soil removal. The burial was not contemporary with, and was probably later than, the big clutch close to it. The pit was separate, at a higher level, and probably the cause of some of the damage to the top part of B.54. The bones were also of different texture and some of the long bones splayed a little over the top of B.54, probably as a result of pressure from the skull (figs. 93 and 95). This may have been aggravated by pressure from above after soil removal, but appeared to be due mainly to an earlier and gradual process preceeding the compaction of the pit-fill — otherwise the upper ends of the long bones would have suffered more damage.

Fig. 95. B.43 (the skull had been lifted) can be seen to splay in over B.54 (the very decayed bones in the top right corner). Note small bones in core of bundle. Camera facing south.

Fig. 96. Same cluster of burials as in figure 93. B.54 here shows between B.43 and B.51. Note the presence of shell in the pit for B.49. Note also serial vertebrae in B.46. Camera facing east.

Fig. 97. B.136 (after lift 1), a horizontal bundle burial. Note dark pit in section, top right corner. Camera facing south.

B.46: A typical vertical bundle-burial in a separate pit, set well below the shell horizon and lacking any trace of shell in its pit-fill. (There were many, but intangible, suggestions of similarity to B.45 near it, cf. fig. 93). The shell horizon was cut through by the pit for B.49, which just missed the bones of this burial but cut a little into the top of its pit-fill (fig. 93).

B.49: The upper part of this burial was cut off by soil contractors and some fragments were found in the disturbed soil, but the base was in situ and the parts left suggest that it was once a vertical bundle-burial. Its pit had been dug through an already well-developed shell horizon, shells from this being scattered in its fill. The lower part of the pit cut into the upper parts of those for B.46 and the clutch B.38+54+51, but without damaging the bones further down (fig. 96).

The relative dating of other burials

In some other cases, it was possible to declare or suggest that one burial must be later than another near it. The burials B.135 and B.136, both sealed below a thin shell horizon, are one rather intriguing example. The latter was a horizontal bundle in a shallow oval pit (fig. 97). The former was also, at first, thought to be a horizontal bundle; the bones were leaning a little, but there was no skull, only a mandible, at the end higher up, which was seen first (fig. 98). The arrangement of the bones in the bundle, including the mandible, was otherwise typical of vertical bundle-burials. The skull

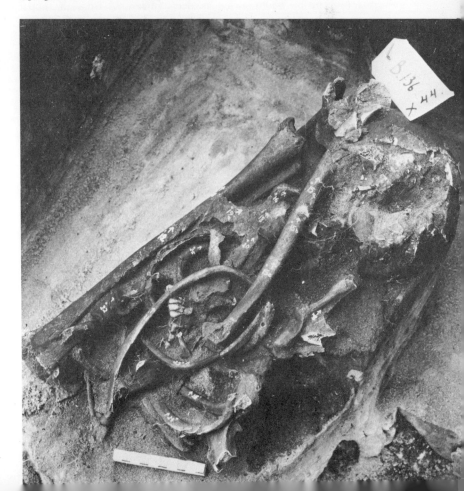

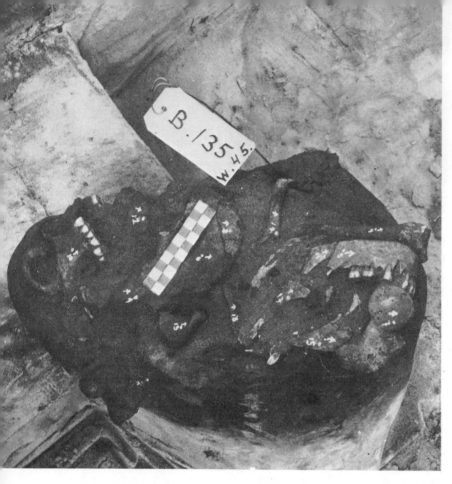

Fig.98. B.135, disturbed burial (after lift 1). Note mandible at upper end, skull at lower end of leaning burial. Camera facing southwest.

was later found at the opposite end, slightly lower, upside down and damaged by the pelvis which had been partly pushed inside it. Teeth were scattered through the burial and the ribs very broken. The pit was found to be about twice as deep (measured from the upper surface of the bones) as the burial itself. Clearly this was once a typical vertical bundle-burial with the skull above the mandible, set at the deep end of a pit of type B. It was accidentally pulled out during the process of digging a pit for another burial. The wrapping had not yet decayed completely but the skull fell off, rolled into the pit (already partly filled by sand trickling back) and the rest of the bundle was put back on top, now almost horizontal, in what remained of the pit, and sand scraped back over it. This sand contained a little fragmented shell and some stone, which indicates that the shell horizon had started forming in the area at the time of the disturbance. There was no shell further down in the pit so the original burial may have taken place during stage O. The pit of B.136 did not cut into that of B.135 (see map 12 and fig. 53), but their borders could not have been more than a few centimetres apart. Several implements and much waste of a striking yellow quartzite were found all around B.136, clearly used in connection with this burial. A little of this material was found just above B.135. It seems probable that it was the people who were burying B.136 who unwittingly disturbed B.135, that they dug a new pit only just far enough away to clear the latter, and that some of the yellow quartzite, already flaked and perhaps used for some early stage of the B.136 ritual, was lost in the process of covering B.135. The remainder was left beside B.136 after the ceremonies had been completed.

Instances of one burial cutting into another were listed in chapter 2, note 10. The main point about the stratigraphical information these give is that a vertical bundle is frequently shown to be later than another burial of the same type. The comments on diagrams A - C, figure 74, have already shown that we are dealing with a burial ground in use over a period of time, not with a case of mass burial. The contemporary nature of different burial types also becomes apparent.

The chronological relationships, if known, of burials not found in diagrams A - C, figure 74, have been listed in table 4. The burials have been divided into three groups according to the quality of the dating evidence. This seems acceptable for burials in group A. For group B it was less reliable. These burials have been assigned the place in the sequence that seemed most probable according to the facts available (given in Appendix D) and my impressions during the excavation. All burials that were too badly damaged or decayed, or for some other reason impossible to refer to a particular stage, have been listed as group C. Note that all burials of type V.1 can be found in diagrams A - C (fig. 74).

Summary of relative dating

The results of these four diagrams can be summarized as follows: All extended or semiextended burials belong to the earliest phase of the burial ground. Some horizontal bundles are very early also, but they occur through stage I into stage II. One case, B.40 and B.52, suggests that the two burial types (one secondary and one primary) overlap in time.

Secondary burial of different types seems to have been the rule during most of the period the burial ground was in use. Vertical bundle-burials *could* all be later than extended burials. However, some details argue against a sharp break in tradition (pp. 32–33).

Horizontal parcels seem to belong to the main stage of secondary burials. They are early within this, but the evidence is not all reliable. Nothing suggests that they were as early as some horizontal bundle-burials.

There have been hints of slight variations within the vertical bundle type of burial, but in only one group does this seem to mean that the burials involved belonged to one short period of time (p. 29). The two cases of cremation belonged to the main period of vertical bundles, but to a late stage within it.

The only clear suggestion of a break in tradition came with the latest, the flexed burials, but even this does not appear to mean that the burial ground was disused for a time or that it was used by a group with different cultural traditions (see the end of chapter 2).

Absolute dating

Radiocarbon dates

There was charcoal in the site but, as mentioned earlier, much of this was of uncertain origin and association. Even charcoal found on the surface of burial pits could, in the case of small crumbs, have derived from a bush fire burning long before the funeral fire.

Table 4. *Relative age of burials not listed in figure 74*

The evidence is good for group A, less good for group B, and nonexistent for group C. The burial types are labelled as in Appendix D.

Stage	Type?	V.2	V.4	V.5	V.6	V.7	V.8	V.9	V.10
				Group A					
II		B.116		B.5,B.36,B.61, B.64,B.65, B.72,B.79				B.68	
I or II				B.85,B.112, B.114					
I				B.4,B.6,B.12, B.60,B.66, B.122,B.123, B.125,B.130, B.133,B.137	B.136				B.15
O or I				B.16,B.23, B.28					
O	B.20,B.42			B.14,B.18, B.21,B.31, B.32,B.103, B.117,B.119, B.121,B.124, B.126,B.128B, B.139	B.132	B.25			
				Group B					
II	B.71,B.90	B.77			B.138				
I or II	B.57			B.35					
I				B.118,B.131			B.48+50		
O or I	B.115			B.0,B.9, B.10,B.13, B.17,B.19, B.22,B.26, B.27,B.44A+B, B.59+69,B.81, B.108,B.109, B.113,B.135					
O			B.2	B.1,B.7,B.8, B.34,B.56, B.89,B.127, B.134	B.91	B.55,B.67, B.70,B.84			
				Group C					

B.3,B.11,B.24,B.33,B.39,B.58,B.75,B.86A+B,B.92,B.94,B.101,B.120,B.129,B.140

Charcoal in intimate and definite association with a burial was rare. Fortunately the best set of samples came from one of the oldest burials — on stratigraphical grounds — B.37, from fires which had clearly burnt in situ on (or just above) the surface of the corpse. More came from two cremations, probably scraped up from fires burning the bodies. Large pieces of charcoal from pit-surfaces over the very latest flexed burials can also be considered examples of definite association. A number of factors are likely to reduce the value of what we have. Some samples of charcoal seem to come from the sides of hollow logs, while others are too fragmented to show whether they come from a trunk or from twigs or branches. The tests can give the approximate date of formation of the wood tissue in question, but they cannot indicate whether this was early or late in the life of the tree, or how long this stood after its death, or how long the log was lying on the ground before a piece was picked up and used. The decay of wood may be fairly rapid in the Queensland climate and termites are very active in the area at present; a time gap of perhaps a hundred years between the death of the tree used — parts of which could be two to three hundred years old — and the lighting of a fire is likely, but would be unimportant, if the site were very old.[14] If all, or some, of the burials were recent, such a time gap would distort our evidence, particularly if one takes into account that the dates given by the tests would not be in terms of specific years, but periods of time within which there is a certain mathematical probability that the absolute date would fall. There are also difficulties in getting reliable results when tests are done on very modern material (less than two hundred years old). This last consideration is important when considering the suitability of the charcoal above the flexed burials.

Bone can also be used for radiocarbon tests. Such tests are nowadays mostly done on the collagen (the bone protein). The latter tends to break down and disappear with time, acid soils being most destructive. The collagen has often completely disappeared in bones more than ten thousand years old. If the burial ground is in fact recent in terms of world prehistory, it should be possible to get good results from the burials themselves. The soil surrounding them is a weak podsol, only slightly acid, tending to neutral in the level of most burials and sometimes a little alkaline owing to the presence of shells in the pit-fill (Appendix A).

There are two difficulties here. The collagen content is small even in fresh bone and large quantities of bone are needed for a test.[15] On the other hand, new methods are coming up all the time in anatomical studies and bones that used to be considered unimportant are suddenly found to be a source of information. Bones would have to be destroyed to be dated; this means destroying useful research material. All bones for a test must of course, in a site like this, come from one burial. The skeletons of small children which were so decayed that their bones would perhaps not give any useful measurements, would not provide enough bone for a test. In some cases, burials had to be treated with PVA in case some of the bones would be possible to measure. The few well-preserved adults in the site are precisely the ones that would provide enough bone for such tests but they are also the most important for anatomical studies.

Some of the importance of the results of the anatomical studies will rest on a knowledge of their absolute age. Bones will have to be tested, but it would seem irresponsible to destroy any bone until it has been fully studied, or to destroy more bone per test than is necessary. It is particularly important to keep this collection of bones as complete as possible, since it is one of the few collections of comparative Aboriginal material from a single site excavated under archaeological supervision.[16]

Shell is also sometimes used for radiocarbon dating, but the results are considered problematic. Marine shells from open beaches are best suited for such tests; most of the shells in the site belong to this category (Appendix C). However, they do not belong to the earliest stages of the history of the site, and it was considered advisable to test our stratigraphically oldest and most suitable material first and also the youngest to get some idea of the time span involved.

Two samples of charcoal were submitted to the Australian National University Radiocarbon Laboratory in June 1966, shortly after its establishment. The first results were so conflicting that they were not published, pending further tests. These have now shown that one of the first results, giving an age of about ten thousand years to a sample that I, on other grounds, believed to be modern, was clearly wrong, probably owing to some mishap with the equipment. (See Appendix G for the full reports on radiocarbon tests.)

One sample, Q1,C.1a, came from the feet of B.37, one of the extended burials. It consisted of many small pieces of charcoal. There is no doubt of the relatively early date of the burial compared to the others, nor about the association of the charcoal with the burial. This sample gave a date of 1290 ± 70 B.P. or A.D. 660 (ANU-68).

The second sample, Q1,C.8, came from the upper part — or original surface — of the pit holding B.100, a very late, flexed burial. This sample gave a date of 450 ± 70 B.P. or A.D. 1500 (ANU-67). In this case we found the pieces of charcoal still forming a slightly curved sheet, suggesting that it was the result of burning a part of a hollow log. Such an origin would make it quite certain that there was a time gap, which could be quite considerable, between the death of the apparently large tree and burning a piece of it, but the curved piece of wood could not in that case have come from the oldest part of the tree.

Three samples have been tested by the Radiocarbon Dating Laboratory, Institute of Applied Science of Victoria. These give very similar results; the dates extracted are slightly younger but of a similar order.

One of these samples was part of Q.1,C.1a, the charcoal at the feet of B.37. The age was calculated as 1110 ± 85 B.P. or A.D. 840 (V-157).

Another sample, Q.1,C.1b, came from the left cheek of B.37, the result of a small fire burnt in situ. The fragments of charcoal were small and its origin in terms of trunk, branches, or twigs could not be established. The age was calculated as 1180 ± 105 B.P. or A.D. 770 (V-162).

Part of sample Q.1,C.8, described above, was also tested, and its age calculated as 50 ± 80 B.P. or A.D. 1900 (V-161).

The results of tests ANU-68, V-157, and V-162 are very similar indeed. If the dates are plotted with the range of one standard deviation, ANU-68 and V-157 are only twenty-five years apart and V-162 overlaps them both. (Note that there are causes of uncertainty which have not been taken into account in calculating the standard deviation.) It must be remembered also that the wood may have come from different parts of the same tree or from different trees.

Thus the results of these radiocarbon tests seem to indicate that the burial ground may have been in use as much as one thousand years ago — if the earliest charcoal came from old trees — or more, if the charcoal came from fresh twigs. At the other end of its history, the samples ANU-67 and V-161 are in less close agreement. This may be due to the difficulties of testing modern samples and other technical causes for uncertainty. It is also, however, possible that they tested charcoal of different origin. Much, but not all, of sample Q.1,C.8 was in the form of a sheet but breaking up. Some of the fragments collected with the larger piece could have broken away from it; others could have come from smaller branches or twigs burnt at the same time. The charcoal was collected with forceps on to several sheets of aluminium foil by one of the students; it would be human nature to first collect the larger pieces on to one sheet, i.e. what was probably once the side of a hollow log. I did not think of this when selecting parcels of charcoal to be sent off for testing. However, the samples agree in showing that the latest burials must have been late indeed in comparison with the earliest ones, and could well have occurred after the arrival of European settlers. This would mean that the period during which this burial ground was in use could be just over twelve hundred years or at least a thousand years, depending on the history of the charcoal samples. Such periods of time seem surprisingly long for several reasons which will be discussed later.

One question remaining is the age of the burials in between. Was there perhaps a long period of time between the very early extended burials and the rest? Stratigraphic and other details seem to suggest that this was not so (see the last section of chapter 2) but we will not be sure until bones from some typical bundle-burials have been dated.

Geological evidence

The processes of dune formation and the emergence of sandy flats and ridges in the low coastal plain described in chapter 1 took place during Later Recent as the result of a coastal emergence;[17] this was preceded by a submergence of at least 2 metres during which the estuarine flats forming portion of this low coastal plain were deposited.[18] Gardner tentatively places the submergence at about 2,500 years, the emergence at about 2,000 years ago. The former may be the one by Sprigg called the Osborne High Sea-level, described as a very recent minor marine inundation of only a few metres, which was followed by a minor regression to below − 1.5 metres (Sprigg 1952). The Osborne High followed the Vincent Low which in its turn followed a high level. Silt deposited in the Yarra delta during the latter contained wood for which a radiocarbon date of 4820 ± 200 B.P. (W-170) has been given (Gill 1962). This picture of relatively rapid minor fluctuations during the Postglacial agrees well with that established in Europe and elsewhere (Zeuner 1958, pp. 95-99). Coaldrake, who has questioned some of the correlations of dunes and sea-levels made by Gardner, found no reason to doubt his conclusions regarding the last three minor highs, and their intervening lows (Coaldrake 1962, p.112). Jennings (in Mulvaney and Golson 1971, p.11) points out that there is no consensus as yet in this matter.

Other evidence

The massive roots of the Forest Red Gum had interfered with some burials (see pp. 39–40 for examples). The tree was identified by the Department of Forestry, Brisbane, whose specialist added this information: "The basic root system in this species is laid down early in the life of the tree and comprises deep anchor roots and a system of lateral feeding roots. These extend and develop side roots as the tree grows in size, but the basic root system is developed at an early age. It would appear therefore that the tree is younger than the Aboriginal burials which you mention."

This means little if the tree was a seedling ca. 200 years ago. The tree was estimated − judging from its girth and normal rate of growth − to have reached an age of ca. 270 years before death. The roots were a little hollow, due to white ants, by the time we excavated the site, but most of the wood in the roots was fresh and sound (fig. 65).

Soil formation had not, in most cases, obliterated the pit. In many pits, e.g. those of the flexed burials, it had barely had time to become noticeable. It need not, however, take much more than a hundred years for a podsol to form in this area to the extent it had formed where it was *not* disturbed by burials.[19]

The bone is in good condition if one considers the forces that must have been at work to destroy it. The ridge is alternately dry or wet, roots and rootlets penetrate in all directions, chemical and bacterial processes are going on all the year through, many insects and small animals − including birds − make their homes in the sand.

I have already discussed the shape of some pits as reasons for believing that European implements were used to dig them. We have not found any object of European origin that could be related to the burials. The traumatic features on some bones may be evidence for damage by European-type weapons, but this requires further investigation. Such things are hard to prove. Dr. I. McBryde, who has had a great deal of experience of archaeological sites in northern New South Wales, has looked at the stone implements found in the site. They could all fit a date within the last millennium, judging from the material excavated in her sites and the dates given these by radiocarbon tests. (See Appendix G.)

Summary of absolute dating

The results of radiocarbon tests suggest a time span of possibly more than a thousand years for this burial ground. Surprising though this may be, it can hardly be doubted when results of three tests by different laboratories on charcoal from different parts of one single burial are in such close agreement. In contrast, the well-preserved bone, the low degree of leaching and soil formation, and the shape of some burial pits have been mentioned as arguments for the low age (in some cases very low) of the material excavated. The area of the burial ground is very limited, occupying only the flat top of the ridge. This could mean that only this part protruded above the marsh to receive interments. This is unlikely. Map 2 shows that the slopes are very gentle indeed. The faunal remains associated with the burials and the floral evidence, such as stumps of ring-barked Forest Red Gums of a girth similar to the one cited and extending for several hundred metres around the site, both suggest that an area of this extent must have been dry enough for a considerable period of time to support rain forest of the coastal type rather than marsh vegetation. The rain forest animals could have come from areas farther away, but few patches of land in the neighbourhood of the site are higher than the burial ground (map 1). Thus, it would appear that out of a larger area available, one small part was selected as a burial ground and its precise position − in an area devoid of striking geographical features − known to a group of people for the whole period of its use. It is amazing that this period could be in the order of a thousand years. The continuity over such a period of burial types and of ritual details, summarized at the end of chapter 2, is also striking and unexpected. (The fact that a total of about two hundred burials would be ridiculously small even for a small group of people over such a period of time means little if this group used several sites in which to bury their dead.)[20]

CHAPTER 4

The living population as represented by its bones

Burials from B.122 on have not been studied at all, not even in terms of age and sex.[1] My own impression is that B.123, B.125, B.126, B.127, B.129, B.134, B.137, B.139, B.140B, and perhaps B.132 are children. Two burials, B.122 and B.128B, are probably adolescents, B.133 on the border of being adult, and burials B.124, B.130, B.131, B.135, B.136, B.138, and B.140A are adults. Of the latter, it is likely that B.124 was female. This list, if correct, would then add ten children, two or three adolescents, and seven or eight adults (one a female) to the numbers discussed in this chapter.

I stated at the outset that I was forced to attempt the complete excavation of the site because of the impossibility of saving any part of it for future investigation. I hoped, however, that the results would be of special value for various statistical analyses of the population that used the site. No such analysis can be included in this chapter, since the study of the skeletal material has not yet been completed. But some of the results of the preliminary studies are of interest here; there are also a number of questions and problems of an archaeological or anthropological character which should be dealt with at this stage, since the answers will affect the value and validity of any such analysis.[2]

If we are dealing with the remains of one group of people, how large was it and from how wide an area were its members drawn? By a group, I mean a number of people who, although not necessarily contemporaneous, possess some genealogical ties, at least indirectly via their offspring. This is important because some features studied may be functionally unimportant while their real significance lay in their being inherited within and typical of such a group – for example a partial or complete dorsal defect of the sacral canal noticed in a number of individuals at Broadbeach. This suggests some inbreeding within a small group, but until other collections from southern Queensland have been studied we cannot know whether this feature was characteristic of the area or restricted to one group within it. Written accounts (cf. chapter 6) suggest that, by the time of European settlement contacts were wide, comprising movement and intermarriage within an area from the Condamine, Dawson, and Comet Rivers to the Clarence.

If the group had a similar genetic background as a result of inbreeding or, more likely in this case, as a result of regular and mutual exchange of individuals between the groups within this area, and if the burials found proved to be a typical sample of the local population, belonging to a short period of time, then one could make certain statements about the amount of variation that existed within such a group in pre-European times. Normal variations have been recorded in detail for many living population groups;[3] only recently have scholars been turning their attention to this aspect of prehistoric populations.[4] Aboriginal skeletal material available for study in the past has consisted mainly of individuals from widely scattered and often unrecorded localities. This is still the case with early fossil material. The tendency was to look for and isolate features that were typically Aboriginal or characteristic of one of the groups into which some scholars divided them.[5]

Do all the bones in the site then belong to one single group? Or was the site used over a long time by a number of groups with perhaps a lapse of time between each period of use? The archaeological evidence suggests that the former was the case. There are many traits that link the various burial types. The differences in burial types are obvious, because the bones are big and quite well preserved. The minor traits may be the result of equally important concepts in the culture of the group, though the expressions of these were less tangible. Such traits were described in chapter 2; their importance may be clarified by evidence presented in chapter 6.

But the absolute dates quoted in chapter 3 indicate that, although the burial ground is not early in archaeological time, its period of use could extend over more than a thousand years. This may mean that even if the burial ground was being used continuously by one group, some of the variation recorded could be due to the additions to the gene-pool from individuals brought in from outside. Even if the exchange over a prescribed area was mutual, there could have been additions from outside this area, either directly or via groups on the borders. There is also the possibility that the exchange had a directional pattern which could have had some effect in time.

Is the sample complete or representative of this local group and its probable changes during the course of time? Almost certainly not. Several factors have to be considered here.

Part of the Broadbeach site was destroyed before excavation. Does this make the remains of the site less representative? I have shown that there is no horizontal stratigraphy (chapter 3 and map 6). All burials were then plotted, using different symbols for males, females, and children. No pattern emerged suggesting that one part of the burial ground was used exclusively for one of these groups. All evidence suggests that the areas removed by soil contractors had a content similar to those we excavated. So the sample we have can be considered representative of what was buried in the site. Apparently this was not every member of the group. Burials of adult males outnumber those of females by almost 7 to 1 (cf. fig. 99). Early European settlers remarked that there seemed to be an imbalance because they noticed more males than females. But their observations did not indicate an imbalance of this magnitude. It is not improbable that there was no imbalance, but that women were kept hidden from Europeans because they feared that they would be stolen. It is more likely that a cultural bias prevented the burial of women in this site. Only the age groups from fifteen years upwards have been studied in detail and it is not possible to say yet whether this imbalance of sexes applies also to the children.

Was there also a selection based on age?[6] A preliminary examination of the reasonably complete burials indicates that all age groups are represented – from neonate to old age. Juveniles and adolescents under fifteen years are slightly in excess of the combined total for subadults and adults. More than 50 per cent of juveniles fall in the under-five category (fig. 100). Among the adults, only a small number of middle-aged and elderly individuals can be recognized. This identification was based on the degree of dental attrition, cranial

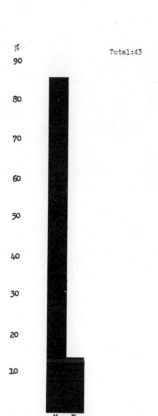

Fig.99. Sex ratio. This was counted on the adult and adolescent burials studied so far.

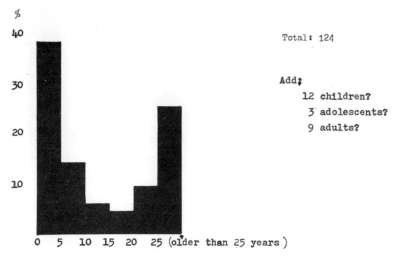

Fig.100. Age ratio. The burials not included in the histograms are either very fragmentary or have been provisionally identified by me without reference to an anatomist.

suture closure, and the presence of osteoarthritis. Most adults belong to the under-forty category. Unless a person's advanced age was the reason for not burying him in this site, as suggested in chapter 6, this indicates that only a few survived long enough to die from old age.

A possible cause of death has been established for only two of the adults so far examined. Both had a fracture of the skull. In neither case were there any obvious signs of healing. One injury (B.6, a vertical bundle) was apparently caused by a blunt instrument,

resulting in a depressed stellate fracture of the right fronto-parietal region. The other (B.100, a flexed burial) consisted of a number of perforating injuries to the skull vault, probably caused by a sharp instrument — for example, a hatchet or heavy knife.

There are a few examples of bone injury or pathology. They will be described later in this chapter. The cause of death rarely left obvious traces in the bones. This indicates that the general health of the group was poor and that the factors causing death probably involved the soft tissues. Poor diet is not a likely cause in a coastal area, where even after commercial exploitation by Europeans fish and shell fish are in abundance. Comparisons with modern primitive communities suggest acute septic, respiratory, and gastro-intestinal conditions as the main killers. No evidence of yaws, tuberculosis, or rickets has been found. Whether malaria or other parasitic diseases were present and added to the mortality cannot be determined.

Two cremated burials, B.15 and B.39, are the only ones in which any evidence has been found that bones were deliberately broken into smaller pieces before they were collected and buried (fig. 33). Other fractures can usually be explained by root action, earth movement, disturbance, excavation or transport.[7]

A small number of ante-mortem injuries have been identified. Two have been cited as the probable cause of death. A third skull had a healed depressed fracture of the frontal bone. This lesion could be due to other pathology. The flexed female, B.100, had as well as her skull injuries, a comminuted fracture of the shaft of the left femur and a cortical shaving removed from the shaft of the right (fig. 48). The fracture on the left side was associated with localized osteoporosis and early new bone formation of the adjacent bone, indicating that it had been sustained some time, probably one or two weeks, prior to death. The generalized osteoporosis noted to be affecting the skeleton as a whole also tended to suggest an enforced period of immobilization, probably accompanied by severe infection, immediately prior to death. The shape and appearance of the bony defect caused by the removal of the cortical shaving on the right side suggested that it was inflicted at the same time as the skull injuries and probably by a sharp instrument. Well-healed fractures of the shaft of a femur, an ulna, and a phalanx, were observed in other individuals (fig. 101). Only one case of probable nonunion of an old fracture was noted, and this involved the mid-shaft of a humerus, a site well known for such a complication.

In most males over the age of fifteen years, the right upper central incisor had been removed before death. In one case the right upper lateral incisor was missing. Dental avulsion was absent in a small number of adult males and generally in females. B.116 is the one female exception but she could have lost her tooth by accident.[8]

The bone collection displayed a limited amount of pathology. Mild to moderate osteoarthritis affecting the vertebral column, hands, and feet was noticed in a number of middle-aged to elderly individuals (fig. 102).[9] An exostosis in the region of the deltoid tuberosity of one humerus was almost certainly traumatic in origin. Most other pathology was associated with the teeth: occasional caries, periodontal disease, apical abscesses, impacted molars, and anterior dental crowding. Apical abscesses were invariably associated with advanced dental attrition and exposure of the pulp cavity. This was probably the main aetiological factor behind the loss of teeth noted

Fig.101. B.102: broken and healed femur. Camera facing south-south-east.

Fig.102. B.73 (left hand removed). Note dental attrition, lipping of vertebrae. Camera facing east.

among the older individuals.[10] No benign or malignant bony tumour was observed in this collection. This description is neither unusual nor unexpected for such a population sample.

CHAPTER 5

The lithic material

Scope of the study

This part of the material from Broadbeach was given rather small attention in the thesis since I was then mainly concerned with establishing traces of burial practices. Here I shall give a rather more detailed picture of the stone artifacts and the technology represented. But some minutiae will be reserved for a later specialized study, involving many sites in the area, in which I will compare artifact types, their proportions, technology, and raw materials. I feel that much information about such aspects becomes immediately more useful and interesting if it can be presented in terms of comparison and the range over a wider area, temporal and spatial, shown.

Here I shall then discuss the presence of stone in the site, what raw materials were present, and what information may be derived from them.

I shall then after a brief discussion of the problems of definition describe the main types of artifacts present. The types defined will, if possible, be referred to stages within the burial ground and the question of whether one or more technological traditions is represented will be discussed.

The use of certain artifact types may be indicated by their position in the burial ground, as well as by some literary references.

The chapter will end with a brief discussion of the lithic material from the burial ground as compared to that from neighbouring areas and other parts of Australia.

Content of the site

All stones, apart from lumps of pumice and possibly small smooth pebbles,[1] which could have been washed there during floods, were brought to the site from a distance.[2] The most common types of material used were quartzites, chalcedonic silica, and basalt. Much of the material shows clear evidence of having been shaped or used by humans, but some stones are very rough and could have broken either through natural weathering or because they were used as anvils or hammers or hearth stones.[3] Map 8 shows the distribution and amount, according to weight,[4] of stone per square; map 9 gives the same information for the portion that showed clear signs of use or knapping. This was 98 kilograms out of a total of 164 kilograms (60 per cent). The proportion remained almost constant over the whole site.

The maps suggest that the presence of stone, whether knapped or apparently unused, was linked with that of the burials. Squares containing more than 1 kilogram of stone were restricted to the area of burials or its very borders. They are the rule where the surface over the burials has not been removed by soil contractors. Patches of low density within the burial ground were confined to such areas of disturbance. (The high density in squares AA 52 - 53 was due to the presence of two very large implements, F.153 and F.214.) Most of

the stone, shown on the maps as occurring outside the borders of the burial area, can be linked with this since pieces of the same materials were found inside burial pits; examples will be given later in this chapter.

Stone waste was found in some quantity just outside the western border of the burial ground. This area seemed a favoured knapping spot. Even the rather slight slope of this ridge may have provided some shelter from sea breezes.

Groups of raw material

It has already been mentioned that groups of raw material were isolated and each piece found plotted. Such grouping was of stratigraphic importance only when several pieces could be fitted together to show their common origin. In some cases, it was possible to build up the better part of a nodule. In the case of some material with veins of different colour in which pieces could be seen to grade into each other but some flakes in between were missing, their origin in the same nodule or from within a few cubic centimetres of the same outcrop was accepted. But one has to be cautious; much stone which appears identical to some used at Broadbeach burial ground is found over a wide area along the coast and inland. This had not become so clear to me when writing the thesis; some of the groups described there I would now hesitate to accept. This grouping and sorting was very time-consuming and perhaps too much time was spent on it. However, when so little good stratigraphical evidence is available in a site, it seems necessary to squeeze every drop of information out of it. The results were used to demonstrate the absence of horizontal stratigraphy. It is worth noting that a number of the groups seem to link certain burials. This aspect was investigated only when the relative sequence of most burials had been established, using all other types of argument. It would not be safe to use the presence of particular stones as a foundation for such a sequence; the stratigraphical evidence cannot be considered as reliable for stones as for burials, unless the former were actually found in deliberate association with the latter. Even such associations could be misleading, since an object may have been found and re-used. What was found in pit-fill could have been discarded during the ceremony associated with that burial, but it could also have been in the sand scraped back, and perhaps derived from another burial pit or simply left on the surface after an earlier ceremony. In a site riddled with root holes and in such loose sand it would also be possible that pieces have moved considerably.

I first tried comparing the presence and absence of certain groups of raw material in the burials. This produced a few patterns of striking similarity, but the numbers of reliable associations were usually too small to produce a recognizable pattern. The next step was to select groups, members of which were found in large numbers in burial pits, and to see which of these associations could be

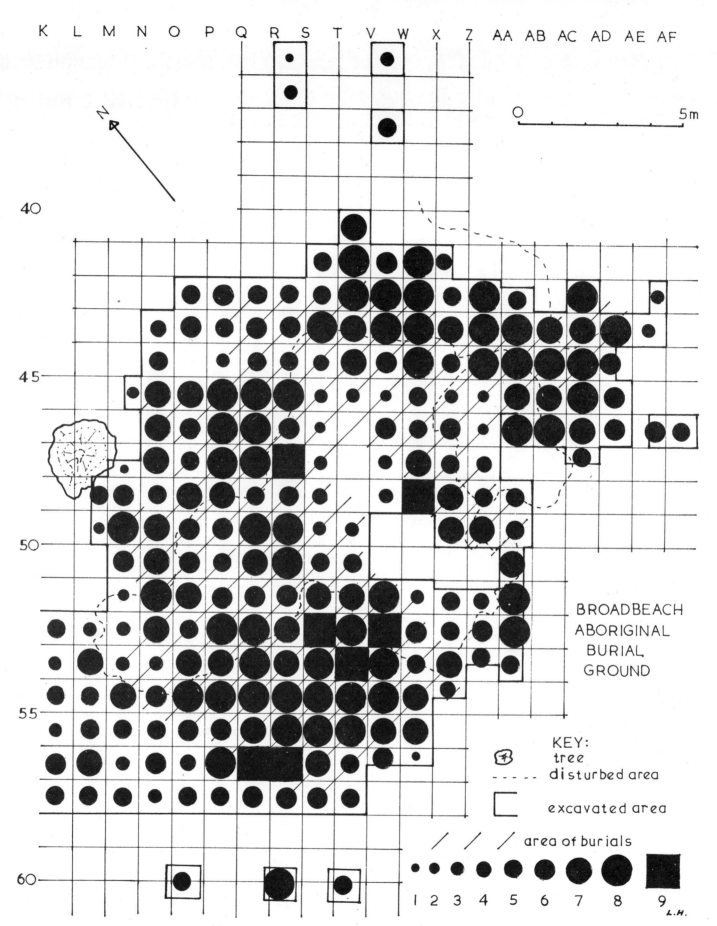

Map 8. Broadbeach burial ground: distribution of stone. Each circle indicates the total amount of stone present in levels 1 and 2 of the grid square.
1. 1—50 grams; **2.** 50—100 grams; **3.** 100—200 grams; **4.** 200—300 grams; **5.** 300—500 grams; **6.** 500—750 grams; **7.** 750—1,000 grams;
8. 1,000—2,000 grams; **9.** More than 2,000 grams.

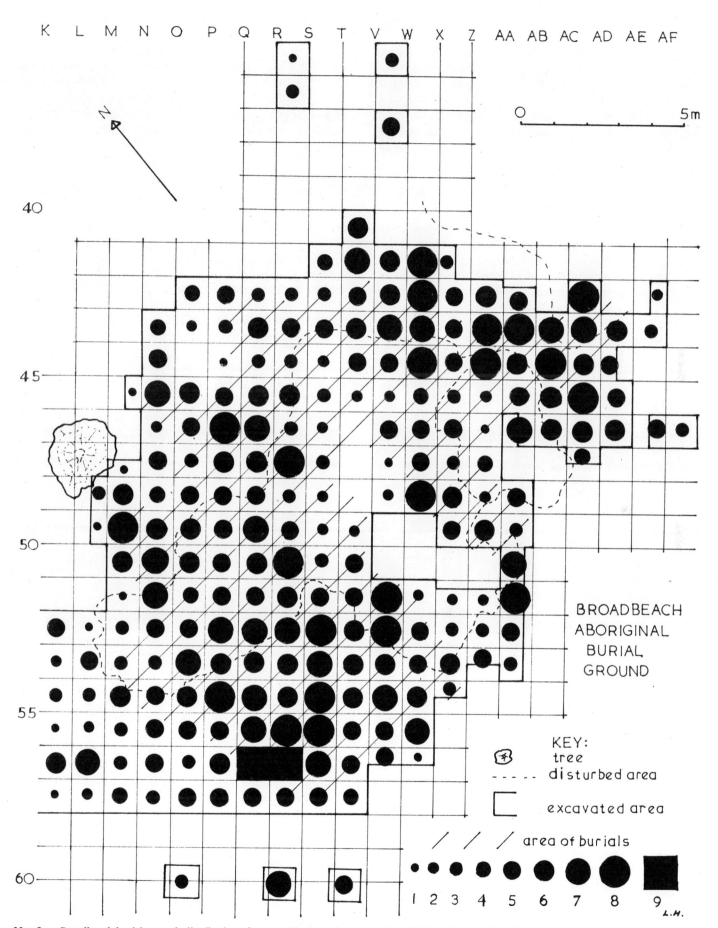

Map 9. Broadbeach burial ground: distribution of stone with signs of use or marks of flaking. Each circle indicates the total amount present in levels 1 and 2 of each grid square.

1. 1–50 grams; 2. 50–100 grams; 3. 100–200 grams; 4. 200–300 grams; 5. 300–500 grams; 6. 500–750 grams; 7. 750–1,000 grams;
8. 1,000–2,000 grams; 9. More than 2,000 grams.

considered original, and which could be fortuitous — the result of pit-digging and infilling — and, when possible, to find from which burial the latter would have derived. This produced a number of burials which were certainly linked, or probably very close in time, in that the persons taking part in the burial ceremonies would have been making use of the same outcrops or nodules of raw material. If burial ceremonies could take place in several stages it is possible that the final ceremonies for approximately contemporary burials could have been combined.

These investigations have been reported in detail in the thesis, including an appendix describing each well-defined stone-group in terms of characteristics and distribution. Many details, however, seem relevant only to somebody who is actually handling the material. I shall therefore here summarize the information derived and quote only some of the more interesting sets of association. (The groups will be called by the same code names as used in the sorting and in the appendix to the thesis.) The study of these groups confirmed the general sequence already suggested. In some cases the temporal relationship between some specific burials was made clearer. Some examples follow, more have been given in my unpublished thesis.

F.21, a neat microscraper, found on the surface of the pit for B.19, fitted into a negative scar on B.38, a half-worn tula, found just under a pocket of shell on the surface of the pit containing B.6 (see fig. 52 and plates 3 and 5). It must have been removed from F.38 before this was buried with B.6, since the shell pockets appear to have been results of the burial ceremonies associated with the latter. On the other hand the burials — or the final ceremonies for them — are not likely to be far apart in time. F.21 measures only 10 millimetres by 13 and would be lost rather easily. That it was not just lost over the B.19 pit is suggested by another link between these two burials, the presence of some grey quartzite of identical hue and grain size.

Group Qo, used first for B.6, became involved in B.12; some pieces from the latter were scraped into the pit for B.73, probably because the contents of this had been dumped in the area of B.12 - 15 - 36 while the burial was inserted. This is borne out by F.858 (a piece of pebble near B.6) which joined a fragment in the B.12 pit and several in the B.73 pit. One can also compare group Qv; some pieces identical in shade of colour with those in B.12 and B.15 were found in the B.73 pit-fill.

Many implements, fragments, and flakes, often fitting together, of several different groups were involved in the next sequence. The only logical explanation of their whereabouts would be something like the series of events to be outlined here. Somebody wanted to dig a grave for B.116 and started digging in the area of B.83/86, near the pit surfaces of B.60 and B.48+50. Soon he struck a skull, B.83, which he dumped back into the hole, a little southwest of its original position. He then tried a little further to the southwest and dug the big pit for B.116, apparently without striking any more burials. The fill was dumped over the area where he had been working (cf. map 12). The pit was then filled again, and some pieces which had been brought up during his first attempts or which had been lying on the surface of that area were put in the big pit as part of the fill. There was for example half a flake of DD in B.48+50 which fitted half in B.116. The small group represented by F.1212 in B.88, an early horizontal

bundle, is particularly interesting in this context.[5] Pieces of this material were found also in B.100 and B.116 and in level 1 over B.48+50 and B.83/86. B.48+50 cut through B.42, an early primary burial (cf. chapter 2, note 3.) It seems likely that the group belonged originally only to B.42, B.88, and possibly other early burials. It ended up in the B.116 pit-fill via B.48+50 (? and in the B.100 pit-fill via some burial that cut into the B.88 pit, see map 12).

There is also a suggestion that of the three adult flexed burials, B.73 was in the ground before B.100 or B.116. F.230 in B.87 was made of a white and cream quartzite with rosy flecks. A few fragments, apparently waste from its manufacture and once left near the surface over the burial (*below* the present surface) were found in the B.73 pit and on its surface. One more big fragment came from the B.116 pit. It had apparently been picked up from the area of the former. A fragment of Qs in B.116 matches several in the B.73 pit-fill; the latter were probably brought up to the surface when the B.73 pit cut through the B.37 trench. A fragment of Qv probably came from B.12 or B.15 via B.73 as discussed, and so on.

B.100 has some links with B.116 but many more with B.73, and since several pieces in its pit-fill can be shown to have been brought up from earlier burial pits by the B.73 pit, this was probably the main source for B.100. A fragment of Dx in the pit-fill of B.100 fitted F.586 from the surface of the B.36 pit, part of which became fill for B.73. Several pieces of Dw in B.100 fitted the core F.501 just above B.62, whose pit was dug into by B.73. (The pieces of Dx and Dw were not flakes but accidental fractures; the original lump must have been hit sharply with something very hard, e.g. a spade.) Both materials were colourful and the pieces broken off may have been picked up intentionally, when noticed. F.503, of Qs, was placed on the arm of B.73 and there were several fragments of this group in the pit-fill; one of them fitted another in the B.100 pit. F.662 of group Dd in the pit for B.100 fitted a flake in B.97A whose pit surface was cut into by B.73 pit. There were several similar links.

Some groupings seem particularly clear even if chance could always have interfered to some degree.

There are many links between B.6, B.12, and B.15 (a cremation) which were all post-shell horizon. As mentioned above, it is likely that B.12 was a little later than B.6. Less numerous but still strong links put B.5, B.29, B.64, B.112, and B.114 in this set; this would fit in with the stratigraphical evidence (cf. fig. 74 and table 4).

Some of the best links are between burials placed far from each other in the burial ground, which makes accidental similarities less likely. Take as an example B.59+69, B.16, and B.112; some of their links have been described in the thesis, but note that a flake of DD in B.59+69 fitted into a negative scar on one from B.112.

Some groups of raw material were represented by implements only and were probably brought to the site in finished form. Examples are the polished axes — certainly some of them — and the pieces made of common opal and of group D.80. These artifacts will be discussed later in the chapter as possibly being gravegoods.

Most of the knapping seems to have taken place on the site and often close to the pit for the pending burial. B.12 is a good example; the pocket of waste flakes, fragments, etc. called F.44 was just outside the pit-circumference. The western (leeward) slope was, as mentioned above, a favourite knapping site. The group represented by F.23 in

B.19 can be given as an example; the latter core came from the same lump of stone as F.4 and F.305 in K.53 and K.54. These were scrapers, one unfinished, one broken during manufacture; there were also matching waste flakes nearby.

Typology

Definitions

The typology of Australian stone artifacts is in a state of flux. Types have so far been distinguished mostly on an intuitive basis. They have been given labels, sometimes descriptive or functional, sometimes derived from Australian Aboriginal ethnography, and sometimes from the artifact typology of some other continent. The labels do not always have the same meaning when applied by different typologists. Few of these types have been analyzed with the help of statistical methods (Glover 1969, Flood 1970). We seem to have a few types which are easily recognized, such as ground-edge axes, and a host of others, whose features overlap. These can be and have been grouped in different ways depending on what features seem most important to the typologist, and on whether he works in terms of ideal types and establishes a series of names for a series of minor variations or in terms of broad categories allowing for much variation in detail within each.

I found myself unable to fit all the artifacts from the burial ground into a system of Australian traditional categories, but hesitate to add to the present confusion by introducing additional labels that do not have backing in careful analysis of large samples involving also statistical methods. The assemblage from this site is not on its own suited to such definitive analysis. It is a fairly large sample — in Australian terms — but also varied. Many types, however defined, are represented by a few specimens or even a single specimen.

Some system of classification is necessary, however, for the purposes of sorting and presentation. My aim has therefore been to evolve a purely descriptive system, flexible, yet possible to expand or, as here, to summarize.[6] I think it will serve, with help of the illustrations, to make clear to any reader the character of this assemblage of stone artifacts although these are not given labels except of a very general kind. Nevertheless the different traits described clearly vary in importance from artifact to artifact. Meaningful clusters of attributes and the relative importance of attributes in such clusters need sorting out before we may hope to get a typology that can be generally used if this indeed will ever be possible.[7] The type of working edge prepared or used appears in some cases of greater importance than the shape or size of the artifact. On the other hand some artifacts have a recurring and distinctive shape but their working edge may be carefully shaped by flaking or retouch or the result of natural cleavage, all showing similar use-wear. Some artifacts of distinctive shape appear to have achieved this before use, others through use. Such recurring shapes or combinations of edges have been noted and descriptions may straddle several groups otherwise separated by traits listed below. To make comparisons easier I have also quoted Australian terms as defined by McCarthy (1967) when these are or may be applicable. Almost all groups or subgroups are illustrated in plates 1 - 6. The few exceptions

Table 5. *Stone: Cores and artifacts*

Group (Type of Working Edge)	Origin P	?	C	CF	TF	Size L	Me	Mi	Total
A: cores	18	39				5	41	11	57
B: utilized edges									
B.1:use polish	7	3				10			10
B.2:bruising	9	7	7	1	1	13	10	2	25
B.3:scalar chipping	3	3		4		3	5	2	10
B.3/4:fabricators	1	1	2	28			15	17	32
B.4:abrupt chipping	3	1	4	2		5	5		10
C:modified edges									
C.5:flaked edges	7	8	2	6		12	11		23
C.6:scalar retouch									
a:straight edge		1	3	17	5		13	13	26
b:concave edge		1		1	1		1	2	3
c:notched edge				4	2		4	2	6
d:convex edge		3		74	12		26	63	89
e:nosed edge				2			1	1	2
f:wavy edge				3			3		3
g:serrated edge				8	1		9		9
h:dentated edge		1		2	1		3	1	4
i:irregular edge		1		5	1		7		7
composite		1	2	14			12	5	17
C.7:abrupt retouch									
a:straight edge		3		5			7	1	8
b:concave edge				3			3		3
c:notched edge				2			1	1	2
d:convex edge	2	4	3	14			15	8	23
e:nosed edge				1			1		1
g:serrated edge		2					2		2
h:dentated edge		1					1		1
i:irregular edge		1	1	3			3	2	5
composite		3	4	13			17	3	20
C.8:grinding axes		7				1-6?			7
D:utilized surfaces									
grinders	3	3				2	4		6
crayons		23					9	14	23
E:modified surfaces									
waisted pieces	3	1				4			4
Total	56	118	28	214	24	61	230	149	440

Key to abbreviations: P — pebble, C — core, CF — chunky flake, TF — thin flake, L — large, Me — medium sized, Mi — microlithic.

are specimens differing only in minor details from some already illustrated.

The terms used in the descriptions are commonly used by typologists, but some will be defined below to avoid confusion or to explain how certain measurements were taken.

Artifact — any object altered by man into something different from its natural shape.

Implement — an artifact that is a tool.

Alter — change by use, accident or with intention.

Modify — deliberately alter.

Edge — the intersection of two planes. The junction of two edges is shown by a sharp change in direction of the line formed by this intersection or in the angle between two planes to one side of it. The latter usually shows as a small projection. Retouch or use may remove the border and reduce the two edges into one, which could be anything from an almost straight line to a full circle. An edge may be:

natural — formed by the intersection of cleavage faces, thermal fracture, or erosion.

flaked — formed by the intersection of one or more flake scars with a natural face, such as cortex, or with one or more flake scars.

used — carrying scars that could not or are not likely to result from natural agencies nor from deliberate retouch.

retouched — the scars of a number of chips so placed that they indicate deliberate modification of the outline and/or angle of the edge.

Chips — small flakes not exceeding 10 millimetres in the direction of the blow.

Flakes — more than 10 millimetres long. They are called chunky (CF) or thin (TF) depending on whether the thickness is more or less than one-fifth of the greatest length or breadth (whichever is the greatest).

Blades — generally in Australian typology flakes are considered blades when the length is twice the width. Blades are few and there is no evidence of specialized flaking techniques to produce blades.

Use-wear — can take the form of:

polish — no grains of mineral removed, only abraded, resulting in a gloss.

bruising — a few grains or very short chips removed leaving rounded or V-shaped hollows.

chipping — see definition of chips. (The term is used even though an occasional scar exceeds the limit.) Chipping can be scalar or abrupt.

Retouch — deliberate shaping of artifact by removing chips or narrow flakes. It can be scalar or abrupt.

Scalar — the chip removed skims the surface of the artifact and ends without a ledge. (Such retouch is often called scraper retouch.)

Abrupt — the chip removed bites into the body of the stone and leaves a pronounced ledge. (Such retouch is often called step-flaking.)

Overthrust — overhanging edge resulting from repeated abrupt retouch or chipping (cf. McCarthy 1967, p.95).

Backing — indicates retouch removing sharp edges or projections to provide better grip or anchorage. It is difficult to identify, the only criteria being the presence of another edge, apparently for use, in a suitable position, and the lack of use-wear on the backed portion. The term is used only in comments on implements, their grouping having been decided on other criteria. Probable backed edges are therefore also counted as working edges.

Edge shapes:

straight — no part of the edge departs more than 1 millimetre per centimetre from the line joining its two ends.

concave — the curve inwards exceeds 1 millimetre per centimetre.

notched — the concavity alters only part of an existing edge.

convex — the curve outwards exceeds 1 millimetre per centimetre.

nosed — a projection has been selected for use or formed by modifying part of one edge or a junction of edges.

wavy — projections and notches come in a series but are too smoothly curved or too far apart to be called serrated or dentated.

serrated — the edge carries up to two points (teeth) per centimetre.

dentated — the edge carries more than two points per centimetre.

burin — as defined by McCarthy 1967, pp.35 - 36.

Angle of edge — measured as the angle between the planes intersecting to form the edge. Retouch, if present, is taken instead as representing the desired plane. In retouch the most typical angle is used, not necessarily the steepest slope, since this often is a scar that bites into the main outline and possibly the result of accident rather than intention. (The angle resulting from use is also measured and may be commented on.)

Angle of striking platform — the angle between the part left on the flake and the bulbar face as represented by two-thirds of this measured from the junction.

Size — most artifacts from this assemblage cluster into three groups in terms of size (but see p. 71):

microlithic — less than 2.5 centimetres in any dimension (Mi).

medium sized — between 2.5 and 7 centimetres (Me).

large — greater than 7 centimetres in at least one dimension (L).

Length — the greatest length in any direction except in the case of unmodified flakes which are measured in the direction of the blow detaching the flake.

Width — measured at right angles to length.

Height or thickness — measured vertically to plane of length and width.

Note: The implements counted in tables or descriptions are whole or so slightly damaged that their character is undoubted.

The artifacts have been divided into five categories:

A. Cores. (Any cores altered by retouch or use are classed as implements.)

B. Implements with unmodified working edges. These may be natural or created by flaking; their character is determined from the presence of use-wear. (Areas away from the edges may also be altered.)

C. Implements with modified working edges (backing included). (Also other areas may be modified and/or used.) These may have use-wear of types 1 - 4.

D. Implements on which one or more surfaces have been altered and which have no working edges.

E. Implements on which one or more surfaces have been modified for use but which have no working edges.

Note: Some implements in groups B and D can be considered poor cousins of similar ones in groups C and E.

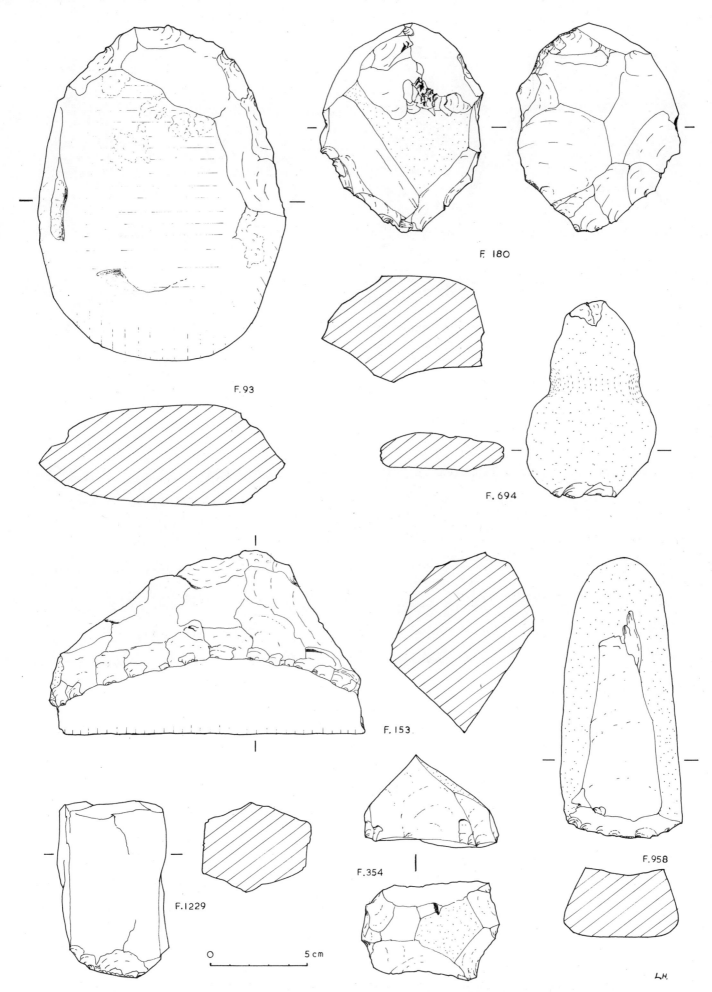

F. 180

F. 93

F. 694

F. 153

F.1229

F.354

F.958

5 cm

L.H.

Plate 1. **F.93**, pp. 73, 75; **F.153**, pp. 71, 75; **F.180**, pp. 72, 76; **F.354**, p. 72; **F.694**, p. 73; **F.958**, p. 71; **F.1229**, p. 71.

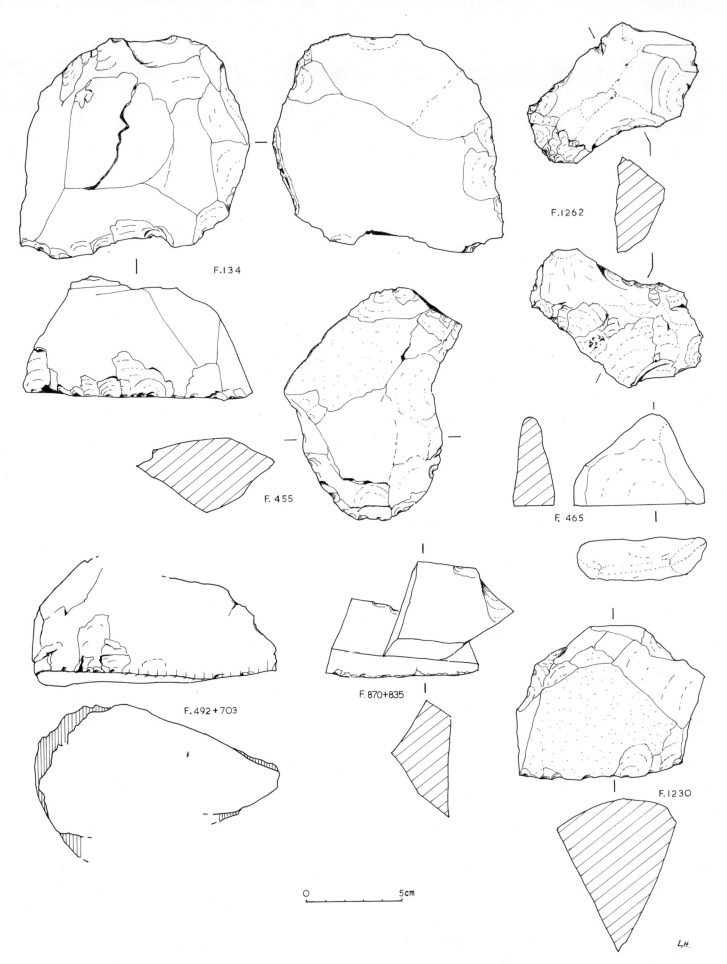

F.1262

F. 455

F. 465

F.134

F.492 + 703

F.870+835

F.1230

0   5cm

L.H.

Plate 2. **F.134**, p. 72; **F.455**, p. 72; **F.465**, p. 73; **F.492 + 703**, pp. 71, 75; **F.870 + 835**, p. 71; **F.1230**, p. 71; **F.1262**, p. 72.

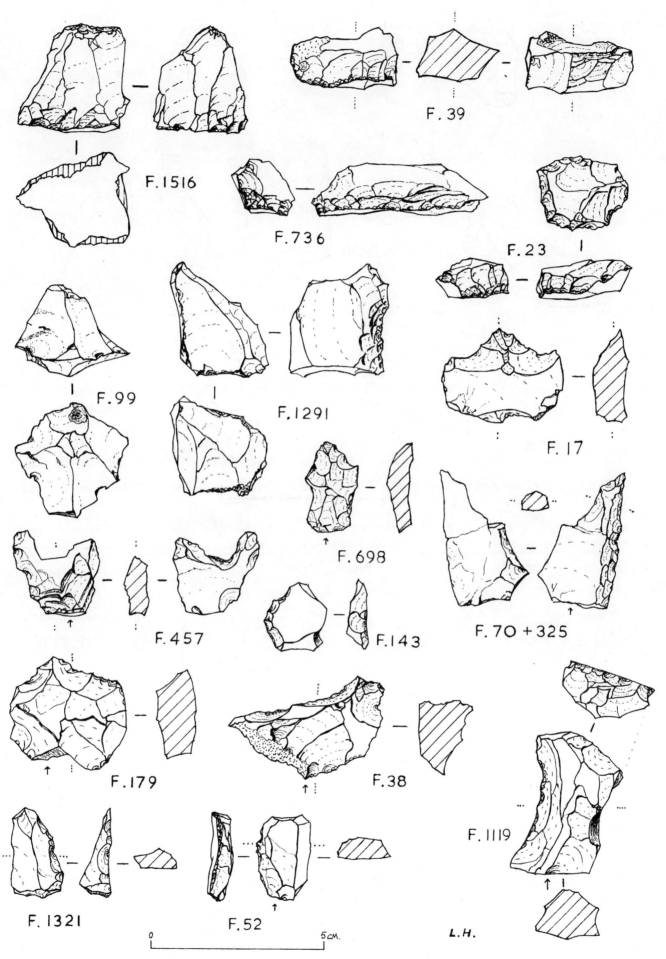

F. 39

F.1516

F.736

F.23

F.99

F.1291

F.17

F.698

F.70 + 325

F.457

F.143

F.179

F.38

F.1119

F.1321

F.52

5 CM.

L.H.

Plate 3.   F.17, p. 73; F.23, p. 72; F.38, pp. 72, 73, 75; F.39, p. 72; F.52, p. 73; F.70 + 325, p. 73; F.99, p. 71; F.143, p. 72; F.179, p. 73; F.457, p. 72; F.698, p. 73; F.736, p. 72; F.1119, p. 72; F.1291, p. 71; F.1321, p. 73; F.1516, p. 71.

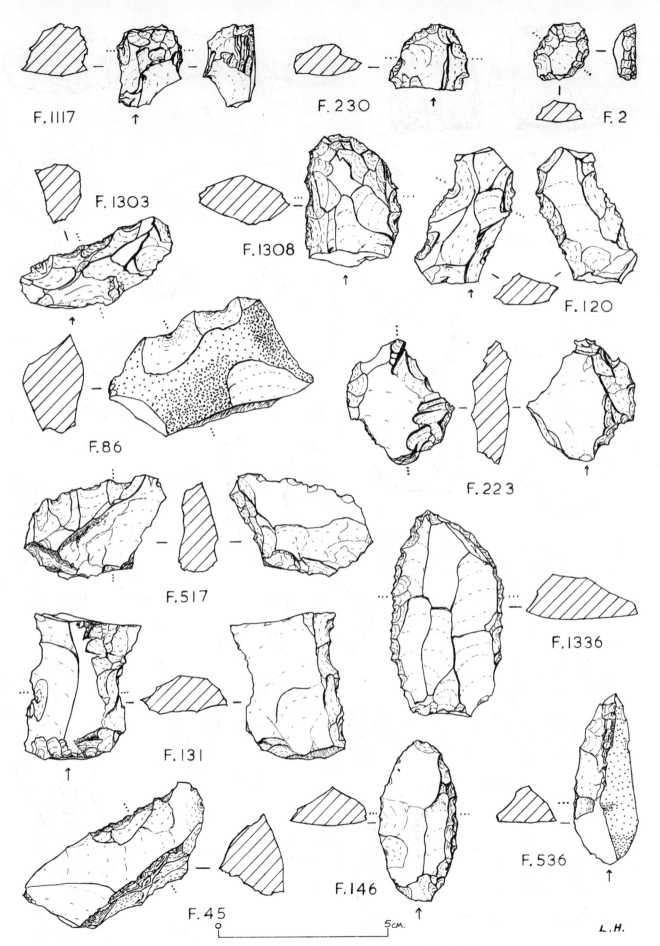

F.1117

F.230

F.2

F.1303

F.1308

F.120

F.86

F.223

F.517

F.1336

F.131

F.45

F.146

F.536

5 CM.

L.H.

Plate 4. **F. 2**, p. 72; **F.45**, pp. 72, 75; **F.86**, p. 72; **F.120**, p. 73; **F.131**, p. 73; **F.146**, p. 73; **F.223**, p. 72; **F.230**, p. 72; **F.517**, p. 72; **F.536**, pp. 73, 76; **F.1117**, p. 72; **F.1303**, pp. 72, 73; **F.1308**, p. 72; **F.1336**, p. 73.

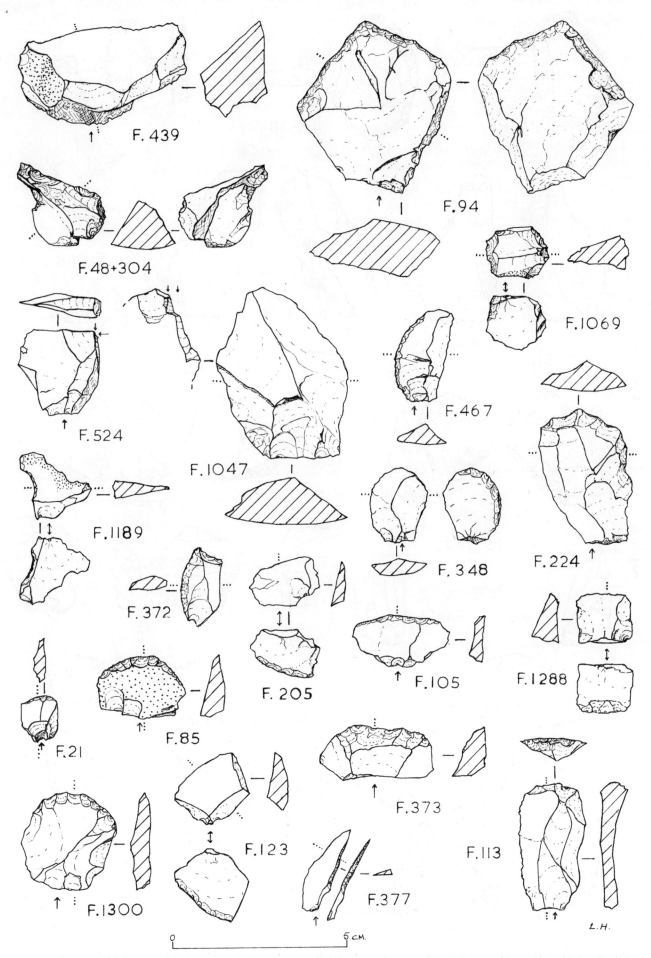

F. 439

F.94

F.48+304

F.1069

F.524

F.467

F.1047

F.1189

F.348

F.224

F.372

F.1288

F.205

F.105

F.21

F.85

F.373

F.113

F.1300

F.123

F.377

0   5 CM.

L.H.

Plate 5. **F.21**, p. 72; **F.48 + 304,** p. 71; **F.85,** p. 72; **F.94,** p. 71; **F.105,** p. 72; **F.113,** p. 73; **F.123,** p. 72; **F.205,** p. 72; **F.224,** p. 73; Г.348, p. 72; **F.372,** p. 72; **F.373,** p. 72; **F.377,** pp. 72, 76; **F.439,** p. 72; **F.467,** p. 72; **F.524,** p. 73; **F.1047,** p. 73; **F.1069,** p. 71; **F.1189,** p. 72; **F.1288,** p. 72; **F.1300,** p. 72.

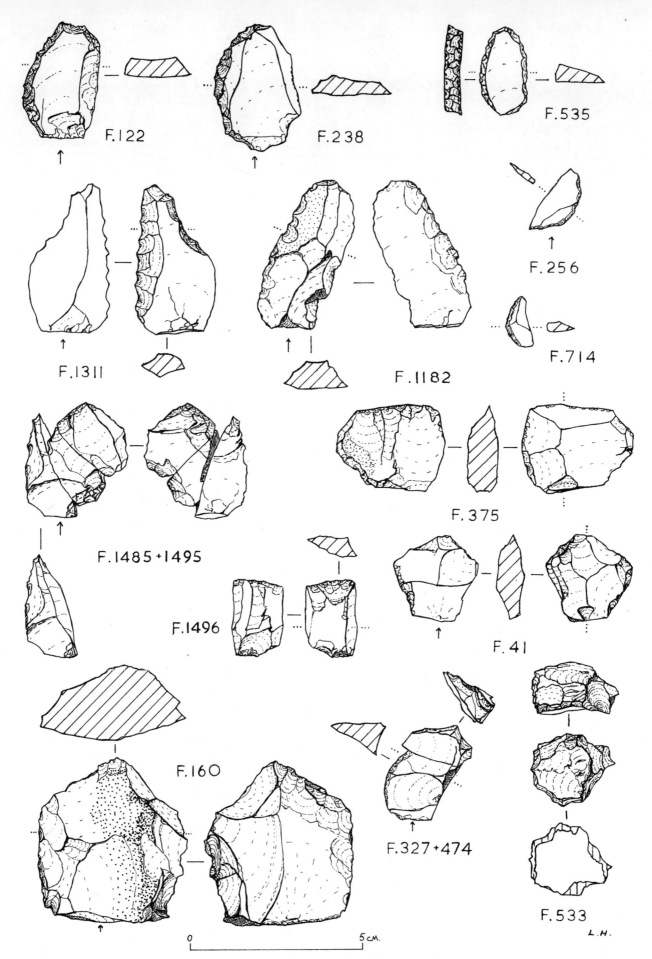

F.122

F.238

F.535

F.1311

F.1182

F.256

F.714

F.1485+1495

F.375

F.1496

F.41

F.160

F.327+474

F.533

0   5 CM.

L.H.

Plate 6.   **F.41,** p. 71; **F.122,** p. 73; **F.160,** p. 72; **F.238,** p. 73; **F.256,** p. 73; **F.327 + 474,** p. 73; **F.375,** p. 71; **F.533,** p. 72; **F.535,** p. 72; **F.714,** pp. 73, 76; **F.1182,** p. 73; **F.1311,** p. 73; **F.1485 + 1495,** pp. 71, 75; **F.1496,** pp. 71, 75.

The next criterion used for subdividing groups B and C is the manner in which the working edges have been altered. Eight categories have been defined; these could be subdivided, cf. Crosby 1971, White 1969.

1. use-polished
2. bruised
3. scalar chipping from use present
4. abrupt chipping from use present
5. flaking modifies edge
6. flaking and/or scalar retouch modifies edge
7. flaking and/or abrupt retouch modifies edge
8. flaking and/or grinding modifies edge

Note: Edges of type 6 - 8 may be further altered by use.

Implements in each of these subgroups were then sorted in terms of straight, concave, notched, convex, nosed, wavy, serrated, dentated, irregular, or burin type edges. The size range, and origin (pebble, chunk, core, chunky flake, thin flake) was noted and used in table 5, but these features were not used for further subdivision. The numbers present are given in the table.

A number of other traits have been noted and measured for use. These are: whether retouch is continuous or intermittent, how much of the available edge was altered, whether a natural or flaked edge was selected, whether retouch or use-wear is unifacial, bifacial, or mixed, what type of face it modifies and from what face retouch was done, whether the artifact is single or multiplane (one or more faces bordered by working edges), how many working edges are present compared to the number of planes, what part of the margin of a flake has been altered, and the length, breadth, thickness, and weight of each artifact. Some reference may be given to such details in the descriptions but they have not yet been studied in all groups.

Descriptions

In the descriptions below references to illustrated specimens are given in the text. The legends to the plates give cross references to the text.

A. Unaltered cores

These may be prismatic (for narrow, oblong flakes) (F.1516, plate 3), alternatively flaked (F.99, plate 3), or irregular (F.1291, plate 3). The last group is the biggest by far in this assemblage. Many cores were altered into implements. Obvious cases have been counted, see table D. Most cores have been worked down to what appears the practical limit; exceptions almost invariably show flaws.

B. Artifacts with unmodified working edges

B.1. Use-polish present
Three shapes (and their approximations) recur.
The segment shaped type (F.153, plate 1) has a straight edge opposed by a rounded back which may be natural pebble surface or created by flaking. The angle of the edge (mostly due to natural cleavage) varies between 60º and 79º, the edge itself is rounded by use and has a distinct polish extending from 5 to 8 millimetres away from the edge on both faces. The segment may be truncated at one or both ends or carry an additional short working edge with use-polish or chipping. The implements are similar to the elouera (McCarthy 1967, p.26) but larger, here up to 18 centimetres long. They are made on pebbles or tabular chunks of rock. The use-polish may be broken by chipping but does sometimes go over scars.

The keeled version (F.492+703, plate 2) has a high rounded back and a roughly triangular flat base enclosed by one or two long use-polished edges and a short flaked and chipped edge. The polish is unifacial or bifacial and the angle of the edge close to 78º.

The rectangular version is similar but has use-polish on two long sides of the flat base. The short sides may be flaked and chipped. The angle of the edge varies from 85º to 93º.

B.2. Bruising (sometimes also slight chipping) present
Straight working edges dominate. The most common version has a short edge transverse to the long axis of the implement (F.958, plate 1; F.1229, plate 1). Its angle ranges from 43º to 90º but the majority are close to the mean of 68º. All examples are found on either split or truncated pebbles or chunks of rock with natural cleavage faces. Compare picks, McCarthy 1967, fig. 9.

Implements with concave, notched, convex, or nosed edges occur in small numbers (F.1516, plate 3). No recurrent shape can be seen. The example shown is a core with a used projection and notches.

B.3 Scalar chipping present
Implements with straight, curved, nosed or irregular edges occur in small numbers, some reminiscent of groups C.6 and C.7. Two examples with straight chipped edge (F.1230, plate 2) are in all other details comparable to segments with use-polish (cf. B.1 above), a third has irregular chipping suggesting a sawing motion (F.870+835, plate 2).

B.3/4 Considerable scalar and abrupt chipping present
This group appears to fit the description of fabricators (F.41, plate 6; F.94, plate 5; F.48+304, plate 5; F.375, plate 6), see McCarthy 1967, p.36. The use-wear is mostly bifacial, mainly scalar in lightly used specimens; more used examples tend to have more abrupt chipping. There is little sign of shaping. The ideal piece selected was square or rectangular and between 2 and 3 centimetres square in size. Many (23 per cent) are wedge-shaped (F.1069, plate 5). Chert or fine-grained quartzite was preferred. The typical use-wear may occur on from one to four margins, but in the majority two opposing edges have been used. The angle of all edges was measured, also on undoubted fragments of this group and is below 60º in 85 per cent. A steep edge is usually opposed by one of more acute angle. The implement often snapped during use producing a characteristic facet (F.1485+1495, plate 6; F.1496, plate 6).[8]

B.4. Abrupt chipping present
One specimen with straight working edge was originally a segment with use-polish. Concave (F.1291, plate 3) notched, convex, or wavy edges are found in small numbers on cores or large flakes.

C.   Artifacts with modified working edges

C.5.   Edges modified by flaking

Straight edges are rare and their use-wear mainly bifacial, scalar, or abrupt (F.160, plate 6). Convex edges are also rare and may be backing rather than working edges.

Wavy edges are found on two sets of artifacts. The high-back examples (F.354, plate 1; F.180, plate 1) have a flat base, partly or entirely enclosed by a working edge of about 95° with abrupt chipping, even overthrust. Other edges may be present, altered by flaking or use (F.134, plate 2).

The second set (F.455, plate 2) has a wavy edge obliquely to or at right angles to the long axis. The angle of the edge ranges from 60° to 72°. Half of the large examples have a notch or slight groove well away from the working edge, possibly for hafting or better grip (F.1262, plate 2). The medium sized examples have a flat facet (for the index finger?) at one end opposite the working edge.

Serrated edges are found on artifacts which grade into the group just described. The working edge with three to five points is opposed by a broad natural back (F.86, plate 4). The range of the angle between the planes forming the edge appears narrow (49° - 58°); the depth and angle of the notches varies more.

C.6 and C.7.   Scalar or abrupt retouch present

Artifacts in these groups were first sorted according to the shape of the retouched edges, and then further divided according to the position of such edges. A visual comparison of all the resulting subgroups brought out several points. Firstly that some members of group C.7 shared all traits except the type of retouch with some members of C.6, and that the abrupt retouch in most of these cases appears the result of repeated retouch, that is a secondary characteristic. Groups C.6 and C.7 will therefore be described together though separated in table 5. Secondly there were clearly several major classes of implements distinguishable by the shape and size of the whole artifact although the shape and position of the retouched edges could vary. Such classes are small scrapers, single plane steep scrapers, multiplane tools, and segments. The descriptions of these will cut across the groups and subgroups and their numbers given in the text. What remains will thereafter be described in order following the system of sorting.

C.6 and C.7: Small scrapers (total seventy) (F.105, plate 5; F.205, plate 5; F.1288, plate 5; F.21, plate 5; F.85, plate 5; F.143, plate 3; F.373, plate 5; F.1300, plate 5; F.348, plate 5; F.467, plate 5; F.123, plate 5; F.535, plate 6; F.372, plate 5). These are all less than 35 millimetres in any dimension. Retouch is in 85 per cent below 71° and angles close to 58° are common. The scraper edge is mostly gently convex (83 per cent) grading into straight. The flakes used are short, as broad as long (42 per cent), slightly elongated (42 per cent) or broad but short. Only five scrapers have more than one edge, since retouch involving several margins tends to be continuous and form one edge. The working edge tends to be opposite a thicker edge which may be the butt (26 per cent), a thick margin (21 per cent) or a steeply retouched (backed) area (13 per cent). (The steep retouch tends to be double, that is from both dorsal and bulbar faces, along all or part

of the margin.) Inverse retouch is found on the scraper edge in just over half of these backed scrapers and of side-and-end scrapers, but is rare in other variants. The left rather than the right margin was chosen for scraper retouch in three cases out of four. There are several cases of two to four scrapers being almost identical in size, technique, and sometimes also of the same material. Each set may well derive from one occasion and maker.

C.6 and C.7: Single plane steep scrapers (total twenty-two) (F.2, plate 4; F.230, plate 4; F.1119, plate 3; F.533, plate 6; F.1117, plate 4). Only one exceeds 35 millimetres in any dimension, and half are microlithic. The base is flat, the sides steep, and the top keeled or flat. Half are discoid or semidiscoid. Those with several working edges tend to have some use-wear on the junction (compare nosed implements). The angle of retouch is in 53 per cent of the edges between 73° and 79°, but ranges between 61° and 96°. All have use-wear, always abrupt chipping, sometimes also bruising. Some overthrust is common. Note that some could be called micro-horsehoof cores; see McCarthy 1967, p.18.

C.6 and C.7: Multiplane implements (total forty-eight) (F.23, plate 3; F.39, plate 3; F.223, plate 4; F.736, plate 3; F.1308, plate 4). None exceed 50 millimetres but only 29 per cent are microlithic. Two planes and two retouched edges are the norm (50 per cent) but up to five planes and five edges occur. The retouch ranges from 49° to 98°, but is in 19 per cent between 68° and 73°, and in 23 per cent between 76° and 82° (notched, serrated, or dentated edges not counted). Straight edges (27 per cent) or gently convex edges (33 per cent) are found in combination with the same type or with concave, notched, nosed, wavy, serrated, or dentated ones, each of these occurring in small numbers only. The retouch may be alternate (12 per cent), that is from two opposing planes on tabular pieces or thick flakes. Inverse retouch on chunky flakes is common (45 per cent) especially for "rods". These form half of the total. They have two planes (often the dorsal face of a flake) at an angle so that the cross section is a lozenge. Most are oblong, a few almost square. Multiplane implements with scalar retouch (41 per cent) almost all have abrupt chipping, sometimes also bruising, as have those with abrupt retouch. Most would probably be called adze-flakes; see McCarthy 1967, p.24.

C.6 and C.7: Segments (F.517, plate 4; F.439, plate 5; F.45, plate 4). A total of seven flakes have a marked crescentic shape, the curved back being thick, the chord thin and sharp. The back is naturally blunt but sharp projections have been removed by steep retouch (close to 90°), in one case from both faces. The chord may have retouch and/or use-wear and its angle is below 57°. The group appears to fit the descriptions of elouera; see McCarthy 1967, p.26.

C.6 and C.7: The remainder.

Straight retouched edges are rare (ten examples). One specimen with steep retouch could be called a backed bladelet (F.377, plate 5). Two others (F.38, plate 3; F.1303, plate 4) fit the descriptions of tula and burren slugs; see McCarthy 1967, pp.27 - 28. The rest are irregular flakes or chunks.

Concave edges are few (five examples) (F.457, plate 3; F.1189, plate

5). These are all on thick flakes and primary retouch was scalar and mostly inverse but further altered by abrupt chipping and retouch.

Notched edges are less rare (eight examples) but range from one or several notches irregularly spaced to a series of notches separated by unmodified projections, that is they grade into the serrated group. Inverse retouch dominates, the first retouch was scalar and at an angle of 50° to 70° but altered by abrupt chipping.

Convex edges are common (twenty-two examples), but of several kinds. The majority conform to descriptions of semidiscoid, end- or side-scrapers and the retouch is clearly for working edges (F.113, plate 5; F.1321, plate 3; F.52, plate 3). In the remainder (nine) the retouch is probably for backing. Four flakes of red jasper have scalar retouch of between 73° and 78° on the left margin and scalar use-wear on the right margin (F.122, plate 6; F.238, plate 6). Three other have steep (ca. 80°) retouch along a curved back and could be called geometric microliths (F.714, plate 6; F.256, plate 6). Two chunky flakes of triangular cross section (F.146, plate 4; F.536, plate 4) have abrupt retouch, partly double, along one side forming a thick back and scalar chipping (some retouch) on the opposite margin. These could be called eloueras or Bondi points; see McCarthy 1967, pp.26, 38.

Nosed implements are rare (three examples). One specimen grades into the serrated group; the retouch is inverse (F.17, plate 3). Two thick pointed flakes (F.698, plate 3; F.70+325, plate 3) have steep (ca. 80°) retouch on both margins; one has been reworked with abrupt inverse retouch, and broken in the process.

Wavy edges are also rare (three examples), but those found are very similar in size and technique. The oblong flakes (F.120, plate 4; F.1182, plate 6) have one or two wavy margins. The retouch is inverse, partly bifacial and close to 68°.

Serrated edges are less rare (eight examples) (F.131, plate 4). The primary retouch is always scalar. Oblong chunky flakes dominate. The angle of retouch is fairly constant; in 75 per cent it is close to 63° on the points and close to 74° in the notches. Bruising is found all along the retouch.

Dentated edges are rare (four examples) (F.1311, plate 6). The retouch may be scalar or abrupt and the angle varies. One example (F.1336, plate 4) also has a convex steeply retouched edge, probably backing, another a natural thick margin opposing the serrated margin.

Irregular retouched edges are few (six examples) (F.179, plate 3; F.224, plate 5) and approximate to nosed or serrated. One had clearly been retouched again after breaking (F.327+474, plate 6).

Burin edges are rare or absent. The two most probable examples have been illustrated (F.524, plate 5; F.1047, plate 5).

C.8.   Artifacts with edges modified by flaking and/or grinding
Axes: There is only one undamaged example (F.93, plate 1) but six fragments are undoubtedly broken axes. These were flaked into shape, pecked and finally ground over part or all of the edges and surfaces, i.e. some are edge-ground, some polished (McCarthy 1967, p.47).

D.   Artifacts with surface only altered by use
High-back grinders: Six chunks (F.465, plate 2) have one oval flat face, the base, further smoothened by rubbing, and opposite this is a keeled or domed, flaked or natural, back. The raw material is gritty

and a faint superficial red tint can be seen on some specimens.

Rubbed chunks of weathered powdery basalt occur. Unbroken examples have striations but no flattened faces.

Crayons of pigment, mainly red ochre, were found in some quantity (twenty-three examples) but often broken. Little or no shaping preceded use. The shape tends to conical or rectangular, see p. 32 and Appendix E.

E.   Artifacts with surface only modified
Waisted artifacts (F.694, plate 1): Four pear-shaped pebbles or flakes have two flaked and battered notches in the narrow part and traces of wear all round forming a barely visible groove. They are reminiscent of net-sinkers (McCarthy 1967, fig. 45:8) but may have use-wear on the broad end.

Miscellaneous. A number of pebbles appear to have use-marks, though mostly faint. Twenty-three were certainly hammer-stones, and nine of these may have been used for grinding also.

Technological tradition

Do the stone implements described reflect one or more technological traditions? We cannot look at the contents of a sequence of layers for an answer, but I shall attempt to indicate by other means that we are almost certainly dealing with one tradition which changed little during the period of the burial ground, except at the very end of this.

Figure 103 shows the range of length, breadth, thickness, and angle of striking platform of unmodified flakes. It is obvious that the great majority of flakes follow the same pattern: short, as broad as they are long, rather chunky, and with a striking platform close to an angle of 100° - 110°. Large flakes were almost invariably retouched. The exceptions, referred to above, are some thick but well-made quartzite flakes with sharp margins. Several of these were found to be definitely related to late burials, see p. 76.

In the typological descriptions above, reference was made to names commonly used in the typology of Australian stone implements. These are generally used as indicators of certain cultural phases.[9] I therefore give in table 6 at least textbook examples from this site with reference to their stratigraphical context. It must be remembered that there is more than one suggestion of re-use of pieces discovered on the surface or through pit digging.

The stages within the sequence are those defined in chapter 3 and used in figure 74 and table 4. A burial number within brackets indicates that the artifact could have been derived from another burial nearby. A burial number in bold type means that more than one implement of this type was associated with the burial.

Some comments on the identifications are necessary. The Bondi point is outside the range of thickness given in McCarthy 1967, p.40, and it may be a very slim elouera. Tulas are thought not to occur in this area, but I have shown F.38 and F.1303 to several Australian archaeologists who agreed that they would call the first a tula and the second a tula slug, see McCarthy 1967, pp. 27 - 28. The examples of uncertain identification would be called steep scrapers or scrapers

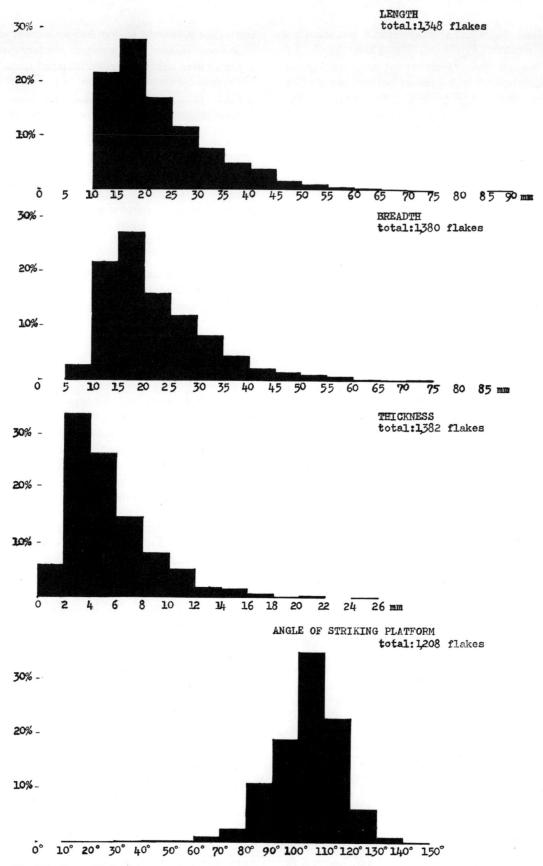

Fig. 103. Unmodified flakes. Length, breadth, thickness, and angle of striking platform shown for the total number of such flakes present in the site which were unbroken or only slightly damaged. Note that flakes less than 10 millimetres long were not measured.

Table 6. *Artifact types present in association with burials*

Name*	Stage O	Stage O or I	Stage I	Stage II
Bondi point (or elouera?)	B.76+82			
geometric microlith			B.60	
backed bladelet		B.28		
fabricator	**B.8**,B.25 or B.31,**B.30**, B.55,B.117, **B.119**	**B.16**,B.23, B.134,**B.136**	**B.6**,**B.15**, B.122,B.125	**B.5**,B.29, (B.116),**B.138**
tula, typical (F.38,F.1303)			B.6	B.138
tula, uncertain	B.25 or B.31, B.87	B.16,B.28, (B.134), **B.136**	B.4,B.6, B.137	**B.5**,**B.36**, **B.116**,**B.138**
elouera	B.25 or B.31		B.12,B.137	B.138
ground edge axe	B.63	B.16		B.79

* Cf. McCarthy 1967.

by most but not by all typologists. The eloueras and the ground-edge axes fit McCarthy's descriptions exactly.

The first four types in table 6 are typical of the middle, the last two of the late phase of McCarthy's Eastern Regional Sequence, see McCarthy 1967, p.91. Mulvaney (1969, p.128) has pointed out that these phases do not appear so definite outside the area near Sydney where they were first defined. I shall comment further on this when comparing the implements in the site with those from other areas. The question here is whether there was any major technological change. The numbers involved are small, but in my opinion the table shows a scatter of each type which suggests that they were all part of the technological tradition all through the period of the burial ground.

The use of some implement types?

It is always hard to discover and frequently foolhardy even to suggest the probable use of the implements found. In this type of site, however, it might be possible to find patterns of association such as whether an implement was most frequently found on the surface of a burial pit or in the burial itself. Such a pattern could suggest uses for the particular type of implement. I looked into this carefully, but in few cases did a convincing pattern emerge. The numbers of each type are too small, and very few of these can be reliably associated with a burial. I shall, however, mention briefly some trends that did emerge. Some further suggestions will be made, and some further elaborated, in chapter 6 with help of written accounts.

The large implements with use-polish (p. 71) were, except for broken examples or where there had been a disturbance, found in level 1 or just below the shell horizon, in the case of B.130 on the edge of the burial pit but in other cases some distance from a pit-surface. This suggests that they were used for some process which did not take place just beside the pit. Such polished edges, stated to be typical of McCarthy's Eastern Regional Sequence, are interpreted by him as the result of working bark or wood or scraping skins. This would be a plausible explanation in this site. It may have been a matter of softening for example tea-tree bark and making it more pliable before using it to cover a corpse or a bone bundle as described in chapter 6. One implement, F.462+456+166a was built up from several fragments. One of these formed part of the B.40 corona. This was one of the early burials in the site, which means that the tradition which resulted in use-polish was early also.

Small steep scrapers and small scrapers do occur in pits and scattered outside burial pits but a notably large proportion are found in level 1 just above the shell horizon or at the top of the pit-fill just below shells. This applies to 41 per cent of such implements. Note that 36 per cent could not be related to particular burial pits. Many of the scrapers are microlithic and could have worked downwards. Some were found wedged inside shell pockets on the surface of burial pits, others all round B.136 at the level at which some funeral meal had taken place, see fig. 53. It seems reasonable to suggest that most of these were in fact used during some such meal to extract shell fish.[10]

Fabricators (p. 71) also occur on pit-surfaces but more often, especially the snapped examples, in the pit-fill. Only 16 per cent were found in level 1 above the pit surface, another 16 per cent were found on the pit-surface itself, and 51 per cent came from deeper down in the pit-fill. (The remainder could not be related to particular burials.) They were often made in several examples, quite possibly at the same time, of the same raw material. This was always extremely fine-grained quartzite or chert. In nine burials they occurred in pairs, that is two to a pit, which were usually of the same material and almost identical in shape and size but not close together in the ground. Their use is hard to imagine but it appears to be something that happened before the bundle was finally interred but close to the pit itself. It is worth noting that the raw materials were used also for other types of implements and flaked on the spot. This, in my opinion, makes it unlikely that fabricators were deposited as gravegoods.

There are, however, finds which I believe could be properly classed as gravegoods. A number of finished implements were brought to the site — at times worn by use — made of raw materials not found or not common in the site and almost certainly deliberately left behind, not forgotten or discarded.

F.45, a well-made, dark green and pink elouera of fine chert, found on the surface of the B.12 pit, is so large and striking in colour that it could hardly have been abandoned accidentally. The same applies to F.38, a half-worn tula of brilliant green common opal. This was found on the pit-surface over B.6. Both are textbook examples of the type and rare or unique in the site. Polished stone axes probably also belong to this category. The best and largest example, F.93, was found on the surface of the B.16 pit, see figure 104. Pieces of another, F.215, were found between the bones of burial B.63 and must have been wrapped inside the bundle. Fragments of a third, F.532, were lying on the skull of B.79. What

Fig.104. F.93, a polished axe, on the surface of the pit for B.16. Camera facing down.

could be a broken axe-blank was sitting near a very decayed burial, B.113, just above where the skull would once have been. The stone shows signs of polish on the ridges between the flake scars, as if some attempt had been made to polish it, before it broke. F.180, large and of unusual shape (see plate 1), was lying on the pit surface over B.61, a burial in many aspects like B.79, just mentioned. The large, plain, and sharp flakes found in little heaps on the surface of burial pits share with the implements mentioned above the characteristics of small numbers, a position on the surface or in the uppermost part of the burial pit with no scatter outside burial pits except in disturbed areas, and also origin in a piece of raw material not used for other finds in the site.

Most examples quoted were found on the surface of burial pits or just below this. Some well-made colourful implements were found in a position which suggested that at a certain stage of filling the pit for some vertical bundle-burials the participants paused to deposit such implements. They were lying about 10 - 15 centimetres away from the bundle, which makes it unlikely that they derived from inside this, and about one-third to one-quarter way down its depth counted from the top of the skull.[11] Ten implements with neat serrations or dentations, made of red jasper or variegated chert, were found in this position. So were six thick-backed flakes, some of which could definitely be called elouera. Four out of eleven burials involved had more than one implement in this position.

Implements of these types were, however, also found on pit-surfaces and rarely far from burial pits except in disturbed areas. It may be worth noting here that red jasper was almost exclusively used for such serrated/dentated implements and for thin backed flakes. The four examples of the latter, made of red jasper, were all found on the surface of burial pits.

Most of the examples mentioned so far have good cutting edges, which suggests that they may actually have been used during a burial ceremony and deposited. Since this could be done before the final filling, it would have been something not related to the eating of shell fish round the pit. They are also striking in colour and well made which suggests that they may have been specially selected or made for some important detail of the funeral processes and therefore not taken away for further use.

Implements and pieces of stone found amongst the bones of a burial may have been placed there deliberately but for somewhat different reasons. This will be elaborated in chapter 6, but I can mention here that in historical times death magic was in this area related to stone, not bone.

Pieces of a stone axe were found amongst the bones of one burial, but also other artifact types and plain flakes were found. These are as a rule pointed or small, thin and sharp, as F.377, the straight-backed bladelet in B.28 and the lunate F.714 in the pit-fill of B.60, apparently fallen out of the bundle. F.536 (which may be a Bondi point)) fell out of B.76+82 when part of the burials collapsed into the B.73 pit. Undoubted points are rare, but two almost identical, oblong pointed flakes were found, F.490 on the skull of B.61, F.503 on the arm of B.73, that is right on the bones. (See also Appendix E.)

Comparison with other sites

A detailed comparison with the lithic content of other sites in eastern Australia would be difficult even if the lithic material from Broadbeach could be divided according to stratigraphical stages, since there are large areas about which we know little or nothing between those that have been studied in some detail by archaeologists. The lack of stratigraphy at Broadbeach makes anything but a general comparison imposssible, since the changes in implement types and in proportions of types present in the strata of a site have been the main criteria used to build up a picture of the cultural development of these sites.[12]

In terms of current Australian typology, the types present are mainly those characteristic of McCarthy's Eastern Regional Sequence, but there are some hints of the inland Tula Regional Sequence — one at least (worn) tula and some probable tula slugs. The pointed bones from Broadbeach are, however, probably not muduks, but combs, see p. 83.

The Eastern Regional Sequence has been divided into three stages. The Broadbeach material includes types belonging to the last two, the Bondaian and the Eloueran. Since there are only a few examples of each of the well-defined types, neither set of types can be said to dominate.

But Mulvaney (1969) has given in some detail the history of the typological and cultural labels used in Australian prehistory. He has also discussed many problems and uncertainties related to these. It seems clear that at least for the time being it would be unwise to try to fit a label to the Broadbeach assemblage. I shall therefore, for the sake of comparison, in Appendix G list sites in eastern Australia which have a comparable lithic content and/or radiocarbon date.

CHAPTER 6

Written accounts versus archaeological evidence

Introduction

This chapter deals with burial customs as described in early accounts of southeast Queensland Aborigines. I shall discuss the quality of the sources and the validity of correlations to be made with the archaeological material. I will then give some examples of how such accounts may fill in details in the archaeological picture of burial customs but also pose new problems.

Problems and limits

The validity of any comparison between archaeological finds and written accounts depends on a number of factors. How reliable is the written evidence? Is it an eye-witness account or merely hearsay? How close in time are the finds and the comments to be compared — would there have been time for traditions to change and, if so, are there indications that change in the study area during that period was rapid or slow? Do the comments refer to the area of the finds — if not, is there any reason to suppose that at a particular point in time cultural connections existed between the area containing the excavation and that described in the literature? Written evidence can deal with happenings that leave no physical trace as well as those that do; how far are we justified in deducing parallels in the former when the archaeological finds agree with the written evidence?

Comments on the reliability of each account will be made as it is quoted. A number of these are first-hand descriptions of Aboriginal traditions as they were when Europeans arrived. The absolute dates for Broadbeach, given in chapter 3, indicate that such accounts may be relevant at least to the last stages of its use. Since, as has been stressed repeatedly, little change could be seen through its history, the accounts could be relevant to most or all of the period in question. Some evidence from archaeological excavations and from modern anthropological research will be quoted when relevant to some part of the area or some topic discussed. The geographical aspect will be considered once I have quoted the accounts and I have given a picture of what was happening in southeast Queensland and northern New South Wales. The extent of my deductions will depend partly on how consistent this picture is. Evidence from outside this area will be discussed at the end of the chapter.

First contact with Europeans

The Aboriginal population of the Moreton Bay district has been estimated as 1,500 at the time the first Europeans arrived.[1] This was probably divided into clans comprising fifty to sixty persons each. Taylor's reconstruction of the clan boundaries and their names, where known, can be found on map 10. Broadbeach burial ground, situated between the Nerang River and the Big Swamp, two of the main features of this area, inhabited by the Kombumerri or Nerang "tribe", was in a fairly central position. The Bundall site was close to its northern border.

In 1823 the castaways Pamphlett, Parsons, and Finnegan came ashore on Moreton Island. From 1824 to 1840, an area centred on Brisbane Town and with a radius of 50 miles (80 kilometres) was an official penal settlement. There were occasional clashes between officials and surrounding natives and some contact between the latter and the prisoners. Pastoralists were moving in quickly after 1840 and most of the suitable land in the Moreton Pastoral District had already been taken up by 1845. Large tracts of land on the coast, however, were left unsettled, either because they were unsuitable for grazing or because they were covered with impenetrable scrub. These areas could support fairly dense populations of Aborigines who here continued to live a more or less traditional life until the end of the seventies.

The Nerang District Show Catalogue of 1946 states:[2]

The first appearance of white men in the Nerang district occurred in 1842, when a party of cedar getters crossed the mountains from the Tweed and explored for cedar. Two young men who had been companions for some time and were on friendly terms with the natives were among the newcomers. They were Edmund Harper and William Duncan. A rafting ground was first established at the mouth of Little Tallebudgera Creek. Later Edmund Harper made his home there to which he brought his mother. Harper and Duncan remained together in the district, and associating with the natives, could speak the dialects of the Tweed and Nerang tribes so well that the blacks could not tell from their speech that they were not of the tribes.

Other timber-getters arrived in the district but no permanent homes seem to have been established there, at that time.

Harper's home was only about 1.5 kilometres north-north-east of Broadbeach burial ground. He is said to have been on good terms with the natives. This suggests that his presence need not have deterred them from using the burial ground. I have found no mention, however, of a native burial ground in that area.

Big groups of natives wandered in the Nerang area as late as 1884.[3] By this time much timber had been cleared in the area and it is doubtful whether it was possible for them to subsist entirely on the vegetation and animal life of the area. Many had already started to lose their old social organization.

Most of the written accounts available refer to neighbouring areas, not to what the Kombumerri did. The few notes extant referring to graves are all late and probably refer to sporadic graves made partly in imitation of European customs.

Written accounts and archaeological evidence from other sites referring to burial customs

The accounts from adjoining areas are sometimes short and cryptic, sometimes long, detailed, and often sensational. From them,

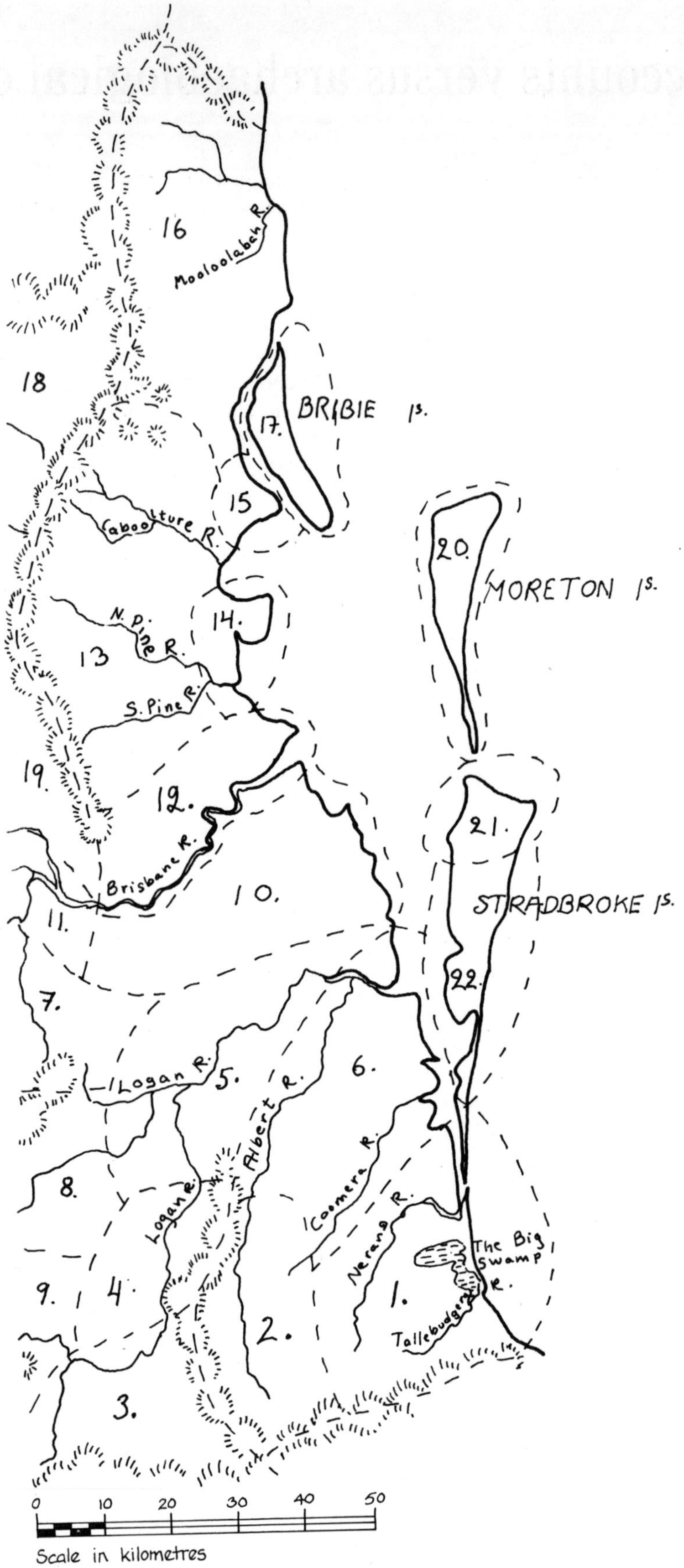

DISTRIBUTION OF CLANS

Possible native name

1. Kombumerri
2. Wangerriburra
3. Migunburri
4. Mununjali
5. Gugingin
6. Bullongin
7. Yagarabul
8. Bukibal
9. Minjangbal
10.
11.
12. Turrbal
13.
14.
15.
16.
17. Ninge Ninge
18.
19.
20.
21. Noonuckle
22. Koenpal

based on J. C. Taylor 1967.

Map 10.   Distribution of clans on the southeast Queensland coast.

it is possible to get some idea of the rituals and permutations of ritual common in southeast Queensland; the ideas behind them were rarely mentioned, much less understood. I shall now quote some of the most reliable of these accounts, taking them according to area and working clock-wise around the Nerang district.

We may start with some accounts from the islands in Moreton Bay (cf. map 1):[4]

... even at the time when Flinders visited Bribie in 1799, the natives on the island were cannibals ... From the birth of a child to the death of an old man or woman, they adopted and carried out customs and mannerisms not known on Moreton or Stradbroke. Their mode of burial was quite different. In the not very far back, skeletons of natives were found in forks of fair-sized trees on the island.

Referring to the Aborigines on Stradbroke and Moreton, Watkins wrote:[5]

... In the case of death, the body was bound with the upper part bent forward towards the knees, and enclosed in a wrapping of tea-tree bark. It was carried to the place of interment slung to a sapling, and followed for a distance by the whole tribe. The burial place was a considerable distance, in one case two or three miles away. About halfway the women and children were left behind. The grave was dug in the sand, and kept from falling in by a framework of saplings. It was lined with tea-tree bark and the body was laid in. This was covered with more bark and saplings and then filled in with bush and sand. The body was set down several times on the journey, when one of the friends who acted as chief mourner and master of the ceremonies, would go to the wrapping, and placing his mouth to the ear, where a hole was made for the purpose, enquire who killed it. Wailing and howling was indulged in to a great extent; and the mourners cut themselves with oyster shell etc., till the blood streamed down. Wailing would be made every evening for some weeks. The women used feathers and down in the hair for mourning. On the occasion of a death, the camp where it took place was deserted and a fresh camp made in another neighbourhood. The name of the deceased was never mentioned, and in the case of a child or other person being named after the dead, such name was altered. After a considerable time, the original name was generally reverted to. In the course of time, the death ceremonies were carried out with less and less of the old forms, until at last some wished to be buried in "white fashion" in the Dunwich cemetery.

In the mountainous area south and west of Broadbeach, the tradition was cave burial. W.G. Curtis stated:[6]

The only burial place I know of is in the cave in the sandstone cliff on the western side of Tamborine Mountain, near Wonglepong, quite close to the old Canungra rifle range... About 80 years ago my father found a skeleton of an Aboriginal in a white ants' (termites) mound near Albert River.[7]

Archie Daniels[8] states that the Migunburri, or Christmas Creek, Aborigines just north of the McPherson Range and west of Beaudesert

... were not cannibals ... The Migunburri buried their dead in caves and rock clefts. At least one proof of this exists [in the Beaudesert area]. These caves are small, being some three feet high and six feet deep, and the dead were placed inside, the entrance being left open.[9]

Further south towards the Tweed, Richmond, and Clarence Rivers, a range of burial types was practised during the period of early European settlement. Some kinds were then no longer in use.

On the Tweed[10] the body was compressed, probably breaking the bones, or at least some ligaments, and placed in a sitting position in a shallow grave in a common burial ground on the side of a hill. The grave was usually covered by bark or sticks. These were meant as a protection from dingoes, but rain often bared the tops of burials. The shallowness of the graves was due to the poor digging equipment, mainly women's digging sticks. A large burial ground at Wardell is said to have been there because the white sand was so easy to dig. But there were also single burials in middens in this area, e.g. at Lennox Heads.

On the Richmond River, the body was carefully doubled up, tied with string or vine, sometimes wrapped in bark, and buried in a sitting position in a shallow grave, usually on the side of a hill. In the South Australian Museum there is a cremation found in a rock crevice in this area (Hiatt 1969, p.109).

The following is a brief summary given of relevant information gathered by Dr. M.J.C. Calley during anthropological research during the mid-1950s and late 1960s on the far north coast of New South Wales and southern coastal Queensland.

Although Aborigines in this area retained more of their old culture than any other group in southeast Australia, it must be remembered that they had been in contact with Europeans for more than a hundred years and that their ideas of traditional culture must have been influenced by this. More important, European settlement meant the cessation of fighting and a much increased geographical mobility among Aborigines. This means that one can never be quite certain whether the description of a rite refers to what was done by an informant's clan or what was done by their neighbours.

Traditional burial rites must have persisted in some areas on the far north coast of New South Wales until well into the 1890s and probably later. Some aspects of the traditional rites persist down to the present day. For example, at the funeral of Danny Sambo at Coraki in 1967, the corpse was "talked to" before the grave was filled and told not to harm the children. It was usual in this area to hold juvenile patrilineal descendants close to, or even in contact with, the corpse while it was told to stay in its grave and not to harm or frighten them. My most complete accounts of traditional burial rites come from two informants, one from the Beaudesert area and one from near Kyogle. Both of these men are now in their nineties and participated in the rites themselves. Though somewhat senile now, both of them were in full possession of their faculties seventeen years ago when this information was gathered, and other elderly men, now dead, who were present at the interviews, agreed that the accounts I was given were correct.[11]

The accounts agree that the discovery of the identity of the sorcerer responsible for the death was an important preliminary.[12] In the Kyogle area one technique was to isolate suspects close to the presumed scene of the murder. The ghost would cause the killer to cry out, indicating his guilt. It seems that this technique could be employed only when suspects were at hand, and as it was usual in this area to accuse people "from a long way away" it may not have been employed very often. The second technique involved asking the corpse questions. In the Beaudesert area, this was done when it was being carried to the grave slung on a pole. In the Kyogle area, this may have happened while it was lying on the ground. The *wiun*, "clever" man, recited the names of suspects and the corpse moved when the culprit's name was mentioned. My Beaudesert informant states that it would buck so violently that the bearers found it hard to keep their feet.

In the Kyogle-Woodenbong-Tabulam area, corpses were buried with their feet to the rising sun. In the Kyogle area, at least, adults were buried extended on their backs, though juveniles might be bundled into a foetal position for ease of transport. It is not improbable that whether the corpse was buried in a foetal position or extended depended on the distance it had to be carried and on the hardness of the soil.[13]

Informants also speak of burials on hill sides "just over the hill", it being suggested that this was so the dead could "look out". A few days after the burial, old men (probably "clever" men) would watch the grave from just behind the crest of the hill and after dark would see the spirit leave the grave. It would appear as a light, bright for men and much weaker for women. I suspect that we have here a third method of establishing the identity of the murderer, though my informants did not say so. That the corpse could "look out" suggests that it was buried sitting.

In this area the individual appears to have had at least two souls. One of these lingered for a while in the grave as suggested above and another went to the land of the dead and "climbed up to Balugan" in the sky. The "clever" man might fly after it on his *bogara* (magic rope) and try to capture it before it reached the land of the dead. He would return it to its body and the dead persons would come to life again. When once it reached the land of the dead, it could not be recovered and the dead person remained dead.

It is likely that a third soul was associated with a person's sacred site *djurebil*. Sick people, particularly if they felt they might die, made every effort to visit the *djurebil* and death might be attributed to their failure to get there in time. I recorded a case of this in 1955. The *moggai (mukwi)*, the "ghost", may have been a fourth distinct spiritual entity haunting the grave and the place of death.

Corpses were wrapped up, possibly in paper bark (later in a blanket) and the bundle was tied with possum-fur string. I have no material suggesting that women were interred differently from men or that there was secondary burial or mortuary cannibalism, though it must be taken into account that such rites "abhorrent" to Europeans would have been discontinued before the events described by my informants or that, if they knew of them, they would have been unwilling to tell me.

In the light of Petrie's account of the flaying of corpses, the use of the word *duggai* for a European may be significant. I have always been told that this meant corpse and it is now a term of opprobrium. It is not improbable that it referred to a flayed corpse which, I suggest, would have resembled a European more closely in colour than an unflayed one. (I haven't seen a flayed corpse so this is speculation.) The word *duggai* is used no further south than Bonalbo in New South Wales; at Tabulam, Baryulgil and, I think, Lismore, the term is *jirali*. Definitely in the Baryulgil area the first Europeans encountered were seen as spirits of the dead *(moggai)*, not as walking (or riding) corpses. I have accounts of these encounters attributed to people occurring in the genealogies I collected. It is likely that *duggai* is of south Queensland origin as Aborigines around Brisbane would have come into intensive contact with Europeans long before those in northern New South Wales. News of Europeans could well have been brought back from bunya feasts, as people from as far south as the mouth of the Clarence River participated in them.

Throughout northern coastal New South Wales and at least as far north as the Mary River, projectile sorcery was a matter of sharp stones. This stone orientation among Aborigines is alive even today. At Cherbourg, they are called *kundri* (Waka-Waka?) and in northern New South Wales *njurum*. This, and the need for sharp stones to draw blood during the mourning rites, could account for some of the Broadbeach lithic finds.

I am at a loss to explain the missing arm in B.116, which is very late in the sequence. As far as I know, bones were not used in sorcery in this area, and it is difficult to understand why anyone would want these bones. Perhaps an explanation lies in the direction of the greater geographical mobility of Aboriginal populations since the arrival of Europeans and the introduction of new ideas. Could it

have been that an immigrant, or one familiar with western Aboriginal populations, was responsible? This secret removal of a bone seems utterly foreign to local ideas of sorcery. The same objection applies to the interpretation of the Broadbeach bone points as magical projectiles. That they were skewers holding bundles together, or hair-teasers, buried with male corpses, seems to me a far more satisfactory, if less sensational, explanation.

My information suggests that most of the personal effects of the dead were destroyed. This was still happening at Tabulam in the mid-1950s, but I have records of small objects (tobacco pipes in particular) being buried with corpses during this period.

It was believed that corpses might be dug up and eaten by female vampire-ogresses *(derangan)*. Some informants held that these were the spirits of women who had died childless, but other accounts suggest that they were not regarded as spirits of the dead but the female counterpart of the male ogre ("hairy man", *boiun*).

The fact that the Aborigines along the coast, north and south of the border, were in close contact makes the use of definite burial grounds in both areas seem a result of common traditions. This is particularly so, since such burial grounds do not seem to have been the rule in areas outside the islands in Moreton Bay and the lower parts of the Nerang, Tweed, and Richmond Rivers. On the rest of the north coast of New South Wales (McBryde 1966, p.218), bodies were buried singly in areas easy to dig or, if none was available, deposited in a hollow tree. In the Tenterfield area, further west, the bodies were wrapped in bark and always placed in trees. Burials were apparently no longer put in caves at the time of European settlement.

On the Clarence River (McBryde 1966, pp.216 - 17), bodies were then buried under tumuli or in graves marked with stone circles. Dr. McBryde has, however, excavated one burial cave at Blaxland's Flat, southwest of Grafton (McBryde 1966, pp.196 - 222). Similar sites are recorded in the Upper Richmond River valley. The burials in this cave were wrapped in bark sheets and packed in with blocks of sandstone. Nine persons were represented — three adults, three children, one adolescent, one foetus, and the remains of one more person — most of these female. There were also bits of burnt and calcined bone. The bone was apparently covered with flesh at the time of burning which had been thorough. The unburnt burials had probably been extended and articulated at the time of burial but disturbed later. We here have at least two different burial rites. The burials were not all contemporary, since different types of bark originating from different areas in the neighbourhood had been used as wrapping material and some calcined bone was found below dry unburnt bark and leaves surrounding unburnt burials. Dr. McBryde concludes that the site was of sacred character and mentions possible connections with other sacred sites nearby, such as a ceremonial ground and two art sites. The time span of the site was probably short. This is indicated by two radiocarbon dates: GaK.463,1090 B.P. ± 60 (A.D.860) and GaK. 464,1230 B.P. ± 50 (A.D.720). These dates are very close to the radiocarbons date for the earliest burials at Broadbeach discussed in chapter 3.

Some findings contrast with those from Broadbeach, e.g. that females were more common than men though the latter were present, and that no artifacts were found in association with the burials. Others seem to point in similar directions, e.g. that the oldest individual at Blaxlands Flat was only ca. twenty-six years old. It may be worth noting that several Bora rings (ceremonial grounds) have been found, or described before destruction, in the Nerang area.

Turning north again but to areas west of Nerang, some of the best accounts we have come from Tom Petrie who spent much of his childhood in the company of Aborigines in the Brisbane area. He knew them, liked them, and did not try to make a good story out of details strange to a European. Unfortunately what he had to say was written down by his daughter who added an occasional, well-meaning, but misguided, touch or sentiment. The information relevant to burials comes in bits and pieces. Some excerpts follow here:[15]

p.30. Whenever the death of an Aboriginal took place, all friends and relatives would gather together and cry, each man cutting his head with a tomahawk, or jabbing it with a spear, till the blood ran freely down his body, and the old women did the same thing with yamsticks, while young gins cut their thighs with sharp pieces of flint stone,

p.31. till their legs were covered with blood. In the meantime, a couple of men would get some sheets of tea-tree bark on which to place the body, and if the corpse was not to be eaten, it would be wrapped up in this bark and tied round and round with string made from the inside of wattle bark. The feet were always left exposed. Then two old men would carry the body, those mourning following behind continually crying all the time. You could hear their cry a long way off. They would go some distance till they came to a tree (generally in a gully out of sight) with a fork in the stem, six or eight feet from the ground. Here they would pause and seek about for two suitable forked sticks to match this tree, and these they fixed in the ground at a little distance from it, making the forks correspond in height with that of the tree. Next two sticks cut about seven feet long would be placed from the forked sticks to the tree fork, and from this three-cornered foundation a platform would be made with sticks put across and bound with wattle-bark string. All being ready, the body would be lifted on to this platform which, without fail, would be made so that when the head was placed next to the tree, the feet would point always towards the west. After this, a space in the ground underneath the body about four feet square would be cleared bare of grass and at one side of it, a small fire would be built. This was that the spirit of the dead man might come down in the night and warm himself at the fire, or cook his food. If the body was that of a man, a spear or waddy would be placed ready, so that the spirit might go hunting in the night; if a woman then a yamstick took the place of the other weapon, and her spirit could also

p.32. hunt or dig for roots ... After that no one went near the body till the flesh had dropped off, when two old women, relatives, again went and, taking it down, they would proceed to separate the bones from each other. Certain of these were always religiously put aside and kept — they were the skull, leg, arm and hip bones — while those of the ribs and back, etc. were burnt. The bones kept were put in a dilly, and so carried to the camp, and this dilly, with its sacred contents, accompanied the old woman relative on all her wanderings for months afterwards ... [Mentions bones

p.33. being chopped with a tomahawk to find the murderer] ... only ordinary men and women of no condition were buried ... [otherwise] the body was carried out a mile away from the camp, and there placed on sheets of tea-tree bark near a fire ... A turrwan ("great man") would take a piece of dry sapwood from an old tree and, lighting it well by the fire, would keep knocking off the red ashes till it burnt with a flame like a candle. With this, he would give the body an extra good singeing all over, excepting the head, until the skin turned from

black to a light brown colour. Then the body would be rubbed free of any singed particles, and turned face downwards and three or four men, who had been

p.34. solemnly standing at some distance from the others, would slowly advance, one by one, singing a certain tune, to the body. Each of these men held a shell or stone knife in his hand and the first would start by slitting the skin open from the head down the neck, then retiring; his place would be taken by the second man, who would carry the opening on down the body, the third man down the legs, and so on till the skin was opened right to the heels, and would peel off in one whole piece. During all this performance never a joke nor a laugh was heard, but everything was carried out with the utmost quietude and solemnity. The body would be cut up when skinned, and the whole tribe, sitting round in groups in a circle, each group possessing a fire ... the old men divided out the flesh in pieces to each lot ... each group would roast and devour it, and in no time "all was over and done". The heart and waste parts would be buried in a hole dug alongside the fire, and this interesting hole was marked by three sticks driven into the ground, standing about a foot high and bound round with grass rope. The hair, ears, nose and the toes and fingers, without the bones, would be left on the skin, which was hung on two spears before a fire to dry ... when ready, it would be blackened with charcoal and grease. After that, the skin was folded up and put into a dilly and so carried everywhere by a relative with the certain bones that were kept. These remains were always carried by a woman relative, who kept them for six months or so, when she tired of the burden, or there was a fresh one ready to carry; and so a hollow tree or a cave in a rock was used as a depository

p.35. .... A tree used in this way was considered sacred, or dimmanggali and no one dared trifle with its contents. The bodies of children

p.36. were never skinned; they were placed up on trees unless in extra good condition, when they would be eaten. Very young children or babies were roasted whole, and women generally ate them ... at death the bodies of cripples were just shoved anyhow into hollow logs.

p.58. ... the Aborigines wore red when mourning for their dead ... Red was put on all over the body, even the face, and then for deep mourning (for instance, if the deceased were a brother or sister) splashes of white clay relieved the monotony here and there ... two stones were rubbed together, and the powder coming from them just rubbed into the skin, but the mourning colour was a dull red.

In the Brisbane area, the dead may not have been buried; a note on Captain Logan's death, however, suggests some tradition of graves similar to that on the coast (Bateson 1966, p.168):

The blacks made him a grave about two feet deep and buried him face downwards; the body had been carefully covered by them ... The grave appeared to have been made with some care, and long sticks were laid on each side of it.

The burial customs further north and northeast, in the Burnett and Wide Bay districts, may have been similar. The most detailed accounts are by Lang (1861), who indicated that he was using information from James Davis (Duramboi), an escaped convict who lived with the Wide Bay Aborigines for some fourteen years. Davis, however, denied giving Lang any information and the accounts given are suspiciously like those of the Brisbane group as given by Petrie, whom Lang knew well. Petrie did, however, also have some knowledge of the Wide Bay area. There seems little purpose in quoting more than the following from Lang's account:

p.351. For the tribe being on the coast, and encamped near some inlet of the sea, where oysters and other shell-fish were abundant, and all that were able being employed in gathering the shell-fish, Davies' companion being in want of a basket or other receptacle for those that he had collected, and observing a dilly, or native basket, hanging in the hollow of a tree close by, took it down and, finding it contained only a quantity of bones, he threw them out and filled the dilly with oysters. These bones, however, were those of a deceased native of the tribe which had thus in conformity with native usage in such cases, been solemnly deposited in their last resting place; and the deed which the white man had done quite unconsciously in removing them and throwing them out was regarded by the natives as the greatest sacrilege and punishable only with death. The unfortunate young man was accordingly surprised and killed a very short while after.

The following description[16] may refer to the practices of the Barambah area, west of the Wide Bay district, but could be taken to suggest that there was an alternative practice in the Wide Bay area (since the deceased came from there), just as there was a little further southwest.

Between the Barambah and the Stuart on a barren scrubby ridge . . . is the dead body of an aged black . . . its face upwards, it rests upon a rude platform composed of small sticks, supported on five forked saplings. A kangaroo net is wound round the trunk and thighs, which are wholly covered with a sheet of bark, curved so that its sides rest upon the platform. The skull is bare, the chest and shoulders in an excellent state of preservation: the abdomen is much shrunk, the bowels having apparently been taken out; the skin, however, appears unbroken, from the shoulders to the knees. The lower bones of the leg, which are not covered by bark, are quite bared and destitute of flesh; the feet, beautifully formed, and remarkable for their unusually high insteps, are shrivelled but still undecayed. On the ground beneath the platform are the vestiges of a very large fire. The Barambah tribes said that the body is that of a Wide Bay black; he is supposed to have been dead about six months.

What follows now are two first-hand accounts, filtered through Lang (1861, pp.360 - 61). His sources are in this case good and the details are probably correct.

The following account of two cases illustrative of the different modes of disposing the dead at Moreton Bay, witnessed and described by the Rev. K.W. Schmidt of the German Mission (centred on Nundah). It does not appear that the body was eaten in the first instance, the individual having died of an odious disease; but the second case strongly corroborates an account given me by Davies —

There are different modes of disposing of the dead. As one instance, a man, who has died of an odious disease, was wrapped up in tea-tree bark and, after being brought to a solitary spot, was put on a framework which was erected for this purpose, about eight or nine feet high; the place underneath was carefully cleared, and a large fire made close by. Before the corpse was put thereon, three men took it on their shoulders, and after an old man had made a hole in the bark, near the ear, and spoken a few words to the corpse, the men ran in the greatest hurry a short distance, and before leaving the place cried and rubbed their eyes until tears ran down their cheeks. The meaning of the words the old man spoke to the corpse was, "If thou comest to the other blackfellows and they ask thee who killed thee, answer, 'None, but I died'." This shows plainly [says Lang] that they believe in immortality.

At another time I witnessed the following ceremony:
A boy about twelve years of age had died of a liver complaint; the corpse was carried by the father to an open place in the forest, a large number of the tribe being in attendance. Three mourning women cleared the place, on which the father put the corpse, and after the women had made a fire close by, six old men placed themselves around the corpse and touched it carefully with firebrands; the whole party had placed themselves in a semi-circle and the mother stood at a distance of four or five yards, howling and leaping.

The six men then plucked off the thin skin and put it into a small bag, which was handed over to the master. Thereafter, the whole corpse, which naturally now looked quite white, was blackened with charcoal and then properly skinned with great expertness, except the hands, feet and head. The whole skin was likewise put into a dilly, and handed over to the mother. After the shoulders and legs were cut off and carefully roasted, the men left the belly, and the father, on opening it and taking out the entrails, observed that the lungs were covered with sores, which he recognised at once as the cause of death. The ribs, and some parts of the entrails were roasted, the rest were put into a little hole, upon which a few sticks were erected, with flowers betwixt them. During this ceremony, all present got up several times, and beat their heads with tomahawks in such an awful manner that the blood was streaming down their shoulders. The mother stood all the while — about three hours — leaping and howling. The branches of the surrounding trees were then broken, in order to let people know what had taken place here. Then they returned to camp, and the parents feasted upon the flesh of their own child, as I was informed next morning by other natives. The skin was afterwards dried on a spear over a fire.

In her article on cremation in Australia, based on both written accounts and archaeological evidence, B. Hiatt mentions that in Queensland cremation occurred in several contexts (Hiatt 1969). Sometimes corpses were burnt and the ashes carried or the corpses were eaten and the remains burnt. Old women were burnt and their remains buried. Some persons were burnt with gravegoods, some corpses were tied before cremation. In eastern Australia, cremation was often part of a compound disposal, that is what I here call composite burial, which means that the disposal took place in several definite stages which could be separated by periods of time.

Comparisons with the archaeological evidence from Broadbeach

All over this area, from the Wide Bay and Burnett districts down to the Clarence River in northern New South Wales, i.e. all around the Nerang River and therefore probably including this area, there was then, at the time of European arrival, a great similarity in burial customs. This is the area from which Aborigines came together in the Bunya Mountains for the well-known bunya feasts and one could expect that such frequent social intercourse, which also involved some intermarriage,[17] would lead to a certain homogeneity in ideas and traditions.

I have shown that there were several different burial customs, but what is important is that the range of customs is similar for different parts of the area and that the constituents, the minor details of the customs, are limited and similar, although arranged and combined in slightly different ways. The choice of rite depended less on geographical than on social circumstances except, possibly, with regard to the use of caves, trees, or burial grounds as final repositories. The latter seem to be a feature only where the ground was easy to dig, especially in sandy coastal areas. The rite accorded depended on several factors: sex, age, physical condition, and social status.

We may now explore these in turn and compare the results with the evidence from Broadbeach.

There are many suggestions in written accounts that women were treated differently from men. If they were buried with the men, they were treated with less ceremony and fewer precautions were taken.[18] Small (1898, p.46) states that no wailing took place and Breton (1933, p.179) that men and women were not buried together. These accounts refer to the southern part of the area. Those referring to the northern parts say that women and men were buried together but that women were given the ritual accorded the socially least important of the men. How do we interpret the imbalance of sexes at Broadbeach? If women were generally not buried here because they were socially inferior, why then do children represent more than 50 per cent of the dead? One would expect these to have been even less important. One of the burials, B.55, may have been stillborn or dead shortly after birth. It was, however, treated with a considerable amount of ceremony, involving wrapping and the use of pigment. The rest of the burials are from categories considered socially important — mostly young and mature, rarely aged, men. To be very old, "close-up dead", or crippled, could again make you somewhat inferior socially.[19] A couple of the burials were of cripples, but one of these, B.102, had been given an unusual, and apparently complicated, type of burial which would, according to literature, signify a socially important position.[20]

The written accounts do not help much in the consideration of these aspects and any interpretation would be uncertain. This also affects interpretations of the medical aspects. The population as represented by the burial ground was neither more nor less unhealthy than would be expected. However, were those of poor health usually placed in the burial ground? There are suggestions that certain diseases were considered obnoxious and that this influenced the treatment of the dead. We have but little evidence of early diseases in this area. Smallpox, however, arrived from the south before the Europeans themselves (Petrie 1932, p.65).

A practice not mentioned by written accounts is that by which a small child is buried with an adult male.[21] No women have been found buried with children unless B.100 and B.77 can be so paired (p. 21).

We will now consider the components of the funeral practices and their possible reflections in the archaeological material. All evidence suggests that the funeral ceremonies occurred in several stages over a prolonged period of time.[22]

Who took part? Modern anthropological studies indicate that this, as well as the role each participant played, would be determined by his relationship to the deceased or by whether he belonged to the deceased's moiety or some such social division.[23] Hints from areas where burial grounds are mentioned suggest that the location of these was kept secret from women although the latter took part in most stages of the burial ceremony. Certainly a great number of people were involved. What determined the roles of the participants in this area is not clear. It is obvious from all detailed accounts, however, that there was a strict division of roles and duties.[24]

One widespread feature is the wailing and gashing oneself at the death of a person and during the various stages of his burial ceremony.[25] The former left no trace; the latter may well explain the presence of some shells, sharp flakes, saw-edged flakes, and stone axes on the surface or in the upper part of burial pits.

Burials were either wrapped in bark from tea-tree or stringy bark and tied up as parcels or they were placed in dillies; B.15, the broken-up cremation, was, judging from its outline, probably placed in a dilly, but almost all the other secondary burials were apparently wrapped up as parcels.

Scorching and flaying would leave no trace since no such tissues have survived in the conditions of the sand ridge. Nor can it be said with certainty that the secondary burials had been eaten or left to rot, or whether both customs had been used. There is no direct evidence from the bones that the burials were dismembered. All accounts suggest that, when such butchering was done, it was done with great skill (Lang 1861, pp.355 - 56), possibly resulting in no damage to the bone, and at least burial B.102 had been so treated.

Some parts of the skeleton are always present in well-preserved burials, while others may or may not be there. Several possible explanations can be given. Petrie states that the skull, limb, and hipbones were always kept, ribs and vertebrae burnt. The former are definitely amongst those regularly present in the Broadbeach burials; the latter may be. Clearly the Broadbeach group made the same kind of distinction as to the importance of certain bones, even if the resulting treatment was not necessarily the same. Petrie states that pieces of skin were distributed to relatives as relics; this is said to have been done with some bones also.[26] The bones were usually carried around for a long time before final disposal. It is possible that some were lost during this time, or even later, on the burial ground, if the burial was opened (see p. 32).[27]

Removal of some bones for use in sorcery seems unlikely, since stones were the instruments of sorcery in this area. Petrie (1932, p.29) states that in the Brisbane area the *turrwan* (great man) used *kundri*, a small crystal stone; in southeast Australia pieces of quartz were said to be projected into people to cause certain illnesses and this belief is said to have been spreading up the east coast of Carpentaria in modern times (Elkin 1954, p.274). This could explain the presence of pieces of milky quartz, smoky quartz, and rock crystal in the burial ground.[28] The pointed bones found in some burials are not likely to be evidence of sorcery; a more mundane explanation is that they were used as skewers or pins[29] holding the wrapping together, or, more likely still, that they are combs. The contents of a man's dilly was described as (Petrie 1932, pp.107 - 8):

... a piece of white clay, red paint, a lump of fat, a honey rag and a hair comb. The latter was a small bone from a kangaroo's leg, like a skewer; it was sharpened at one end by rubbing on sandstone, and was used to comb out a man's hair. If the man was a *turrwan*, he also carried his crystal or *kundri* in the dilli.

This list includes two more types of object found in some burial pits: white clay (if this is a correct description of the lumps of white powdery devitrified chalcedonic silica) and red pigment. (Appendix E describes the occurrence of the different types of object mentioned here.) Were the contents of a man's dilly buried with him? One group from near Brisbane is said to have buried all possessions of the dead except for a few objects given to near kinsfolk.[30] The belongings of a dead person were generally avoided, destroyed or purified (Elkin 1954, pp.301 - 2). This seems a possible explanation for some beautiful implements found abandoned on the surface of, or inside, the burial pits. Some probably belonged to the dead person, others may have had to be avoided because they had been used in the burial ceremony.

The bones of the dead were sacred and must not be interfered with. A grave was avoided (Elkin 1954, p.302). Both points are borne out by the evidence from Broadbeach. The interpretation of several cases must be that great care was taken to avoid disturbing earlier burials and that, if this happened despite the care, it was necessary to treat the disturbed bones with respect and ceremony. This suggests a continuing tradition, a continued knowledge of the whereabouts of the burial ground which would preclude its use as a campsite. The small amount of food refuse present, which can often be seen to be directly related to a burial pit, agrees with this interpretation.

What was the function of this food refuse? Was it from food meant for the dead or remains of what had been eaten by participants? Weapons and digging sticks were placed ready to be used by the dead while decaying. If the purpose of this was to make the spirit content and willing to leave completely after the final rite (Elkin 1954, p.318) — the interment of the bare bones — there would seem to us to be no logic in providing food for the dead at this stage. The Aborigines, however, may have reasoned differently. But when pockets of shell were found intact, they often contained a number of valves stacked inside each other which could not have been done until the soft content had been removed. They also often contained animal bones, sometimes completely charred, and charcoal, as if the remains of a meal had been scraped together.

Fire seems to have played a part at almost every stage of the ceremonies and it is somewhat surprising that there was so little charcoal in the site. Most stages of the ceremonies could have taken place elsewhere, either some distance away or just outside the area used for burials, or both. There is some evidence for the latter in the form of waste from stone knapping. There were traces of fire over some pits. An account from Port Stephens area, further south, states that the widow made a fire by the graveside and mourned every night until grass was growing on the grave (Scott 1929, p.47). Precautions preventing the spirit of the dead from following the participants from the grave could include passing through a smoke screen or brushing each person with smoking twigs. The fires lit close to the bones of the dead (e.g. B.37 or B.88) are more difficult to explain; a fire to warm the dead[31] while he waited for his due ceremonies would hardly have been lit intentionally where it would scorch him.

One cannot completely discount the possibility that a fire below or near a corpse exposed on a platform[32] may have got away and partly burnt the corpse. But this does not seem a likely explanation for the two cremations in this site. B.15 had had its bones distinctly reddened with haematite before burning. (B.39 was more charred, fragmented, and discoloured by the soil.) At the moment we do not know whether the burning took place before or after the bones were broken into pieces. However, the burning does seem to have been one of the last stages of a composite rite (cf. Hiatt 1969, p.109).

The red pigment, haematite, is ubiquitous in the site; it was found colouring the bones or as crayons, lumps, or crumbs (see map 4). I have already suggested that the pieces found in the pits could have been part of the dead person's belongings. Some were found close to or on the surface of pits. It is mentioned in many texts that participants painted themselves red for mourning.[33] This could have taken place also at the graveside. It is also stated that the corpse was often completely smeared with red ochre and this was at times used *repeatedly* on the bones.[34] One such occasion may have been immediately before final burial. This could have involved opening and rewrapping a bundle if this had been carried around for some time. The slightly shiny facets on the crayons suggest contact with something smooth and dense, such as bone, rather than rubbing against a more or less gritty stone to make powder.

Some other details about some of the burials hint at beliefs discussed in anthropological literature, such as the necessity of preventing the spirit of the dead from returning and disturbing the group. The stones placed as a "cap" over the vertical bundle-burials B.36 and B.112, or on the arms of B.37 and B.73, both primary burials, could have been meant to weigh down the body so that it would not be able to wander (Elkin 1954, p.302). The legs of B.102 and probably B.42 were folded right back and perhaps tied. Those of the flexed burials were apparently forced beyond the normal limits of bending one's knees and perhaps also tied in that position (fig. 55). All tying was probably executed to prevent the return of the spirit.

A form of mummification, practised on the east coast of Australia, involved drying the corpse (sometimes flayed) in the sun or over a fire, carrying the dried corpse, packed, bound up, and often painted, and then after some time, disposing of it (Elkin 1954, pp.292, 313). The corpse was sometimes first disembowelled. This rite was usually reserved for important people, the "clever men". Only one burial, B.102, seems to fit this description (fig. 17). Disembowelling could, however, be carried out for the purposes of inquest to find the cause of death, and so the murderer.

Only a few accounts mention the orientation of a corpse as important. East-west seems to be the important axis, but in some areas it is the head, in others the feet that should be at the eastern end.[35] The study of the practices at Broadbeach indicates that orientation was of importance but there was some variation and the directions were only approximate. The orientation of the tree-stage has been described; also the pit to hold the burial seems to have had a prescribed orientation.

Many accounts mention that graves were shallow due to the poor digging implements available. Petrie[36] mentions sharp sticks and tomahawks in use for digging out the centre of a *kippa*-ring, and Enright (1937, p.88) that boomerangs were used for heaping up mounds. On the Tweed, women's digging sticks were used (Sullivan 1964). An account from the Port Stephens area describes how the natives wrapped a corpse in "Titree" and stringy bark bound with vines, *borrowed* a spade and buried the corpse only a few yards above high water mark (Scott 1929, p.46). This last account may well be relevant to the last, flexed, burials at Broadbeach. Harper's home was not far away and if he was a good friend of the natives, he may have lent a spade at times. The presence of Europeans would also perhaps explain the sudden change from secondary to primary burial; neither mortuary cannibalism nor rotting corpses in the neighbourhood is likely to have met with the approval of Europeans.

To sum up: the accounts quoted here are probably relevant to the Broadbeach site because of its position both in time and space. Some difficulties involved in the comparisons attempted are due to the differences in type of material used. Certain details described in literary accounts could not have left physical traces. There are also discrepancies between what was described as common in this area and what was observed during our archaeological investigations. How far are these due to actual differences in ritual tradition between the areas of the accounts and the Nerang area? How far is it a case of people believing and saying that they did certain things which were not in fact done? To what extent did Aborigines deliberately mislead Europeans when asked about rites of which Europeans were likely to disapprove? How many of the European settlers whose accounts have come down to us were really able to communicate with the Aborigines in their own language?

It will be obvious, comparing accounts by early settlers, etc., who were not trained in anthropological methods, with those of modern anthropologists, that a straightforward step-by-step description of a ritual, though often helpful in identifying archaeological features, cannot give an adequate picture of the ceremony. Too much remains intangible, unexplained; the remnants of mythology collected in recent years indicate that this was certainly no less rich some centuries ago. There are many beliefs to choose between if one wants to try to understand the background to some ritual detail. It is also clear that such beliefs have changed and travelled, occasionally introducing new rites, at other times a new explanation of a traditional rite.

Evidence from the Sydney area

The evidence quoted, whether from early accounts, archaeological excavations, or modern anthropological research, has dealt almost entirely with southeast Queensland and northern New South Wales. I have stressed that this evidence is meagre and incomplete, often contradictory and difficult to interpret. But the evidence available from eastern Australia outside this limited area is even more meagre, and what there is refers mostly to an area centred on Sydney.

Aboriginal skeletons have turned up in several places, but rarely was an archaeologist present or even later asked to investigate the circumstances and the find location. Some scientifically recovered remains come from Megaw's excavations at Curracurrang in the Royal National Park and at Gymea Bay, Port Hacking, both south of Sydney.[37] The Gymea burials were of two young women, 27 ± 5 and 18 ± 2 years; the second skeleton was badly decomposed and very incomplete. Both were lying on the left side, legs tightly flexed and probably once tied. A fragment of what appeared to be leather thonging could not definitely be identified as such. No pit had been dug to hold either corpse which had been left lying on what was then the surface of the midden. The site goes back some 1,200 years and

the badly decayed skeleton came from the earliest stage of its history. The stone industry was characterized by small flakes, fabricators as the dominating implement type, and a small number of burins, elouera adze flakes, and ground-edge flakes. The skeletal remains from Curracurrang were less well preserved and mostly badly disturbed, but contained at least one adult, two juveniles, and one infant (> 3 years) from one investigation and, from another, skull fragments of a juvenile (possibly part of one mentioned above), an infant of ± 3 years, the skull of a female (30+ years) and a young adult. The last skeleton was earlier than and less disturbed than the others and was associated with a Bondaian level of occupation. Charcoal from this level gave a date of 2360 ± 90 B.P. (GaK-688). None were buried in pits or gave evidence suggesting an intentional grave except for one infant in the midden. Some blocks of stone around this skeleton could be intentional or accidental rock fall from the roof.

Some points of special interest with reference to the Broadbeach material are that the corpses had apparently been left to decompose, but had not been taken to a special site for this process, nor had they been interred or deposited somewhere else thereafter. Although the site may have been avoided for some time while the corpse decayed, the bones must still have been visible when the sites started being used again. This is in sharp contrast to the use of special burial grounds or depositories, such as burial caves or trees, cited from further north. Some of the corpses had clearly or probably been placed on the ground with legs bent and probably tied. This is the case only for the last burials at Broadbeach from a period of, I suspect, increased geographical mobility and hence possibly a result of an influx of new ideas. It is worth noting also that the burials at Gymea and Curracurrang were of females or children and that none was older than forty-five years of age.[38] This can be compared with the predominance of females and young people at Blaxland's Flat and of males and children at Broadbeach. Elderly people seem to be absent or rare in all these sites.

In an article discussing the use of historical sources in archaeological research,[39] Megaw shows that both cremation and inhumation were probably practised in the Sydney area during the early period of European settlement. Inhumation appears to have been used for the young and cremation for the old people. The archaeological finds suggest that sex may also have been an important factor in the choice of burial rite. The Aborigines of the area were said to shun and fear their dead. It is possible that the lack of burial pits for the excavated burials indicates that these were for some reason treated in yet a third way. A skeleton found in a midden by a person without archaeological training would, however, probably be assumed to have been buried in a pit. But Megaw quotes early accounts which include the digging of a pit as a part of the burial process. He also quotes an early French description of a corpse being wrapped in bark before burial, in the manner found at Blaxland's Flat and assumed for the Broadbeach burials.

Evidence from South Australia

The excavation of an extensive burial ground at Roonka Station on the Murray River in South Australia is still in progress (Pretty

1971). This site may produce a corpus of skeletal material of a size similar to or larger than that from Broadbeach and probably spanning a greater period of time. Comparisons in terms of cultural traits can only be of a general and cautious kind, considering the great distance between the sites. Primary burial of extended or crouched bodies in some position from fully horizontal to fully vertical appears to be the rule, however, with cremation as the only exception. A comparison of the anatomical analyses of the populations as represented by their burials is more likely to be of scientific interest and importance, but this will have to await the completion of such anatomical studies.

Comparisons between areas as far apart as southeast Queensland and South Australia — or the area near Sydney — would always be tenuous, but could be of some interest and value if we have a wealth of material to compare and some evidence also from the areas in between. Some more such evidence is likely to be available when Mrs. Betty Hiatt publishes the interesting results of her search through Australian archives and early sources.[40]

Conclusion

The site described in this report at first appeared unique in Australian archaeology; a study of literary sources and reports now coming in suggests, however, that many more such sites are being and will be found.

The following is a summary of what would appear to be the most important results of our excavations. The site is a proper cemetery and may have contained about two hundred persons before modern disturbance. It was in use for the last millennium before the arrival of Europeans. There is no suggestion that the site was ever used for purposes other than burial and attendant ceremonies. There is no sign of any period of neglect or disuse; all evidence suggests that it was used by one group of people whose traditions changed but little over this period of time. Variations and marked differences in rites (e.g. between primary and secondary, or between vertical or horizontal burial) were found but seem to be mostly a matter of possibilities of choice; this could have been linked to factors such as age, sex, and social position of the deceased. Burial rites were apparently prolonged and complicated, consisting of many separate features which could be combined in different ways on different occasions. The use of haematite to redden the burials, the lighting of fires, and a final meal at the side of the filled burial pit seem to have been almost standard features. It was also usual to deposit some good quality implements with the dead; literary evidence can be interpreted to suggest that these had belonged to the deceased or been used in the funeral ceremonies. Arrangements of stone or shell occur but within, not on the surface of, the burial pit; there is no evidence that the graves were marked in any way. Earlier graves were occasionally disturbed but the bones they contained were treated with care and respect. There is no horizontal stratigraphy: no part of the site was used for a certain period only nor for a certain sex or age group.

Written accounts by early European settlers in southeast Queensland, and New South Wales just south of the Queensland border, can be used to give a fuller picture of the funerary ceremonies, since the site apparently was in use up to the time of settlement and probably for some time thereafter, and since cultural traditions were very similar in this area at that time. Written accounts and archaeological evidence sometimes appear conflicting. Many details noted during the excavations must result from traditions or preferences to which no reference has been found. The ideological background is rarely mentioned in such descriptions and can only be inferred, with caution, from the results of modern anthropological studies.

The skeletal material will form an important corpus of comparative material since it clearly belongs to one single population; not every member of this population was buried in this site, however, and the long time-span involved may have affected its value with regard to statistical analysis.

The lithic material is varied, and includes most types known from archaeological sites in neighbouring areas. Some implements were brought to the site in finished form. These may have belonged to the deceased or may have been meant for important details of the funerary ceremonies. Some knapping was carried out on the site and this can also be seen to have been related to these ceremonies. But we cannot group implement types as belonging to certain stages within the burial ground. Even when an implement was found in association with a burial, there can be no certainty that this association was original.

Many of the conclusions and inferences are tentative and will always remain so. A few may be confirmed by evidence from other sites.

Sand and soil in the ridge

Sand

Five samples were tested by the Geological Survey of Queensland. This was a matter of grain-size analysis to see whether any difference in physical characteristics could be found which might indicate that the ridge had been built up in different stages. The shape and character of the sand grains were also studied to see if there was any suggestion of differential weathering.

The samples submitted were:

S.s.47 and 49 from AF 47, a test pit close to but outside the burial ground, showing the typical undisturbed podsol profile (see section on soil). S.s.47 came from just below the turf line (1 - 12 cm below the surface), S.s.49 came from the redeposition zone (29 - 47 cm below the surface). S.s.26 and 29 from Q 56, within the area of the burial ground; there was a shell horizon but no burial pit just here. S.s.29 came from just below the turf line (1 - 8 cm below the surface) and S.s.26 from the redeposition zone below the shell horizon (35 - 42 cm below the surface). S.s.10, as a check, came from O 53, just below the base of B.4, a vertical bundle-burial.

All samples showed fresh, unweathered, quartz grains; the size range was very small, the sand being extremely well sorted and very fine, a large proportion being close to the silt grade. The five curves were almost identical, the only difference noticeable being a fraction more fine material in S.s.10 which also contained some haematite from the burial. Compare fig. 105.

Soil

The site was visited during excavation by Mr. J.E. Coaldrake from the C.S.I.R.O. laboratory in Brisbane. His comments on the soil development have been quoted in the text (p. 55).

He advised that there would be little point, for our purposes, in testing factors other than acidity and colour; he also lent the equipment necessary.

I have so far tested forty-seven samples for acidity, sixty-four for colour; such a number was not necessary to establish the character of the normal soil horizon of the sandy ridge in comparison to that of the part containing burials. It soon became apparent, however, that some other interesting information could be gleaned from the results.

I used as standard a column, S.s.47 - 51, taken in AF 47, a test

Fig.105. Size of sand grains in the ridge. Typical curve.

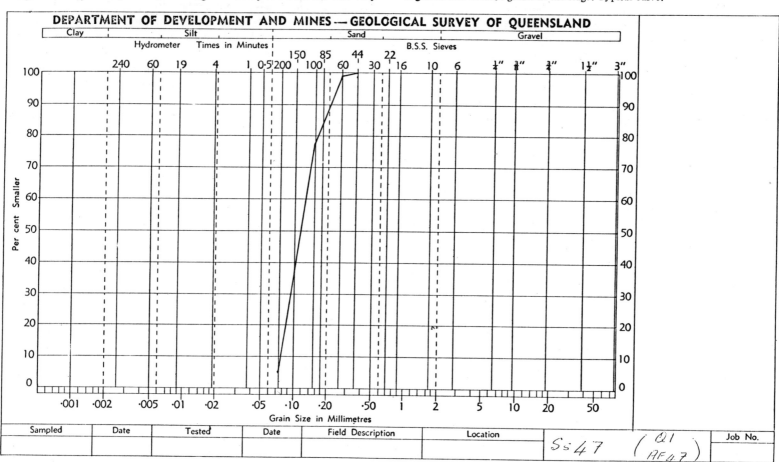

pit just outside the actual area of the burial ground. The results, tabulated below, can be compared with those from the column S.s.29 - 24 from Q 56 (within the area of the burial ground), with S.s.14 - 20 taken through the pit of B.16 and with S.s.1 - 6+10 from inside and just outside the pit for B.4.

The turf level has a constant pH value of 5.8 - 5.9, unless it has been disturbed recently; outside the burial ground this acidity decreases gently and steadily to pH 7 in the sterile quartz sand at the base of the ridge. Whenever a shell horizon was or had been present, the acidity decreased much more rapidly, the result showing immediately below the shell horizon or within if this was thick. The sand inside the skull of a vertical bundle-burial would show the same acidity as the surrounding soil or a little more alkalinity, particularly if there had been a concentration of shells near the skull. The sand in a skull retained the traces of such influence longer than the surrounding sand. This fact was used successfully in a number of cases, in areas of modern disturbance, to check the assumption that there had been a shell horizon present above a burial until recently.[1] The pH value of the sterile parent sand ca. 50 - 60 cm below the surface was mostly slightly alkaline in the burial area, especially just below or near pits. This is probably due to the concentration of shells over the surface of pits as well as, in some cases, to the presence of shells in the pit-fill.

In the case of B.73 two columns were taken, one just outside, one inside the pit; both showed the same sequence (S.s. 37 - 46): pH 5.9 at the turf line, pH 7 - 7.3 at the level of the shell horizon and then a steady increase in alkalinity to between pH 7.7 and 7.8 at a depth of ca. 90 cm below the surface. A certain amount of leaching, but only of the most soluble constituents, had clearly taken place in the pit; the colour differences were still sharp.

The use of the colour chart brought out many instances of the use of haematite when the traces left were so faint that one might suspect the red tinge to be a matter of imagination. The natural colour range of the parent sand, sterile or affected by humus, leaching, redeposition, etc., was from 2.5 Y to 10 YR; presence of pigment immediately changed this to from 5 YR to 7.5 YR.[2]

Sample No.	Depth below Surface	Description	Colour	pH
47	1 - 12 cm	turf line (A_0 horizon)	10 YR 5/1	5.8
48	13 - 28 cm	pale band (A_2 horizon)	10 YR 5/2	6
49	29 - 47 cm	dark band (B horizon)	10 YR 4/1	6.5 - 6.6
50	48 - 57 cm	paler, blotchy band (B/C horizon)	10 YR 6/2	6.6
51	below 58 cm	pale sterile sand (C horizon)	10YR7/3	7 - 7.1
29	1 - 8 cm	turf line	10 YR 3/1	5.9
28	11 - 18 cm	shell horizon	10 YR 3/1	6.1
27	23 - 30 cm	dark sand below shells	10 YR 2/2	6.7
26	35 - 42 cm	dark mottled sand	10 YR 4/1	6.9
25	47 - 53 cm	pale mottled sand	10 YR 6/2	7.3
24	59 - 65 cm	sterile pale sand	10 YR 7/3	7.5
19	6 : 10 cm	turf line	10 YR 4/1	5.8
18	13 - 17 cm	shell horizon	10 YR 4/1	6.6
17	23 - 27 cm	dark sand below shell horizon, pit	10 YR 4/1	6.6
16	31 - 36 cm	ditto	10 YR 4/1	6.7
15	45 - 49 cm	mottled sand	2.5 Y 5/2	7.1
14	56 - 61 cm	pale sterile sand	2.5 Y 7/2	7.3 - 7.4
20	30 - 35 cm	from skull of B.16	10 YR 3/1	6.6
1	1 - 10 cm	below turf line, disturbed	10 YR 3/1	6.1 - 6.2
2	ca.20 - 30 cm	pit-fill, dark sand, B.4	10 YR 4/1	6.3
3	ca.20 - 30 cm	outside pit, dark sand	10 YR 5/2	6.3
4	ca.55 - 65 cm	pale sterile sand, outside pit	2.5 Y 7/2	7.2
5	ca.55 - 65 cm	pit-fill below S.s.2	10 YR 3/1	7
10a	ca.70 - 78 cm	sand below base of burial	7.5 YR 4/2	7.6
b	ditto	ditto	5 YR 4/3	7.5
6	ca.22 - 28 cm	sand in skull, B.4	10 YR 5/2	8

Faunal remains excavated from site Q1, Broadbeach, southeast Queensland

By Alan Bartholomai, Director of the Queensland Museum

Faunal material recovered during the course of the excavation of the Aboriginal burial site, Q1, in the Broadbeach hinterland, southeastern Queensland, is dominated by remains of extant marsupials, together with minor representation by eutherian mammals, reptiles, and some teleosts. No bird remains were identified. (*Note:* The bones submitted for analysis were those recovered during the first three seasons of excavation.)

In general, preservation is exceedingly fragmentary, with the most completely preserved elements comprising marsupial mandibular rami. Identification of skull fragments, apart from isolated dentigenous remains, has not been generally possible, nor has it been desirable to determine many of the marsupial postcranial remains to levels lower than that of family. No attempt has been made to identify considerable quantities of bone splinters.

The collection presents little evidence to suggest natural death and accidental burial in situ of any of the animals from which the skeletal fragments were derived. Only very small proportions of postcranial elements from the one individual are represented, and these are very rarely associated with identifiable cranial remains. An incomplete series of ophidian vertebrae referrable to ?*Morelia* sp. represents the only exception to the complete absence of articulated remains. Postcranial remains, in general, show considerable evidence of postmortem fracturing, while some are fire damaged, and the assemblage suggests that the collection is largely the relics of Aboriginal food sources. This conclusion is supported by the presence of identifiable marine teleost fragments in the site.

Among the marsupials represented, *Isoodon macrourus,* the largest bandicoot on the mainland, numerically constitutes the most abundant material excavated. It is now found mainly in open forest and woodland areas under natural conditions. The Long-nosed Bandicoot, *Perameles nasuta,* rarely present in the site, is found in both rain forest and sclerophyll forest areas. Both forms are solitary nocturnal animals, but of the two, *I. macrourus* is more abundant in southeastern Queensland at the present time.

Occasional specimens of the Brush-tailed Possum, *Trichosurus vulpecula,* are encountered, but of the larger marsupials, macropodids make up most of the remaining material. Of these, the Pademelon, *Thylogale* sp., is most common. Specific identification of remains of these animals has not been possible because of the general similarity in identification in the mandibular rami of the two species currently found in the southeastern portion of Queensland. These species, *Thylogale stigmatica* and *T. thetis,* occur sympatrically in the rain forest and wet sclerophyll forest. A single maxilla of the Potoroo, *Potorous tridactylus,* was present together with more common remains of the Red-necked Wallaby, *Macropus rufogrisea.* The Potoroo is found in rain forest and wet sclerophyll forest while the Red-necked Wallaby is mainly a dry sclerophyll dweller. Both are relatively common at present.

Among the native eutherian mammals, only the native rodents, *Rattus fuscipes, R.* cf. *R. lutreolus* and *Rattus* sp., are represented. *R.*

rattus, R. norvegicus, and *Mus musculus,* the introduced sewer and ships rats and house mouse, are not represented, suggesting, but in no way proving, that the bulk of the burials were made prior to white settlement. However, a single bullock tooth, recovered from area A (disturbed) indicates that at least some overlap may have occurred.

Reptilian vertebrae are relatively widespread, but generally rare throughout the site, with the exception of vertebrae of *Morelia* sp., a carpet snake, which are more common. Apart from ophidians, the only other reptilian group represented is the Lacertilia. A single cranial fragment of the lizard, *?Tiliqua* sp., was recovered, while indeterminable lacertilian vertebrae are rarely present.

Of importance are the widely dispersed fragments of marine teleosts, with both cranial and postcranial remains being present. Where identifiable, they have all been derived from representatives of the Family Spariidae, which includes the snapper and sea bream, and some have been determined as ?*Rhabdosargus* sp.

It is evident from the foregoing discussion that animals from a wide variety of habitats are included in the site. However, it is likely that all such habitats were originally present within reasonable distance of the site, and no problems are believed to exist with the present association.

Identifications are outlined in the following list.

R 53:1	Ramus *Isoodon macrourus*
	Indet. teleost occipital
	Indet. teleost vertebra
	Indet. postcranial and cranial fragments
	Indet. lacertilian jaw fragment
	Partial macropodid upper molar
R 53:2	Ramus *Isoodon macrourus*
	Indet. lacertilian vertebra
R 53:2 in B.65	Ramus *Isoodon macrourus*
	Partial macropodid M4
	Maxilla *Rattus* cf. *R. lutreolus*
R 53:2 assoc. B.71	Ramus *Isoodon macrourus*
	Ramus *Thylogale* sp.
	Indet. postcranial fragments
R 53 in B.72	Indet. postcranial and cranial fragments
R 54 B.47	Mandibular fragment, *Isoodon* sp.
	Indet. fragment
R 54:1	Associated rami *Isoodon macrourus*
	Indet. fragment
R 54:2	Upper premolar *Isoodon macrourus*
R 55:2	Partial upper molar, *Macropus* sp.
	Indet. teleost vertebra
	Indet. postcranial fragments
R 55:1	Indet. postcranial fragments
R 56:1	Partial upper molar, *Thylogale* sp.
	Macropodid tibial fragment
	Indet. teleost spine and vertebra
	Indet. postcranial fragments
R 56:2	Ramus *Isoodon* sp.

	Ramus *Thylogale* sp. Macropodid cervical vertebra, fibula Maxilla *Rattus* cf. *R. lutreolus* Indet. Rodent pelvis Ophidian vertebra, cf. *Morelia* sp. Indet. teleost vertebrae and fragments Indet. cranial and postcranial fragments
R 56 B.36	Lower molar *Macropus* sp. Indet. fragment
R 58:1	Indet. fragment
S 51:1	Premaxilla *Thylogale* sp. Indet. cranial and postcranial fragments
S 51:2	Ramus *Isoodon macrourus* Macropodid tibia and fourth metatarsal Indet. teleost vertebrae Indet. fragments
S 51 B.77	Macropodid tibia
S 52:2	Ramus *Rattus* cf. *R. lutreolus* Indet. fragments
S 52:1	Upper molar *Isoodon macrourus* Peramelid ramus Ramus and maxilla *Rattus fuscipes* Indet. teleost vertebra Indet. fragments
S 53	Indet. teleost vertebra Indet. fragments
S 53 in B.105	Molar *Isoodon macrourus* Indet. teleost vertebra Indet. fragments
S 53 B.96A and B	Ramus *Perameles nasuta* Maxilla *Thylogale* sp. Indet. teleost vertebra Indet. fragments
S 53 in B.87	Molar *Thylogale* sp. Indet. calcaneum
S 53 - 54 B.97	Indet. teleost vertebra Indet. fragments
S 54	Indet. teleost vertebra Hominid tooth
R - S 54 in B.62	Indet. fragments
S 55:2	Indet. teleost vertebra Indet. fragments
S 55:3	Ramus *Isoodon macrourus* Indet. teleost vertebra Indet. fragments
S 57:2	Indet. molar Indet. fragment
S 58:2	Indet. teleost vertebra
T 51	Macropodid vertebra Ophidian vertebrae, cf. *Morelia* sp. Lacertilian cranial fragment Sparid premaxilla, ?*Rhabdosargus* sp. Indet. teleost vertebrae Indet. fragments
T 52:1	Ophidian vertebra cf. *Morelia* sp. Indet. fragments
T 52:2	Ophidian vertebra Indet. teleost vertebra Indet. fragments
T 52	Ramus *Isoodon macrourus* Macropodid phalanges Indet. fragments
T 52:3 in B.100	Ramus *Trichosurus vulpecula* Indet. rodent ramus Ophidian vertebra Indet. fragments
T 53:1	Ramus *Isoodon macrourus*
T 53 in B.99	Ophidian vertebra
T 53 in B.107	Sparid dentigenous plate Indet. fragments
T 54:1	Rami *Isoodon macrourus* Macropodid limb fragments Indet. fragments
T 54 in B.104	Ramus *Isoodon macrourus* Indet. fragments
T 54 in B.93	Indet. teleost vertebra
T 55:1	Indet. teleost vertebra
T 56:1	Maxilla *Isoodon macrourus* Maxilla *Thylogale* sp. ?Sparid dentary Indet. fragments
T 56 in B.69	Ramus *Rattus fuscipes*
T 57:1	Indet. fragment
T 58:2	Indet. fragment
T 58:1	Indet. teleost vertebra
V 52:2	Indet. teleost vertebra Indet. fragment
V 52	Ramus *Macropus rufogrisea* Macropodid tibia, fourth metatarsal Indet. phalanges Indet. teleost vertebra
V 55:1	Maxilla *Isoodon macrourus* Indet. fragments
V 55:2	Indet. calcaneum
Q 50 in B.81	Indet. fragments
Q 50 in B.56	Fragment *Thylogale* sp.
Q 50	Ophidian vertebrae, cf. *Morelia* sp.
R 49:1	Ophidian vertebra
R 50	Maxilla *Potorous tridactylus* Indet. tooth Indet. fragments
R 50:1	Indet. fragments
S 50	Macropodid upper molar Indet. fragments
S 50 in B.92	Ramus *Thylogale* sp. *Rattus* sp.
T 42	Macropodid molar Indet. fragment
T 50:1	Indet. fragment
T 50:2	Maxilla *Rattus* sp. Indet. reptilian vertebra Indet. teleost vertebrae Indet. fragments
W 46	Left M^4, *Macropus* cf. *M. rufogrisea*
W 47	Indet. fragments
Z 49	Indet. fragments

Z 50	Indet. teleost vertebra
in B.39	Indet. fragments
AA 49	Indet. fragments
R 52	*Isoodon macrourus*
	Ramus *Thylogale* sp.
	Rattus sp.
R 52:1	*Isoodon macrourus*
	Indet. macropodid fragments
	Rattus sp.
	Indet. fragments
R 52:2	Thylogale sp.
	Indet. fragments
R 51	Indet. fragments
in B.64	
R 51:1	*Isoodon macrourus*
	Indet. fragments
R 51	*Isoodon macrourus*
	Rattus cf. *R. lutreolus*
	Indet. teleost vertebrae
	Indet. fragments
R 51:2	Indet. fragments
R 51:1	*Isoodon macrourus*
Q 57	Macropodid molar
above B.16	
Q 57:2	*Isoodon macrourus*
	Rodent fragments
	Indet. teleost vertebra
	Indet. fragments
Q 56:1	*Isoodon macrourus*
	Macropus sp.
	Indet. fragments
Q 56:2	*Isoodon macrourus*
	Ophidian vertebra
	Lacertilian jaw, ?*Tiliqua* sp.
Q 55:1	Macropodid premolar
	Ophidian vertebra
	Indet. fragments
Q 55	*Thylogale* sp.
Q 55:1 - 2	*Isoodon macrourus*
	Indet. fragments
Q 54:1	*Macropus* sp.
	Macropodid postcranial fragments
	Rattus sp.
	Ophidian vertebrae
	Teleost premaxilla, ?*Rhabdosargus* sp.
	Indet. teleost vertebrae
	Indet. fragments
Q 54:2	*Isoodon macrourus*
	?Lacertilian vertebrae
	Indet. fragments
Q 54	*Rattus* sp.
	Indet. fragments
Q 52 - 53	*Rattus* sp.
in B.57	Rodent fragments
Q 52	Reptilian vertebrae
in B.45	Indet. fragments
Q 52	Macropodid molar
in B.49	Indet. teleost vertebra and spine
	Indet. fragments
Q 52:1	*Isoodon macrourus*
	Thylogale sp.
	Macropodid teeth

	Macropodid postcranial fragments
	Rattus sp.
Q 53	Teleost dentary, ?*Rhabdosargus* sp.
	Indet. fragment
Q 53:1	*Isoodon macrourus*
	Thylogale sp.
	Macropodid tooth
	Rattus sp.
	Indet. fragment
Q 51:1	*Isoodon macrourus*
	Indet. teleost vertebra
	Indet. fragments
Q 51	Indet. fragment
in B.51	
Q 51	Indet. fragments
in B.54	
Q 51	*Isoodon macrourus*
in B.44A and B	*Macropus* sp.
	Rattus sp.
	Indet. teleost vertebra
	Indet. fragments
P 55:1	*Thylogale* sp.
	Indet. fragments
P 55:2	Indet. fragments
P 55	Indet. fragments
in B.22	
P–Q 54:2	*Macropus* sp.
in B.15	*Rattus* sp.
	Indet. reptilian vertebra
	Indet. teleost vertebra
	Teleost premaxilla, ?*Rhabdosargus* sp.
P 54	*Macropus* sp.
	Indet. fragments
P 53	Teleost premaxilla, ?*Rhabdosargus* sp.
in B.30	
P 53:1	*Isoodon macrourus*
in B.29	Indet. fragments
P 53	*Macropus* sp.
P 53:1	*Isoodon macrourus*
	Thylogale sp.
	Rattus sp.
	Indet. fragments
P 52	*Isoodon macrourus*
P 52:1	*Macropus rufogrisea*
	Thylogale sp.
	Rattus sp.
	Indet. teleost vertebra
	Indet. fragment
P 51:1	*Macropus rufogrisea*
O 56	Ophidian vertebra
O 55	*Macropus* sp.
	Ophidian vertebra
O 54	*Macropus* sp.
O 53 - 54	*Macropus* sp.
in B.19	
O 53	*Macropus* sp.
in B.4	*Thylogale* sp.
O 52	Indet. fragments
N 57	Indet. molar
N 56	*Macropus* sp.
N 52:1	*Macropus* sp.

N 51:1	Macropodid tooth, *Macropus* sp.
L 54	Macropodid tooth, *Macropus* sp.
M 56	Macropodid tooth, *Macropus* sp.
K 56	Macropodid tooth, *Macropus* sp.
K 55	Macropodid tooth, *Macropus* sp.
K 53	Indet. reptilian vertebra
P 53, F.33	*Macropus* cf. *M. rufogrisea*
P 52, B.28 F.512	Macropodid fibula
AA 51 F.135	Bullock tooth

O 54:½ at 124 cm, F.434	Macropodid incisor
T 50:2 F.433 in B.109	Macropodid fibula
Q 51, F.645 in B.54	Macropodid fibula
T 54:2 in B.102, F.619	Indet. fragments

Alan Bartholomai
Director, Queensland Museum

Shells present in the burial ground

The usual methods of sampling, such as taking a small column in each square of the grid or taking the total contents of a number of separate squares, did not seem adequate for this site for several reasons. The presence of shell was probably intimately connected with burials (chapter 3), the shell content of each square usually relatively small compared to what would be normal in a midden, and there was also a possibility that the presence of certain species was linked with one or more groups of burials (chapter 2). I have, therefore, weighed and identified the total content of the area excavated. This amounts to 41.6 kilograms. The shells were dry but had not been washed; some sand remained clinging to the shells but the resulting error would be fairly uniform for all the site. A couple of examples of each species were selected and handed to the Queensland Museum for identification. I thereafter identified and counted other members of these species with the already identified examples as a guide and a check. Any errors regarding numbers are thus due to my mistakes and to the sometimes very fragmentary state of the shells.

Eighty per cent of the weight consisted of wedge shells, mostly *Plebidonax deltoides* Lamarck, the common pipi or ugari. There were also some examples of the much smaller *Amesodesma angusta,* the Elongate Small Wedge Shell, but it would have been impossible to establish their relative proportions when so many of the shells consisted of eroded fragments. Both species are very common on ocean beaches from Queensland to Western Australia.

A fairly fresh and unbroken pocket of such larger and smaller wedge shells weighing ca. 480 grams contained ca. 350 shells, representing ca. 175 live examples. This suggests that the whole sample of such shells from the site represent a living population of at least 15,000 individuals. It must be remembered that some shells were removed by soil contractors. Even so, that is not a large quantity for a site that spans at least one thousand years of time.

The rest of the shells can be tabulated as follows:

Family Ostreida, in some cases certainly *Crassostrea commercialis,* but mostly too fragmentary for exact identification   9 per cent
Other species   11 per cent
(The species included under this heading are tabulated below and their proportion within the 11 per cent given, but this time calculated on numbers present, not weight.)

Pyrazus ebeninus	90 per cent
Pyrazus australis	4.5 per cent
Polinices incei	4.5 per cent
Dicathais orbita	0.5 per cent
Anadara trapezia and	
Trisidos semitorta	0.5 per cent

The members of the oyster family which like rocks on the open coast and in estuaries could have come from the rocks at Knobby's Beach not much more than 1.5 kilometres away (map 1). The dunes, sandy ridges, and marsh areas in between are free from rocks.

Dicathais orbita also belongs to rock platforms and is very common from southern Queensland to Victoria.

Pyrazus ebeninus belongs to the muddy foreshore and is very common in eastern Australia. *Pyrazus australis* occurs commonly with the former in sheltered areas but is very much smaller.

Anadara trapezia prefers mud flats and estuarine beaches. Since it is very common, it is somewhat surprising that so few examples were found in the site. There are creeks and shallow estuaries not very far away.

Nothing suggests that any great climatic or topographical changes have taken place since the shells were collected except for, in the last few years, the interference with creeks and lagoons due to property developing schemes associated with the building of canals and dredging. *Note:* All the information about living habits and distribution come from McMichael 1965. The names are not all those used in his book since nomenclature has changed and I have tried to incorporate such changes by referring to the Queensland Museum.

Police investigation

The original map made on this occasion (cf. chapter 1) was burnt in a fire, but a copy of the notes on which it was based remained. Nobody could remember, however, exactly what they meant. I was shown one of the two trees used in the plotting and the main area of activity.

The distances and degrees from a certain point given on the list were plotted on tracing paper. The result was placed over a map of burials excavated by us and swivelled around, keeping the reference point within the circumference of the big tree stump, until the best possible agreement between the facts as we had found them and the information we were given had been reached.

The burials removed under police supervision (numbered P.B.1, etc.) could then be plotted (map 12) and the list annotated as follows:

P.B.1 "Original find (wholly removed)": was probably in S 46, the northwest half, near the centre; the soil was very disturbed here.
P.B.2 "Police (photographed)": was probably in T 46, the east corner. This could be the clearly modern pit seen by us east of B.131, cf. fig. 3.
P.B.3 "Skull only removed": was probably in W 47, near the centre. This could have been B.35 (unlikely since young and fragile) or scatter from B.11, already broken up and disturbed, but very solid. His skull could have been dropped but remained whole.
P.B.4 "Parcel destroyed — fragmented": in S 50, south corner? Note that B.92 here was completely broken up and spread around whilst B.101 consisted of a few fragments only. The most likely identification is with B.92 or with both burials.
P.B.5 "Untouched": in V 56, northwest quarter, near centre. This could refer to either B.60 in T 56 or B.83/86 in V 55, but probably the former, since the burials were located by "probing", and since the skull of B.60 was found smashed to pieces although unusually thick-boned. The disturbance of B.83/86, two small, fragile, but relatively undamaged children, was probably more ancient (cf. p. 62).
P.B.6 "Head removed. Police": in T 53, northwest half, near centre. This could be the skull of B.106B, a leaning bundle, protruding into level 1 (cf. p. 48).
P.B.7 "Not assessed": in M 54, southeast border, near centre. Probably refers to F.20 in N 54, northwest third, some human bones waiting for identification.
P.B.8 (No comment, which was said to mean "untouched"): in S 46, southeast border. Probably refers to B.131 in T 46, north corner, but could refer to some burial already removed.
P.B.9 (No comment): two readings given which indicate an area between T 44, east quarter, and V 45, the centre of line 45. There was a complete vertical bundle, B.124, at the northern end of this

area and scattered fragments of a burial, B.128A, to the south of this, which could explain the data.
P.B.10 (No comment): a spot over B.100 pelvis. Almost certainly refers to this burial but just possibly to B.91 instead, the latter being without a skull and the disturbance fairly recent.
P.B.11 (No comment): in R 50 on line 50. No burial nearby but area very disturbed. Perhaps removed after the police investigation.

We know that some burials were removed by locals, not soil contractors, after the police investigation. This probably happened in the area Z - AA 53 - 54, judging from the pieces of bone, the pigment, and the shells found at a depth normal for the base of a burial pit.

Excavated burials

Much of the information is repetitive. Some is given in table 7. Information given for sequences A to C, pp. 41–51, has not been repeated here. The table is followed by notes on each burial. These are meant to clarify the table, when needed, and to add data which cannot easily (or not at this stage) be tabulated.

Table 7 gives the number of the burial, its position in the grid (compare map 12), and the depths below the surface of the site of the top and the base of the burial. The pit type is given as A, B, or C (cf. fig. 38) when applicable, otherwise briefly described, and its long axis stated. Then follows the probable place of the burial within the sequence of stages described in chapter 3 (cf. also fig. 74 and table 4). (Stage O or I means that the burial probably belonged to a late part of stage O or an early part of stage I, etc.) The burial type is shown in the form of a code, given below. The next columns show the long axis of the burial itself, which for vertical bundle-burials means the long axis of its cross section but for burial types V1, V2, V3, and V6 the long axis of the skeleton with the head end mentioned first, and the direction in which the skull was facing. Then follow sex and age of the burial, if these have been established. Adult here means more than twenty-five years old, juvenile means somebody not yet thirteen, and adolescent refers to the group between these age limits. The comments will indicate whether the adult was young, middle-aged, or elderly, if this has been established. In the last columns, the presence of red pigment or the charring of some bones will be indicated. Note that this charring does not refer to cremation but to the slight blackening that may suggest the lighting of a fire over the bones of the burial. Some data are put within brackets. In the third column, bracketed figures indicate the probable depth of soil removed in modern times, elsewhere that the data have or may have changed since the burial ceremonies were completed. A question mark shows that the feature or fact tabulated was indistinct or difficult to establish with certainty.

Table 7. *Data for well-preserved burials*

Burial No.	Position	Depth	Pit	Axis of Pit	Stage	Burial Type	Axis of Burial	Skull Facing	Sex	Age	Red Pigment	Charring
B.0 (= F.127)	S 57	28 - 87 cm			O or I?	V.5		(E)	M	20 - 25 years	X	
B.1	X 46	0 - 40 cm (+40)	C?	NE - SW?	O?	V.5		N		7 years		
B.2	X 47	0 - 34 cm (+40)	A		O?	V.4		E		10 - 11 years	X	
B.4	O - P 53	18 - 64 cm (+20)	B		I	V.5	NE - SW	SE	M	15 - 20 years	X	
B.5	O 54	6 - 39 cm (+30)			II	V.5	NW - SE		M	adult	X	X
B.6	N 55	24 - 71 cm	B	W - E	I	V.5	W - E	W	M	20 - 25 years	X	
B.7	O 52	11 - 44 cm (+20)	A		O?	V.5	N - S	N		8 - 9 years	X	
B.8	O 52	24 - 35 cm (+20)	B	W - E	O?	V.5	N - S			1 - 2 years	X	
B.9	O 51	17 - 41 cm (+12)			O or I?	V.5	NW - SE	NW		5 - 10 years		
B.10	O 51	17 - 42 cm (+12)			O or I?	V.5	NW - SE?			3 - 4 years		
B.12	P 56	30 - 68 cm	A?		I	V.5	NE - SW	SSW	M	adult	X	
B.13	Z 48	0 - 17 cm (+43)			O or I?	V.5	N - S			2 years?	X	
B.14	N 51	24 - 48 cm			O	V.5	NE - SW			10 - 15 years		
B.15	P 54	35 - 66 cm	B	NW - SE	I	V.10			M	15 - 20 years	X	
B.16	Q 56	23 - 56 cm	A		O or I	V.5	W - E	E		4 - 5 years	X	
B.17	Z 47	11 - 37 cm (+45)	B?		O or I?	V.5	NNW - SSE		M	adult	X	
B.18	N 52	38 - ? cm (+14)			O	V.5				1 - 2 years		
B.19	O 54	3 - 31 cm (+29)	A		O or I	V.5	NW - SE			3 years	X	
B.20	R 57	30 - 39 cm			O	?			F?	15 - 20 years		X
B.21	N 51	50 - ? cm			O	V.5				2 years?	X	
B.22	P 55	42 - 63 cm			O or I?	V.5?				0 - 1 years	X	
B.23	Q 56	34 - 77 cm	B	N - S	O or I	V.5		S		7 - 8 years	X	
B.25	S 58	28 - 39 cm	B	N - S	O	V.7	NW - SE	SE		5 - 6 years		
B.26	P 51	10 - 46 cm (+24)	B	NW - SE	O or I?	V.5		NW		5 - 10 years	X	
B.27	P 51	13 - 33 cm (+24)	A		O or I	V.5	W - E	S		2 - 3 years	X	
B.28	P 52	24 - 79 cm (+17)	A		O or I	V.5	NW - SE	NNW	M	20 - 25 years	X	
B.29	P 53	0 - 34 cm (+15)	A		II	V.5			M	adult		X
B.30	P - Q 53	42 - 90 cm (+11)	B	N - S?	O	V.5	NW - SE	NW	M	adult	X	
B.31	S 58	37 - 51 cm			O	V.5?		NNW		3 years		
B.32	Z 49	26 - 62 cm	A	NW - SE?	O	V.5	W - E	E		7 - 8 years		
B.33	X 50	16 - 36 cm (+13)				V.5?				2 - 3 years		
B.34	X 50	11 - 40 cm (+13)				V.5?				3 - 5 years		
B.35	W 48	10 - 23 cm (+15)			I or II	V.5?				5 years	X	
B.36	R 56	23 - 50 cm	A	NNW - SSE?	II	V.5	NW - SE		M	adult	?	
B.37	Q 54 - 55, R 55	49 - 72 cm	trench	NNE - SSW	O	V.1	SSW - NNE	E	M	adult		X
B.38	P - Q 51	8 - 48 cm (+15)	B	W - E	O	V.5	N - S	N	M	adult	X	
B.39	Z 50	30 - 60 cm				V.10				adult	X	
B.40	Q 53	39 - 60 cm (+5)			O	V.6	NNE - SSW	N?		6 - 7 years		
B.41	R 55 - 56	27 - 48 cm	B?	N - S?	O or I	V.5?			M	adult		?
B.42	T 57 - 58	41 - 50 cm			O	V.2 or V.3?				adult		
B.43	Q 51	9 - 60 cm (+17)	C	W - E	O or I	V.5	W - E	E	M	20 - 25 years	X	X
B.44A	Q 51	30 - 50 cm (+16)	B	NW - SE	O or I?	V.5	N - S	N		2 - 3 years	X	
B.44B	Q 51	30 - 50 cm (+16)				V.5				0 - 1 year	X	
B.45	Q 52	34 - 80 cm (+16)	B	W - E	O	V.5	W - E?	E	F	20 - 25 years	X	
B.46A	Q 52	28 - 83 cm (+20)	C	NW - SE	O	V.5	NW - SE	WSW	M	adult	X	
B.47	R 54	29 - 73 cm	B	N - S	O or I	V.5			M	20 - 25 years	X	X
B.48	T 57	22 - 68 cm	A		I?	V.8	NW - SE	E	M	adult		X
B.50	T 57	22 - 65 cm				V.8		W	F	adult		?
B.49A	Q 52	15 - 50 cm (+15)			II	V.5	NW - SE		M	adult		X
B.51	Q 51	33 - 60 cm (+17)	B	W - E	O	V.5	WSW - ENE	SW		1 - 2 years	X	
B.52	Q 53	68 - 84 cm	trench	NNE - SSW	O	V.1	SSW - NNE	NW	M	adult		
B.53	P - Q 51	? - 65 cm			O	V.5?				4 - 5 years	X	
B.54	Q 51	45 - 60 cm (+17)	B	W - E	O	V.5	N - S	N		12 - 14 years		
B.55	Q 51 - 52	68 - 75 cm (+17)	C	N - S	O?	V.7	N - S			neonate	X	
B.56	Q 50	30 - 60 cm (+20)	B?	NW - SE	O?	V.5		W		0 - 1 years	X	
B.57	Q 52 - 53	0 - 41 cm			I or II?					2 - 3 years		
B.59A	T 56 - 57	23 - 70 cm	C?		O or I?	V.5?	NE - SW			10 - 15 years	X	
B.60	T 56	19 - 50 cm			I	V.5			M	adult		
B.61	R 52	17 - 73 cm (+5)	B	NW - SE	II	V.5	NW - SE	W	M	adult	X	
B.62	R - S 54	33 - 54 cm	A?		O or I	V.5		(E)		7 - 8 years		
B.63	S 55	26 - 61 cm	A		O	V.5	NW - SE	N	M	adult	?	
B.64	R 51	2 - 50 cm (+16)	B?		II	V.5	W - E	E	M	15 - 16 years	X	
B.65	R 53	22 - 66 cm	A	NNW - SSE	II	V.5	NNW - SSE	(W)	M	adult		
B.66	R 52 - 53	32 - 57 cm	A?		I	V.5	N - S	W		3 - 4 years	X	
B.67	S 55 - 56	37 - 47 cm	A?		O?	V.7	NE - SW	NE		0 - 5 years		
B.69	T 56	42 - 64 cm			O or I?	V.5	NE - SW	W	F	adult	X	

Table 7 *continued*

Burial No.	Position	Depth	Pit	Axis of Pit	Stage	Burial Type	Axis of Burial	Skull Facing	Sex	Age	Red Pigment	Charring
B.70	R - S 53 - 54	37 - 50 cm			O	V.7	N - S			3 - 4 years		
B.72	R 53	41 - 72 cm	B	N - S	II	V.5	N - S	SSW	M	15 - 16 years	X	
B.73	R - S 54 - 55	109 - 130 cm	triangular		II	V.2	W - E	SW	M	adult		
B.76	S 54	41 - 59 cm			O	V.5		S		20 - 22 years	?	
B.77	S 51	26 - 34 cm (+21)	trench	ENE - WSW	II?	V.2	NE - SW	NW		4 - 6 months		
B.78	S 55	28 - 47 cm	A?		O or I	V.5	NW - SE			10 - 15 years	X	
B.79	S 52	15 - 56 cm	B		II	V.5	NE - SW	SSE	M	adult	?	
B.81	Q 50	24- 67 cm (+21)	B	W - E	O or I?	V.5	W - E	ESE		8 - 9 years	X	
B.82A	S 54	(20 - 66 cm)			O	V.5			M	adult	?	
B.82B	S 54	20 - 66 cm			O	V.5	W - E	E	M	adult	?	
B.84	R 50	28 - 39 cm (+28)			O?	V.7	NW - SE			0 - 1 year		
B.85	S 53	13 - 43 cm			I or II	V.5			M	adult	X	
B.86A	V 55 - 56	(23 - 42 cm)				V.5				7 - 8 years	X	
B.86B	V 55 - 56	(23 - 42 cm)				V.5				7 - 8 years	X	
B.87	S 53	37 - 59 cm	A?		O	V.5	N - S			4 - 5 years	X	
B.88	V 53 - 54	36 - 50 cm			O	V.6	ENE - WSW	NW	M	23 - 25 years		X
B.89	R 49 - 50	26 - 39 cm (+28)	B?		O?	V.5	NW - SE	NNW?		1 - 2 years	X	
B.91	V 52 - 53	30 - 42 cm (+19)				V.6	WNW - ESE			(10) - 15 years	X	
B.93	T 54	25 - 56 cm	A		I	V.5				6 - 8 years		
B.95	T 54 - 55	14 - 57 cm	A	NW - SE?	I	V.5	NW - SE	E	M	adult	X	X
B.97A	S 53 - 54	27 - 38 cm			I	V.5				0 - 2 years	X	
B.97B	S 54	27 - 38 cm	A?		O	V.5				4 - 5 years	X	
B.98	T 53	17 - 76 cm	C	WNW - ESE	I	V.5	NW - SE	NW	M	23 - 25 years		
B.99	T 53	17 - 59 cm			I or II	(V.5)				15 - 20 years		
B.100	T 52 - 53	65 - 97 cm	oval	NE - SW	II	V.2	SW - NE	NE	F	20 - 25 years		X
B.102	T 54	58 - 67 cm			O	V.3	SSW - NNE	NE	M	adult	?	
B.103	S - T 50	26 - 57 cm (+30)	B	W - E	O	V.5	W - E	W		8 years	X	
B.104	T 54	25 - 41 cm	A	W - E?	O or I	V.5	NW - SE	NW		4 - 5 years		
B.105A	S 53	30 - 39 cm			O	V.5				4 - 5 years		
B.108	T 50	26 - 62 cm (+25)	B	WNW - ESE	O or I	V.5	W - E	ENE		1 - 2 years	X	
B.109	T 50	16 - 67 cm (+25)	B	NW - SE	O or I?	V.5	NW - SE	NW	M	20 - 25 years	X	
B.112	O - P 50	6 - 30 cm (+19)	C?	NE - SW?	I or II	V.5	NE - SW	NE		8 years		
B.113	N 51	38 - 55 cm	B	NNW - SSE	O or I?	V.5	NE - SW	E?		2 - 3 years	X	
B.114	P 49	35 - 81 cm	B	N - S	I or II	V.5	NE - SW	ENE		12 - 14 years	X	
B.115	O 50	24 - 47 cm (+11)	B	NNE - SSW	O or I?	V.5				4 years		
B.116	W - X 54-55	81 - 97 cm	oval	NE - SW	II	V.2	NE - SW	SE	F	adult		
B.117	N 50	38 - 72 cm	B	W - E	O	V.5	N - S	N		4 years		
B.118	O 50	17 - 52 cm (+10)	B	NNW - SSE	I?	V.5	N - S	(NNE)		8 - 9 years	X	
B.119	M 50	38 - 64 cm	B	W - E	O	V.5	(W - E)			3 years	?	
B.121	M 51	47 - 65 cm	A?		O	V.5	N - S	N?		2 (-3) years		
B.122	N - O 49	30 - 75 cm	B	ENE - WSW	I	V.5	N - S	N		adolescent?	X	
B.123	Q 48 - 49	40 - 80 cm	A?		I	V.5	NE - SW	ENE		juvenile	X	
B.124	T 43 - 44	19 - 62 cm	A?		O	V.5	WNW - ESE	(ESE)	F?	adult?		
B.125	Q 48	27 - 69 cm	C	W - E	I	V.5	W - E	W		juvenile	X	
B.126	Q - R 48-49	53 - 92 cm	C?	W - E?	O	V.5	W - E	WSW		juvenile	X	
B.127	V 43	21 - 33 cm	B	N - S	O?	V.5?				juvenile	X	
B.128B	V - W 44	24 - 56 cm	B	NNW - SSE	O	V.5	NNE - SSW	NNE		adolescent?	X	
B.129	S 49	10 - 17 cm (+26)	B	W - E		V.5?				juvenile		X
B.130	O 47	33 - 81 cm	B	W - E	I	V.5	W - E	W		adult?	X	
B.131	T 46	0 - 34 cm (+40)			I?	V.5	N - S	(S)		adult?	X	
B.132	O 47	55 - 68 cm	oval	NNE - SSW	O	V.6	N - S	W		juvenile?	X	
B.133	Q 45 - 46	40 - 78 cm	C	N - S	I	V.5	N - S	N		adolescent	X	
B.134	R 47	20 - 43 cm (+10)	B	W - E	O?	V.5	W - E			juvenile	X	
B.135	W 45	12 - 42 cm (+12)	B?	W - E	O or I?	(V.5?)	(N - S)			adult?		X
B.136	X 44 - 45	34 - 54 cm	oval	WSW - ENE	I	V.6	WSW - ENE	N		adult?		X
B.137	P - Q 44	56 - 93 cm	C	W - E	I	V.5	N - S	S		juvenile	X	X
B.138	Z - AA 46	15 - 28 cm (+45)	oval	NNE - SSW	II	V.6	SSW - NNE	NW		adult?		
B.139	N 46	41 - 57 cm			O	V.5?	W - E			juvenile	X	

Burial type, V.1 - 10 (descriptions in chapter 2)

V.1   Fully extended, bones in correct anatomical position
V.2   Flexed, bones in correct anatomical position
V.3   Partly extended, partly flexed, disjointed
V.4   Tightly flexed vertical bundle

V.5   Disarticulated vertical bundle
V.6   Disarticulated horizontal bundle
V.7   Disarticulated horizontal parcel burial
V.8   Disarticulated double vertical burial
V.9   Disarticulated child inside adult burial
V.10 Disarticulated partially cremated burial

Very fragmentary or disturbed burials have not been included in the table but details can be found in the specific comments. Some comments on the arrangement of bones may appear repetitive, but to tabulate them would be misleading until all burials have been studied in detail. In the descriptions "serial" means that the bones were found in correct anatomical relationship, indicating that they were still articulated at the time of burial.

A number of abbreviations have been used in the comments. These are:

SH — shell horizon
PS — pit-surface
PP — pit-periphery at level of pit-surface
PF — pit-fill
OCS — oval cross section
RCS — round cross section

B.0. (originally F.127). This area much disturbed (cf. B.20, B.24, B.58) but not in modern times. SH thin or disturbed, no shells in PF. Skull missing, maxilla present, probably in situ. Phalanges and vertebrae present in core.

B.1. Much soil removed recently. No SH, could have been removed, no shells in PF. Skull broken, tight bundle, all skeletal parts represented. See p. 105.

B.2. Much soil removed recently. No SH, could have been removed, no shell in PF. OCS, poles of long bones, mandible arched below skull, core of smaller bones but all bones could have been articulated at time of burial. See pp. 15, 30, 105.

B.3. Scatter of bone in modern disturbance, traces of pit to the north.

B.3A fragments, mainly skull and teeth, 2 - 5 years, red pigment present.

B.3B fragments, skull only, adult.

B.4. Modern disturbance did not reach burial. No SH but pockets of shell above skull and scattered shells in upper quarter of PF, i.e. associated with burial process. Early in stage I? OCS, poles of long bones but some long bones at sides also, ribs, phalanges and vertebrae in core, pelvis with sacrum at base. Much attacked by curl-grubs. Four scrapers (two microlithic) on PS, animal bones in PF and shell pocket. See pp. 88, 89, 105.

B.5. Modern disturbance cut into burial, skull would have been partly in level 1. No SH but shells also in undisturbed PF. Upper ends of long bones cut (by shovel?), OCS, poles of long bones, bundle tight, phalanges and vertebrae (3 serial) in core, pelvic bones at base. Middle-aged adult. See p. 105.

B.6. Pockets of shell above burial, some shell in PF. OCS, poles of long bones, phalanges and vertebrae present, pelvic bones at base. Left and right ribs in two opposed bundles placed on south side, heads adjacent. F.38 (tula?) and five scrapers (one microlithic) on PS, cf. fig. 52 and pp. 26, 57, 62, 75, 105.

B.7. Modern disturbance removed SH (once present), no shell in PF. OCS, long bones mainly on western aspect, ribs and vertebrae on eastern aspect of bundle, mandible arched below skull. See p. 105.

B.8. Pit well below level of SH, here recently removed, no shell in PF, large root across part of PS. OCS, fragments of skull present, bones badly decayed but most of skeleton represented. See p. 105.

B.9. Top of burial once just below SH, a little damaged when this removed in modern disturbance, no shell in PF. OCS, poles of long bones, lifted in toto, apparently fairly complete.

B.10. As B.9 but more damaged, only fragments of skull present, some long bones broken.

B.11. Scatter, partly within mark of shovel or spade. Burial was lifted in modern disturbance and dropped again. Adult male, definitely not from B.17. See p. 95.

B.12. Thin SH over pit but also some broken shells in PF, some stacked shells north of burial being remains of shell-pocket. OCS, poles of long bones, mandible arched below skull, ribs and vertebrae (8 serial) but no phalanges in core, pelvic bones at base. Fragmented and decayed, skull tilted. Young mature adult. F.106, microscraper, under base of skull. One cluster of four microscrapers and one of fragments and flakes on PS just northeast and west-south-west of burial. F.45 (elouera) on western PP, two microscrapers on north PP, two more on northwest PP. See pp. 26, 62, 75, 105.

B.13. Modern disturbance cut into burial. No shell in remaining undisturbed PF. OCS, poles of long bones, ribs in core, pelvic bones at base, lifted in toto.

B.14. SH just above top of burial, no shell in PF. Skull fragmentary through decay.

B.15. SH went across pit, two pockets of shell were on PS, some shell also in PF. Phalanges and vertebrae present, most stones in PF are broken and probably accidental but four implements (steep scraper, small grindstone for pigment?, microscraper, and microcore) are whole. Animal bones, some charred, were amongst the bones of burial and in PF. See pp. 16, 21, 24, 26, 32, 53, 57, 62, 83, 84, 105.

B.16. A thin horizon of shells and charcoal was present across the pit, pockets of shell were on the PS and some fragments of shell were in the PF. OCS, lifted in toto. F.93 (polished axe) lay on south PP, four scrapers (three microlithic), a small chopper (?), and a crayon of red pigment on the PS. Two microscrapers were found in the PF. See fig. 52 and pp. 26, 33, 62, 75, 89, 105, 106.

B.17 Modern disturbance cut into burial. No shells were found in what remained of PF or in disturbed sand above burial. OCS, poles of long bones, phalanges (3 serial) and vertebrae (3 serial) in core, pelvic bones at base. Middle-aged adult.

B.18. SH present well above burial, no shells in PF. Undisturbed but decayed, some long bones vertical, lifted in toto. A steep scraper was found close to the bones.

B.19. Modern disturbance removed most of SH over burial. No shells were found in the PF. Crushed but not dug into. OCS, poles of long bones, most skeletal parts represented, lifted in toto, F.21, microscraper (on flake from F.38 in B.6), F.23, small core scraper, and F.70+325, awl, lay on PS or just below this. The two parts of the awl came from opposite ends of PP. See pp. 62, 105, 106.

B.20. Burial was disturbed before the formation of a thin SH which went over and a little above the bones. F.99, a core of fused termites nest, was close to the bones and a pocket of charcoal just southeast of them.

B.21. Pit-shape obliterated by leaching. SH present well above burial, no shell further down. Decayed, incomplete, lifted in toto.

B.22. Pit-shape obliterated by leaching. SH present above burial, one small fragment of shell in PF. Very squashed, incomplete but not disturbed, lifted in toto. See p. 105.

B.23. Thin SH over pit about 10 centimetres above burial, two small fragments in PF, a pocket of shells just east and some charcoal just northeast of burial on PS. RCS, tight bundle, most skeletal parts represented (ribs in core and long bones on two sides of this), lifted in toto. A fabricator, two microscrapers, and a serrated flake came from the PS, a pocket of charcoal from below this at the level of the vault. See p. 105.

B.24. No clear SH in this area, soil churned up, ancient disturbance. Skull and half of mandible only. Elderly adult. F.120, serrated implement lay near skull. See chapter 2, note 3.

B.25. Clear SH 5 centimetres above burial, no shells in PF, pocket of shell on south PP. The skull was lying on its right side. See p. 105.

B.26. Most of level 1 and SH removed by modern disturbance. No shells in remaining PF. Burial would have been well below level of SH. RCS, lifted in toto, skull leaning to left side.

B.27. See comments for B.26. OCS. A scraper was found at level of PS, matching flake in PF.

B.28. Thick SH, no shells in PF, pockets of shell on northeast PS. OCS, poles of long bones, mandible arched below skull, ribs, phalanges and vertebrae in core. F.373, scraper, was inside burial, F.377, backed bladelet, pointed, in PF close to bones. See pp. 28, 42, 105, 106.

B.29. Burial was partly in SH with many shells in PF. A large pocket of shell northeast of burial also contained animal bones. Top removed, lower half in situ but leaning. No phalanges or vertebrae were found. The PF contained a scraper, two cores, and an implement with serrated edge which could all be accidental. Two fabricators further down probably belong to the B.30 PS. See pp. 40, 43, 62, and fig. 73.

B.30. SH across that part of the pit not cut by B.29. No shell in PF. OCS, poles of long bones, mandible arched below skull, ribs, phalanges and vertebrae (serial, 4 - 4 - 6) in core, pelvic bones and sacrum at base. Middle-aged adult. Fabricators F.41 and F.375 (of same raw material) probably belonged to PS as well as two scrapers. See pp. 40, 42, 105, and fig. 73.

B.31. Pit partly obliterated by surrounding burials and leaching. Partly below B.25, buried before B.0 or B.25, pits differ in depth and character of PF. Somewhat tilted and disturbed, skull leaning to left. Lifted in toto, skull separate.

B.32. Pit slightly oval. Thin SH sealed pit, no shells in PF. OCS. Note F.131 (serrated edge) in PF near bones almost halfway down. See p. 105.

B.33. Level 1 and SH removed by modern disturbance, sand above burial not in situ, top of burial removed. No shell visible in remaining PF. Mainly long bones left plus some ribs, the mandible, and loose teeth, all disturbed. Lifted in toto.

B.34. Comments as for B.33, damage less severe. Skull missing. Lifted in toto.

B.35. Level 1 and SH removed by modern disturbance but much shell present in dark matrix around and between bones. Fragmentary,

lifted in toto. See p. 95.

B.36. Burial once partly in level 1, pushed over and squashed, shells mixed into the PF all through pit, a few amongst the bones. OCS, skull squashed, phalanges and vertebrae present. Note "cap" of rough stone fragments over skull. A pocket of large flakes and a microscraper were on PS, a scraper and an elouera with serrated edge were near the bones almost halfway down. See pp. 26, 62, 84, 105.

B.37. Most of pit-outline obliterated by later pits. Young mature adult. Note stone on left wrist, charcoal on left ramus and left ankle. See pp. 24, 28, 33, 43, 53, 54, 84, 106, and fig. 11.

B.38. In same pit as B.51, B.54, cut into B.53. OCS, poles of long bones, mandible arched below skull, opposed ribs, phalanges and vertebrae in core, pelvic bones at base. Middle-aged adult. See pp. 16, 49, 105.

B.39. Area disturbed, no SH. Shells amongst bones could be recent intrusions. Bones mostly in small fragments, sex uncertain. Some charred animal bones present. See pp. 16, 26, 32, 53, 84.

B.40. Pit obliterated by later pits and leaching. Lifted in toto, skull separate. Face down but approximately to the north. Note pelvic bones and mandible close to skull. A corona of stones included two pieces of pebble, a large rectangular flake and a fragment with use-polish. See pp. 28, 32, 33, 42, 52, and fig. 54.

B.41. Disturbed by B.73. Skull missing. No phalanges or vertebrae. Pelvic bones at base. See p. 43.

B.42. Pit obliterated by leaching and cut into by that for B.48+50. Bones were lying in lens of dark soil. SH was present above these over most of the area. Very fragmentary. See p. 62 and chapter 2, note 3.

B.43. OCS, poles of long bones, mandible placed below skull, phalanges and vertebrae (9 serial) in core, pelvic bones at base. See p. 50.

B.44. Level 1 and most of SH removed by modern disturbance but the pit was well below this level and there were no shells in PF. See p. 16.

B.44A. Fairly complete. OCS, poles of long bones.

B.44B. Fragments of skull and a few other bones packed close to those of B.44A.

B.44C. Fragments of adult, probably from upper disturbed soil.

B.45. Pocket of shell on southwest PS. OCS, poles of long bones, mandible arched below skull, ribs, vertebrae and phalanges in core, burial discussed on p. 41. See also fig. 11.

B.46A. OCS, long bones massed on northern aspect, ribs, phalanges and vertebrae (4 serial) on southern aspect of bundle. Skull inclined down and to the left. Young mature adult. See p. 51.

B.46B. Loose teeth, skull fragments and a few other fragments, all small and definitely from B.49B, buried just above.

B.47. Tilted, skull in fragments but looking upwards. Almost complete serial vertebral column with sacrum in correct position at base. No phalanges. OCS, poles of long bones. Area disturbed by B.73 pit. See pp. 43, 105, 106.

B.48. No clear SH over pit, no shells in deeper part of PF but a few near the top. Certainly later than B.42 or B.59+69. Long bones bundled with those of B.50 (axis of burial that of the two combined), vertebrae present. Young mature adult. Only flakes and fragments of implements found in PF. See pp. 16, 21, 62, and fig. 32.

B.49A. Base very close to the top of B.46. OCS, skull missing. No phalanges but vertebrae present. See p. 51.

B.49B. See B.46B. Most bones lifted with those of B.49A. Probably a V.9 burial, 4 - 5 years of age.

B.50. See comments for B.48, pp. 16, 21, 62, and fig. 32.

B.51. Compare B.38 and B.54, buried in the same pit. See pp. 16, 49, and fig. 32.

B.52. Pit obliterated by later pits and leaching. Skull tilted on its left side. Young mature adult. See pp. 9, 21, 41, 52, and fig. 11.

B.53. On north side of and partly below B.38 (see B.38). Bones disturbed but some long bones vertical. See pp. 16, 49.

B.54A. Buried with B.38 and B.51. Inverted but probably accidentally. OCS, mandible near skull, phalanges in core. See pp. 16, 49, 105, and fig. 32.

B.54B. Vertebrae of smaller child, 0 - 1 years.

B.55. Pit well down below SH, here partly removed by modern disturbance. No shells in PF. Skull missing. Neonate or premature. F.971 fits F.355 in O 52 and flake in B.100, together form fabricator. See pp. 19, 32, 83.

B.56. SH here partly removed or disturbed. The pit was well below this disturbance and no shells were found in undisturbed PF. Skull fragmented and tilted to the right. RCS, vertebrae form core, long bones all round this, all set below skull.

B.57. Pit was disturbed, shallow. The bones were scattered.

B.58. S 56 - 57, 27 - 42 cm, area disturbed, pit-shape and stage unknown, bones disturbed. Age: ca. 3 years.

B.59A. Cut into by pits for B.60 and B.48+50, probably contemporary with B.69. No shell in undisturbed PF. Pit very deep. Skull destroyed by root. Teeth of maxilla remained in anatomical relationship. Mandible present. Stones – see description of B.69. See also p. 105.

B.59B. = B.69.

B.60. Pit cut into that for B.59+69 but was partly obliterated by later disturbance. It cut through SH mixing shells into fill. Burial must have protruded into level 1 before it was pushed over and broken. The skull was shattered. OCS, poles of long bones, pelvic bones at base. Middle-aged adult. A microscraper was on the PS, an oval flake amongst the bones, and F.714, a lunate, very close to these. See pp. 28, 62, 76, 95, 105.

B.61. Pocket of shell over skull, shells all through PF. OCS, poles of long bones, ribs in core, no phalanges or vertebrae, pelvic bones at base. Skull lying on its right side, placed so originally. Note B.68 inside burial. F.180, large core, was on PS, F.490, pointed oblong flake, was lying on the centre of the skull. A microscraper, a piece with serrated edge, and a core came from near or amongst the bones. See pp. 16, 28, 29, 33, 76, 105.

B.62. Disturbance caused by B.73 pit and by root. The skull was shifted away from the burial, lying on its right side, facing up. RCS, tight bundle with ribs in the core. F.185, a neat but broken scraper was at the base of the burial. See pp. 30, 45, 62.

B.63. Charcoal on the PS could belong to the B.73 PS. A shell pocket was on the south PP. OCS, poles of long bones, mandible arched below skull, ribs present, pelvic bones at base. Burial tilted, skull pushed over on its left side, broken by a root. Middle-aged adult. F.215a and b, pieces of a polished axe, were found inside the burial. F.587 in S 56:1 probably belonged to the same axe. See pp. 28, 33, 45, 75.

B.64. Pit was almost round. The burial originally protruded into level 1 and the PF contained much shell. OCS, poles of long bones, mandible arched below skull, ribs in core, pelvic bones at base. Skull pushed over on left side, originally higher up and vertical, maxilla left behind at top of bundle. See pp. 29, 62.

B.65. Pit slightly oval, PF full of shells. OCS, long bones bundled together on northern aspect, mandible, pelvic bones and ribs on southern aspect of bundle. Skull to southeast and above core but pushed over by root on to its left side and shattered. Young mature adult.

B.66. The surface was sagging because of modern disturbance nearby, so a few centimetres should be added. The pit was slightly disturbed, shallow, and contained shells. OCS, leaning to the west with the skull leaning over on its left side.

B.67. Its pit intersected with that of B.63 in the upper part and it was not clear which came first. There was a thin SH over the pit and no shells in the PF. The skull had been placed upside down. See p. 105.

B.68. Inside B.61. A V.9 burial, 0 - 1 years of age. See p. 16.

B.69. (B.59B in anatomical field notes). In same pit as B.59A. Skull had tilted face down, pushing long bones apart and moving downwards. Elderly adult. Associated stones for this and B.59A: two round flakes of fine chert were lying on the B.69 skull, a third found further down fitted F.293 in J 55, and a flake in B.112, Q 50. There were fragments from the same core amongst the bones. With these was also F.688, a broken fabricator. See pp. 62, 105.

B.70. The pit was obliterated by leaching with a faint SH above it and no shell in the PF. The burial was decayed, but not disturbed. Most parts of the skeleton were represented amongst the fragments.

B.71. R 53, 37 - 47 cm, but not in situ. Dug up and dumped again by soil contractor? Much shell in surrounding matrix so a late burial? Skull only. See p. 106.

B.72. Shell pockets on the PS and much shell in the PF. Note a shell corona around the skull. OCS, ribs, phalanges and vertebrae in core, pelvic bones at base. Skull on its right side, placed so originally. See pp. 29, 30, 33, 105.

B.73. Pit subtriangular, steep-sided. Late in stage II. Charcoal on PS. Lying on its right side. Elderly adult. Note F.503, an oblong, pointed flake, lying on the left humerus. See pp. 9, 19, 28, 33, 45, 53, 62, 76, 84, 89, and fig. 5.

B.74. R 55, 108 - 113 cm in B.73 pit. The fragments were of a child. See p. 45.

B.75. R 53, 27 - 30 cm, add another 5 cm removed by modern disturbance. Fragments of child, type or stage of burial unknown.

B.76. Parts of the burial came down in a collapse with some from B.82A+B. Probably buried with these. The skull remained in situ after the collapse, tilted on its right side. It must have been sitting to the east of the bundle of postcranial bones. Sex uncertain. See pp. 44, 76, 105.

B.77. Disturbance uneven here. The pit was a subrectangular steep-sided trench with flat floor. Much of level 1 and the SH had been removed but there was much shell in level 2 also, below the level of disturbance. Lying on its right side, lifted in toto. See pp. 9, 19, 21, 83.

B.78. Disturbed by B.73. OCS, leaning to northeast, no vertebrae, some skull fragments to the east. See p. 44 and fig. 5.

B.79. Almost round pit. Pocket of shell on western PP, thin SH and much shell in PF. Note shell corona around skull. OCS, poles of long bones, ribs in core, pelvic bones halfway down. Skull on its left side, placed so originally. Young mature adult. F.532, part of polished axe, was lying on the centre of the skull. A joining piece came from S 53. See pp. 29, 33, 75, 105.

B.80. S 55, 60 - 65 cm, in the B.73 pit. Adult. See p. 45.

B.81. Most of level 1 and SH removed or disturbed, but there were no shells in PF below that level. OCS, poles of long bones but some also in the core with ribs and other smaller bones. Note mandible sitting above the face on the skull. Lifted in toto.

B.82A. Involved in collapse with B.76. No phalanges or vertebrae in burial. Young mature adult. F.536, a Bondi point or elouera, appeared to come out of this bundle when part of it collapsed. See pp. 45, 76, 105, 106.

B.82B. Top part damaged by B.73 and B.93 pits. OCS, vertebrae present (8 serial). Skull tilted to the right and back, facing up. Young mature adult. See pp. 45, 105, 106.

B.83 = B.86B.

B.84. Deep pit partly obliterated by leaching. No shell in PF, parts of SH left over burial. Decayed, not disturbed. Very fragmentary skull, long bones, ribs.

B.85. Pit shallow and cut into, burial partly in level 1. Skull smashed, some bones broken. Middle-aged adult.

B.86A+B. Some disturbance of the soil here. The skull of B.86B (=B.83) was found a little southwest of the bundle itself. Pit-shape and stage unknown. Bone arrangements disturbed, but still clear that they were of V.5 type. No vertebrae or extremities represented. See pp. 62, 95, 105.

B.87. Skull in pieces, skeleton almost complete, all bones much decayed. Note that central core contained long bones. F.230, neat steep scraper, was found close to the bundle. See pp. 28, 30, 49, 62.

B.88. Pit cut into by others. Pelvic bones and two teeth were at opposite end to skull. There were no phalanges or vertebrae but a few ribs in the core between the major long bones. Note corona of rough fragments and a thick oval flake around the skull. See pp. 28, 33, 47, 62, 84.

B.89. Most of level 1 and SH removed here, no shell found in the PF below this level. The burial was well below the disturbance. OCS, decayed and crushed but not disturbed, skull very crushed, no vertebrae present. See pp. 30, 32.

B.90A. S 52 - 53, 30 - 38 cm, burial disturbed, partly removed. If base was in situ the burial must once have protruded into level 1. Fragments only. Age: 0 - 2 years.

B.90B. Skull fragments of adult found amongst the juvenile bones.

B.91. There had been recent disturbance of level 1 and SH but no shells were seen below that level or amongst the bones. The burial was probably early, cf. B.88. The skull had been removed but the rest of the burial was undisturbed. The pelvic bones and the mandible had been placed as a core between major long bones. See pp. 32, 95, 105.

B.92. S 50, 1 - 24 cm, add ca. 35 - 37 cm removed by modern disturbance. The burial lifted and dropped again. Most of skeleton there but bones jumbled. Age: 5 - 10 years. Red pigment present. See p. 95.

B.93. Pocket of shell just above burial. Leaning and fragmented — because of pressure from above? — skull crushed, no vertebrae found, pelvic bones at base. See pp. 45, 47, 48.

B.94. Found in area C. Scattered fragments of middle-aged adult.

B.95. Pit slightly oval. OCS, poles of long bones, ribs in core, pelvic bones at base. Skull broken, facing up. Two pockets of large flakes, F.F.682a - e and F.706a - b, were lying on PP. See pp. 26, 48, 105.

B.96A+B. S 53, 30 - 38 cm, some disturbance here. Stage O or I? Burial type uncertain, bones too disturbed; Age (for both): 1 - 2 years. Red pigment present. See p. 49.

B.97A. Disturbed. A quartzite flake, an oblong pointed flake (F.539), and a microlithic triangle (?) of milky quartz were found amongst the bones. See pp. 28, 48, 62, 105.

B.97B. Crushed. See pp. 48, 105, 106.

B.98. Skull crushed. OCS, poles of long bones, mandible below skull, but not arched, ribs in core. No phalanges or vertebrae. See p. 48.

B.99. Disturbed by the B.100 pit. Skull upside down, one bone fragment from B.107 fits a bone in B.99. Some bones do not belong to burial. Sex uncertain. See p. 48.

B.100. Pit oval and steep-sided with a flat floor. Late in stage II. Charcoal in PF and on PS. Face down. Stones in PF all fragmentary and apparently accidental. See pp. 9, 19, 21, 33, 48, 53, 54, 57, 62, 83, 95, 106, and figs. 15 and 90.

B.101. S 50. Scatter of bone fragments just below surface. Adult? See p. 95.

B.102. Pit cut into by others. Young mature adult. Red pigment could derive from B.95. See pp. 9, 33, 48, 83, 84, 105, 106, and fig. 17.

B.103. Modern disturbance cut into top of level 2 here, but below this there were no shells in the PF. The pit was deep. OCS, poles of long bones, tight bundle, ribs in the core, lifted in toto.

B.104. Pit slightly oval. OCS, poles of long bones, no vertebrae present. Skull crushed by pressure. F.238, a neat flake scraper, was lying on PS. See p. 48.

B.105A. Pit cut into by others. Skull crushed by B.97A. See p. 49.

B.105B. A few fragments of a smaller child, consisting mainly of teeth.

B.106A. T 53, ? - 47 cm, probably not in situ, no clear pit but some evidence of disturbance. (Stage O?) Skull only, facing north. Adult male. See p. 48.

B.106B. S - T 53 - 54, 18 - 56 cm. Some disturbance here. Bundle leaning. See pp. 48, 95.

B.107. T 53, from ca. 25 cm below the surface, not in situ but part of B.100 PF. See pp. 48, 106.

B.108. Level 1 and top of level 2 removed or disturbed here, shell mixed into disturbed sand but no shell below this level, pit deep. OCS.

B.109. Comments as for B.108. OCS, poles of long bones, serial vertebrae (many) and opposed ribs in core. See pp. 28, 105.

B.110. S - T 53, T 54, 62 - 70 cm. In pale sand which dribbled out under B.106A, no pit visible. Bones apparently horizontal when buried. Stage O. Probably type V.7. Age: 0 - 2 years? See p. 48.

B.111. No burial (no human bones).

B.112. Top part of burial must have been in level 1 before being pushed over. Much shell in PF also amongst bones. Leaning to southeast. OCS, poles of long bones, ribs in core, pelvic bones at base. Note "cap" of stones over burial. See pp. 26, 62, 84, 105, 106.

B.113. No shell in PF, little above. OCS, tight bundle, badly decayed, teeth in anatomical relationship. Note F.1040 (axe-blank?) in PF near burial. See pp. 33, 76, 105.

B.114. Pit cut through well-developed SH. Charcoal and burnt animal bones on PS. RCS, tight bundle, long bones below skull. Note notched scraper near bones. See pp. 26, 62, 105.

B.115. No shells in PF, no SH above (removed by pit for B.112?). Type uncertain, burial fragmentary, lifted in toto. Oblong flake of quartzite lying just above burial.

B.116. Pit oval and steep-sided with flat floor. There were lenses of shell in the PF, and charcoal all over the PS. Burial was lying on its left side. Note that the right scapula and armbones, but not the hand, were missing. Elderly adult. Many stones, mostly fragmentary and probably derived, were in the PF. See pp. 9, 19, 23, 53, 57, 62, 105, 106, and figs. 12 and 44.

B.117. Burial was partly below massive root. SH went over root and PS. Soil horizons across pit. Skull squashed and pushed to northeast by the root. Lifted in toto. OCS. Two microscrapers were found just below PS. See p. 39.

B.118. Once partly in level 1. Not much shell in PF. OCS, poles of long bones, mandible arched below skull, ribs in core. Skull had slipped down onto western aspect of bundle, tilted to the east, leaving tooth behind on top of bundle. Two big flakes of milky quartz were found near the skull on opposite sides and just below PS. See p. 105.

B.119. Pushed by same massive root as B.117, skull in pieces. Note several concentrations of shell or rough stone fragments, probably once on PS but pushed about by large root.

B.120. X 55, fragment of skull in B.116 PF. Age: ca. 14 years. See p. 62.

B.121. In deep-set pit below SH, no shells in PF. Bones badly decayed but teeth in anatomical relationship. Lifted in two blocks. A probable burin was lying on PS. See p. 105.

B.122. Parts of vault scattered in level 1, disturbed by roots and probably by digging though this was not as recent as the main disturbances. No SH over pit but fragments of shell in the fill. A thin SH in the area around the pit appeared broken by this. The PF was dark but showed developed soil horizon right across pit. Only skull damaged, parts of vault detached, the rest mainly squashed. OCS, mandible arched below skull, poles of long bones, proximal ends upwards, ribs surrounding scapulae form the core, pelvic bones at base. *Note:* root pushing from northwest and swelling moved the

northeast part of the base of the bone bundle to the southeast and upwards, causing it to tilt to the west and probably causing some of the damage to the skull. There was a concentration of stones on the south PP level with the top of the skull. See pp. 26, 39, 56, 105.

B.123. No clear SH, but fragments of shell in the PF and pockets of shell on the PS; some SH had formed before burial; note incipient soil horizons across the pit and root through base eroding the bone. OCS, poles of long bones, tightly packed. *Note:* leaning to northwest due to push from root. See pp. 39, 56.

B.124. Level 1 thin on the slope of the ridge. Pit broad-based with gentle slopes all round. No clear SH but faint SH to south of pit and over southwest part of pit. (PF was dark without shells. Note incipient soil horizons across pit.) Upper part of burial fragmented, eroded by roots, skull sunk over core, basal part most. This twisted to the southeast, pushing over one long bone, leaving face and vault higher up. OCS, mandible arched below skull, poles of long bones, pelvis at base, ribs in the core. *Note:* soil horizons across pit sag where skull had sunk. There was some charcoal on the southeast to south part of PS. See pp. 26, 56, 95.

B.125. Pit-outline blurred by roots in parts. No SH but some fragments of shell in PF. Incipient soil horizons went across burial. Upper part and base of burial were eroded by roots. OCS, tight bundle, poles of long bones, mandible arched below skull, ribs in core, lifted in toto. Much red pigment. *Note:* base of bundle pushed to north-north-east by expanding root. See pp. 39, 56.

B.126. Upper parts of level 1 disturbed over southeast half of burial, but most of the PS was intact. Shape of pit obscured by root, steep end to the west. Clear thin SH over area of PS, no shell in PF. The bundle was definitely buried before any root from the big tree had reached the area. The burial was almost "wrapped" around southwest side of big root, the skull squashed by the swelling root, its lower part pushed inside the vault, and all bone for 4 cm eroded away by root. The mandible was pushed inside the skull. OCS, tight bundle, poles of long bones, pelvis and phalanges at base of core, ribs further up. Much red pigment. *Note:* there was some charcoal just below and in SH over pit. See pp. 26, 39, 56, 105, 106.

B.127. The base of the pit was another 22 cm down — the bone had eroded away? Steep slope of pit to the north. No SH but roughly concentric bands of scattered shell found on south part of PS at level of SH. (They may have existed over all PS though not noticed by worker.) No shell in PF. Burial very eroded. The bones left were vertical, and tightly packed. Much red pigment. See pp. 26, 56.

B.128A. T - V 44; 25 - 28 cm (level 1 was undisturbed over the bones recovered but part of the burial may have been removed by modern interference [cf. map 12]. Note F.95, ca. 2.5 metres further south, a series of eroded serial vertebrae, possibly dropped from a shovel [cf. the case of B.11] after being lifted from elsewhere. This was possibly the southwest end of B.128A, the consistency of the bone being very similar.) No pit visible. A faint SH with scattered stones was present a few centimetres above the bones. Stage O or early I? Type of burial unknown but several bones were found in position of articulation though now held together by roots, not by sinews. Bones present: parts of two feet, finger bones, patella, lumbar, cervical vertebrae. *Note:* it is not certain that the person was buried. A corpse could have been left on the surface to decay, parts getting scattered and other parts getting embedded in the sand, later to be covered by the developing shell horizon. See p. 95.

B.128B. (The skull was first thought to belong to B.128Á.) The pit was almost round, the burial at the northern steep end. A SH was present, but no shells were in PF. The bones were eroded, especially the upper ends, the skull squashed by pressure. OCS, tight bundle, mandible arched below skull, poles of long bones, upper ends splayed by sinking skull, core of ribs etc. Note tooth and pelvis at base of burial. See p. 56.

B.129. Covered by ca. 10 cm of sand churned up by modern soil removal. Shallow pit, steeper end to the west. Scattered shells in disturbed sand and in PF. Not very early in sequence of burials. A few fragmentary bones present, some vertical. Vault fragments uppermost. Burial crushed but apparently not disturbed by digging. See p. 56.

B.130. Pit had broad rounded floor, steep end to east. Clear SH (whole, more fresh-looking shells over pit and around it, outside pit more eroded shells below these). Shells in PF, soil horizons across pit. Burial very crumbling due to roots and curl-grubs — and time? Top of vault almost gone, some face left, core of bundle least decayed. OCS, tight bundle, mandible arched below skull, poles of long bones, core of ribs, vertebrae, pelvis at base. *Note:* shell pocket on PP to north-north-west, charcoal 55 cm below surface just west of burial. See pp. 56, 105.

B.131. Modern soil removal cut into top of vault. Pit cut into from northwest and west, cf. P.B.8, and from east and southeast, cf. P.B.2, but broad-based with very dark fill. Some shell in PF. Burial complete except top of skull, face pushed down by recent pressure and wrapped round heads of long bones. OCS, tight bundle leaning to east, mandible arched below skull, poles of long bones, one pelvic bone at base, one high up, opposed groups of ribs forming oval on one side of bundle. See p. 56.

B.132. The pit was an oblong oval trough. SH was present (thicker to southwest, cf. B.130). There was no shell in the pale grey PF. The burial was pre-SH and pre-B.130. Clear soil horizons went across the pit. The burial was badly eroded, the southern end almost disintegrated. The skull was at the northern end, with parallel long bones south of this, and the mandible next to the skull. The red pigment is not likely to derive from B.130. *Note:* a red stone was lying on the skull. See pp. 28, 32, 33, 56, 105.

B.133. SH was present all round and over the pit but less thick on the PS. The shells were not very eroded; some were in PF. The skull was fractured by pressure from above. OCS, tightly packed bundle, mandible arched below skull, poles of long bones, pelvis at base, vertebrae in core. *Note:* pockets of shell on southwest part of PP. See p. 56.

B.134. Modern soil removal disturbed another 5 cm. The burial was at the western steeper end of the pit. Scattered fragmentary shells over the area of the burial — remnants of a SH. There were no shells in the PF. The burial was fragmentary — especially the skull — due to erosion and pressure. OCS, tight bundle, mandible arched below skull, poles of long bones, core of ribs. Skull too fragmentary to establish orientation. See pp. 56, 105, 106.

B.135. Soil contractors removed ca. 12 cm of humus. Lower undisturbed parts of pit suggest that it was oval, deep end to the west. SH was present but thin, clearest over southwest part with much stone and shell in a layer 16 cm thick just below modern interference. There was no shell in the PF. Axis of burial was N - S, skull at southern end, facing up and west. Note that arrangement of long bones, ribs, pelvis, and mandible fit the dominant pattern of V.5, but that the skull was at the opposite end to the mandible, upside down and damaged by the pelvis being pushed into it. Teeth were scattered through the burial and the ribs very broken. Burial, when found, was leaning but not horizontal, and clearly not disturbed in modern times. (Suggested interpretation, see p. 51.) *Note:* there was a suggestion of charring on some bones and some charcoal in the PF to the west, below the burial. See p. 56.

B.136. The surface of the ridge here sloped to the northeast. Level 1 was disturbed over the southwest end of pit, probably by work in earlier seasons as well as by modern soil removal. The pit was roughly oval, with a flat floor. SH was present in the area around the pit, many shell pockets were just above the bones in the pit area. Early in stage I? The skull was crushed and some other damage to the bones was due to pressure from above and work in earlier seasons. The burial was first found at the end of season V and covered up, but most bones were in situ and horizontal from the time of burial. The arrangement was a neat rectangle of suboval cross section, with the skull at the west-south-west end. The bones do not follow the dominant V.5 plan: the long bones are roughly parallel but the mandible away from the skull and pelvic bones, the scapulae and the ribs were scattered through the centre. The skull was facing into the bundle. *Note:* some charring on the upper faces of the bones, flakes, fragments and implements around bundle. See pp. 26, 33, 51, 56, 105, and fig. 53.

B.137. Burial was in the centre of the pit. SH was present all around the pit, a few shells on PS, pockets of shell on PP and some shells in the PF. SH formed before the pit was dug, more shells added at time of burial. The pockets not scattered, probably because burial was on outskirts of burial ground, i.e. slope of ridge. Soil horizons went right across pit. Charcoal, flakes, animal bone, and fragments of shell about 14 cm above vault but below PS could derive from a stage of the burial ceremony or could have been scraped in from the surrounding surface during the filling of the pit. The bone was undisturbed but fragile. OCS, tight bundle, mandible arched below skull, poles of long bones, vertebrae in core, one pelvic bone at base but one higher up. Sutures in the skull, even in the base, were not fused. Much red pigment present. The shell pockets on the western, southwestern and southern parts of the PP contained also charcoal and bone. There were some human phalanges in the southwest pocket. Much charcoal was scattered to the south and on PS, some also in PF. See p. 56.

B.138. The pit was an oval trench with a flat floor. There were shells in the PF and amongst the bones. Modern soil removal had interfered with all but 15 cm of soil above the burial. The burial was undisturbed, tightly packed with the skull at the southwest end. One tibia and femur on either long side, two humeri together on upper face, below these the ribs to southeast and the scapulae to northwest. The mandible was close to the skull, the pelvis at the opposite end. The skull was lying on its left side. Proximal ends of long bones were towards the skull. No pigment could be seen but the PF was very dark. There were no stones close to the bones but implements and shell pockets to northeast and east; some of these may belong to B.136. See pp. 32, 56, 105, and fig. 53.

B.139. Pit obscured by leaching. SH present all over pit-area and near this, thickest to southeast and thinning to northwest, the border of the burial ground. No shells were found in the PF. The bones were badly eroded. Probably a V.5 type burial since the long bones were tight together and almost vertical. Most of the skull had disappeared but it had clearly once been above the long bones. OCS but few bones easily recognizable. Note that juvenile teeth were found scattered to the east and northeast of the burial from 30 - 40 cm below the surface. If these belong it could be a matter of early disturbance or root activity. See p. 56.

B.140A+B. AC 44, 39 - 50 cm. Level 1 very disturbed, especially to the east, pit-shape obliterated by this, burials also disturbed. Stage in sequence not known. Bones of adult to northeast and those of a child to the southwest. The latter was least disturbed and its bones vertical, perhaps once a V.5 burial. The adult could either have been disturbed by recent soil removal or when the child was buried. No pigment could be seen. There was a shell pocket west of the burial on PP. See pp. 56, 105.

Bone points, quartz, pigments, and small flat pebbles

Reference to objects which may have been used for sorcery or may have been part of a man's dilly bag (p. 83) are scattered through the text. This appendix aims at collecting and listing such information in one place to facilitate interpretation and comparisons.

Bone points

These have been found in burials B.28 (F.512), B.54 (F.645), B.102 (F.619), and B.109 (F.433 a,b). More may turn up when the bones of all burials have been studied. B.54 was adolescent, sex not known, but the other three were all young males.

Quartz

Because of written accounts of the use of small chips of stone in sorcery and because there were a number of pieces of clear or milky quartz in the site, often in burial pits, I thought it worthwhile to plot all occurrences of quartz, whether cores, artifacts or small chips down to about 4 millimetres in length. Very few pieces were retouched or showed much sign of use and few were above 3 centimetres long. The distribution map, presented in the thesis, was not very enlightening, except in terms of showing a general connection with the burials.

Fig. 106. Bone points found inside burials.

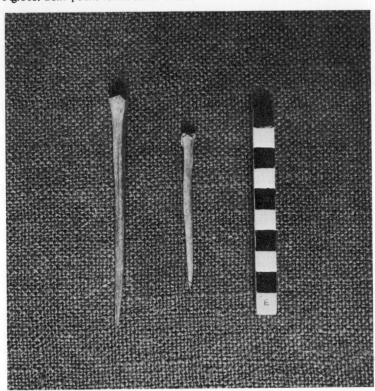

There was a scatter all over and through the area of the burial ground but not far outside its borders. It should be noted that a very large proportion of the quartz chips found did not come from burials or burial pits. This does not, however, exclude the possibility that some were intentionally associated with burials.

Quartz was found amongst or close to the bones of burials B.1, B.6, B.12, B.15, B.16, B.22, B.23, B.28, B.30, B.59A, B.67, B.69, B.97A (a microlithic triangle?), B.102, B.112, B.113 (a core), B.118, B.122, B.130, B.136. It was in the pit-fill of B.32, B.36, B.91, B.95, B.114 (rock crystal), B.121, and probably also in the pit-fill of B.4, B.19, B.25, B.61, B.72, B.79, and B.86, though close to the floor or periphery of the pit.

Some burials contained small, sharp flakes which may belong in this context. The raw material was fine translucent quartzite (B.28, B.38, B.60), white banded chalcedony (B.19), or colourful chalcedonic silica or jasper (B.5, B.6, B.59A).

Red pigment

The various forms of this and its connection with burials was discussed in some detail in chapter 2. I have suggested that some larger chunks without facets of polish which were found near or amongst the bones of burials could have been part of the content of a man's dilly bag rather than used in the funerary ceremonies (cf. pp. 83 - 84). The lists below give the incidences of this.
A: chunks of haematite amongst the bones of a burial: B.2, B.15, B.22, B.47, B.140.
B: chunks of haematite near the bones of a burial: B.4, B.6, B.7, B.8, B.12, B.76+82, B.91, B.95, B.130, B.132.
From identifications made so far, we know that burials B.4, B.6, B.12, B.15, B.47, B.82, B.95 are male; burials B.2, B.7, B.8, B.22, B.91 juveniles or adolescent; the sex or age of B.76, B.130, and B.132 have not been established.

Other pigments

We found twenty-four pieces of chalcedonic silica, so devitrified that it powders easily when scraped with a fingernail or, in some cases, from a mere touch. This degree of devitrification does not occur on any other pieces in the site, waste or implements. Most pieces are shapeless lumps, but there are three thick flakes among them. One, F.137, has steep retouch (backing) along one margin. Margins and surfaces appear worn by rubbing. F.97 is pale turquoise, the remainder white. The former was lying on the pit-surface over B.16. Six of the white pieces came from amongst the bones of burials (B.16, B.19, B.28, B.97B, B.112, B.134), another seven from close to the bones (B.16, B.116?, B.126, B.134, B.136, B.138). Six pieces were scattered in the area of the B.73 pit (Q 54, R 54 - 56) as if brought up and broken by the digging of this. The remaining four came from areas of recent disturbance, one from near B.97B and one from near B.83/86 (see Appendix D).

These pieces of white soft stone must clearly be considered associated with burials and could well be the white pigment mentioned on p. 83. Note that B.28 was a male, burials B.16, B.19, B.83/86, B.97B, B.112, B.126, B.134 were juveniles or adolescents. B.116 was a female but stones in the fill of her pit are all likely to be derived from elsewhere in the site.

Pebbles

Small flat water-worn pebbles from about 1 to about 5 centimetres in length were found quite frequently. To test my impression that they were most frequently found near burials, I plotted the occurrence of each pebble on map 11. (Note that they are plotted in terms of grid square, not position within this square.) They were most frequent where there were most burials and they did not occur far outside the burial area. Their distribution is clearly linked with that of burials, their purpose a mystery. Since they are flat and smooth, it is possible that they were used as spatulae for applying powdered pigment, but many are rather too small to get a good grip on. Some were found close to the bones of burials: B.16 (two pebbles), B.37, B.47, B.71, B.82 (two pebbles), B.100, B.107, B.102. A little over half of the pebbles, however, were found in or just above the shell horizon.

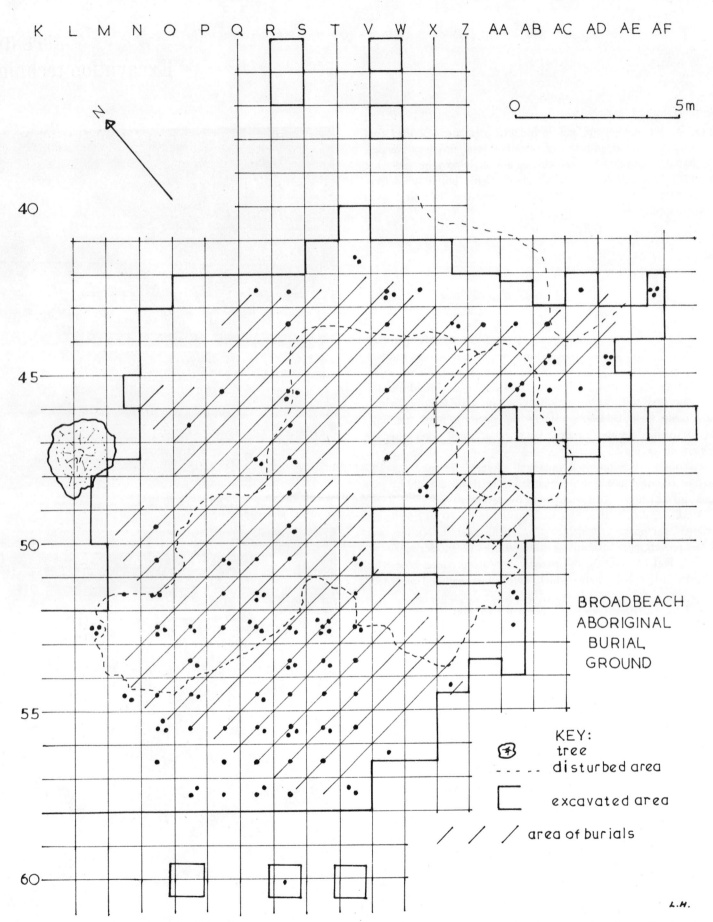

Map 11. Broadbeach burial ground: distribution of small flat pebbles. Each dot indicates one pebble. Note that these were plotted according to grid square, but the position within this has not been shown.

Some of the equipment and techniques used are described first and then the whole process of clearing and lifting a vertical bundle-burial, showing what difficulties are likely to arise and what steps might be taken to counteract these. Other burial types were relatively easy to lift and the techniques described here were used only when applicable.

Equipment

Compressed air

When the bone was damp or wet, it was often so soft that even gentle brushing with a fine artist's brush would abrade it as some of the sand would stick to the brush. A well-aimed puff of air was safer, making the grains of sand jump away from the bone without injuring it. For our first tests we used ordinary air-mattress inflators, which worked fairly well. However, usually the operator must use both hands to manipulate the inflator. We then acquired compressed-air equipment consisting of:

1. Cylinders of compressed industrial oxygen. We used the 220 cubic foot (6 cubic metre) size which could be handled easily by two persons and which provided enough gas for several days.

2. An air-regulator valve. This we adjusted to ca. 10 - 12 lbs/inch² (83 kilopascals) pressure, which was sufficient to shift even very wet sand, but proved more efficient as the moisture content decreased.

3. Fifty feet (15 metres) of specially reinforced plastic hose. This was divided into three lengths which were joined with a T-piece (see 4).

4. A T-piece. This allowed two operators to work from the same gas supply.

5. Two pen air-guns with triggers to turn the oxygen flow on and off. (A modern type, the pm-pistol, type T, has the refinement that air is blown out sideways also, preventing the sand from jumping into the eyes of the operator. This was found unsatisfactory in that the "screen" was not very efficient and much oxygen was wasted. It was difficult to get the power required in spite of increased flow of oxygen. In the end, we put adhesive plaster over the side-vents and used goggles.

6. A cylinder key.

7. Hose-clips to join hose to valve, T-piece, and air-guns.

We made stands of iron reinforcing with hooks of wire at the top. These were stuck into the sand and held the air-guns and goggles to prevent sand from fouling the trigger mechanisms and outlet barrels or from scratching the goggles. It was essential to use goggles, especially when the sand was dry (figs. 107 and 108). The air-regulator valve was always kept covered by a plastic bag because of flying sand and dust. When a new cylinder was opened, a short

Fig.107. The pm-pistol used for compressed air.
Fig.108. Compressed air equipment.

sharp release of gas from the cylinder was used to clear the outlet before the valve was attached.

We found that short, sharp bursts of air were more efficient in removing the sand and also more economical of gas than prolonged jets. Where the surface of sand to be removed was very wet or smooth, it was loosened a little first with a dentist's probe. It was, of course, wise to avoid using the compressed air near any surface recently painted with preservative. The flying sand would otherwise produce a burial coated like emery-paper.

Preservatives

The bones were hardened, when necessary, with Vinalak 5249, polyvinyl acetate (PVA) dissolved in alcohol, or with Vinamul 9807, PVA with a wetting agent. The former was used on dry or slightly damp bones, the latter on very wet bones. Vinamul is awkward to use, taking much longer to dry. The bones remain soft until the solvent has evaporated completely. Vinalak, on the other hand, will not penetrate into bone if this is very wet. Both are supplied as thick viscous fluids which have to be diluted with ethyl alcohol (maximum strength 96 per cent, see Plenderleith 1957) before use. The proportions vary a little depending on weather conditions and objectives desired, but are approximately 1 part PVA to 3 parts alcohol. A very thick solution will not penetrate very far but may be useful to form a protective cradling film. A very thin solution may go through the bone too readily, forming a clump below the object to be hardened. The treated bone can be softened again by simply applying alcohol. The softening can be done selectively and if an acetone-based glue, such as Tarzan's Grip, is used to stick fragments together, it is possible to clean or remove piece after piece of a bone or a bundle without risking the collapse of all the parts. (Acetone is, however, a solvent for PVA also.) Note that since this time research has been done on preservatives available in and suitable for Australian conditions (Ambrose 1968). The comments on consistency and application may remain valid, but it is likely that other brand names are more suitable. The ones mentioned above were not without their problems, but were the best we could find at short notice.

The PVA was usually applied with a small artist's brush, dripping or brushing it on to the pieces to be hardened. When a surface was very flaky or when a part had to be hardened from below or reached through a narrow opening – as in the case of the interior part of the facial skeleton – this application was made much easier and safer by using a syringe full of Vinalak in a manner similar to a water-pistol (figs. 10 and 109). A 20 cubic centimetre syringe holds enough to avoid constant refilling, but is still easy to manoeuvre. The solution has to be kept thin, especially when the weather is hot and the bore of the needle very fine. The best size for this is a matter of experiment. The aim is to get a fine unbroken jet. Using a syringe also makes it easier to apply small amounts and to judge exactly how much preservative has been used. If the syringe is kept in a polythene bag or glass tube with a few spoonfuls of alcohol and the needle is stuck into cottonwool soaked in alcohol, the equipment will not clog or dry for quite a few hours. If it is not to be used again for several days, it is advisable to clean it with alcohol immediately after use.

Fig.109. Use of syringe to apply PVA.

Supports

The burials were supported when necessary (fig. 110). We used lengths of ¼ inch and 3/8 inch steel rods which, when pushed well down into the sand, stayed firmly in place. To these were fixed, using clamps and boss-heads (normally used for laboratory apparatus), specially made pads of foam plastic covered with gauze and mounted on strips of malleable metal. This had to be soft enough to bend easily into the required curve but solid enough to actively support the weight of a skull full of sand. These were set on short steel rods which could be held by the clamps.

Clearing a vertical bundle-burial

Once the first evidence of the burial – generally the upper ends of the long bones or the vault of the skull – started appearing in the horizontal plane, it was a matter of deciding where the section should go. The sand on one side of this line was removed to a depth of a few centimetres at a time, watching the section to see if anything unusual or very typical appeared. When three-quarters of the skull was clear, the section was photographed (and drawn, if it contained stratigraphical details that might not show up in a photograph). The sand on the other side of the line was then removed in the same way. Trowels were used for the main work, but only dentist's probes, fruit-knives, brushes, and compressed air once the work was going on close to bone. The sand was loosened a little with a probe or a knife, any rootlets cut with small, pointed, sharp scissors and the sand then

Fig.110. B.81, supported, impregnated with PVA and drying before being lifted as a block. Camera facing north.

brushed or blown away. A half-inch paint-brush and an artist's brush No. 3 were most in use. The orbits and the nasal region were cleared of matrix only if the surrounding bone seemed in very good condition. Compressed air was used for this and the pressure lowered by about half unless the bone seemed exceptionally solid. In other cases, the matrix was left and this as well as the adjacent bone set with PVA to provide support for the facial skeleton. Any teeth showing signs of coming loose were fixed firmly into their sockets, preferably with the acetone based glue.

If the skull was cracking badly but the fragments still in situ, the skull was mapped. Each fragment was numbered and symbols painted across the fracture lines. The fragments were then painted with PVA. If there seemed to be any chance of getting at an opening in the skull through which the sand in it could be removed, we avoided letting the PVA penetrate into this sand. This was done by painting over the fragments with a solution which was thicker than usual, which penetrated a little but which also formed a surface film. Once the PVA was dry, clamps were shaped to follow the cranial contour as closely as possible to ensure an even distribution of pressure and placed around the skull to take the weight. Their positions depended on whether the skull was leaning and in which direction. If possible, one was put against the occiput and another against the frontal bone, both of which are usually relatively solid. One arm of one clamp was placed as far as possible underneath the skull. Some of the sand in the skull was then removed if there was a suitable gap. First it was loosened bit by bit with a probe, rootlets were then cut, and then it was lifted out with a long fine curette or a spoon. The facial skeleton was disturbed as little as possible, since many of the bones in this

area are very fragile. The inner surfaces of any vault fragments were then hardened with PVA if they could be reached. This was done a little at a time, allowing each part to dry before proceeding to the next to avoid softening of the whole dome and the risk of collapse.

The neighbouring sand was then cleared, first on one, then on the other side of the section line, down to the level of the base of the skull which was then undermined. Most of the undermining was done with compressed air. If the foramen magnum became visible, sand was removed from inside the skull through this opening also, by using compressed air and probes alternately. While undermining, if was particularly important to free completely the teeth, the palate, and the pterygoid regions from the embedding soil matrix. (No sand was removed from the ear holes to avoid loss of the "hammer" bone. Adhesive tape was used to cover the opening if the bone was solid, otherwise the sand inside was set with PVA before the skull was moved.) The skull was ready to be lifted when all visible rootlets joining it to other bones or the surrounding matrix had been cut and — if PVA had been used — after a few drops of alcohol had been applied to soften any areas of adhesion to other bone or matrix. The lifting needed two operators; one supported the skull with both hands while the other loosened and removed the clamps. The former then gently and carefully lifted the skull in the direction previously decided while the latter stood ready to remove any obstacles appearing or to cut any rootlets still holding the skull. The skull was then inverted and placed, vertex down, in its box. This was specially made and had been marked with the number of the burial. The bottom was first padded with woodwool forming a little nest and this was covered with newspaper. Rolls of crumpled newspaper were placed between the skull and the sides of the box to eliminate movement. Fragile parts of the now exposed skull base were cleaned and treated with PVA is necessary. The skull was allowed to dry completely before storage, and any remaining sand run out and collected in a plastic bag (to be used for various tests). The sand would flow freely once it had dried. It was not advisable to leave any sand inside a skull unless both bone and sand were well impregnated with PVA; such impregnation, although occasionally necessary, is a nuisance. A small pad of Kleenex tissue was placed across the orbits (or any other very fragile parts) between the bone and the newspaper once the bone was quite dry.

The skull was sometimes so firmly wedged between the upper ends of some long bones that part of the underlying bundle had to be lifted before any attempt could be made to remove it. It was then particularly important to support both skull and bundle since any sand left inside the skull made it very heavy and the bundle below was largely unsupported by its surrounding matrix.

If the bundle was leaning at all, it was best to approach it from the upper face. Since the long bones often protruded well up to or above the level of the skull, it was usually possible to take the direction of lean into account when deciding where the section should go. The sand was, if possible, removed from this side of the bundle, still working in spits of about 4 centimetres. Care was taken not to undermine any part of the bundle, and the lower part of a bone to be lifted was left embedded in the sand for as long as possible. Compressed air was particularly useful for removing the sand between and behind the bones. Long fine dissecting forceps or converted sponge-holding forceps were used to reach in between the bones still in situ, when small bones and fragments freed by the air blast had to be removed. Bones were marked before any treatment with PVA. White ink was found to run less on wet bone. Wet bone sometimes became stronger on drying, but too long exposure of the bundle increased the risk of collapse, and uneven drying, that is of part of the outer surface only, caused cracking and splitting. Wet bone was sometimes lifted and allowed to dry before packing, being turned over now and again. Eroded ends of long bones were treated with PVA, the sand filling the crevasses being left in situ. Bandaging the ends with gauze soaked in PVA, as tried at first, did more damage in the end, since the gauze took bits of bone with it when removed, however well it was softened with alcohol first. Scapulae were usually treated with PVA, whatever the condition of the rest of the burial, since they would otherwise fragment during lifting or transport.

One bone at a time was freed from sand and rootlets, lifted and packed. Long bones and pelvic bones were wrapped in newspaper. This was ideal for any but the most fragile bones. These and loose teeth, fragments, etc. were wrapped in Kleenex tissue and placed in polythene bags. Vertebrae were arranged in rows with newspaper between them, or, if very fragile, put in separate polythene bags, as were the scapulae. (We avoided using cottonwool unless it had been wrapped in tissue first. It tends to get entangled in small projections of bone or caught on flaky surfaces and does much damage while being removed. Sawdust is useless.) The bags were left open, or opened later, until the bone inside was quite dry. The postcranial bones were placed in specially made stout cardboard boxes long enough to hold the longest femur. Bottom and sides were first lined with crumpled newspaper and a pad of this placed on top, before putting on the lid. The boxes and all plastic bags used were marked with the burial number and the label used in photographs of the burial was placed inside the box.

Recording

The method employed for recording the position of bones in each burial was to number each bone as it became visible, using black or white drawing ink, depending on the colour of the bone. Arrows pointing upwards or towards the skull were added on the shafts of the long bones to assist in later identification of orientation. A list of numbers was kept for each burial and each number ticked off when used on a bone and again when the bone was finally lifted. Badly cracked skulls were mapped as shown in figure 18. The whole burial was photographed, if possible from several different directions so as to display all markings, and the bones then removed in lifts (a small number of bones at a time). Rarely were bones lifted that would not have been showing in the last photograph taken of the burial. After each lift, any new bones showing were marked and another photograph taken. The bones removed were listed for each lift or packed as a group labelled, for example "lift 1". The photographs were listed and described in a separate register as well as on the appropriate burial form. Each photograph included a scale of 10 centimetres or 1 metre and a label showing the number of the burial, its name and its place in the grid. The photographic register listed the serial number of the photograph, the film used, the direction in which the camera was pointing, the number of the burial, its position in the grid, any special feature to be noticed, and anything else that might be useful in interpreting the photograph later on.

This method was, however, not without its problems. Taking the photographs was a full-time job for one person. A great number of repetitive photographs had to be taken since there was always the chance of some technical mishap such as wrong exposure or slipping film. This was a major problem in the early seasons when we had only an old and worn camera. It was often a matter of getting the camera into very odd angles and difficult corners. The tripod had to be positioned in such a way that it could not topple onto the burial, while providing room for the photographer to work. Flash-guns proved unsatisfactory, particularly when the bone had been treated with PVA and the surface was somewhat shiny. Reflectors were used to eliminate shadows when photographs were taken in the open. In sunny weather, the sharp contrast between the light-coloured dry sand and the dark pit-fill and bone made shading with tarpaulins necessary. In rainy weather, the light was poor, particularly since tarpaulins had to be kept erected over the trenches. The coloured tarpaulins distorted colour photographs, so colour film was used only under favourable conditions, which were rare indeed. The bones, especially those in the upper part of the ridge, were often almost the same colour as the surrounding matrix, particularly when wet, and careful undercutting along their contours was necessary to make them show on a photograph. We have on an average seven photographs per burial, but this in fact means two or three each for scanty remains set with PVA and lifted in toto, and a dozen or more for the better preserved examples.

Note: The preservatives were supplied by Reichhold Chemicals Inc. (Aust.) Pty. Ltd., 49 - 61 Stephen Road, Botany, New South Wales.

Skull boxes were 10 inch x 8 inch x 8 inch (depth) and made of 2/16 inch cardboard.

Boxes for long bones were 21½ inch x 15½ inch x 6 inch.

Five samples from the burial ground have been tested so far. The results are as follows:

ANU - 67   450 ± 70 B.P. (A.D.1500)

Description of sample and site reference:	Charred wood or bark, Q.1, C.8, Broadbeach burial ground, Queensland.
Details of pretreatment:	Charcoal pieces were penetrated with rootlets. These were removed under a microscope and the charcoal flakes washed in 2N HCl, rinsed with distilled water, and dried.
Statement of error involved and other comments:	Three independent benzene liquid scintillation determinations were carried out on your sample.

ANU - 67/1   14/11/66 resulted in an erroneous age of 10200 ± 300 B.P. due to a then unobserved equipment error. Because of this two further independent determinations were made.

ANU - 67/2 25/10/67   440 ± 100 B.P.   Counting time: 1220 min.

ANU - 67/3 22/3/68   460 ± 100 B.P.   Counting time: 980 min.

The result ANU - 67 is reported as the mean value of the two last determinations, and the error is ± 1 standard deviation based on the total counting time of these two determinations of 2200 minutes.

ANU - 68   1290 ± 70 B.P. (A.D.660)

Description of sample and site reference:	Charcoal, Q.1, C.1a, Broadbeach burial ground, Queensland.
Details of pretreatment:	No rootlet contamination observed. Sample washed in 2N HCl followed by a distilled water rinse and drying.
Statement of error involved and other comments:	Two independent benzene liquid scintillation determinations were carried out.

ANU - 68/1   10/11/66   1190 ± 100 y   Time = 1200 min.

ANU - 68/2   25/ 3/68   1390 ± 100 y   Time = 1020 min.

The result ANU - 68 is reported as the mean value of the two determinations (which are in excellent agreement), and the error is ± 1 standard deviation based on the total counting time of 2220 minutes.

The ANU report form states:

By international agreement all radiocarbon ages are reported using Libby half-life of 5568 y and 95% of the measured activity of the Oxalic Acid C - 14 Standard as Modern reference sample.

The stated error is based upon uncertainties of physical measurements of the Standard, Background and Sample and does not include the half-life error, or the uncertainty of the half-life determination itself. The error is quoted as 1 standard deviation.

The radiocarbon reference year is A.D. 1950 and this applies both to the ages expressed Before Present (B.P.) and the laboratory calculated Christian calendar age.

V - 157   1110 ± 85 B.P. (A.D.840)

Description of sample and site:	Broadbeach burial ground, Queensland. Charcoal lying on ankles of extended burial B.37; from just above C horizon. Sample Q.1, C.1a.
Sample pretreatment:	Hydrochloric acid.
Reference Standard and errors:	Age calculation has been based on the C - 14 half-life of 5568 yr and uses a reference activity of 0.950 NBS oxalic acid standard.
	The quoted uncertainty in the age (1 standard deviation) is derived from the counting statistics and does not include the uncertainty in the half-life figure. No correction has been made for isotopic fractionation of the sample.

V - 161   50 ± 80 B.P. (A.D.1900)

Description of sample and site:	Broadbeach burial ground, Queensland. Charcoal from upper part of pit holding burial B.100. Sample Q.1, C.8.
Sample pretreatment:	Hydrochloric acid.
Reference Standard and errors:	As above.

V - 162   1180 ± 105 B.P. (A.D.770)

Description of sample and site:	Broadbeach burial ground, Queensland. Charcoal from left cheek of burial B.37. Sample Q.1, C.1b.
Sample pretreatment:	Hydrochloric acid.
Reference Standard and errors:	As above.

Table 8. *Selected radiocarbon dates*

Site	Lab. No.	Date B.P.	Date B.C. or A.D.	Reference	Comments
Bendemeer I (N.S.W.)	GaK-569	410 ± 40	A.D.1540	Mulvaney 1969	Latest backed blades (including geometric microliths)
Burrill Lake (N.S.W.)	ANU-139	1660 ± 70	A.D.290	Mulvaney and Golson 1971	Backed blades (plus elouera, fabricators, flakes with use-polish, thumbnail scrapers and larger scrapers)
Capertee (N.S.W.)	V-33	2865 ± 57	915 B.C.	Bermingham 1966	Backed blades
Curracurrang (N.S.W.)	GaK-688	2360 ± 90	410 B.C.	Megaw 1966	Earliest backed blades) (Also elouera, geometric microliths, microscrapers.
	GaK-689	840 ± 90	A.D.1110	Megaw 1966	Latest backed blades) Fabricators and edge-ground axes persist later)
Graman:B:1 (N.S.W.)	GaK-1188	3950 ± 80	2000 B.C.	McBryde 1968	
	ANU-54	2760 ± 65	810 B.C.	McBryde 1968	Backed blades (plus geometric microliths, scrapers, burins, grinding stones)
	GaK-1187	2040 ± 70	90 B.C.	McBryde 1968	
Graman:B:4 (N.S.W.)	GaK-1190	2480 ± 80	530 B.C.	McBryde 1968	
	ANU-56	2290 ± 62	340 B.C.	McBryde 1968	Blade-tool industry dominated by Bondi points and geometric microliths
	ANU-55	2050 ± 55	100 B.C.	McBryde 1968	
	GaK-1189	1750 ± 80	A.D.200	McBryde 1968	
Gymea Bay (N.S.W.)	NSW-6	1220 ± 55	A.D.730	Megaw and Wright 1966	Backed blades (Plus burins, adze-flakes, ground-edge axes. Fabricators dominate. Note flexed burials present.)
Kenniff Cave (Q.)	NPL-65	3830 ± 90	1880 B.C.	Mulvaney 1969	Earliest backed blades) (Also geometric microliths, elouera, grinding techniques,
	NPL-32	2550 ± 90	600 B.C.	Mulvaney 1969	Latest backed blades) some tulas and a burin)
Lapstone Creek (N.S.W.)	ANU-10	3650 ±100	1700 B.C.	Mulvaney 1969	Backed blades (Bondi points) present (type site for Bondaian)
		2300 ± 100	350 B.C.	Mulvaney 1969	Bondi points disappear, elouera present
Seelands (N.S.W.)	V-11	2850 ± 50	900 B.C.	Bermingham 1966	Blade tools (including Bondi points, geometric microliths), uniface pebble tools
	V-25	870 ± 80	A.D.1080	Bermingham 1966	Blade and uniface pebble tools
	V-10	625 ± 85	A.D.1325	Bermingham 1966	Uniface pebble tools and blade tools (including geometric microliths)
	V-26	350 ± 60	A.D.1600	Bermingham 1966	Uniface pebble tools and blade tools
The Tombs (Q.)	NPL-31	3600 ± 93	1650 B.C.	Mulvaney 1969	Pirris and backed blades
Wombah (N.S.W.)	GaK-568	3230 ± 100	1280 B.C.	Mulvaney 1969	Shell midden with uniface pebble tools and Bondi points

Table 8 gives some radiocarbon dates from other sites in Australia, selected because they may be of interest with regard to their age and their content of stone implements.

Chapter 1. The Burial Ground

1. Ordinance Survey map, 1 inch:1 mile, series Queensland and N.S.W., "Springbrook", 602201. Australia 1:50,000, sheet 9541 - 1, ed. 1, series R 733,56JNP411983.
2. Gardner 1955, p. 17: "They appear to have originated, as the dunes did, through the silting of an earlier bay and a consequent seaward advance of the shore-line. Apparently each sand ridge represents a sand-spit or sand-bar that extended northward from the southern end of the bay at about the outer edge of the surf-zone, enclosing on its landward side the former beach and a narrow strip of shallow water, now the swamp."
3. Personal communication from Dr. F.W. Whitehouse, who has visited the site. This type of rain forest is also called vine forest.
4. It is only now that, having excavated the top of the ridge and some of the surrounding slope, we can be reasonably certain that the burial ground was limited to this flat, top part.
5. The Aboriginal Relics Preservation Act of 1967 was gazetted in May 1968.
6. The beetles feed on eucalypt foliage, but the curl-grubs live in the soil, feeding on roots and decaying organic matter.
7. For other known burial grounds being excavated see Gill 1967 and Pretty 1971.
8. We wanted to investigate more of the surroundings but it seemed urgent to save the burials first.
9. All sand and soil was sieved and everything but fresh rootlets kept.

Chapter 2. The Burials

1. The terms primary and secondary burial can have several meanings in archaeological usage. I am following the anthropological tradition, see Winick 1958: "Burial, secondary. A final burying of a person's bones, after the first temporary burial during which the flesh has decomposed..." Note that according to written accounts, quoted in chapter 6, the first stage did not necessarily, in Australia, involve interment. Mrs. Hiatt (1969) divides burials in terms of simple or compound procedures. Her compound burials were disposed of in two or more stages which took place at different times over varying periods of time. It is quite possible that the primary burials at Broadbeach were compound burials just as were the secondary burials.
2. Fuller references to individual burials mentioned in the text are given in Appendix D.
3. The very fragmentary and decayed remains of B.42 could belong to a similar burial judging from the pieces left. The skull, never found (unless it is B.24 or B.50) should have been to the south, the legs were bent back almost parallel with the trunk and all but the feet removed by the pit holding the later burials B.48+50.
   Dr. Wood comments: "It is possible that the more important and better preserved bones of B.42 (e.g. skull and long bones) could have been lifted by whoever dug the pit for B.48 and then included with the latter to make the unusual double burial B.48+50. If B.42 were originally similar to B.102, the greater compactness of the bones in the burial would allow all or most to be fortuitously exposed in a pit for a vertical bundle, hence the major part could well have been lifted as opposed to only the leg bones of B.52. There were only a few small vertebral fragments in the B.48+50 complex and no hand or foot bones. The remnants of B.42 were rather light in structure and probably from a female — B.50?"
4. Vertical bundle-burials, see type V.5 in table 7. There were eighty-three certain and thirteen probable cases. Note that some were multiple and some which were counted as single may be found to be multiple.
5. Differences in the directions of alignment in long bones have not yet been studied and tabulated and it is not known whether these show any observable regularity.
6. Burials of this type can be found in the collections of the Queensland Museum.
7. B.40, B.88, B.91, B.132, B.136, B.138, total: 6.
8. B.25, B.55, B.67, B.70, B.84, total: 5.
9. See Appendix D. Burials of unknown type form 25 per cent of the total.
10. Burials B.38, B.45, B.48, B.73, B.100, B.116, and probably B.136 caused major damage to other burials; B.29, B.43, B.49, B.60, and B.97 minor damage; and burials B.25, B.30, B.41, B.71, B.95, B.104, and B.130 caused no visible damage.
11. The left humerus of B.52. It was photographed when the burial was found and it could not be a case similar to that of B.116, p. 23.
12. Level 1 was too shallow to have held all of a burial and too few parts of the body were represented amongst the fragments to make this at all likely. See chapter 3 for descriptions of levels 1 and 2.
13. These have not been counted and cannot be discussed in this report. It may later be possible to try to match them with disturbed burials and to estimate how many persons could be represented by the remainder.
14. Composite burials: the term is equivalent to compound burials as described by Hiatt 1969.
15. Dr. Wood comments: "She must have been in the ground long enough for the soft tissues to be completely decomposed, i.e. some considerable time, probably 3 - 6 months, must have elapsed between burial and subsequent disturbance. The Aborigines obviously knew just how long a body had to decay before it was ready to be disarticulated and bundled. Such a period would not be long enough for grass to obliterate the outline of the pit."
16. Over B.77 this surface had been removed by soil contractors.
17. In the thesis these were mistakenly quoted as *Amesodesma angusta*. The latter form only a small proportion of the wedge shells present, see Appendix C.
18. Noted for burials B.6, B.12, B.15, B.16, B.23, B.25, B.28, B.29, B.45, B.63, B.79, B.123, B.130, B.133, B.136, B.137, B.138, B.140.
19. Noted for burials B.4, B.15, B.16, B.61, B.93.
20. Possible implications are discussed in chapter 6, p. 83 and in Appendix E.
21. Note that a small baby, B.68, was found inside B.61.
22. Chapter 3 contains the stratigraphical evidence.
23. A detailed discussion can be found in my thesis, p. 48.
24. These shells have sharp edges. Compare the presence of sharp flakes in some burials, Appendix E.
25. A couple of very decayed burials which may but need not have been of V.5 type have been excluded from the count. The presence (x) or probable presence (?) of red pigment is shown in table 7.
26. These are B.1, B.9, B.10, B.14, B.32, B.112, B.117, B.125.
27. The presence of red pigment indicates that cremation was part of a compound procedure (see Hiatt 1969).

Chapter 3. Stratigraphy, Relative and Absolute Dating

1. Compare the ratio of artifacts to weight of shell in these two sites; the second a shell midden:
   Broadbeach burial ground: 1 artifact per 100 grams
   Cascade Gardens: 1 artifact per 65,380 grams.
   This site was published as Haglund-Calley and Quinnell 1973; see plate 27.
2. Weighing the shells seemed the best way to get a picture of the quantities present. A straight count of numbers would have been misleading since the shells vary in size and condition, some being broken into minute fragments. Note, however, that shells lose weight with time under conditions such as in this site.
3. The only shells found in test pits several metres outside the area of burials were along a modern track used by soil trucks and the shells are most likely to have spilled off loads taken away from the burial ground.
4. It is unlikely that many late burials had been removed from the north and northeastern parts of area A, since the soil disturbance here was shallow and the lower part of any disturbed pit showed up below this.
5. See discussion on pp. 59, 62.
6. Compare also maps 8 and 9, showing the total weights of stone present in the site and the total weight of stone with marks of use or retouch.
7. Note that the position of a burial in these diagrams shows its relation to

another, *not* its actual depth in the ground. Map 12 shows the horizontal relationships.

8. The trench floor for B.52 was flat and there was no elevation of head and feet above trunk level. This suggests that the sand was wet when the trench was dug. B.52 could not be later than B.37 or it would have caused the feet of the latter to shift from the position in which they were found.

9. Compare the discussion of B.116 on p. 23.

10. The anatomical details and relationships of burials B.99, B.107, B.106A, and B.106B remain to be studied.

11. Compare the notes on B.73, pp. 45, 47 and B.116, p. 23.

12 When the details of the police investigation were available and plotted it became obvious that the skull belonging to this bundle could be one removed by the police (Appendix D, P.B.6).

13. Even at the time of excavation, when many little rootlets, bigger roots, and the general compaction of the sand helped to consolidate the bundles, it was always necessary to support them to prevent collapse.

14. Compare the age of the Forest Red Gum, p. 55. An age of three hundred years before death would not have been unusual for some species growing in this area before it was cleared by Europeans.

15. The Australian National University laboratory asks for 1,000 grams of bone per test. All the bones in the body are studied and may be important in supplying information on disease or injury. However, once the pathology has been studied, the ribs, which are put to less use in comparative osteological studies than other postcranial bones, are generally the first to be released for radiocarbon and other tests. Ribs in an adult well-preserved burial weigh about 300 grams. But see Sellstedt, Engstrand, and Gejvall 1966, for a method of determining the exact quantity of bone needed per test by determining the nitrogen content in a small sample.

16. For reasons already given, we cannot embark on a programme involving a series of bone sample tests until a later date. However, 300 grams of ribs from B.37 will soon be tested by the laboratory at the Institute of Applied Science in Melbourne to complement the tests done on charcoal associated with this burial.

17. The sea level has been rising and the 0.6 metre emergence meant a sea level only slightly below the present, the 2 metre submergence a sea level about 0.6 metres above the present; cf. Gardner 1955, p.35.

18. Gardner 1955, p.16 and tables 14 - 16.

19. Personal information from Mr. J.E. Coaldrake, C.S.I.R.O., who visited the site during excavation. He saw some typical sections, including the one through the flexed burial B.116, and commented that from his experience this burial must be fairly recent.

20. Less than 3 kilometres further north, at Bundall, were the very disturbed remains of what had clearly been a burial ground of the same kind, though less extensive even before disturbance. A brief report was included in my unpublished thesis as Appendix H. This site was published as Haglund 1975.

Chapter 4. The Living Population as Represented by Its Bones

1. This chapter remains almost entirely as in my unpublished thesis. Further work has been done on the skeletal material but the results are not ready for publication.

2. Dr. Wood has very generously allowed me to use and quote all results from his studies of this skeletal material that may be relevant to this chapter. The diagrams of age and sex distribution are directly based on his findings; descriptions of injury or pathology are almost direct quotations. Comments on the anthropological or archaeological aspects are my own responsibility.

3. Preliminary studies of the Broadbeach material indicate that it falls well within the normal range of variation published for Aboriginal skeletal remains. Compare: Fenner 1939, pp.248 - 306; Krogman 1932, p.399; Wood-Jones 1929, pp.353 - 55; idem 1934, pp.323 - 30; Morant 1927, pp.417 - 40; Larnach and Macintosh 1965.

4. Compare the following; Webb 1946; Snow 1948; Santiago 1960, p.205; Johnston and Snow 1961, p.328; Snow 1962, p.69; idem 1965, p.328.

5. A good summary of the problems and theories referred to here can be found by N.W.G. MacIntosh in Berndt and Berndt 1965, pp.29 - 70.

6. Some references to this type of bias will be found in chapter 6.

7. No long bones had been split, nor had the foramen magnum been enlarged nor any other attempts made to produce artificial openings in the skull. Compare references to mortuary cannibalism in chapter 6.

8. Not all skulls have been examined and the following list is not complete,

but can be used to indicate trends.
   R. Upper Central Incisor removed: B.0, B.11, B.15, B.37, B.52, B.63, B.72, B.82A, B.82B, B.98 (total 10).
   L. Upper Central Incisor removed: B.47, B.48 (total 2).
   Both Upper Central Incisors removed: B.43 (total 1).
   R. Upper Lateral Incisor removed: B.64 (total 1).

9. Only three definite cases have been recorded — viz. B.5, B.38, and B.73 — but most burials have not yet been fully examined for this condition.

10. Only four cases of caries have been recorded so far. Four other cases of apical abscess were probably due to excessive dental attrition, not caries. The above findings are based mainly on the mandibular dentition.

Chapter 5. The Lithic Material

1. Note, however, a suggestion in Appendix E that the presence of pebbles was also related to that of burials.

2. Written accounts and recorded reminiscences suggest that it may be possible to find quarry sites or areas of origin for some of these. This will be a time-consuming task. It forms part of my present research project.

3. One form of use for these could have been to mark graves (cf. chapter 6).

4. This was done by weight and not by number of pieces, since the unused stone particularly had often rotted badly and was falling to pieces even after collection.

5. It was part of the corona and the association can not be doubted.

6. I am most grateful to the Reverend E.D. Stockton for his helpful suggestions, interesting discussions, and the loan of manuscripts describing his own system.

7. The present spate of articles querying traditional typological systems suggests that we may do well in sorting out our aims before starting on the methods (cf. White 1969, pp.18 - 19).

8. White 1968 challenges the assumption that fabricators were actually implements and suggests that they were cores. Note, however, the typical use-fracture on a large number found in the burial ground. Some fabricators found here were made on rather thin flakes, some on core-tablets, and some may have started as cores. Note that they are of a standardized shape and that this shape is not reminiscent of any group of cores found.

9. See McCarthy 1967, p.36 and pp. 90 - 93 and in Berndt and Berndt 1965, pp. 73 - 80.

10. Such small scrapers were among the few implements found in the Cascade Gardens shell midden, see chapter 3, note 1.

11. The following burials had more than one well-made artifact in this position: B.16, B.32, B.36, B.138.

12. I have not yet been able to study Dr. McBryde's Ph.D. thesis in detail to compare the artifact content of the burial ground with that of sites excavated by her. See, however, p. 55 for her comments.

Chapter 6. Written Accounts versus Archaeological Evidence

1. This account is based on Taylor 1967.

2. Written by a local school teacher, McCarthy, who had access to private collections of diaries and letters not yet available to scholars.

3. Lenz, n.d., p.11. J.C. Taylor considers him a reliable source, having investigated other claims made in his memoirs.

4. Welsby 1937, p.114. Not a reliable source, but this account is confirmed by others.

5. Watkins 1890 - 91, p.47. A methodical, reliable eye-witness.

6. W.G. Curtis, North Tamborine, seventy-seven years old in 1963. He was in the Nerang area while there were still Aborigines wandering around.

7. Burial in ant hills crops up in several reminiscences, but it is not explained whether this was done to some classes of people (e.g. only women). The wife of "King Jacky" of the Logan and Albert Rivers was buried in this way. She was a cripple. (Personal information from J. Colvin.)

8. Resident of Beaudesert for some fifteen years. He has collected much information in the area; the accounts are second- or third-hand but collected with circumspection and care.

9. When I saw this cave some years ago it was still almost undisturbed by humans but animals had clearly scrabbled in the deposit. The bones had but a thin cover of soil; the visible part appeared due to relatively recent weathering of the roof above.

10. The following information is taken from Sullivan 1964; this gives detailed references to sources, mostly letters and press-cuttings, in the Richmond River Historical Society archives.

11. One of these informants has recently died.

12. Cf. Petrie 1932, pp.32 - 33. Part of many eye-witness accounts quoted in this chapter, but left out of some for lack of space.

13. Jenny, described as a "black gin from Kyogle", had this treatment: "... hands and feet were tied together and the body slung over a stick." See E.J. Johnson, The life story of William Martin Johnson of Casino; and other reminiscences, 29 June 1957. Typed MS, Richmond River Historical Society archives, p.4.

14. Cf. Lang 1861, p.356: "The cuticle ... peeled off ... and as the cutis vera, or true skin, is, in all varieties of the human family, prefectly white, the corpse then appears of that colour all over; and I have no doubt whatever, that it is this peculiar and ghastly appearance ... that has suggested to them the idea that white men are merely their forefathers returned to life again ... "

15. Petrie 1932. Some "sentiments" have been left out.

16. *Moreton Bay Courier,* 12 May 1849.

17. It is frequently stressed that women came from outside the "tribe"; this is perhaps important to the anatomical interpretations. Cf. Petrie 1932, pp.11 - 12, 16, 59 - 60, 137.

18. E. Bray, History of Lismore. Typed MS, Richmond River Historical Society archives, p.1.

19. Hiatt 1969, p.109 and table 4, quotes sources and tabulates evidence suggesting that females and very young or very old members of the group were considered less important. They were therefore often cremated in areas where this was a treatment given the less important of the dead. See also Elkin 1954, p.315 and Petrie 1932, p.36.

20. Petrie 1932, p.19: "... they never failed to eat anyone killed in fight, and always ate a man noted for his fighting qualities, or a *turrwan* (great man), no matter how old he was, or even if he died from consumption!! ... The tough old gins had the best of it; no one troubled to eat them; their bodies weren't of any importance, and had no pity or consideration shown them ..." Cf. also Elkin 1954, pp.292, 317.

21. At Roonka, however, grave no.50 contained a fully extended adult man with a crouched infant across his body. Cf. Pretty 1971.

22. Apart from the accounts quoted see also Elkin 1954, pp.313 - 14 and Hiatt 1969, pp.104,109, for composite burial rites as characteristic especially of north and east Queensland.

23. See Elkin 1954, pp.298 - 99 and note 203.

24. Petrie 1932, p.34 and Lang 1861, pp.355 - 56.

25. Cf. Petrie 1932, p.30; Lang 1861, p.354; Curr 1886 - 87, vol.III, p.165; and J. Ainsworth (1847 - 1922), Reminiscences. Typed MS, Richmond River Historical Society archives.

26. Berndt and Berndt 1964, p.401. Cf. also Petrie 1932, p.35 (how Tom Petrie was given pieces of skin) and pp.197 - 200 (Wanangga wills away his skin; his bones are later collected by relatives).

27. We cannot say, until all bone sheets for the burials are completed, whether there is evidence of removal of finger joints or whole hands, as suggested in some sources. Cf. Petrie 1932, p.57; Curr 1886 - 87, vol.III,p.138 (for Mooloola groups); and Berndt and Berndt 1964, p.399. Phalanges were certainly present in some burials.

28. There are records of burials being marked with stones, e.g. at Limpinwood in the Tweed Valley where the grave had white lumps of chalcedony marking its centre; according to local information this was an inhumation, sitting, dating from the first period of cedar-cutters, after the late 1840s. The "Grave of the Aboriginal Giantess" at Terragon in the Tweed district, marked with bright lumps of light coloured rocks, is said to be a grave predating European settlement. This information comes from McBryde 1966, pp. 216 - 17, who comments that it is somewhat uncertain that these features are in fact graves.

29. This is the label given some similar bones held by the Queensland Museum in Brisbane; note, however, that one such bone came from inside the lower part of the core of B.28.

30. Berndt and Berndt 1964, p. 390. But see p. 80 of this book.

31. As suggested in Petrie's account.

32. Such fires are sometimes said to have been quite big.

33. Elkin 1954,p.299. Note that he mentions that in some areas red, white, or black was used, the choice depending on one's relationship to the dead person. Cf. also Curr 1886 - 87, vol.III, p.138. He states that the Mooloola "tribe" (on the coast a little north of Brisbane) colour themselves red for mourning, skin the dead, eat the flesh, and deposit the bundled bones in a tree.

34. Berndt and Berndt 1964, pp.390,405. The emphasis of the word "repeatedly" is mine.

35. Berndt and Berndt 1964, p.398: "Victorian tribes are said to have placed the body on the funeral pyre with the head to the east."

36. Petrie 1932, p.49. Kippa-ring means initiation ground, *kippa* being the local term for first degree initiation.

37. Reports on these sites: Megaw 1965,1966,1967a, and Megaw and Wright 1966.

38. These facts are stressed in the article quoted in note 39.

39. Megaw 1967b. He shows how useful – though difficult – such comparisons can be and that far too little attention has been paid to the possibilities they offer.

40. This material is now available as a thesis (Meehan 1971, pp.265 - 66, figs.23 - 27). The author has summarized the results from archaeological excavations revealing burials. For detailed comparisons it is necessary to turn to original excavation reports. Sites from the same period as Broadbeach listed by her are: Ball's Head, Blaxland's Flat, Cape Otway, Curracurrang, Currarong, Fromm's Landing, Gidgealpa, Gymea Bay and Kurnell, all from the southeast quarter of Australia.

Appendix A. Sand and Soil in the Ridge
1. The skull of B.4 was just below the pocket of shells.
2. The Munsell Soil Colour Chart was used to measure colour.

Bibliography

Ambrose, W.
1968. Conservation in the field. *Kalori* 35:34 - 45.
Bateson, C.
1966. *Patrick Logan, tyrant of Brisbane Town.* Sydney: Ure Smith.
Bermingham, A.
1966. Victoria natural radiocarbon measurements I. *Radiocarbon* 8:507 - 21.
Berndt, R.M., and Berndt, C.H.
1964. *The world of the first Australians.* Sydney: Ure Smith.
Berndt, R.M., and Berndt, C.H., eds.
1965. *Aboriginal man in Australia.* Sydney: Angus and Robertson.
Bowler, J.M.; Jones, R.; Allen, H.; and Thorne, A.G.
1970. Pleistocene human remains from Australia: a living site and human cremation from Lake Mungo, western New South Wales. *World Archaeol.* 2, no. 1:39 - 60.
Breton, H.W.
1833. *Excursions in New South Wales.* London: Richard Bentley.
Coaldrake, J.E.
1962. The coastal sand dunes of southern Queensland. *Proc. R. Soc. Qd* 72:101 - 16.
Crosby, E.
1971. Suggestions for the re-evaluation of some Australian scraper types. *Mem. Qd Mus.* 16(1):153 - 70.
Curr, E.M.
1886 - 87. *The Australian race,* I - IV. Melbourne.
Elkin, A.P.
1954. *The Australian Aborigines: how to understand them.* 3rd ed. Sydney: Angus and Robertson.
Enright, W.J.
1937. Notes on the Aborigines of the north coast of New South Wales. *Mankind* 2, no.4 (June).
Fenner, F.J.
1939. The Australian Aboriginal skeleton; its non-metrical morphological characters. *Trans. R. Soc. S. Aust.* 63:248 - 306.
Flood, J.M.
1970. A point assemblage from the Northern Territory. *Arch. & Phys. Anthrop. in Oceania* 5(1):27 - 52.
Gardner, D.E.
1955. Beach-sand heavy-mineral deposits of eastern Australia. *Commonw. Bur. Miner. Resour. Aust. Bull.* 28.
Gill, E.D.
1962. A.N.Z.A.A.S. meeting Sydney, 20 - 24 August 1962. Typescript, p.2.
1966. Aboriginal sitting burial near Swan Reach, Victoria. *Victorian Nat.* 83, no. 3:48.
1967. The Chowilla project. *Newsl. Aust. Inst. Aboriginal Stud.* 2, no. 6:35 - 41.
Glover, I.C.
1969. The use of factor analysis for the discovery of artifact types. *Mankind* 7, no. 1:36 - 51.
Haglund, L.
1975. Aboriginal relics at Bundall near Surfers Paradise, Queensland. *Occ. Pap.* 4, Anthrop. Mus. Univ. Qd, pp.105 - 16.
Haglund-Calley, L., and Quinnell, M. C.
1973. A shell midden at Cascade Gardens, Broadbeach, southeast Queensland. *Mem. Qd Mus.* 16(3):399 - 409.
Hiatt, B.
1969. Cremation in Aboriginal Australia. *Mankind* 7, no. 2: 104 - 19.

Johnston, E.E., and Snow, C.E.
1961. The reassessment of the age and sex of the Indian Knoll skeletal population; demographic and methodological aspects. *Am. J. phys. Anthrop.* 23:328 (Abstract)
Krogman, W.M.
1932. The morphological characters of the Australian skull. *J. Anat.* 66:399.
Lang, J.D.
1861. *Queensland, Australia.* London: E. Stanford.
Larnach, S.L., and Macintosh, N.W.G.
1965. The craniology of the Aborigines of coastal New South Wales. *Oceania,* monograph 13.
Lenz, C.F.O.
n.d. Memoirs and some history. Mimeographed.
McBryde, I.
1966. An archaeological survey of the New England region, New South Wales. Ph.D. thesis, University of New England, Armidale.
1968. Archaeological investigations in the Graman District. *Arch. & Phys. Anthrop. in Oceania* 3, no. 2:77 - 93.
McCarthy, F.D.
1967. *Australian aboriginal stone implements.* Sydney: Australian Museum.
McMichael, D.F.
1965. *Shells of the Australian sea-shore.* Brisbane: Jacaranda Press.
Meehan, B.
1971. The form, distribution and antiquity of Australian Aboriginal mortuary practices. M.A. thesis, University of Sydney.
Megaw, J.V.S.
1965. Excavations in the Royal National Park, New South Wales: A first series of radiocarbon dates from the Sydney district. *Oceania* 35, no. 3:202 - 207.
1966. Report on excavations in the south Sydney district, 1964 - 65. *Newsl. Aust. Inst. Aboriginal Stud.* 2, no. 3:4 - 15.
1967a. Radiocarbon dates from Curracurrang Cove, New South Wales. *Newsl. Aust. Inst. Aboriginal Stud.* 2, no. 5:26 - 30.
1967b. Archaeology, art and Aborigines. *J. R. Aust. Hist. Soc.* 53, no. 4:1 - 28.
Megaw, J.V.S., and Wright, R.V.S.
1966. The excavation of an Aboriginal rock-shelter on Gymea Bay, Port Hacking, New South Wales. *Arch. & Phys. Anthrop. in Oceania* 1, no. 1:23 - 50.
Morant, G.M.
1927. A study of Australian and Tasmanian skulls based on previously published measurements. *Biometrika* 19:417 - 40.
Mulvaney, D.J.
1969. *The prehistory of Australia.* London: Thames and Hudson.
Mulvaney, D.J., and Golson, J., eds.
1971. *Aboriginal man and environment in Australia.* Canberra: Australian National University Press.
Petrie, C.C.
1932. *Tom Petrie's reminiscences of early Brisbane.* Sydney: Angus and Robertson.
Plenderleith, H.J.
1957. *The conservation of antiquities and works of art.* Oxford: Oxford University Press.
Polach, H.A., and Golson, J.
1966. Collection of specimens for radiocarbon dating and

interpretation of results. *Aust. Inst. Aboriginal Stud.*, manual no. 2, Canberra.

Pretty, G.L.
  1971. The excavations at Roonka Station, Murray River, South Australia, 1968 - 70. FEPA Symposium 1, *Fossil and recent man in Asia, Australia and the Pacific,* Canberra, January 1971 (Abstract).

Santiago, G.T.
  1960. Revaluation of age, stature and sex of the Tepexpan remains, Mexico. *Am. J. phys. Anthrop.* 18:205.

Scott, W.
  1929. *The Port Stephens blacks.* Dungog, N.S.W.: *Chronicle* Office.

Sellstedt, H.; Engstrand, L.; and Gejvall, Dr. N.-G.
  1966. New application of radiocarbon dating to collagen residue in bones. *Nature, Lond.* 212:572 - 74.

Small, J.F.
  1898. Customs and traditions of the Clarence River Aboriginals. *Sci. Man* 21 March.

Snow, C.E.
  1948. Indian Knoll skeletons. *Uni. Ky Rep. Anthropol. Archaeol.* 4, no. 3: Part II.
  1962. An old Hawaiian population on Oahu. *Am. J. phys. Anthrop.* 20:69 (Abstract).
  1965. Vital statistics based on the skeletal remains from Sudanese Nubia. *Am. J. phys. Anthrop.* 23:328 (Abstract).

Sprigg, R.C.
  1952. The geology of the south-eastern province, South Australia, with special reference to Quaternary coastline migrations and modern beach developments. *Geol. Surv. S. Aust. Bull.* 29.

Sullivan, S.
  1964. Aboriginal culture in the Richmond-Tweed districts of northern New South Wales at the time of white settlement. B.A. Hons. thesis, University of New England, Armidale.

Taylor, J.C.
  1967. Race relations in south-east Queensland, 1840 - 1860. B.A.Hons. thesis, University of Queensland.

Watkins, G.
  1890 - 91. Notes on the Aboriginals of Stradbroke and Moreton Islands. *Proc. R. Soc. Qd* 8:40 - 50.

Webb, W.S.
  1946. Indian Knoll. *Uni. Ky Rep. Anthropol. Archaeol.* 4, no. 3: Part I.

Welsby, T.
  1937. *Bribie — the basket maker.* Brisbane: Barkers Bookstore.

White, J.P.
  1968. Fabricators, Outils écaillés or Scalar Cores? *Mankind* 6, no. 12:658 - 66.
  1969. Typologies for some prehistoric flaked stone artifacts of the Australian New Guinea Highlands. *Arch. & Phys. Anthrop. in Oceania* 4, no. 1:18 - 46.

Winick, C.
  1958. *Dictionary of anthropology.* Ames, Iowa: Littlefield, Adams and Co.

Wood-Jones, F.
  1929. The Australian skull. *J. Anat.* 63, no. 3:353 - 55.
  1934. Contrasting types of Australian skulls. *J. Anat.* 68:323 - 30.

Zeuner, F.E.
  1958. *Dating the past.* London: Methuen.

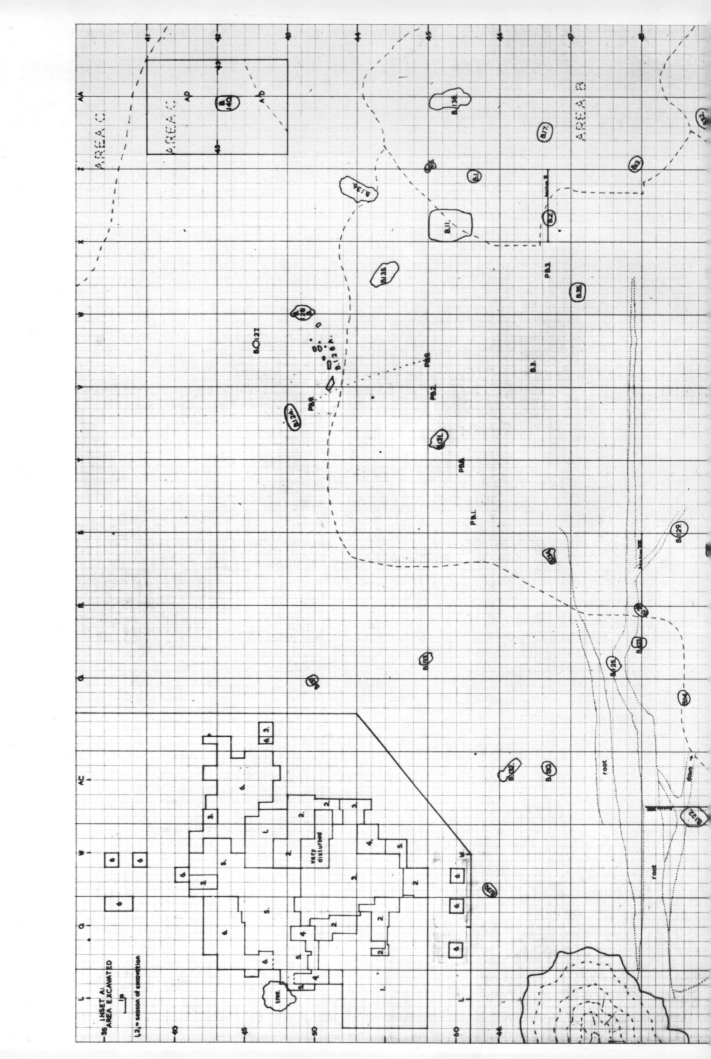

Kate Greenaway

Kate Greenaway

CATALOGUE OF AN EXHIBITION OF
ORIGINAL ARTWORKS AND RELATED MATERIALS SELECTED FROM
THE FRANCES HOOPER COLLECTION AT THE HUNT INSTITUTE
WITH ESSAYS BY MISS HOOPER, RODNEY ENGEN AND JOHN BRINDLE
AND A SUMMARY REGISTER OF THE FULL COLLECTION

EDITED BY ROBERT KIGER
COMPILED BY BERNADETTE CALLERY, MICHAEL STIEBER,
JAMES WHITE AND ELIZABETH MOSIMANN

HUNT INSTITUTE FOR BOTANICAL DOCUMENTATION
CARNEGIE-MELLON UNIVERSITY

PITTSBURGH   1980

ISBN 0-913196-33-9

CONTENTS

PREFACE

It was a complete, and completely delightful surprise. Those of us now at the Institute knew Frances Hooper, of course, but mainly in connection with her effort to build a collection of Linnaeana in English for the Chicago Horticultural Society. Not only did we not expect an offer of her Kate Greenaway collection, we did not know she had one! Our founding Director, Dr. Lawrence, knew Miss Hooper from an earlier period and surely was aware of her collection, but never had occasion to mention it to us before his much-lamented death in 1978. More remarkable is that, as best any of us can recall, Miss Hooper herself never chanced to mention it during her contacts with us in recent years. Considering her passion for Kate Greenaway, this forbearance must have required great effort—or else her keenness for things Linnaean, the concern of the moment in those contacts, must have temporarily overshadowed the longer-standing one. (Like Mrs. Hunt and Dr. Lawrence, Miss Hooper holds back nothing by way of commitment when she decides to undertake something—Linnaeus was and is getting full measure and more from her apparently bottomless store of enthusiasm.) So, when a call from Miss Hooper was announced last November, I picked up the phone anticipating nothing other than one of our pleasant Linnaean interludes.

She soon came to the point, but in an uncharacteristic, almost timid fashion, rather like a driver backing a car into a parking space of problematic dimensions. She had this little collection, she said . . . this accumulated evidence, as it were, of an extended self-indulgence (I am putting words to her implications, not in her mouth) . . . perchance I had heard of Kate Greenaway? (charitably allowing me what would have been, but fortunately was not, a colossal ignorance) . . . just perhaps, we might be willing to consider her giving it to the Institute . . . Greenaway did flowers too, as well as all those lovely children . . . she had thought to call on the off chance we might think her little collection not incompatible with ours; we needn't fear hurting her feelings if we didn't want it (!!). Indeed we would love to have it, I quickly assured her, with what grace I could muster in the aftershock of surprise.

Forthwith Miss Hooper put her lawyer to the details of preparing papers and arranging for an appraisal. Not too long after Sothcby-Park Bernet had finished the latter, and just as spring was underway, we went to Miss Hooper's home in Kenilworth for three hectic but exhilirating days of reviewing, sorting and packing the collection—and of her unstinted hospitality. Well before that we had come to realize just how consequential, just what sort of treasure, is this "little" collection of hers. (The only thing "little" about it is the diminutive scale of Kate Greenaway's art.) As we have noted elsewhere, it was surely the best and most extensive such assemblage in private hands anywhere. Among institutional collections, it must yet be counted in the first rank, and we are exceedingly proud to have it at the Hunt Institute. We are grateful for this fine compliment to Mrs. Hunt, Dr. Lawrence, and their creation—for this ultimate accolade at Miss Hooper's bestowal. We, too, trust that the collection is well placed here, in an active research environment which reflects still, we hope, something of Mrs. Hunt's dignity and elegance.

This catalogue and the exhibition it accompanies mark the formal installation of the Frances Hooper Kate Greenaway Collection at the Hunt Institute. As well, they are meant to convey a realization of the Collection's extent and diversity, of its aesthetic and historical richness. As a context for more fully appreciating these materials and their assembly, we here include two invited essays, as well as a briefer retrospect by our own John Brindle.

Miss Hooper herself has kindly provided a very personal view of the Collection's making, of her motivations, experiences and concerns in that regard. Her account affords a variety of vignettes charmingly revealing of ideas, times, places, occurrences, other people—above all, of Frances Hooper the impassioned collector and concerned donor. Without collectors like her—bent on very personal satisfactions in avowed partiality— we should have far less such material aggregated to any consequence; without patrons like her we should have many fewer such collections held intact for future study and edification. (In this case, "edification" is perhaps too staid; "delight" is more apt.) We are also fortunate to have Rodney Engen's scholarly survey of Kate Greenaway's life and work, which draws upon his extensive research for a forthcoming biography of the artist, and upon his already published studies of other Victorian illustrators. Taken together, Miss Hooper's contribution and Mr. Engen's betoken the complementarity of two quite different but equally rewarding approaches to the subject of such a collection: that of the impassioned partisan and that of the objective researcher. A collection like this one, approached from both directions, supports a kind of cultural symbiosis, one in which passion becomes ever more informed, dispassionate inquiry ever more appreciative.

As with all our other holdings, the Frances Hooper Collection will be not a dead but a living one, actively maintained and used. It will be available for consultation by all qualified researchers whose uses are legitimate and appropriate. For the broader public's enjoyment of this treasure, we are planning other exhibitions drawn from it, to be shown periodically both here and elsewhere in North America. Another major goal is to produce an annotated catalogue of the entire Collection as soon as possible. For general reference until that work is completed, we have here supplemented the suite of entries for the exhibited items with a summary register of the Collection's full content. Upon request, we will be happy to provide more detailed information about any of the materials listed there. As time goes on, we also expect to be publishing a variety of other works drawing upon the Collection's rich resources; almost surely those will include an edition of the unpublished autobiographical notes and a volume devoted to the Greenaway-Ruskin correspondence.

It belabors the obvious to note that we could be doing and planning none of all this were it not for Miss Hooper's magnificent generosity in giving these wonderful materials to the Institute. Less immediately obvious, perhaps, but none the less crucial, are the 30 years of dedication and effort, fitted into an otherwise amazingly busy life, that are integral to the Collection as well. Along with the tangible items, Miss Hooper has bestowed a portion of herself, also in perpetuity. And she remains yet actively involved with the Collection, now that it is here in Pittsburgh. This makes especially appropriate her appointment as Honorary Curator of The Frances Hooper Kate Greenaway Collection, which I am most pleased to record here.

For Miss Hooper's beloved collection, we intend the best of care, the most appreciative and productive of use. For Miss Hooper herself, ever youthful of spirit, we wish an unending Kate Greenaway springtime.

Robert Kiger, *Pittsburgh, September 1980*

Kate Greenaway (1846-1901). From a photograph taken about 1880, original print in the Hooper Collection.

"How did you happen to collect Kate Greenaway?" I might begin an answer to this familiar question by saying that I hardly know who collected whom—whether I collected Kate Greenaway or she collected me. She came to fascinate me—her endless capacity to create the new and different on her recurrent and inseparable themes of children and flowers. Her creative ideas and elegant delicacy entranced me—those thousand-and-one expressions of the new and beautiful, her jets of fancy, her many ways of bringing smiles to both grownups and children. Of one thing I am very sure: I did not set out to build a Kate Greenaway collection; I only wanted to accumulate some of her best, most characteristic work. There is a big difference between an accumulation and a collection.

Long before I started accumulating, then finally *collecting* Kate Greenaway materials, I had known of her work. In fact, rather early in my adult life I had inherited a copy of Spielmann and Layard's definitive work on the artist.[1] From owning and reading that book, as well as from a general acquaintance with Kate Greenaway's published works, I knew her art and knew I liked it. But it was to be a long time before my interest in her became an active one, before my Spielmann and Layard volume had a collection to belong to.

From those pre-collecting years, I also have Gladys Clarabell's hat, a leghorn after the manner of Kate Greenaway. It was made by a modish Detroit milliner for a little Michigan girl's doll. The little girl, her mother and Gladys Clarabell were customers of the milliner. All five—the doll, the little girl, the mother, the milliner and Kate Greenaway—were Victorians when the artist was all the vogue for adults as well as for the very young in England, France and Germany, and here in our own country.[2]

Harriet, the little girl, grew up. The doll and her Kate Greenaway hat came to me. Harriet's brother, Clarabell's "uncle," grew up too, and became Governor Comstock of Michigan. The pink plume on the hat I suspect of being no more than a plain old feather salvaged from among odds and ends in the milliner's workroom. By the time it became mine, mice had nibbled at it until it was almost eaten up. The mice wouldn't have quibbled over "plume" or "cast-off feather," but that hat might appear in more pristine condition if they had quibbled and not nibbled.

But time was...Time was when the doll was new and the plain everyday feather on her hat could have passed for a pink plume. Makes me think of Eugene Field's "Little Boy Blue." Remember it?

"The little toy dog is covered with dust,
But sturdy and stanch he stands;
And the little toy soldier is red with rust,
And his musket moulds in his hands.
Time was when the little toy dog was new,
And the soldier was passing fair;
And that was the time when our Little Boy Blue..."[3]

It was furthest from my mind, as I said, to build a Kate Greenaway collection. I just began to accumulate some examples of her finest work. Then came the day I had to call in a carpenter to add shelf space in my library to accommodate the Greenaway accumulation. And after some time, I bid him return to build a row of bin-like cupboards for the larger scrapbooks of original study sketches and first drafts and art in finished and unfinished form. Also there were the larger watercolors, mounted with wide gold mats and thick, carved, gilt Victorian wood frames, in bulky bundles, the frames padded for protection. After five or so years I felt that what I had should be file-catalogued, and I was able to persuade the earnest, sincere, scholarly Laurence Gomme of New York to come to Chicago for the task.[4] He had been closeted with the accumulation for only a day when he began to refer to it with dignity and great respect as "Your Collection" or "The Collection." I fell in line, referring to "My Collection" or "The Collection," and I began to be very much interested in the enjoyment of building it consistently and constantly.

That was in 1957, and after Mr. Gomme's return to New York, no one could have been more surprised than I when in a summary he sent to me he wrote, "Let us say at the outset that this is the most important and comprehensive collection of this artist's work ever to be brought together in private hands." Much more recently, when my collection went to the Hunt Institute, Sotheby-Parke Bernet's appraisal called it "matchless." And the Institute, in announcing its acquisition of these original artworks, books, letters and other manuscript materials, characterized the collection as "one of the finest and largest of its kind in the world." It is as exciting as it is unexpected for the attainment, or dare I call it achievement, of my Greenaway collection to be held in such high regard. But I did not make it alone.

The great Walter M. Hill was my bookman, and while I have also had other bookmen along the way, there has been only one Mr. Hill. How did I meet him? Was an appointment made, an introduction arranged? Or what?

Here let me digress to speak of the affection and admiration felt for Mr. Hill by J. Christian Bay of the John Crerar Library, who called him "The Old General." Mr. Bay wrote that "of two of our country's greatest bookmen, one was Dr. Rosenbach of Philadelphia, other other, Walter M. Hill in Chicago." The house of Hill, we learn, was for almost half a century "hospitable to all friends of the literary arts. It created many friendships and much pleasant cheer and it was instrumental in helping to build up a number of very important collections of books."[5] Mr. Hill didn't have Dr. Rosenbach's million, but many among his coterie of clients did have such means. One of them was our own brilliant, bookish Chicagoan Mrs. Edith Rockefeller McCormick. The magnificent wrought-iron grill that surrounded her mansion on Lake Shore Drive was worth as much as a king's ransom (once the symbol of *real* worth). Her home was a museum, with its signed furniture, its tapestries and chandeliers. Her staff included footmen and butlers, in livery—velvet tailed coats with gilt braid, velvet knee breeches, white stockings, shoes with buckles. At her dinners there was a butler behind every chair. When the occasion warranted it, her magnificent Pauline Bonaparte silver service for 24, which was one of the showpieces of the Chicago Art Institute, was brought out and returned under guard. At the Chicago Opera she appeared in her box wearing a stomacher set with Catherine of Russia's emeralds. This was living in fashionable elegance.

To resume the story about how I came to meet Mr. Hill: There was no appointment, no arranged introduction. The meeting was ordered by a just-right juxtaposition of the stars; it was a work of perfect serendipity. What happened was that by mistake I got off on the wrong floor of a Loop office building. The doors closed behind me, I heard the elevator continuing on up, and there I was in the hall opposite an enticing bookshop. Its door stood invitingly open, and I stepped in to look around.

Mr. Hill met me with a cordiality which I later learned was very characteristic, but at the same time there was an aloofness, which Mr. Bay said was to cover up a heart of wax.

Mr. Hill—"Is there anything in which you are particularly interested?"
Me—"No, I just thought I'd like to look around."
Mr. Hill—"Do so. You might find something you may want to get."

I went into another room lined with shelves filled with interesting-looking books arranged more as in a home than a regular bookstore. It didn't take long to realize I was in a rare-book place for bibliophiles. I was drawn to a slim green volume which I took off the shelf; upon opening it, I saw that the publisher had my own name, *Hooper*. It would be fun to have a book whose publisher had my name, and when Mr. Hill came into the room I told him I would like to get it. He cocked his head to see what book I was holding. He said, "Oh yes, Thackeray's essay on Cruikshank. You'll like this." I replied, "But not for that reason." While he was having the book wrapped, I continued to look. Upon his return, Mr. Hill brought with him a most attractive little five-volume set of Pepys diaries, which he placed on a table.

Mr. Hill—"I want to give these to you."
Mr—"In looking around, I've found this is a bookshop for book collectors. I'm not a book collector."
Mr. Hill—"Perhaps not now, but I know a book collector when I see one."

On the way up to my office, which was on Michigan Avenue at the River, I had to pass Kroch's book store. I was feeling in a holiday mood with my three interesting companions—Mr. Thackeray, Mr. Cruikshank and Mr. Pepys—and so we turned in at Kroch's. Miss Jones, my bookseller there, saw me come in the door and with a big smile came toward me. "I've been thinking of you today. I have something you'll just love." It was a self-portrait of Cruikshank. "Look," she demonstrated, "you turn the frame around and here is another self-portrait of him." I told Miss Jones I was indeed interested, and bought it. That night I read the essay, and enjoyed the many small black-and-white pen sketches and the two self-portraits.

The next morning was Saturday. The office wasn't open but I went down to it anyway to make up for all the playing I did the day before. The telephone rang. "It's Miss Jones. I took a chance you'd be there. I have something else you'll just love." She said she was sending it right up with a boy who would wait to bring it back in case I didn't want it. She must have dispatched him by breeches-buoy, he arrived at my door so speedily, carrying a package the size and shape of a shoe box. It held a complete set of Cruikshank's little almanacks, which I had been reading about just the night before. I told the boy I was keeping the package. What was going through my head was that all three of these Cruikshank items coming together like that seemed like a sign—something nudging me to collect Cruikshank. On a hunch I guessed that was what I should do, I would have a Cruikshank collection.

At this point you are undoubtedly wondering what all this has to do with how I happened to collect Kate Greenaway. As a matter of fact, I am not far afield, which I will explain presently. However, first let met say that on Monday I returned to the office building where I had gotten off on the wrong floor—this time to get off on the right floor. My business accomplished, I went back to the wrong floor which had become a right floor and went into Mr. Hill's bookshop. And by an impossible coincidence, Mr. Hill had a Cruikshank pocket sketch-book he had put aside for me were I to return within a reasonable period. (Cruikshank always had a pencil at hand to sketch down notes he might use at a future date.)

I still had no idea I had been with the great Walter M. Hill. I doubt if I had ever heard of him. Instead of his giving me Mr. Pepys or thinking I might be interested in Cruikshank, for the sake of my story he should have "divined" something to do with Kate Greenaway. But this would have been truly occult. It was magical enough that I had met Mr. Hill. My not knowing who he was was not important; in due course that took care of itself. Meanwhile, I wasn't to begin my Greenaway collection quite yet. I had three more years of learning and growing before that came about.

Collecting Cruikshank's work, as I had set myself to doing, eventually proved not right for me after all. His work, though extremely interesting, was just too voluminous; I could not realistically expect to assemble any significant portion of it. But meanwhile I was learning from that and other experiences, and Mr. Hill, I believe, was trying me out. In his reserved but sensitive way, he was testing to see what I *should* collect—what *would* be just right for me.

Mr. Hill had soon perceived my long-standing love of illustrated works and fine printing (hence, for example, his picking out the Cruikshank almanacks for me). It only remained, as I am sure he realized more clearly than I, to discover what in that vein would especially suit my particular sensibilities and circumstances; then I would be on my way. And in good time, through my association with Mr. Hill, that happened.

A group of dedicated Midwest bibliophiles came together at Mr. Hill's, for literary banter and serious discourse. Different vocations and avocations were represented; the common denominator was that they were all book lovers and collectors. I came into the group very late, but was on hand to celebrate Mr. Hill's 77th birthday, for which Leon Godchaux arranged the collation. (He and Mrs. Godchaux owned a small, very fine Kate Greenaway collection, acquired through Mr. Hill, which in time became part of mine.)

Writing about this group in his *The Bookman is a hummingbird*, Mr. Bay described another of its members, Arnold Shircliffe, as "Chicago's foremost restaurateur, who collects menus, lectures on food in colleges and universities, a scholastic scholar, and still author of a monumental work on salads." What began to interest me was that Mr. Shircliffe had a small but exceptionally fine collection of Kate Greenaway watercolors. And it so happened that I generally had my lunch at the Wrigley Building Restaurant, over which he presided, and not infrequently he stopped at my table to exchange the pleasantries of the hour. One day I told him how much I would appreciate seeing his Kate Greenaways, and straightaway I received an invitation from him and his wife to visit their home.

On a wall at the Shircliffe's was a framed watercolor of a typical little Kate Greenaway girl in an old-time red pelisse, probably Kate's favorite child-model, her little Mary.[6] She captivated me instantly; I wanted to take her right home. Then, after I saw the rest of the collection, I wanted everything. But no, Mr. Shircliffe wouldn't part with a single item, much less all of the collection, not for anything in the world. Arnold Shircliffe was a sparingly

Unpublished pencil and watercolor drawing signed ''KG Sept.
1894,'' 83 x 60 mm. The first Kate Greenaway original artwork
acquired by Frances Hooper.

built person like President Coolidge. In fact he looked like the President, and when he chose to say "No" he meant what he said. However, I was hooked and wasn't going to accept this—I would play the long game. I decided to mount a persistent campaign (with tact and delicacy), hoping that repetitive suggestion would eventually work to get me at least the one picture, if not the entire collection, and eventually it did.

My opportunity came on the first day of Spring after a miserable long winter —cold, blizzards and grey skies. A person could have wondered if the sun had abandoned our Midwest forever. But it finally returned on this particular miracle of a First Spring Day. The sky was blue, there was warmth in the air, and Mr. Shircliffe was Mr. Sunshine himself. In celebration he had decked the restaurant tables with yellow tablecloths, yellow and red tulips, and yellow daffodils. As jocund as the daffodils, he stopped by my table and set his own trap: "I feel so happy today, I feel like making everyone I see happy." I didn't lose a minute. "Perhaps then," I said jauntily, "this is the day you will make *me* happy by letting me have your Kate Greenaway watercolor of the little girl in the red pelisse." It was almost unbelieveable, his immediate reply: "Yes! This is the very day. You can have the little red pelisse picture and all the rest of the watercolors. I'll see that everything is taken over to Mr. Hill for you, tomorrow." What a considerate, gentlemanly way to arrange the transfer of ownership! Never would either of us have to discuss the matter monetarily. We both had utter faith in Mr. Hill's fairness and judgement, and all three of us were made happy thereby and thenceforth (and forever, we hope).

I have always thought of the little girl in the red pelisse as the cornerstone of what became my collection's main edifice, its "showpieces," most of which were painted for exhibitions. Among them are watercolors heretofore unpublished, and three of the Surrey cottage paintings. In the latter connection, art critics have pointed out with indulgent smiles that Greenaway kept changing her sights, but I dare say each would have loved to own one of those Surrey cottages, with the little wildflowers in the foreground which remind people of "Botticelli's grass" (his tiny wildflowers no lovelier than hers) and, not dominating the picture, one of Kate's pretty young mothers with her little children on a happy outing in the sunshine, carrying small baskets for flowers they might want to pick.

Kate Greenaway could bewitch people—her imagination could beget such appealing children! Robert Louis Stevenson was inspired by her little pictures to create his delightful classic, *A child's garden of verses*.[7] And Boutet de Monvel, the inimitable French artist, was inspired by Greenaway's books and pictures to try his own hand at doing books of children and flowers. One of the most charming is his *Vieilles chansons pour les petits enfants.* A copy came to me just this year from an artist friend, Eleanor Tobin, who had loved it when a child, literally loved it to pieces. Comparing it with Kate Greenaway's work is interesting; it is easy to see where and how Boutet de Monvel was inspired by her, yet each artist's work is plainly identifiable as his own—each has created in his own manner and style. De Monvel's youngsters stand on their heads, kick up their heels, aren't still a minute. (Even his beetles dance hilariously, and stand on their heads, too.) Kate Greenaway's are dream children. The illustrations of both artists have an elegant daintiness, and the costuming is of their own designs.

Whether de Monvel's flowers are accurate or not, I cannot say, but they do look as though they might be de Monvel hybrids. When the English botanist William T. Stearn and Mrs. Stearn visited me and were looking at my Greenaways, I asked him if Kate's flowers were accurate, for she was not a botanical illustrator. His reply was that they were "not inaccurate." We know Greenaway loved flowers and loved to work in her flower garden. Whether de Monvel had a green thumb, a garden, or thought much one way or another about rendering flowers accurately, I have no idea.

After luncheon one day with my friend Madeliene Mayer in her New York apartment, my eyes travelled to a small framed painting on the wall, of a little girl posed on the order of a Greenaway portrait, but unmistakably by Boutet de Monvel. "Madeliene, that must be a de Monvel!" "Yes, when he made a visit to Chicago we were living there; I was a little girl and my parents had him paint my portrait." Since I thought it one of the cutest things I had ever seen, Madeliene had a color photograph made for me. It is now part of a group of such Greenaway-related items in my collection. A drawing of "Little Dinkie," one of Locker-Lampson's characters in his book of popular poems London lyrics, is also there, as is a sketch by Randolph Caldecott, another Victorian illustrator supreme.

Greenaway and Caldecott, born in the same year, were friends and admirers of each other's work. Once when they were guests at the same country house, Caldecott appeared with a sketch done in the Greenaway manner. It amused Kate so greatly that she kept it the rest of her life—so it is said, and I believe it true. When I bought the sketch in London, the auction was sponsored by Kate Greenaway's grand-nephew, who had inherited it. In presenting the sketch, Caldecott is said to have told the company present that he had lost his power of working in his own style and everything came out Greenaways.

The Kate Greenaway revival that is going on today has spawned a number of new so-called "Kate Greenaway books." These are superficially attractive editions using her drawings, but enlarged (she was master of the Small, the Little, the Tiny), and the layouts are completely different and have nothing of the artist's originality or charm. I doubt if Kate would be pleased. She was so popular in her lifetime, and copyright laws were so lax, that she was plagued continually by being copied, others using her style and characters and claiming them as their own. Some of her works were actually pirated—stolen outright. There were periods when the fakes glutted the market, much to her financial hurt.

But back to the little girl in the red pelisse. She may be Mary, Kate Greenaway's favorite child-model, whose activities, like those of the Greenaway dog, Rover, were so often reported in letters to Ruskin and other friends. Working with this particular child was difficult: she talked incessantly, moved her little feet constantly. Here I can't resist quoting Kate's letter to Joanie Severn ("Saturday" 1887?) in which she described Mary's conversation while modeling one morning. It was monologue about the trials and tribulations of her parents' cab business, and it nearly drove the artist to distraction. But Kate's report reveals her sense of humor and understanding of the working of little person's mind:

"I have had little Mary this morning—and I think I have learned every detail of the Cab trade so that I could set up myself. it seems the father has

15

invested in too many Cabs—and is not equal to the business so he drives a Cab and the mother does all the business Part. the Cabmen who hire the Cabs and horses—seem to object to pay for them—
And Enemies report the Horses to have the Glanders—Perhaps says Mary you dont know what this is—I said I didn't—She said its large lumps on their chests—and they come out at their noses—she says if you go near a Horse with the Glanders you die—even if he's a mile off.—also she says one Horse eats a sack of corn a day—which costs 9-6[.] then also they require chaff and straw—she also said the Cabmen had cut up four of her fathers Horses with Gutta Percha [whips?]—she also described one of the Cabmen's wives—as of such a temper that she went about like a Lion— There. I've put it down so badly it doesn't seem a bit funny[,] and it was so funny as she told it—"

I wish, sometimes, that I had held back that little pelisse picture—not included it with the rest of the collection when it went to the Hunt Institute— because I so love looking at it. But at the same time I know that the collection, red pelisse and all, is where it belongs, and I believe Kate Greenaway would have felt happily satisfied to have her art still being honored (after a hundred years) by being welcome in Mrs. Hunt's distinguished treasury.

I wanted my Greenaway collection to be at the Hunt Institute for a number of reasons, but the principal one is Rachel McMasters Miller Hunt herself. She was one of the great women of her era. She did everything with taste and elegance. She was thorough, clear thinking, imaginative, creative, and scholarly minded, always feminine, but equally practical. It is to be wondered how so much could be undertaken and achieved in a single life span. Dr. Lawrence wrote of her "doughty grit," and that "When conversing in areas of mutual interest, one's awareness of her grasp of a subject was immediate, and her enthusiasm was infectious; that she was well-read was obvious…"[8]

Like the young Linnaeus, early in her life Mrs. Hunt wanted to know the names of the wildflowers and trees. As Dr. Lawrence reported, "She later prided herself on knowing the Latin names of the species grown in her gardens, and of the wildflowers, and in her later years would chide the visiting botanists who would condescend to use vernacular names of plants when Latin names were more precise. Throughout her life, her love for nature and all that composed it received as much of her interest as did her love for literature and the arts."[9]

The range of Mrs. Hunt's interests is amazing, various major botanical, horitcultural and related fields being chief among them. Her significant collections in these areas had a very important place in her private library, and now have permanent and internationally recognized status in the Hunt Institute. But Mrs. Hunt could also be enthusiastic about collections of materials that were not of major scientific or scholarly importance, for instance, that ample body of publications on the language of flowers. In this connection Kate Greenaway helped supply a number of the volumes that Mrs. Hunt collected.

"A fascinating group of little books even if of peripheral botanical significance, is that known as the Language of Flowers books, of which more than sixty titles and editions have been collected by Mrs. Hunt. These rather Victorian items, much prized then by the distaff side, flourished in England, France and America from about 1820 to 1860.

16

Many were published anonymously, with the simple title Language of Flowers. *Perhaps the longest run of these is the British series first published and illustrated by Kate Greenaway, titled* Kate Greenaway's Almanack for 1883, *with publication continued (with corresponding change of title) even until 1927. These volumes are usually provided with colored copperplate engravings or other types of colored plates, accompanied by verses or quotations about flowers. Some titles and editions are extremely rare, and collecting them has become a speciality.*"[10]

College or university education for women was not extraordinary when Mrs. Hunt was of that age, but it was not as common as it is now. She regretted not having had a formal higher education, but was well educated nonetheless. She was taken on frequent journeys to Europe, and travel was an education, learning languages a passion. Also she was an avid reader. Few women, with or without college degrees, have held the multiplicity of honorary citations that were bestowed upon her.

Mrs. Hunt was a director of The Garden Club of America from 1934 to 1939, and its book review editor 1937 to 1957. She also served for many years as an elected trustee of the John Carter Brown Library at Brown University. She was a member of the founding committee of the Carl Purington Rollins Printing Office of the Yale University Press—a special unit for the production of works to exemplify the finest in typography and printing. Through membership in the Manuscript Society of New York she was active in fostering and stimulating interest in collecting and preserving autograph letters and manuscripts; she herself assembled a collection of over 400 letters of nearly 200 botanists and horticulturists (most of which date from prior to 1850).

When no organization existed and one was needed, Mrs. Hunt would become one of the founders. I belong to two such groups. One is the Limited Editions Club. In its early years she was active in its promotion and production of works that reflected the best in typography, fine printing, and the graphic arts. The other organization, and one which I enjoy almost beyond all others, with one exception, is the Hroswitha Club, based in New York City. Mrs. Hunt, one of its six founders, helped bring together a group of women outstanding in this country for their book collecting activities, and served as president from 1949 to 1953. This small organization might be described as a feminine Grolier Club. We are closely associated with the Pierpont Morgan Library in New York City, and our books by members are kept in Director Ryskamp's own office. The Club takes its name from the 11th century Saxon abbess Hroswitha. Albrecht Dürer did a woodcut of her in the robes of her order, kneeling before her King Otto and presenting him with one of her books or manuscripts.

I missed ever meeting Mrs. Hunt personally, but I did have the pleasure of knowing George H. M. Lawrence, the Institute's first director, and Miriam, his wife and one of my Hroswitha sisters, who became my friends. Recognizing Dr. Lawrence's outstanding work as a professor of botany and as director of the Bailey Hortorium at Cornell University, Mrs. Hunt had sought his advice in connection with her collections and activities in botany, horticulture and kindred subjects. Later, Mr. and Mrs. Hunt tapped Dr. Lawrence to help them bring into reality her dream for a Hunt Botanical Library (the name it still had at the time of my first visit to Pittsburgh). As its first director, Dr. Lawrence guided the Library's establishment as an active

17

research center, one which quickly achieved international recognition for its highly successful program. After ten years (just when the name was changed to the Hunt Institute, reflecting more accurately the full extent of the enterprise he had so capably fashioned), Dr. Lawrence retired as director and moved back to his native Rhode Island. But he remained an active member of the Institute's staff, devoting practically his full effort to compiling and editing, with Dr. Strandell of Stockholm, a massive, detailed bibliographic catalogue of the Institute's Strandell Collection of Linnaeana. Mr. and Mrs. Hunt had passed on, but Dr. Lawrence was still in the flower of his vigor and creative work when he invited the Hroswitha Club to visit the Hunt Botanical Library. It was a memorable day, and in the evening Mr. and Mrs. Hunt's sons and their wives had a dinner for the visitors. That occasion marked the beginning of my admiration for the standards and quality of this unique institution, the dream of one small powerhouse of a woman. I had seen the same effect of her personality and high ideals reflected in the character of the Hroswitha Club.

Recently, I received a letter from one of my Hroswitha sisters, Ruth Brown—Mrs. John Carter Brown of Providence, Rhode Island—who knew Mrs. Hunt well. She began her letter:

"What a joyful piece of news that your magnificent Greenaway collection will have a permanent home in the Hunt Institute . . . and I think you have made an excellent choice. I am sure dear Rachel Hunt would be most happy to know that it will join her wonderful collection."

I too believe that Mrs. Hunt would have welcomed my Kate Greenaway collection among her treasures. Those two women had much more in common than being hardly-five-feet-tall dynamos. They also shared elegance, originality and thoroughness. Had they ever met, I think they would have sincerely admired each other.

Our Hroswitha visit to Pittsburgh had strengthened my intention to collect only Kate Greenaway materials which had a personal appeal to me, and only her best and finest works. This was the way Mrs. Hunt had collected—selecting everything from personal taste and appeal, and informed astute judgement. I did not care about accumulating the largest collection or the most comprehensive. I was only collecting what I personally wanted and could find pleasure in, and had no notions about a gift to any art museum or library. But a private home is really not the place for such things, for all the care they must have, including safeguards against fire, excessive humidity and acidity, ultraviolet rays, tiny creatures that survive on paper and leather, and even chemical enemies in the air.

Whoever has a collection such as mine—of original artworks, first editions, holograph letters, etc.—owes it to the originator of those materials as well as to posterity not to let the collection be neglected or purloined—to try to safeguard it into the future in every possible way. The most obvious safeguard that my collection has at the Institute that I could not provide with equal care is an ultramodern fire detection and suppression system. I live in a wood house. Three times a sturdy oak on my parkway has been struck by lightning. Once a ball of St. Elmo's Fire came into my study. We try to remember to unplug the televisions and other electric appliances when there is an electrical storm, and we have an electrician go over the house annually to check for loose connections and crossed wires; yet even French-frying potatoes for dinner could cause a conflagration. Then there is humidity, which is said to be Enemy Number One, and is closely related to temperature. Despite thermostatically controlled heating and air conditioning, we can never hold an even temperature; the house is always either over- or under-heated. The Institute controls temperature *and* humidity to tolerances (68-75 °F, 45-55% RH) not possible for private homes, generally speaking. Also, it has sophisticated intrusion and video-monitoring security systems; for obvious reasons, the details of those are not for publication. Finally, the Institute operates its own fine bookbinding and conservation facility, to provide all the services necessary for the physical preservation of its collections, including deacidification.

Besides this safety provided my collection above and beyond anything I could pledge it, I like thinking about and visiting it in such a beautiful place. Everything about the Institute's Penthouse base reflects Mrs. Hunt's taste and concern for elegance and beauty. For example, serviceability and at the same time loveliness are expressed throughout the Rare Book Room. On the floor are three Savonnerie carpets handwoven with a mille-fleurs pattern whose flowers and yarn colors Mrs. Hunt personally selected. Upholstery material and green silk damask draperies were woven in Lyon to match those in Mrs. Hunt's library at home. The furniture, antique and custom-made, and its arrangement recreate the atmosphere of her library. She loved to entertain her friends at tea in the Gallery, and for this she had commissioned a special tea service with a Linnaean motif. You can see how the Hunt Institute appealed to me as a permanent home for my collection.

Rachel Hunt was one of the great greats in private collecting, with interests both broad in scope and aesthetic in emphasis. What has become the Hunt Institute "is more than a simple library; it is an assemblage of interlocking collections..."[11] So Dr. Lawrence reported in 1961, and I like to think of my own collection now joined with those others, enhanced by them and at the same time contributing something of its own to that most distinguished assemblage.

How I happened to collect Kate Greenaway is now told, and also why I wanted it to go to the Hunt Institute. It remains to say just a bit about other collections, and collecting. Along the way I also collected, or started collecting, other subjects that were sooner or later abandoned, but I enjoy having the portions of them that I did assemble. I began collecting egg cozies just for fun—little felt ones I picked up in Vienna on my first trip to Europe. After that I got more whenever I came upon any, and had a long shadow box built to display them in the dining room. But my friends got the idea I was collecting egg *cups,* which they began to get me whenever they saw one in their travels or at home. This was another sort of collection—too many people in the act. Both cups and cozies are now in my go-down awaiting...I don't know what they are waiting for. I've already told about starting to collect Cruikshank, but having to give that up because there was too much of it. I would have needed a warehouse until I could open up an entire museum or library (like the Folgers). I also began on the ever fascinating Lewis Carroll and *Alice in Wonderland,* but I was too late. Good pieces were rare (and dear Dr. Rosewald paid a million dollars for the original manuscript) and I felt I couldn't acquire enough within my lifetime. What I have I wouldn't part with, but I soon learned this also wasn't for me to pursue as a collector.

My principal quarry at present is works by Virginia Woolf, and those in English by and about Carl Linnaeus, the latter for our Chicago Horticultural

Society Library. Linnaeus, you know, wrote only in Swedish or Latin, but the users of that library are for the most part garden club members, teachers and students who are not familiar with those languages.

Even greater than the pleasure of having a Kate Greenaway collection or any other has been that of the collecting itself and the people and episodes contingent. One thing, one friend leads to another new one, thence to yet another, and it never seems to end. So if one wants a whole new galaxy of interesting friends and delightful experiences, just begin a collection.

Frances Hooper, *Kenilworth, Illinois, September 1980*

NOTES

1. Marion H. Spielmann and George S. Layard, *Kate Greenaway*, London, 1905. This is a yet unexcelled source by authors who knew the artist and lived her times. Contributors were friends; they lent letters and drawings, and told anecdotes about Kate Greenaway, not from reading about her, not from hearsay, but from firsthand knowledge. The book is long out of print now, but many libraries have copies, and now and then it appears in antiquarian catalogues.

2. Sales of Kate Greenaway in the United States exceeded even those in England. This may be attributed to our having had a larger population, with more people who could read (due to our universal public schools and compulsory education).

3. From Eugene Field, *The poems of Eugene Field*, New York, 1911, p. 248. Field was born in St. Louis in 1850, when Kate Greenaway was a little four-year-old over in England. Both rose to fame and fortune during the Victorian age of expansion and opulence, and both paid attention to children themselves. They painted and wrote poems, each in his own way, which showed children cute and loveable, as they are, featuring their whimsies and their ways. They didn't preach at them; they entertained them. And they presented them to adults. This was a new approach.

4. Laurence Gomme was a bibliophile. Professionally he was an authority on rare books and fine bindings, and he specialized in appraisals.

5. From J. Christian Bay, *The bookman is a hummingbird* and *Book collecting in the Middle West and the house of Walter M. Hill*, privately printed for the friends of the Torch Press, Cedar Rapids, Iowa, 1952. Edition limited to 400 copies.

6. A pelisse was a wide-collared woman's fur, fur-lined or fur-trimmed coat or cloak that went straight down to the ankles or ground.

7. It might be regretted that Stevenson could not have written the verses around Greenaway's ideas and illustrations, and it is surely regrettable that she did not illustrate *A child's garden of verses*. But neither the poet nor the artist liked to work with another's ideas, and indeed each was marvelously creative unto himself.

8. From his perceptive and evocative gem of brief biography "Rachel McMasters Miller Hunt—1882-1963," *Huntia* 1: 5-15, 1964.

9. *Ibid.*

10. From [George H. M. Lawrence], *The Rachel McMasters Miller Hunt Botanical Library...*, Pittsburgh, 1961, p. 15.

11. *Ibid.*, p. 5.

21

Kate Greenaway's studio at 39, Frognal, Hampstead. From an original photographic print in the Hooper Collection.

Towards the end of her life, Kate Greenaway (1846-1901) wrote a defiant verse to describe her single-minded attitude to the startling age into which she had been born:

"There are sometimes moments when I see
A sort of divinity in it for me,
To keep me separate and alone;
To hold away and keep my heart
All for my work, set aside and apart,
As if I were vowed away to Art."[1]

It was clearly a stubborn refusal to submit to the "clatter and bang" of the Victorian period that had brought unparalleled wealth and poverty to the British people. Since she retained her faith in escaping through her very special view of that world, her life and career as an artist must then be seen in this light, bathed in the memories of the blissful rural past she tried to recreate each time she put brush or pen to paper.

By the time Queen Victoria firmly took her place on the throne in 1837, memories of Regency England were fast fading, and a belief arose that the eighteenth century, with its squires and elegantly gowned ladies, had been England's Golden Age, a period of supreme style and grace. It inspired such Victorian novelists as Thackeray and Trollope to set their novels in Bath crescents or on the vast country estates that began to be transformed into productive farm factories during their own lifetimes. Soon the vogue for eighteenth-century literature, architecture and painting grew in leaps and bounds. Queen-Anne styled architecture borrowed heavily from the period, with Norman-Shaw-designed mansion houses built to accommodate the Regency frills of the past, complete with carefully clipped gardens and shrubbery. The vogue for Gainsborough- and Reynolds-inspired portraiture (often of the latest industrial magnate and his family) brought with it a boom in the sale of engraved prints after their more popular paintings, and artists built whole reputations on recreating the period with so-called "Dorothy pictures"—of a demure, elegantly dressed lady seated in her garden before a Regency buck. These became very popular, and countless variations were sold as prints or book illustrations, spawning the careers of Randolph Caldecott and later Hugh Thomson, to name just two artists who worked in the formula.

The strong influence of Kate Greenaway's contribution to the eighteenth-century revival, though coming somewhat later, cannot be denied. She tapped the Victorian public's desire for refined, harmless escapism by setting her innocent children in a pastel-tinted dreamland recognizable to all those, like the beleagured city dweller caught up in one of the numerous urban prisons, who longed to escape the world around them. "There are no railroads in it to carry the children away, are there?" remarked the great art critic John Ruskin in an Oxford lecture on Kate Greenaway's pure vision. Above all, he continued, there were "no tunnel or pit mouths to swallow them up, no league-long viaducts— blinkered iron bridges. There are only winding brooks, wooden foot- bridges, and grassy hills without holes cut into them...And more wonderfully still,—there are no gasworks! no waterworks, no mowing machines, no sewing machines, no telegraph poles, no vestige, in fact, of science, civilization, economical arrangements, or commercial enterprise!!"[1]

Ruskin here pinpointed, in his typical effusive manner, the diseases of urban, industrial England that he believed would culminate in a great "Storm Cloud." The industrial smoke and fumes of too many people living in too small an area would ultimately destroy the life-enhancing benefits of Nature and civilization as he knew it: "But our cities, built in black air which, by its accumulated foulness, first renders all ornament invisible in distance, and then chokes its interstices with soot; cities which are crowded masses of store, and warehouse, and counter, and are therefore to the rest of the world what the larder and cellar are to a private house; cities in which the object of men is not life, but labour . . . cities in which the streets are not the avenues for passing a procession of happy people, but the drains for the discharge of a tormented mob, in which the only object in reaching any spot is to be transferred to another; in which existence becomes mere transition, and every creature is only one atom in a drift of human dust . . ."[3]

This was Ruskin in his most outraged mood, but it was just such sentiment which the young Kate Greenaway had read and on which she wholeheartedly agreed, tempering her response but never losing the desire to escape her own life in the city. "For oh, I love the country—the beautiful country. Who'd live in a London street when there's the country?" she wrote in *Marigold garden.* She was in fact born on 17 March 1846 at Hoxton New Town in a row of workman's houses in the heart of London's industrialised East End—just the sort of urban spawl Ruskin so viciously attacked. Hoxton's famous seventeenth- and eighteenth-century market gardens had by the 1840s given way to rows of uniform brick terraces built to accommodate the rush of population to the city: by mid-century 170,000 farm workers had invaded London in just twenty years and many had found work in areas like Hoxton. The neighbourhood was soon known for small businesses (and remains so today), with furniture and cabinet makers sharing premises with makers of everything from corsets to musical instruments and lampshades, each family intent on climbing its way up the ladder of wealth and into the growing middle class. Moreover, with so much of the country's population migrating, long-distance travel was no longer confined to the wealthy, and the growth of railway networks transformed the country: "Distance has disappeared. England so long a great country, is fast becoming one great city, and we may reach London from Nottingham in less than it would take a person to walk from one extreme of the great metropolis to the other," claimed one newspaper in the year of Kate Greenaway's birth.[4]

The Greenaway family was in many ways typical of the London immigrants. Both Kate's mother and father had their family roots outside London, but the call of the city had been heard and obeyed. Kate's paternal grandfather had abandoned a prosperous shipping business at the Royal Dockyards, Sheerness, to struggle as a "rag and bone merchant" in Southwark, south London. There her father, John Greenaway, the eldest of nine children, had been forced out of the house at fifteen by a drunkard stepfather and forced to fend for himself (and later to support

Kate Greenaway's house at 39, Frognal, Hampstead, designed for her by R. Norman Shaw. From *Kate Greenaway* by Spielmann and Layard.

his sisters and ailing mother), first apprenticed to Robert Brandard, the London stationer, then to Ebenezzar Landells, with whom he learned wood engraving. Soon the firm, rebellious independence in his nature broke through (it was a family legend that he was related to the infamous Father Greenway, implicated in the Gunpowder Plot of 1605 to blow up the houses of Parliament), and John worked hard to set himself up in his own engraving business, which he had achieved by the early 1840s. He then married Elizabeth Jones, the daughter of a violent-tempered, Welsh-born butcher who had a shop in the East End until his untimely death at his daughter's coming of age. Although little is known of Elizabeth Greenaway, she was the dominant figure in the family. She had inherited staunch religious principles from an eccentric Welsh mother (herself a wealthy countrywoman) and maintained a stubborn independence in the face of the many upsets and traumas that beset a family of four children growing up in a London backstreet.

The first of these upsets came shortly after Kate was born. Her mother agreed to take her two children to relatives in the country, leaving her husband undisturbed to work on a promising new engraving commis-

25

sion and to set up the new house he had rented on the strength of its success. As it happened, this visit, when Kate was but six months old, first exposed her to the scene of the most important experiences of her life, for it marked the beginning of her love affair with the idyllic rural life of Rolleston, a small village near Newark in Nottinghamshire. There each summer the "Little Lunnoner," as she was known, tramped the corn fields and hedgerows and learned the old world ways of relatives living in a rural backwater as yet unmarked by the changes of the nineteenth century. The visits, religiously observed each year, continued to provide the experiences and, later, drawings that became the Greenaway vision.

From the outset, young Kate was expected to adapt to the country ways and prejudices of her mother's Rolleston relatives. She was in fact the niece of one of the area's wealthiest farmers and, while the more humble villagers treated her with awe and respect, she soon learned to attach herself to those less fortunate but more sincere members of the community. Above all she loved her guardians, the Chappells, a poor dairy farming husband and wife who treated their young charge as if she were the child they never had. With her wide brown eyes, dark hair and precocious personality she soon became something of a village legend, well remembered by the locals long after she had returned to London. She responded joyfully to her country home and helped gather the cows early in the morning, tried to give the hay harvest her full attention, and even delivered the dairy produce her guardian sold for a living.

These were remarkably impressionable years, unequalled in their enchantment, as she later recalled. "In these early days all farm things were of endless interest to me . . . I had a tiny hayfork, a little kit to carry milk in, and a little washing-tub, all exactly like big real ones, only small."[5] This was written for her autobiography, and the childhood journal she devised in preparation was filled with favourite Rolleston attractions: "the swing in the barn," "the dressing in (sic) the hob ring," or playing the endless games her inventive young mind had devised, like "sailing caterpillars in tubs—on leaves" and "playing hide-and-seek in the stock-yards." There were also visits to Southwell, the market town nearby, renowned for its church carvings (praised by Ruskin) and its display of summer roses and rural crafts; or visits to the larger market town of Newark, approached in a bouncing horse and trap filled with squawking ducks and chickens, fruit and cheeses for the famous weekly cheese and sheep market. Here too were maltings, corn mills and the linen factory that produced the farmer's smock-frock fashions that inspired the Greenaway dresses in later years.

Kate Greenaway's impressions of country life remained those of a starry-eyed child, oblivious to the rampant hardships endured by most Victorian farmers and their workers, however remote their farms. To her, "Everything was done slowly at Rolleston, and bustle unknown;" and yet Rolleston suffered hardships and disasters like any other village, despite its backwater reputation (electricity was not installed there until 1931). To Kate it was merely an enchanting world of farmers in smock-frocks tending sheep and cattle, their wives waving from scented gardens, dressed in long dresses and poke bonnets ("Charity bobs"). There was indeed some element of the idyllic in the village setting. Rolleston was mentioned in the Domesday Book and, although the local manor house had since been destroyed, the village green with its stocks was still there, surrounded by several quaint thatch-roofed cottages, a Saxon church and bell tower. But the eternal struggle against natural elements prevailed, despite Kate Greenaway's ignorance, and the local papers were filled with horrific accounts of floods, destruction by fire or wind, droughts or deaths among agricultural workers, many of whom slept six to a room and survived on little more than bread, dripping and tea. One of the Greenaway relatives squandered his wealth on drink, no doubt defeated by the relentless pressures of country life, while on the other hand, her aunt and uncle flaunted their wealth by leaving some of their fields unharvested, or keeping a number of servants. Such were the class distinctions even among yeoman farmers, but curiously the Greenaway memory did not recall such things, and the hard, dull, daily drudgery of farm life was seen through rose-coloured glasses all her life. Even when as an older woman she ventured outside London and saw the terrible hardships of country life, she refused to alter her original interpretation of blissful, idyllic Rolleston; reading Thomas Hardy she was plunged into deep disgust at such "horrible" descriptions and senseless distortions.

Such a relentless belief in her own vision, however distorted, was strengthened while walking in the flower gardens she loved all her life, or by recalling the Sunday afternoon strolls along a Rolleston hedgerow, where wild docks became "tea" ("we used to have a tea-shop and weigh it out and sell it for tea") and purple mallow became "cheeses" ("sweet little flat green things"). The country garden of the Fryers at Rolleston remained her ideal, with its large stone house, convolvuluses climbing the walls and windows, and peacocks strutting the long gravel paths to oval flower beds kept seasonal by the Fryer's large staff of servants. There in the apple, pear and plum orchard, young Kate experienced a strange transformation while peering up at the blue sky through clouds of fruit blossoms. It was to her a unique experience, repeated each spring, as she often told her friends. "You can go into a beautiful new country if you stand under a large apple tree and look up to the blue sky through the white flowers—to go to this scented land is an experience," she recalled, adding why it remained so potent an experience: "I suppose I went to it very young before I could really remember and that is why I have such a wild delight in cowslips and apple blossom—they always give me the same strange feeling of trying *to remember*, as if I had known them in a former world."[6] Indeed this eternal spring setting was transferred into the pastel greens and pale pinks of many of her finest book illustrations and watercolours, as were the rural scenes of many of her verses. "The impression was so great it could never go away again," she admitted to Ruskin three years before her death, and vividly described one scene in particular that had haunted her all her life: "Go and stand in a shady lane—at least, a wide country road—with high hedges, and wide grassy places at the sides. The hedges are all hawthorns blossoming; in the grass grow great patches of speedwell, stitchwort, and daisies. You look through the gates into fields full of buttercups, and the whole of it is filled with sunlight. For I said it was shady only because the hedges were high. Now do you see my little picture, and me a little dark girl in a pink frock and hat, looking about at things a good deal, and thoughts filled up with such wonderful things—everything seeming wonderful and life to go on for ever just as it was! What a beautiful long time a day was! Filled with time—."[7]

Kate Greenaway's return to London, after such a period in the country, proved somewhat traumatic. The grim rows of terraced Hoxton houses saddened her memories of sweeping fields filled with butterflies and birds, these now replaced by a cruel rectangular patch of brick-walled yard where she was allowed to sit amongst the laundry defiantly hung to dry in the yellow fog-clogged air. She soon developed a stoic attitude to her urban surroundings, suffering them because she had no other choice, while her heart remained in the country. She wrote in *Marigold garden*, of this very real disappointment:

"I live in a London street, then I long
To be the whole day the sweet Flowers among
Instead of tall chimney-pots up in the sky,
The joy of seeing Birds and Dragon Flies go by...

Life in London for the Greenaway family was indeed hard and disappointing, especially when John Greenaway failed to support his family with his wood-engraving. He had placed all their hopes on an enterprising project, engraving from John Gilbert illustrations for a series of reprinted Dickens novels, but the publisher soon went bankrupt and left him with his fee unpaid, his time wasted, and a growing family to support. His wife, in her typical no-nonsense manner, accepted the situation and opened a fancy goods shop in Upper Street, Islington, an area noted for its drapers, stationers and millinery shops that were crowded each Saturday with fashionable ladies and their daughters intent on restocking their wardrobes and linen cupboards. There the family moved and grew, two more children being added, and happily Mrs. Greenaway's shop prospered. Gradually young Kate overcame her disgust with city life, and with her new brother and elder sister she explored the many delights of Islington's streets—shops filled with picture books, toys and games, and the noisy din of the street entertainers, whose instruments and songs later found their way into the Greenaway book verses.

Meanwhile, John Greenaway was forced to work day and night to recover his losses, by engraving for the growing number of illustrated books, newspapers and magazines that began to appear at the time. It was the heyday of the black-and-white illustrator, throughout the 1850s and 1860s, brought on by the advent of steam-driven printing presses and rapid printing schedules that meant news items could appear in print, often with illustrations made on the spot, within days of their happening. Papers like the *Illustrated London news*, later the *Daily graphic*, established themselves on topicality, and John Greenaway was often sent out with woodblock to sketch some enthralling scene—perhaps a murder trial or a royal event—then to rush home to engrave the block, working all night to have it ready for the early morning deadline and publication the next day. It was a hard regime for such "special reporters," and many succumbed to drink and ill health. But the numbers of illustrator-engravers rocketed during this ten-year period, and by all rights John Greenaway should have built up a successful business by then, for he had trained with the best of the master engravers, Ebenezzar Landells, who founded the *Illustrated London news*, and many of his fellow apprentices (such as Edmund Evans) had become very successful. However, his heart was often elsewhere, especially at the theatre he loved, and while he worked hard it was often half-heartedly, engraving the children's books full of Harrison Weir animal drawings for which he became well-known.

His despondency was overcome when young Kate, his favourite daughter, took a growing interest in his work and nursed him through his all-night engraving sessions. She tried to comment and to learn the engraver's skills; she studied her father's large collection of prints and illustrated magazines, making drawings on slate, then with pencil on paper, of her favourite fairy or gnome-like illustrations. She pored over early issues of *Punch* with their John Leech street urchins, the dignified cartoons of John Gilbert, and the sprightly fairies of Richard Doyle and Kenny Meadows, and on the whole preferred these fantasy illustrators. The real world, of murders, tragedies and disasters, she took too much to heart, and her extreme sensitivity to suffering—she never allowed any living creature to be killed—meant she could be consumed with terror while just reading the papers. The horrific accounts of a massacre of women and children by Sepoy rebels at Cawnpore, accounts written by eyewitnesses in most graphic detail, transfixed the young artist, and she felt it her duty to at least imagine that the victims had survived and were now well. "I could sit and think of the Sepoys till I could be wild with terror, and I used sometimes to dream of them. But I was always drawing the ladies, nurses and children escaping. Mine always escaped and were never taken."[8] Fear and terror played an important role in her development, as her childhood reminiscences recall a "fear of water taps," a delicious longing to hear the penny-dreadful stories of bloodthirsty pirates like Blue Beard, and a month-long depression brought on by the apocalyptic visions of John Martin prints. Among her worst fears, it seems, were those of her early days at a succession of four dame schools which she sporadically attended, trying all the while to convince her mother that her teachers were terrible, frightful individuals with glass eyes and unbearable tempers. And yet when left to her own devices, young Kate achieved considerable successes at the piano, with her French lessons, and of course with her drawing.

Kate Greenaway's art lessons were first suggested as an experiment when, at the age of twelve, she accompanied her obstinate cousin to evening classes. While the cousin soon abandoned the work, Kate accepted the difficult lessons with zealous delight and eventually became a day student at the local Finsbury School of Art, where she won several book prizes and medals for her perseverance under the rigours of a daunting training scheme. The National Art Training Scheme, as it was called, was set up in the mid-1840s as an alternative to the highly competitive fine-art training offered at the Royal Academy schools, where painters, sculptors and other "fine artists" were taught from classical casts. Through a system of local schools established throughout the country and controlled by a central school at South Kensington in London, a national scheme was devised to train artist-craftsmen, as opposed to fine artists. The course comprised twenty-three stages, based on geometric principles of design and its application in ornament, progressing from drawing geometric shapes on cards to drawing outlines of three-dimensional objects like plaster casts, plants, shells, birds and minerals. The primary principle was outline, so that designs could be applied to the plethora of manufactured "artistic" objects—wall and floor tiles (stage twenty-three was to design a set of floral tiles), wallpapers, fabrics, plaster ornaments, and the bric-a-brac so popular among the rising middle class. Much of this vogue for ornamental design had arisen out of the Great Exhibition of 1851 in Hyde Park, where the work of silversmiths, cast-iron manufacturers, cabinet makers and glass blowers was displayed and regarded in a new, artistic light; it was hoped thereafter that a distinct national style of decorative design would emerge, perpetuated by the National Art Training Scheme, to produce objects to rival the utilitarian manufactures of Germany and France.

The national training scheme was not without its critics. The series of twenty-three stages involved a painstaking patience even the most devoted pupil found almost impossible, some stages taking up to two years to complete. Charles Dickens parodied the scheme in Chapter 2 of *Hard times,* where a government art inspector (based, it was said, on Henry Cole, pioneer of the national scheme) was "A mighty man at cutting and drying [flowers for outline drawing]" who lived by the claim that geometry and mathematics were the sole basis for all good art, at the expense of creativity and individual inspiration: "You must use for all purposes combinations and modifications (in primary colours) of mathematical figures which are susceptible of proof and demonstration. This is the new discovery. This is fact. This is taste." Despite this soul-destroying regime, however, Kate Greenaway raced through all twenty-three stages in about six years, and her works entered in the National Competitions alongside others from local schools were judged so successful in echoing the prescribed national style that they were purchased by the national school for use as examples for future students. In 1864 alone she was awarded a bronze medal for her "Analysis of Flowers" and an honourable mention for a floral watercolour as well. She had clearly succeeded where so many of her fellow students had floundered and failed, and to a certain extent all her future work was done under the shadows of the national training scheme's outline and geometric dictums.

She had now proved herself capable of designing for industry, but like so many of her fellow students, she had more adventurous ambitions in the realms of painting as an end in itself. During summer holidays at Rolleston she had spent hours sketching the Chappell farm and surroundings, practiced her outline pencil technique on blackberry branches and primroses, and drawn realistic portraits of her guardians and members of her family. She therefore decided to enroll in a series of lessons which tried, to some extent, to broaden her outlook, to stretch her copyist skills for a more individualistic approach to her art.

She first enrolled in the Central School at South Kensington, but the most valuable lesson learned there was to work alongside equally ambitious female students from different, often artistic family backgrounds, girls like Elizabeth Thompson, destined to become Lady Butler on the strength of her remarkable recreations of battle scenes, for which Queen Victoria offered the highest praises. Lessons at South Kensington were rigorous, but still choked the inspiration or inventiveness from the students' work, since they were taught from colour manuals and remorseless copying in the "South Kensington style" of chalk drawing. This gave the school an unfortunate reputation which, by the 1880s,

30

Gilbert and Sullivan parodied in *"Patience"*: one character exclaimed to another, "Oh! South Kensington!" where they "*taught* too much and educated too little." The ordeal was best described by George Moore in *Modern painting,* where he pointed out the folly of the "stumping technique" of drawing endured by Kate Greenaway and her fellow students: "I shall never forget the scenes I witnessed there [at South Kensington]. Having made a choice of a cast, the student proceeded to measure the number of heads; he then measured the cast in every direction, and ascertained by means of a plumbline exactly where the lines fell. It was more like land-surveying than drawing, and to accomplish this portion of his task took generally a fortnight, working six hours a week. He then placed a sheet of tissue paper upon the drawing, leaving only one small part uncovered, and having reduced his chalk pencil to the finest possible point he proceeded to lay in a set of extremely fine lines. These were crossed by a second set of lines, and the two sets of lines elaborately stippled, every black spot being carefully picked out with bread. With a patience truly sublime in its folly, he continued the process all the way down the figure, accomplishing, if he were truly industrious, about an inch square in the course of an evening . . . After three months' work a student began to be noticed; at the end of four he became an important personage." Most important of all, the resulting drawing was a "flat, foolish thing, but very soft and smooth." Despite its opponents, this drawing method continued well into the 1890s, when the sixteen-year-old Augustus John was awarded a certificate attesting to his success at perpetuating the folly, making him a "Master Stumper Third Class."[9]

The alternatives for more ambitious art study were few. Kate Greenaway enrolled for a short period in the famous Heatherley's (formerly Leigh's), off Oxford Street, where she added life classes to her South Kensington lessons. There she joined the only school in London where women and men worked together from the model, unhampered by professional or class distinctions. Struggling beginners worked alongside well-established professional painters and illustrators, and the ranks had swelled to include the young Walter Crane, Frederick Walker (idol of 1870s art students), Henry Stacy Marks, and Simeon Solomon, all presided over by the ghostly figure of Thomas Heatherley, pale-bearded, dressed in heavy gaberdine gown and slippers, who shuffled between student and model most days of the week.

Women students in life classes had long been a controversial topic; indeed by as late as 1863 there were only eight British art schools with life classes of any type, and those strictly limited to male students. Sexual discrimination had even invaded the local Finsbury School of Art, where women students were regarded as "ladies or potential governesses" a full cut above the vulgar artisan classes of male students, who were kept quite separate of course. By 1852 a Female School of Art and Design was established, but there too the students were usually ladies in search of temporary diversion until marriage, or at least daughters of working class families forced by circumstances to train as governesses or art teachers. Few had hopes of becoming fine artists; as the *Art journal* of 1861 pointed out, "the art education of working class girls is hopeless." Nevertheless Kate Greenaway persevered in evening classes at Heatherley's, and about 1872 she enrolled in the adventurous new Slade

School of Art, a school established under Edward Poynter to counteract the stilted regime of South Kensington. There models were drawn for their poses, and the movement and interpretation a student could bring to his drawing was a refreshing if not confusing change from Kate's previous experience. There she laboured long and hard under the school's primary dictum: "Pictorial art is everything—ornamental Art comparatively nothing." It was a difficult lesson to learn, for it meant reversing almost thirteen years' training.

During these difficult years as an art student, Kate Greenaway tried to apply her lessons in those commercial venues open to a woman with artistic ambitions. She eagerly accepted black-and-white illustration commissions her father secured for her from among his publisher employers; her colour studies were applied to illustrations of favourite children's tales for the Warne series *Aunt Louisa's London toy books* (1870), in which she struggled to avoid the garishness of previous, similar publications. Colour, especially watercolour, was a medium she wholeheartedly enjoyed and practiced all her life, from art-school lessons to her last coloured sketches for a series of unfinished books. It was the one medium the Victorian art world thought suitable for women artists. Several had broken ground by exhibiting watercolours at the prestigious Royal Academy exhibitions, although such works were relegated to separate rooms and it was long believed that a watercolourist—whether male or female—could never be admitted to full membership in the Academy. The medium itself demanded total dedication and privacy to regulate and build up the layers of quick-drying colour washes around a preliminary pencil drawing. It was the method Kate Greenaway used while working in the small backstreet studio room she had taken by the 1870s, rented from a woman with a Pre-Raphaelite beauty of a daughter, who was immediately pressed into modelling. Her frizzy red hair and endearing smile appeared in many of the watercolour portraits Kate successfully exhibited in London at that time—at the Dudley Gallery, the Royal Institute of Painters in Watercolour, and finally the Royal Academy itself.

Painting for exhibitions soon became one of Kate's major concerns; exhibition was a goal which many art students, however successful as decorative designers, strove to achieve. The London galleries offered the successful painter a respectability that the commercial designer-illustrator, tainted by the vulgarity of working for industry, could seldom attain. Artists like Millais, Rossetti, Holman Hunt, and Walter Crane therefore earnestly pursued their painting for exhibitions, while doing illustrations, often only grudgingly, for the money. Women artists then, had to labour under a double burden, since circumstances confined most of their efforts to commercial designing, while the fact that their few exhibition works were done by women hindered their chances of recognition. Nevertheless there were a few woman painters who managed to build reputations in the London galleries, women trained at South Kensington and the Slade, as well as the Royal Academy Schools. They included the portrait painter Clara Montalba; Mary Backhouse (later Mrs. W. E. Miller), painter of "Spring" (RA 1871) and "Maidenhood" (RA 1872); and the influential Helen Paterson (later Mrs. William Allingham), painter of rustic cottage scenes that eventually challenged the Greenaway reputation. Many of these women painters had the advantage of painter parents or brothers who could ensure that a daughter's or sister's works were associated with their own reputations and hung when those by others, with unknown names and amateur status, were ignored.

The exhibition venues open to women artists were noticeably few. Apart from the Old and New Watercolour Societies, there was the Royal Society of Painters in Watercolour, founded in 1821 to promote a medium neglected by the more prestigious galleries. Although Kate Greenaway never exhibited there, it was important as a centre for new artists, especially females; this unfortunately gave the gallery a frivolous reputation, as Thackeray pointed out when he visited it early in the period: "In the first place, you never can enter it without finding four or five pretty women, that's a fact; pretty women with pink bonnets peeping at pretty pictures, and with sweet whispers vowing that Mrs. Seyfforth is a dear, delicious painter, and that her style is 'so soft.'" Another gallery was the Society of British Artists (Suffolk Street), founded in 1824 by a rebellious group of painters (including the biblical painter John Martin) "for the purpose of Low Art, at any rate for the exercise of greater realism than was supposed to be favoured by the Royal [Academy]." As such there was a decidedly second-rate quality to the works exhibited there, and its hanging committee was often criticised for lacking sound artistic judgment. For example, the artist Weedon Grossmith, co-author of the Victorian classic *The diary of a nobody*, recalled sending his student studies of Royal Academy School models to Suffolk Street. If painted in fancy costumes and feathers, elaborately framed and titled "Marie" or "Clarice," these "were frequently bought by men who felt the pictures reminded them of old loves, known before marraige—(if one could invite men without wives to private views, one could sell double the number of pictures)."[11] Into this rather jaded atmosphere were sent the eleven child portraits Kate Greenaway successfully exhibited at Suffolk Street from 1870 to 1876, each one an idealised watercolour of a child or an adolescent, with titles like "A Peeper," "Little Watercress Girl," or "A Fern Gatherer," and all based on the local Islington street urchins she had pressed into modelling. The Dickensian character of her subjects and their settings—some were posed against a grimy street wall with tattered posters—were occasionally tempered with an old-world pastiche of a medieval garden, planted with Pre-Raphaelite madonna lilies or roses, the child dressed in heavy tapestry gown and eighteenth-century mob-cap.

When these works failed to sell at Suffolk Street, they were sent to the even more adventurous Dudley Gallery. Situated in the heart of London, in the Egyptian Hall, Picadilly, from 1865 to 1882 the Dudley served a vital role by exhibiting the works of amateurs and professionals unable to exhibit at the more prestigious galleries, and, most important of all, exhibited the rising number of artist-illustrators who worked for book publishers and magazines. There, from 1872, for the first time in any major British gallery, were hung works by popular black-and-white illustrators such as Randolph Caldecott, Walter Crane, Millais, Walker and other "Sixties School" artists. Kate Greenaway first exhibited there in 1868; her fairy painting and a group of six drawings on wood, the drawings based on studies of her masters Doyle, Meadows and Dadd, were hung alongside a "poetic though peculiar" Walter Crane painting, designs by Henry Stacy Marks, and rows of Christmas card designs. Her designs were singled out by the *Art journal* and bought by the editor of *People's magazine* (Reverend Loftie), who subsequently published four in his new family magazine.

Kate Greenaway continued to exhibit at the Dudley until its reputation began to wane. In 1879 the gallery's open-ended hanging policies came under attack, and even with her four watercolour children's portraits hung alongside works by Tenniel and Stacy Marks, the *Atheneaum* critic could describe the atmosphere only as "an agreeable lounge-place," the pictures lining its walls not to be taken seriously. Fortunately, by that time Kate Greenaway had successfully broken into the prestigious Royal Academy exhibitions, again with child portraits, which the art press called "charming," or painted in "powerful colour." This was a considerable achievement, since only 7% of the Academy exhibitors had been women in 1850, the number increasing only to 28% by 1903.

Works sold at annual exhibitions could scarcely support a thirty-two-year-old single artist, and, on her own admission, Kate was forced to undertake whatever "hack work" she or her father could find for her. She contributed black-and-white illustrations to children's periodicals like *Little folks,* published by her father's employers Cassell, Petter Galpin, and tried her hand at illustrating those domestic drawing-room dramas and romances made popular by Millais and Walker illustrations, her anguished figures dressed in contemporary costumes taken from her mother's dress shop, their faces often modelled on her brother's and father's. She adapted her style to fit a series of childhood reminiscence books by society ladies, like *My school days in Paris* and *The children of the parsonage*, and skillfully managed to suggest the backgrounds of places she had never visited. Other commissions were developed from her own childhood love of fairy tales, and she devised variations on gnomes and fairies to frighten the innocent child readers of *Starlight stories told to bright eyes and listening ears.* Gradually she steered her work to illustrating predominately for children, and a formalised "Greenaway face" emerged on her figures, probably borrowed largely from the vast doll collection she kept. She also studied the round-faced, pastel-tinted children's faces in portraits by Gainsborough and Reynolds in the National Gallery, and by the early 1870s had freely adopted Tenniel's popular "Alice" formula in her own fantasy-parody on the humorous papers she knew so well.

Also by the early 1870s, the Christmas card boom had begun to provide design work for amateur and professional artist-illustrators. The boom had been sparked off by the introduction of the postcard in 1870, and by the perfection of the colour lithographic printing used to produce such cards. Although at first most cards were printed in Germany, eventually British firms began to make inroads into the market. The most famous and respected of these was the Belfast-based Marcus Ward. They produced cards, calendars, and, later, colour-plate books to fill the bookshops and stationer's windows with elaborate pastiches of current artistic taste, either edged in lacy frills or printed in pale aesthetic tones, all designed largely by an anonymous staff under the art direction of Thomas Crane, Walter's brother. By 1880, prizes were offered to promote card designing among amateur artists; that year the firm of Raphael Tuck offered £500 for the best design from among 2,000 frames exhibited in one London gallery. By 1890, it was confidently asserted that one could earn £500-900 annually as a card designer, and by then even the Royal Academicians and other successful painters were tempted to design for such a lucrative market.

As an art student Kate Greenaway too had worked on card designs, no doubt using her ornamental design training in the samples she submitted to Marcus Ward's London office. Despite the firm's reservations about her garish colouring and the mawkish accompanying verses, these designs were eventually published (with colours altered, verses omitted), and several years' steady employment began for Kate. Some of these cards were issued singly, others in sets with elaborate envelopes or running stories, some even sewn into small booklets. She was eventually awarded the ultimate accolade of her design profession and allowed to display her initials in the corner of each design, but she never succeeded in getting her card verses accepted. Indeed, despite repeated insistences with Ward and numerous attempts at writing to formulas—hadn't the Poet Laureate himself been offered £1,000 for a card verse at this time? —she failed; and yet she continued to write verses, largely love sonnets, all the rest of her life, confident that she could develop her literary talent.

Gradually Kate's career began to advance and her remuneration grew from a ten-shilling commission here, two pounds five shillings there, to as much as 20 guineas for a Dudley picture sale. However, she never received adequate payment for the greeting card designs, and this caused the row that abruptly ended her relationship with Marcus Ward; her designs, though, continued to appear (she had no control over their use), and even were reissued as colour plates in a giftbook series. Her greatest achievement in this vein, however, was designs with Walter Crane for valentines in *The quiver of love* (1876). As a result, by 1877 she had not only attained a staggering £300 annual wage but had gained significant footholds in such influential papers as the *Illustrated London news* and *Graphic*, periodicals by then famed for their illustrations.

Despite Kate's success, her personality had changed very little; she was still deeply shy and awkward with strangers. But these were in fact the very qualities that endeared her to her friends and neighbours, like the artist Mrs. Miller, who claimed she was always "gentle, patient, industrious, exquisitely sensitive, extraordinarily humourous, while under and over it all was an indomitable will." A strong will is an essential attribute in any artist's life, with its continual upsets and disappointments, not to mention worries over finances, and Kate often used the panacea "Never mind" in a dismissive tone when some deadline forced her to trudge the grim, dark backstreet to her lonely studio. She took her task philosophically, always recalling how easy it was to escape each time the pen or brush touched the paper and a primrose or apple blossom appeared. Then, she insisted, "I am in fairyland."[12]

Most important of all, Kate Greenaway doggedly refused to accept the label of "paintress"—a term bandied about in a condescending manner by her male painter colleagues, descriptive of the rising number of female artists exhibiting in the London galleries. She firmly believed in her own private vision and maintained an almost obsessive insularity, in later years attacking the so-called "shrieking sisterhood" of suffragettes and women artists bent on redressing the imbalances in a male-based society. Nevertheless, the prejudice did exist, as exemplified in 1857 when the *Illustrated London news* reviewed a Society of Female Artists Exhibition and proclaimed that, "strength of will and power of creation belonging to the other sex, we do not of course look for the more daring efforts in an exhibition of female artists." Thirty years later, however, Kate Greenaway was proudly cited as a key examplar of perseverance and dedication to her work, her success embraced by female art students (4,000 by 1903) who had risen out of the era of prejudice and had learned that, according to a contemporary art career manual, "There is more hope for a girl with a very little talent and an infinite capacity for taking pains, than for one who has natural gifts but who lacks industry and perseverance. And it is almost impossible to say whether there is talent or not until the power of working hard has been exercised for some time."[13]

This was clearly a restatement of Kate Greenaway's own principle of perseverance, which by the late 1870s she had successfully put into practice. Ignoring the objections of her father, who believed she had found her role in piecemeal illustration and should go no further, Kate nurtured a private dream to have her own book of drawings and verses published—it was in one sense the result of failing to have her illustrated card verses published. She carefully (and secretly) prepared forty-nine watercolour drawings of children in the rural settings she knew so well, with verses based on moral tales and her essential life-long preoccupation with right and wrong, and presented the result to her father for an opinion. He was not at first impressed, but did show the rough pencil drawings to his early engraving colleague Edmund Evans, by then a master colour printer of Crane toybooks and Birket Foster rustic scenery, with a rising reputation that would make him the foremost colour printer in Britain. Always eager for a new project—he had just begun to commission children's books himself—Evans saw the commercial potential in Kate's naive drawings and agreed to produce a book from them. He showed them to his publisher-distributor, George Routledge, who objected to the verses (it seemed inevitable), but agreed to the venture. Evans had the verses slightly altered, engraved the pictures in the pastel colours that had made him famous, titled the book *Under the window* (from the opening verse), and printed a staggering 20,000 copies. These were sold out even before a second printing could be ordered, much to his collegues' astonishment, and eventually the book sold over its 70,000 second edition, was published in numerous foreign editions, and is still today in print. It earned its author over £1,500 and set her on the crest of a wave of fame and fortune that would break only some 45 books and 15 years later.

The overnight popularity of *Under the window* is difficult to explain today, but clearly Kate Greenaway had answered a largely neglected longing for nostalgia in the book-buying public, doing so with a fresh, if not startling, new naiveté of design; previous gift books had been over-produced, with overly-ornate engravings and smeared, garish colour plates. Kate's formula shows most of her childhood and student preoccupations, including eighteenth-century costumes (derived to a certain extent from discovering a trunk of old dresses and dolls at Rolleston) and the firmly outlined children of her greeting cards, their dresses modifications of oddments studied in her mother's shop. She also introduced appropriate contemporary notes with peacock feathers, sun-flowers, Pre-Raphaelite lilies and long, free-flowing pastel gowns made popular by followers of the burgeoning Aesthetic Movement. Her verses, on the other hand, were a mixture of greeting card sentiment and nursery-rhyme morals, tempered with the unexpected but very real melancholia so much a part of childhood: "Heigh Ho!—time creeps but slow;   I've looked up the hill so long; None come this way, the sun sinks low   And my shadow's very long." This image accompanied the self-portrait vision of young Kate, in pink frock, forlornly standing at a garden gate, and was among those verses the critics singled out as "piquant and fluent," accompanying "first-rate" designs. The real competition when *Under the window* appeared, in December 1879, were the Crane toybook series and the first of Caldecott's picture books. In spite of what the *Art journal* called a severe depression in the art market ("The worst we have experienced for many years"), the book sold very well, even at six shillings a copy. It was indeed a fairy tale come true, which is the way Kate Greenaway decided to accept her good fortune:

"For the world had found a new and lovely voice
To teach and train me in her secret ways,
And I saw beauty in all things that are
And knew that I was blest for all my days.

Above the world now, above its good and ill,
I ventured on a new and lovely life—
Sesame! had been said and I passed in,
My soul and body no more waged a strife."[14]

The world into which *Under the window* emerged so successfully was rapidly filling with children's books, intended for artistic parents with childish longings. The Elementary Education Act of 1870 had made school education a public service—by 1880 school attendance was compulsory—and the demand for children's school books had been met by a plethora of illustrated textbooks and so-called children's classics, many of which were poorly produced religious tracts or horrific reworkings of time-honoured nursery tales. "Most of the children's books published during the last quarter of the century [were] hurtful to children," claimed Henry Cole, pioneer of the first educational children's book series, Felix Summerley's Home Treasury. Produced from 1843, of well-known nursery favourites illustrated by Royal Academician friends, the series was intended to restore "elements of a child's mind, its fancy, imagination, sympathies, affections . . . ." By the 1860s, Walter Crane had begun to formulate his influential theories on illustrating for children, a discipline which he clearly loved for its freedom: "the imagination is singularly free, and let loose from ordinary restraints, it finds a world of its own, which may be interrupted in a spirit of playful gravity," but which evolved from his belief in preserving "the child spirit."[15] Randolph

Caldecott followed suit, and by the 1880s he, Crane and Greenaway were lumped together in the public's mind as the "Nursery Triumvirate" who would revolutionise the illustrated book and elevate the role of the book illustrator; by 1894, Henry Stacy Marks could confidently claim, "It is impossible for a child now-a-days not to be influenced by the admirable specimens of draughtsmanship he sees in most illustrated books and periodicals. A child's book today is a work of art."[16]

On the strength of *Under the window* and *A day in a child's life* (1881), *Mother Goose* (1881) and *Little Ann* (1883), the *Art journal* claimed Kate Greenaway had earned a remarkable reputation and "has obtained a position of standing among the artists of the present day"—the *artists*, not illustrators; clearly she had elevated herself from the prejudices surrounding illustration. That same year even her friend and colleague Randolph Caldecott lamented his rival's rise to fame, as she cut seriously into his book sales and had taken away "some of the necessary luxuries of life."[17] And to her own chagrin, this success had meant abandoning the watercolour pictures she loved to paint for exhibitions, as the demands on her talent as a book illustrator left little time for such speculative ventures.

The business of planning and preparing sequels to *Under the window* and subsequent books proved increasingly difficult. Fortunately Kate Greenaway had a series of well-meaning older "gentlemen advisors" who were well-versed in business, publishing and the unpredictable nature of fame, and who willingly offered advice to steer her away from the commercial exploitation a person in her new, vulnerable position might easily suffer. Apart from her father, constantly interested, there was Edmund Evans, who readily accepted his role as business partner, always searching for and suggesting new book subjects, pressing for deadlines to be met. In response, Kate spent many weekends working at his country home near Witley in Surrey, where the landscape, with Hindhead and gentle gorse-covered heath, became a constant delight; the Evans household, with its five vivacious children and constant houseguests, from Caldecott to George Eliot, lured her to return whenever she could manage the time from book work in her studio. Moreover, Evans himself was an endearing father-figure who loved the countryside; he would walk miles at the weekends delighting in "the effects of sunset, storm and sylvan beauty" that led to his printing a series of nature-guide books and promoting his neighbour, the rustic artist-illustrator Birkett Foster, whose works he also printed. Clearly, Evans and his new discovery, Kate Greenaway, had much in common, including a staunch belief in the essential goodness of their fellow man now and in afterlife, and the friendship lasted throughout their lifetimes.

Another personal advisor was the aristocratic poet and retired civil servant Frederick Locker (from 1885, Locker-Lampson), author of *London lyrics* and the *Under the window* verse revisions commissioned by Routledge and Evans. This early collaboration with Kate Greenaway led to a respectful admiration of her work, and a deepening friendship ensued, Kate showering him with watercolours, dedicating books to his children and, whenever possible, visiting his Rowfant, Sussex country estate and the wild and windy seaside retreat he built at Cromer in Norfolk. The seaside sequences in her later books, the forest scenes and heathland landscapes, were all inspired by such visits, and her later verses were in fact reworkings of conversations held with the Locker children.

Frederick Locker's chief rival for Kate's attention was the outspoken art critic John Ruskin, who had been so struck by an exhibition of *Under the window* drawings in London that he immediately wrote to congratulate their creator. This letter, written in 1880, was the spark that kindled a 20-year artistic and private friendship, the flames flaring as Ruskin's bouts of madness dominated their postal communication, the fire smouldering as Kate tried to finish a book and keep Ruskin content by submitting to his nearly impossible demands for nature study. Ruskin's influence on the Greenaway books and paintings, and indeed on her life and career in general, cannot be overestimated. As the foremost art critic in the country, he commanded an army of devoted followers who embraced his nature aesthetic, the Pre-Raphaelite painters he had once championed, and the lessons in seeing Italian art through an obsessed Englishman's eyes. By the 1880s, however, his followers were mainly female and his career as art critic had diminished as he succumbed to illnesses and self-imposed exile from London in his Lake Coniston house in the Lake District. Nevertheless, Kate Greenaway had earnestly read and agreed with Ruskin's writings, especially the attacks on urban decay and the death of the countryside, and when his letter arrived, filled with praises for her work, she readily became his devoted student and he her "Master." She was always willing to drop her brushes and rush to his side, to prepare the tea on his infrequent visits to her studio or to board the train for a long-awaited visit to his lakeside home. When he became dangerously ill, her letters arrived daily to inform him of her concern and her progress on books and watercolour lessons he had sent her. In some instances she supplied him with carefully constructed drawings of his favourite "girlies," which rekindled his nympholeptic fantasies; in others she learned a greater social conscience and responded with the drawings of beggar children or acts of charity that appear sporadically throughout her books.

Ruskin's primary aim for Greenaway was to alter her artistic vision, to make it more naturalistic in detail and colouring. He believed that colour in nature was merely a mosaic of pure, simple hues, as his beloved Turner had shown, and that by combining clear colour with abundant detail, all pictures could succeed—as his beloved Pre-Raphaelite friends Rossetti, Holman Hunt and, later, Burne-Jones had proved. In Kate's case, this pure colour was to be combined with angelic innocence, figures of tiny girls in long white nightgowns, wreaths of roses in their hair, and the result, according to Ruskin's view, would be "High Art" to rival the Italian masters (with whose works he often compared her pictures). To the uninitiated, this was stretching credibility to some extent, but his instructions to Kate were determined enough to make even the most sceptical look for the truth in nature: "Yesterday I saw quite blindingly bright pure greens, over acres of fresh warm grass. Can you do me a group of children in a hayfield, with pure green grass and *blue sky,* and flowers in ruby red and gold and purple?"[18] It was a typical Ruskin directive and Kate responded with watercolours and carefully composed book illustrations derived from them. These culminated in a painting for *The pied piper of Hamelin* (1888), with the piper in a vibrant green orchard, pale-pink-and-white-gowned children dancing among the bright meadow flowers. It had been created as a tonic to revive Ruskin's flagging spirits, its Pre-Raphelite figures and architecture using the perspective lessons he had tried, somewhat in vain, to teach her; it was, in Ruskin's view, a "Paradise Scene" worthy of all his efforts with her. On those rare occasions when they met, it was a marriage of two minds, and agreement was often forthcoming on such vital issues as Wordsworth's poetry or current literature and art, for theirs was a singular vision. In 1898, Kate tried to find words to describe this to Ruskin, then marvelled how "there goes on the wonderful world all the time, with its wonders hidden to, and uncared for by so many. How is it that I have got to think the caring for Nature and Art of all kinds a *real* religion?"[19] The answer of course was in Ruskin's 20-year domination of her life and art.

The Greenaway books continued to increase in number throughout the 1880s, each one a careful variation on the proven Greenaway formula, their formats sometimes suggested by Evans or by Kate's perusal of her book competition. When she started the almanack series in 1882 (published annually from 1883 to 1897, excluding 1896), she merely elaborated on her familiar greeting-card formula of figures and text, trying each year to vary the presentation somehow: one year figures were placed in open windows, another year in seasonal landscapes or composed in the geometric shapes borrowed from her art school lessons. Many books were specifically aimed at pleasing Ruskin, and his favourite roses and cherubic children predominated. Others were purely commercial, from the *Kate Greenaway painting book* of line drawings for colouring taken from previously published books, to the tiny *Kate Greenaway alphabet*, this reprinted from the financially unsuccessful *Mavor's English spelling book*. There were even two collaborations with Ruskin, the headpiece drawings for his *Fors clavigera: Letters to the working men of Britain*, and a series of new woodcuts in the reprinted classic *Dame Wiggins of Lee*, to illustrate the new verses Ruskin had written.

Botanical drawing played an important role in Kate Greenaway's early career, as we have seen, when she spent days at Rolleston perfecting drawings of flowers and hedgerow plants for her art lessons. The floral motifs in *Under the window* are a direct result; these rather stark cutouts pasted against white borders were followed by blown-up roses, daisies and chrysanthamums in the borders of *A day in a child's life* (1881), an enchanting but financially largely unsuccessful book. Both exemplify the Victorian emphasis on floral decoration and symbolism; that period produced some of the most ornate floral paintings and prints we know. For example, V. F. Bromley's "Flora," a seductive bare-breasted nude posed in a garden of hundreds of flower varieties, with a sunflower for a halo, was extremely popular when engraved and sold as a drawing-room print. Moreover, codebooks of floral symbols emerged with the greeting-card boom—especially at the introduction of the valentine—and Greenaway's *Language of flowers* (1884) was intended to offer this information in a convenient form, illustrated with the sentiments symbolized: the rose meant "love," but the forget-me-not meant "true love." The following year, *Marigold garden* appeared with its floral designs, but the emphasis had shifted to pastiches of Gainsborough children romping in silk dresses in a field of lambs. (Ironically, the book was dedicated to those children, both rich and poor, whom Ruskin had taught her to acknowledge as the true victims of senseless economic barriers.)

This book also marked the beginning of Kate Greenaway's preoccupation with the countryside surrounding her new home in Hampstead. She had chosen a buttercup field high above the smoke and fog of London—Hampstead Heath was known as "London's Lung"—and there, along the edge, perched her Norman-Shaw-designed house and studio, with its large walled garden. She never tired of daily walks to the heath, following in the footsteps of her famous past neighbours like Constable, Romney, Rossetti, Ford Madox Brown and Whistler; occasionally she even called in on the *Punch* cartoonist George du Maurier, who lived nearby.

Eventually competition and plagiarism of the Greenaway formula—a plethora of imitation Greenaway books appeared from early 1880—severely threatened Kate's livelihood. Also, the advent of the photoengraving process, which reproduced drawings photographically on metal blocks, meant thousands more copies could be printed from single, easily produced blocks than from those painstakingly hand-engraved wood blocks that were used for the Greenaway, Crane and most of the Caldecott books. There were also unauthorised uses of her designs for dolls, dresses, china and silver, sanitary wallpaper, towels and shoes, and in America, Greenaway drawings advertised toilet soaps, gloves and even pianos. By the 1890s, the situation had turned her bitter and forced her to consider other ways of earning her living; yet she was then only in her mid-40s and was still willing to work hard, as she wrote Ruskin: "I would like to work very hard but in a different way so that I was more free to do what I liked, and it is so difficult now that I am no longer at all the fashion."[20] She returned first to her early watercolours and concentrated on landscapes with few figures, relying no doubt on Ruskin's devoted advice and counsel. These paintings began to appear at the Royal Institute of Painters in Watercolour, a new gallery incorporating the Dudley, whose members included her beloved Millais (honorary member), the remarkable horse painter Rosa Bonheur, Tenniel and Walter Crane (who later resigned). Kate had been elected to membership in 1889, and during the following years she submitted some of her most effective landscapes, processional figure groupings inspired by classical friezes, and groups set in faded sunsets. One was "Gleaners Going Home," with Pre-Raphaelite maidens and storybook children wistfully returning from the fields—a work that followed similar ones hung at the Royal Academy and in two studio clearance sales of her sketches and paintings held at the London Fine Art Society in 1891 and 1894. Unfortunately, these latter were not wholly successful, for the public snapped up only those slight sketches and reminders of a once-popular book illustrator; most of the new watercolours remained unsold, and moreover they were attacked by the art press as too much in the vein of Helen Allingham, the acknowledged master of cottage scenes. This was a pity, since Kate's pictures in this style are among her most charming, and reflect a lifetime's practise and understanding of a difficult watercolour medium. She employed the controversial "knifing-in" process, cutting areas of flowers and folding the paper back for maximum contrast, and

41

she freely used body colour, that opaque white paint abhorred by many of her colleagues. True, her figures retained many of their anatomical faults—the knees too far down the leg, the pointed chins and marble-shaped eyes—but she believed, perhaps rightly, that this was what her public had grown to expect from her pen and brush.

Much of this later work was clearly created in a firm defiance of the changes going on in the British art world at the end of the Victorian period. Those staunch Victorian institutions like the Royal Academy and Royal Watercolour Society were then under attack by a new generation of artists who believed such places crushed creativity and employed out-dated standards of taste. The giants they had produced, Leighton, Millais and the other Pre-Raphaelites, were similarly attacked, and London galleries held requiem exhibitions of these masters as one by one the gods fell from their pedestals. Nevertheless, Kate Greenaway retained her belief in the merit of these Olympians and continued to work from their moulds. There was in fact something of a crusader's air about her attitudes then, and each time she returned disgusted from the London galleries she grew even more determined to champion the naturalism she and Ruskin so deeply believed in. "It isn't realism, it isn't all imagina-tion, it's a queer giving something to nature that is possible for nature to have, but always has not," she maintained.[21] But it was a difficult strug-gle in the face of Beardsley's influence ("Tell Mr. Ruskin I hate Beardsley!"), and of George Moore's and the New English Art Clubs's fer-vent belief that "The [Royal] Academy must be destroyed, and when that is accomplished the other Royal Institutes will follow as a matter of course."

Kate's exhibition disappointments meant that by 1897 she turned to oil portraits of children, her models taken from the long lists she gathered over years of spotting angelic "Italianate" faces in tube trains and on buses. Her close friends—many of them high-born and important literary or government wives—tried to help secure commissions, but the struggles to re-adopt what was basically an entirely different discipline proved too much. Her fresh watercolour technique failed now, the children's faces ("smooth, sticky things") turning into chalky or at worst muddy messes that required scraping and repainting. When her last watercolours appeared at the Royal Institute, despite modest prices of £25 they were unsold and berated by the art press; the *Athenaeum* called them "as before," predicting that "Even her faithful public may end up getting tired of her quaintly clad girls and her groups of children."

Then in early 1900, John Ruskin died, and with him went Kate's own will to live. Their crusade had lost its thrust and she retreated into her studio to write increasingly morbid verses ("A lonely soul, I am ever alone"), which culminated in the lines she designated for her gravestone: "Heaven's blue skies may shine above my head, while you stand there and say that I am dead." Shortly thereafter, on 6 November 1901, she died. The true end of the Victorian period had come, Queen Victoria having died a few months earlier. The artistic world that had increasingly chosen to ignore Kate Greenaway rallied to her graveside, only then to pay full tribute to the singular vision of the artist who had earned the accolade "Pre-Raphaelite of the Nursery."

Rodney Engen, *London, July 1980*

NOTES

1. M. H. Spielmann and G. S. Layard, *Kate Greenaway*, 1905, p. 260; hereafter cited as S & L.
2. John Ruskin, "In Fairyland," in his *The art of England*, 1883.
3. See John Ruskin's essay, "The study of architecture in schools."
4. *Nottingham review and general advertiser*, 3 April 1846.
5. S & L, pp. 28-29.
6. S & L, p. 189.
7. S & L, p. 235.
8. S & L, p. 41.
9. See Michael Holroyd, *Augustus John*, 1974, vol. 1, p. 34.
10. See Thackeray's "Second lecture on the fine arts," *Fraser's magazine*, 1840.
11. Weedon Grossmith, *From studio to stage*, 1913, pp. 34-35.
12. S & L, p. 52.
13. Florence Reason writing on "Art," in Lady Jeune's *Ladies at work*, 1893, pp. 45-46.
14. S & L, p. 260.
15. See *The Imprint*, 1913, and the *Easter art annual*, 1898, for Crane's comments on children's illustration; his work is surveyed in R. K. Engen's *Walter Crane as a book illustrator*, 1975.
16. H. S. Marks, *Pen and pencil sketches*, 1894, vol. 2, pp. 141-142.
17. For a survey of Caldecott's work see R. K. Engen's *Randolph Caldecott: Lord of the nursery*, 1976.
18. Undated letter, Ruskin to Kate Greenaway, Pierpoint Morgan Library.
19. S & L, p. 234; for a complete discussion of the Greenaway-Ruskin relationship see R. K. Engen's *Kate Greenaway: A biography*, (forthcoming, 1981).
20. S & L, p. 232.
21. S & L, p. 209.
22. George Moore, *Modern painting*, 1893, p. 248.

Frontispiece illustration from *Language of flowers* by Kate Greenaway.
Wood engraving in color by Edmund Evans.

Illustration from *A day in a child's life* by Myles Birket Foster,
illustrated by Kate Greenaway, p. 20. Wood engraving in color by Edmund Evans.

In the century since the instant success of her first book, Kate Greenaway's reputation has survived widespread imitation and outlived periods of neglect. The child-world of her private vision strikes a note of universality. Though firmly embedded in Victorian taste and sentiment, her special world still has a fresh appeal. While the names of her equally talented contemporary artist-illustrators are scarcely known to the general public, Kate Greenaway books and greeting cards still appear regularly in bookstores. If the appeal of her art has proved durable, so, too, has been the appeal of the subjects she favored. Childhood may have lost the nearly cult status it had in the 1880s, but toys still support a thriving industry, and while the "language of flowers" is no longer familiar lore, flowers themselves are still favorably regarded. Her innocent children, in old-fashioned costumes, reminded a Victorian public of a brighter and happier age, and today, while we may agree with the modern wit who assures us that nostalgia is not what it used to be, it still counts in the marketplace.

Kate Greenaway's books captivated Victorians, and still have the power of seduction, not only because of her gift of seeing in a new and special way, but because her intuition and hard-earned skills matched that vision and gave it fresh artistic expression. While Ruskin was sometimes overly critical of details of execution, he did recognize the essential charm and originality of her art. Her shortcomings of draughtsmanship are often cited, but do we look at children's books for training-school studies of drapery and anatomy? More academically correct rendering of gowns and limbs might well have done harm to the general decorative effect of her illustrations. At the technical level, Kate Greenaway commanded a sensitivity of line and an aptness for composition of figures, singly and in groups, that are essential to coherence; she made use of simple, pastel color harmonies which greatly heighten the enchantment of her illustrations.

It has been suggested that if the bird subjects were cut out of Audubon's great *Birds of America,* there would remain a respectable collection of botanical illustrations. Kate Greenaway without children is unthinkable, of course—even though she did illustrate the famous Piper piping the children out of Hamelin. But her pages, even minus their leading actors, would still offer rich backdrop scenes of meadows, orchards, streets and interiors, and in the foreground and margins, a varied assortment of flowers and plants—bouquets, nosegays, beribboned garlands, swags and wreaths, floral borders and individual plant portraits. *The language of flowers,* of course, *A day in a child's life* and *Marigold garden* are notable examples in which flowers act powerfully in the general decorative effect so characteristic of her art. The skills developed in Kate's early years as a designer of greeting cards (and where would greeting cards be without flowers?) were used with telling effect in the major books of the best years of her career. John Ruskin, Kate's self-appointed champion and mentor, shared her passion for nature in general and flowers in particular. Along with the steady barrage of praise, criticism, advice and admonition that the awesome author-critic aimed at the modest artist were a multitude of suggested projects, one of which called for collaboration on a handbook of field botany, she to furnish the illustrations and he the text. (Unfortunately, nothing came of it.)

Kate Greenaway arrived on the scene too late to catch the great period of flower-book production earlier in the century, a period in which several women—Mary Lawrence, Mrs. Withers, Mrs. Bury—made notable contributions as illustrators. For Kate's generation, the things in demand were greeting cards and children's books, and a good living was to be made by hard-working women trained to meet those demands. As student and as artist, Kate Greenaway was, indeed, hard-working.

Considering the only art training available to young women of Kate's day— rigidly structured schooling of deadening stodginess (a curriculum described in Rodney Engen's essay)—it is astonishing, and a measure of her stubborn resolve, that she was able to emerge as an individual and as an original artist whose fanciful vision of infancy and childhood created an idyllic world that transcends her period.

Compared to the masters of flower painting, Kate Greenaway must be considered a floral miniaturist, an eclectic adapter of manuscript illumination and of the seventeenth-century decorative and florilegium traditions. Her own floral art was based on close and sympathetic study of plants drawn from life, and drawn with an artless freshness, an unaffected spontaneity that makes it a fitting complement to the solemn-faced, quaintly-costumed creatures that live and dance on the pages of her books.

Kate Greenaway's career is a reminder that the artist who would make a living from book illustration is subject to the technologies and economies of the publishing trade. Drawings and paintings themselves do not illustrate books (not since the fifteenth century, anyway). Books are illustrated by printed replicas of original artworks, produced with whatever degree of fidelity the publisher can manage at a cost low enough to allow a small profit from expected sales.

Kate was notably lucky in attracting the attention of Edmund Evans, a perceptive, sympathetic publisher and judge of talent who had enlisted both Walter Crane and Randolph Caldecott, the two leading children's book illustrators of the age. Evans also happened to be the foremost color printer in England. Ink line and watercolor wash was the medium best suited to realize the fresh quality of Kate Greenaway's images, and the chromolithography then in general use was inappropriate for its reproduction. Thomas Bewick (1753-1828) had long since developed wood engraving as a vehicle for black-and-white illustration. Using engraver's tools and working on fine-textured end-grain blocks, Bewick achieved a great refinement of the traditional woodcut technique in which a knife is used to cut the design into a relatively coarse plank block. By the 1870s Evans had successfully adapted the medium to color printing through the use of a separate block for each basic color. Careful planning and delicate cross-hatch engraving of each block enabled him to superimpose one color over another in a

THE LITTLE QUEEN'S COMING.

Illustration from *Marigold garden* by
Kate Greenaway, p. 35. Wood engraving
in color by Edmund Evans.

UNDER ROSE ARCHES.

Illustration from *Marigold garden*, p. 47. Wood
engraving in color by Edmund Evans.

close pattern, the separate colors blending to produce additional shades.[1]
Using no more than three or four separate blocks, Evans was thus able to
reproduce virtually the full range of pastel colors so characteristic of Kate
Greenaway's art. His great contribution was in capturing with remarkable
fidelity the freshness of her originals, and in doing so with an equally
remarkable economy of means. This was crucial to the production of
children's books at prices within the reach of the large middle-class
market.[2]

Kate Greenaway was, of course, well known as an artist, apart from her illustrations and books. Over the years of her career she painted in various
modes; her drawings and paintings were often on exhibition and sold in
galleries. But her name would scarcely be remembered on this account. It is
chiefly through the medium of her children's books that the general public
then and since has come to know and prize her art.

John Brindle, *Pittsburgh, August 1980*

NOTES

1. Several of his blocks for Greenaway illustrations are included in this exhibition.
2. In the 20 years after 1878 the Greenaway-Evans partnership issued, in book form alone,
   some 932,100 copies.

47

CATALOGUE OF THE EXHIBITION

Asterisks following the entry numbers indicate items illustrated in this work. For those reproduced or quoted in *Kate Greenaway* by M. H. Spielmann and G. S. Layard (London, 1905), that work is cited in the entries as "S.," together with the relevant page number(s).

Heights of books are given to the nearest half-centimeter. Dimensions given for artworks (height preceding width) are of mat openings, unless otherwise stated.

Greenaway's signed initials, rendered variously in the originals, are cited in the standardized form "KG."

Complete citations for primary and secondary sources mentioned in the catalogue entries and not cited fully there will be found in the Summary Register under the appropriate headings.

THE SUNFLOWER

1* Sunflower. Ink and watercolor, 67 x 64 mm, for *Language of flowers.*

2* Sunflower. Ink and watercolor, 91 x 49 mm, for *A day in a child's life.*

3* Sunflower. Watercolor sketch, 182 x 146 mm.

4 Myles Birket Foster. *A day in a child's life.* Illustrated by Kate Greenaway. Music by... London, New York, George Routledge and Sons, [1881].
  25 cm. Light green glazed pictorial boards, bevelled edges, olive green endpapers.

5 Kate Greenaway. *Language of flowers* illustrated by... Printed in colours by Edmund Evans. London, George Routledge and Sons, [1884].
  15 cm. Green glazed pictorial boards, with red background, brown endpapers.

THE ARTIST AND HER CIRCLE

AUTOBIOGRAPHY

6* Autobiographical journal, pp. [1-183]. Verbatim excerpt, p. [61], concerning the garden at Rolleston.
  round the House window, always new Convolvulus—the biggest the most intensely coloured I have ever know[n]—

lovely deep blue Flowers with Pinky stripes deep Pink ones with white stripes—and they were new every day—I never went there without going to see what Convolvulus were out—I could look at them a long long time—a grape vine also grew over the House at the back. Then began the Garden divided by a gravel Path from the House.*2 [Added reference here is to note on opposite page by G. S. Layard: "(In later life her letters were filled with just such catalogues of flowers GSL)."] First came to your left a large oval bed—with Roses, Pinks Stocks Sultans—the brown Scabous I mean, white Lilies Yellow lilies Red Fuscias[sic] Roses—and in earlier Summer Monster Tulips The loveliest double white Narcissus Peonies Crown Imperials Pansy Wall Flowers—indeed all lovely Flowers seemed to grow here—and the scent—there were the largest Box Borders I have ever seen here—thick and bushy and nearly a yard high—we used to sit down on them and they never gave way with you—then Past the large oval bed a long gravel walk went straight down to the bottom of the Garden bound by the box border. Flowers grew all the way down—both sides—while beyond was the orchard on your left and Kitchen Garden on your right—Apple Pear Plum trees—with bushy Filberts—then the entrancing—white and red currants han[g]ing in the shining transparent bunches—and the Pretty little stalks—then Strawberries and Gooseberries—and the Patch of Scented herbs—and the Feather[y] asparagus. *it was* an enchanted Place—and I think From these early impressions that the enchantment has still in a measure remained with me for all such Places. The house stretched on into barnlike Places. That was one lovely thing in all these Country Houses the Vast Space. The Monster barns and store places—which of course are no longer required. (vide note on opp page)*1 [Added reference here by G. S. Layard is to note by KG on opposite page: "People took a Pride in keeping Corn unthreshed[;] it showed they didn't need the money."] The Corn of course being then kept for some time often in the Barns—and threshed—which took a long time

11

3

7* Lilies. Watercolor sketch, 220 x 131 mm.

8* Rose trellis. Watercolor sketch, 275 x 215 mm.

9* Poppies. Watercolor sketch, 96 x 96 mm, for *Book of games.*

10* Apple blossoms. Watercolor sketch, 243 x 132 mm, for *Language of flowers.*

11* Narcissus. Watercolor sketch, 134 x 114 mm.

12 Marion Harry Spielmann and George Soames Layard. *Kate Greenaway.* London, Adam and Charles Black, 1905.
   28 cm. White cloth, gold-stamped, illustrated endpapers. Number 10 of the limited edition of 500 copies, signed by John Greenaway, including two original watercolors by Kate Greenaway, one a study for an Almanack.

FLOWERS AND GARDENS

13 *Mother Goose or the old nursery rhymes* illustrated by Kate Greenaway, engraved and printed by Edmund Evans. London, New York, George Routledge and Sons, [1881].
   17 cm. Beige cloth, printed in green and brown, olive green endpapers. Illustrated salmon dust wrapper. Bookplate of Cortlandt Bishop. Includes watercolor copies, slightly enlarged, of illustrations on half-title and title pages.

14 Jane and Ann Taylor. *Little Ann and other poems.* Illustrated by Kate Greenaway. Printed in colours by Edmund Evans. London, New York, George Routledge and Sons, [1883].
   23.5 cm. Half green cloth with cream glazed pictorial boards, yellow endpapers. Presentation copy with original watercolor signed "KG" on verso of first illustrated page, inscribed "Eileen Ponsonby From Kate Greenaway" on recto.

15 Jane and Ann Taylor. *Little Ann and other poems.* Illustrated by Kate Greenaway. Printed in colours by Edmund Evans. London, New York, George Routledge and Sons, [1883].
   23.5 cm. Cream glazed pictorial boards, yellow endpapers. Presentation copy inscribed "Lionel Tennyson From Kate Greenaway 1895" on first illustrated page.

16 Kate Greenaway. *Under the window.* Pictures and rhymes for children by... Engraved and printed by Edmund Evans. London, New York, George Routledge and Sons, [1878].
   24 cm. Blue cloth, gold-stamped, blue floral endpapers. Includes original watercolor drawings for two illustrations, one signed "KG." Bookplate of George Lille Craik.

50

round the House window, always New Convolvulus. the biggest the most intensely coloured I have ever known. lovely deep blue Flowers with Pinky Stripes deep Pink ones with white Stripes - and they were new every day. I never went there without going to see what Convolvulus were out. — I could look at them a long long time - a grape Vine also grew over the House at the back. then began the Garden divided by a gravel Path from the House *2 First came to your left a large oval bed - with Roses, Pinks Stocks Sultans. the brown Scabous I mean, white Lilies Yellow Lilies Red Fuscias Roses - and in earlier summer Monster tulips the loveliest double white narcissus Peonies Crown Imperials Pansy wall Flowers - indeed all lovely Flowers seemed to grow here. (and the Scent - - - - there were the largest Box Borders I have ever seen here. thick and bushy nearly a yard high - we used to sit down on them and they never gave way with you — then Past the large oval bed a long gravel walk went straight down to the bottom of the Garden bound by the box border. Flowers grew all the way down - both sides. while beyond was the orchard on your left And Kitchen Garden on your right - Apple Pear - Plum trees - with bushy Filberts — then the entrancing - white and red Currants hanging in shining transparent bunches. and the Red little shallot - then Strawberries and Gooseberries — and the Patch of Scented herbs. and the Feathery asparagus. it was an enchanted Place — and I think From these early impressions that the enchantment has still in a measure remained with me for all such Places. The house stretched on into barnlike Places, that was one lovely thing in all these Country Houses the vast Space. the Monster barns and store places which of course are no longer required. the Corn of course being then kept for some time after in the Barns — and threshed). which took a long time

[61]

6

26

22

17* Envelope illustrated with topiary, poppies and lattice-work fence, addressed "Violet Dickinson." Watercolor, 92 x 118 mm.

18* Envelope illustrated with topiary, blue birds and poppies, addressed "Oswald • Dickinson • Esq." Watercolor, 92 x 118 mm.

19* Topiary. Watercolor (sketchbook page), 87 x 125 mm.

20* Woman holding child in garden with fox-gloves. Watercolor, 252 x 156 mm.

21 ALS: 21 July 1897, Witley, Surrey to John Ruskin. Envelope and eight pages. Pen sketch of the countryside at head of first page.

> Greenaway, in recounting her visit to the family of Edmund Evans, her publisher, tells of touring the residence next door which once belonged to the "Birket Fosters" and of being quite taken with the Burne-Jones and Rossetti windows in this house, the former depicting the four seasons and the latter Chaucer's dream of fair women. Then, she describes her visit on the 20th to Gertrude Jekyll's home: "There were numbers of Alpine Flowers such deep colours at least the blue ones—it is a great enjoyment to go to her Garden—She showed me the most exquisite Carnations in the world[,] white with colour running round every Petal[;] it was called dainty Lady and there was

one with the Finest thread of red. So beautiful—The Hollyhocks here are enough to make You long to Paint Holly-hocks For ever. They are such colours and look so Fresh and beautiful. ¶I wish You had some time seen this Place—it really is perfection and the Cottages and Farm Houses are so very beautiful with their tall chimneys and wooden beams."

22* ALS: 30 November 1886, 50, Frognal, Hampstead, N.W. to John Ruskin ("Dino—My Dear, My Dear"). Four pages. Pencil and watercolor sketch of a girl's head in stock-ing cap at head of first page. S., pp. 160-161.

> She tells him how much she is enjoying *Praeterita*. She then speaks of going to see Mrs. Allingham, "who was in town for a few days—with such a lot of beautiful drawings—they *were* lovely—the most truthful, the most like—things really look and the most lovely likeness—I've felt en-vious all the hours since—There was one Cottage and Garden with a deep back-ground of Pines—it was a marvel of Paint-ing—then such a Rose bush—then a divine little Picture—of her own beautiful little boy sitting on a Garden seat with a Girl picking red Currants—a background of deep Laurels—you Cant think the beauty of it—and *Many Many Many* More—all so lovely—so beautiful—she asked Me could I tell her anything—give her advice and I could not help saying—I

37

19

can give you nothing but entire praise and the deepest admiration . . ." Then she recommended that Mrs. Allingham send Ruskin one of her paintings of a little girl with a cottage, or one of a cottage garden.

23   ALS: 8 April 1882, 11, Pemberton Gardens, Holloway, N. to Lily Evans. Four pages, with undated half-page note by Lily Evans. S., pp. 107-108.

She talks of the flowers in her garden and in the "boxes of dirt" which Lily Evans said (in the attached note) were "window boxes for plants to grow in which I as a country child had never before seen." Greenaway writes: "I've a real hope that I do see Golden Rod coming up at last—or does a witch live in our Garden and is it flox [sic] after all[?]"

24*   ALS: 22 March 1896, 39, Frognal, Hampstead, N.W. to Violet Dickinson. Three pages. Pencil and watercolor sketch of five women in a field of crocuses at head of third page. S., p. 189.

She describes somewhat poetically how "You can go into a beautiful New Country if you stand under a large Apple tree—and look up to the Blue sky through the White flowers—to go to this scented Land—is an experience. ¶I suppose I went to it very Young before I could really remember—and that is why I have such a wild delight in Cowslips and Apple Blossom—They always give Me the Same

strange Feeling of trying *to remember*—as if I had known them in a Former World. ¶I always feel Wordsworth must Have Felt that a little too—when he wrote the Intimations of Immortality—I mean the trying to remember—¶It's such a beautiful world especially in the Spring—Its a Pity it's so sad also—I often reproach the Plan of it[.] it seems as if some less painful and repulsive end—Could have been found—for it's Poor helpless inhabitants—considering the wonderfulness of it all[.]"

25   ALS: 22 April 1897, 39, Frognal, Hampstead, N.W. to Lady Maria Ponsonby, Envelope and four pages. S., p. 212.

She describes her hard work in the garden ("My enthusiasm led me to do too much in the Garden consequently now I can hardly move") and complains that she should be painting backgrounds. "I seem not to do things well, and whatever I do Falls so Flat. it is rather—unhappy to Feel you have had Your day.—Yet if only I had just enough Money to live upon. I could be so very happy Painting Just what I liked and no thought of Profit[.]"

26*   ALS: 18 April 1899, 39, Frognal, Hampstead, N.W. to John Ruskin. Envelope and eight pages. Pen sketch of a woman's head at head of first page.

Greenaway wants to spend all her time at oil painting. She comments on Rover at

53

28

39

54

the window, and speaks of the translation of Dante's sonnets and of her reading Le Gallienne's *Young lives.* She describes the heath as "...a large Orchard Filled with beautiful Flowering Trees Apple, Pear, Plum, Just all coming into Flower. I'd like to Paint [these?] only it takes so long to Paint Flowering things and I feel I ought to devote myself to the Portraits and the verses." She speaks of her attempts to write stories and plays, and comments on her affection for flowers: "it is Curious but Certain Flowers are to me almost like books I like that every now and then I Feel I Must read over again—so I Feel with Certain Flowers. I must Possess some—to look at For a day or two—it's the Feeling of seeing Someone You Care For again—There are certain Flowers I never look on without Feeling an extraordin[a]ry sort of affection For them."

27   Flowering fruit trees with moon, brook. Watercolor (sketchbook page), 185 x 237 mm; signed "KG" in pencil, partly erased.

28   ALS: 11 August 1897, 39, Frognal, Hampstead, N.W. to John Ruskin. Envelope and eight pages. Pen sketch of a woman sitting by a lake at head of first page.
       She complains of being tired and hot, and of her brother being unwell. She thanks Ruskin for sending his love to her, describes the flowers of Amersham and

Witley, talks of painting flowers in the garden under "two umbrellas," and says that she "seems to have made backgrounds to everything. Of flowers which of course are twice as much work as anything else. I dont know why I do it[.] I suppose I like the Flowers—and dont think when I Put them in[.]"

VIEWS ON ART

29   ALS: 12 July 1896, 39, Frognal, Hampstead, N.W. to Lady Maria Ponsonby. Envelope and four pages. S., p. 209.
       After commenting at length on how Lady Ponsonby's kind letter "revived" her, Greenaway digresses on art: "Yes the Pleasure Art gives us is so strange—all the Most beautiful things in every way—And—I can Never define what Art really is—in painting I mean—it isnt realism[:] it isnt all Imagination[;] its a queer giving Something to Nature—that is possible for Nature to have but always has not—at least thats my idea—its what Burne Jones does when he twists those Roses all about his People in the Briar Rose. They dont often grow like that but they could. And it's a great Comfort to like such things—at least I find it so[.]"

30   AL Fragment: 4 October 1896, 39, Frognal, Hampstead, N.W. to Violet Dickinson. Two pages. Pen sketch of a woman walking at sunset at head of first page.

54

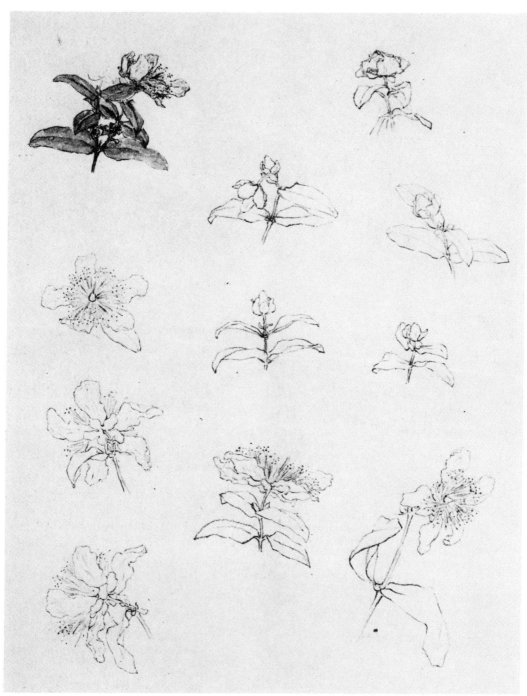

34

55

57

She speaks of how much Violet will learn in her travels and how fortunate she is to be in Venice now. After describing some of the exhibits of the Arts and Crafts, whose Private View she attended, Greenaway proceeds to discuss the current fashion for imitating the art of the past: "They go back and take too much of the old—without its meaning—the Old People *were* trying to copy real things—while these try to make things just as they *dont* see them. ¶Im quite sure there is No one in the whole world *can* love the old things more than I do[.] They could not give More joy to anyone than they do to me—but I do feel all this im[it]ation strikes a False Note—They Follow slavishly where—they ought only to be inspired—I'm sure all distortion is False. Art is a queer thing and I think quite undefinable—it must be true—with an Ideal of the Most beautiful Part of Everything."

31* ALS: 21 October 1896, 39, Frognal, Hampstead, N.W. to John Ruskin. Envelope and eight pages. Pen sketch of a young woman with landscape background at head of seventh page. S., p. 209.
   Greenaway speaks of rarely being able to put a book aside once she has begun to read it, even if she dislikes it. She digresses on the difficulties she has in painting certain colors: "The Heath looks

wonderful[;] it is all so brilliant—Red Orange and Emerald Green—Rosettis Green. it always makes me think of Rosetti. I see the Colour He *tried* For—and How difficult it is—You cant think what Colours to Paint it with because it always looks so cold when it is done—not a bit like the real Colour—I despair over grass[.] I cant do it—I dont know what it is. I dont know what blue to use—or what Yellow.—I'm so longing to try More body Colour[.] it's a Curious thing[.] Everybody runs it down—Yet—all the great water colour People (The Modern ones) have used it . . ."

32 ALS: 8 March 1899, 39, Frognal, Hampstead, N.W. to John Ruskin. Eight pages. Pen sketches (two portraits), called by her "The new thing," at head of first page. S., p. 240.
   She tells him that illness has taken up much of her time for the past month. She describes a tearful farewell to her friends the Tennysons who left for Australia. She is enjoying reading Browning's letters and reports a visit to the Spielmanns, mentioning their portraits of Ruskin. Then she rants against the modern taste in art, contrasting it with the greatness of John Millais: "The Poor Artists—cant afford to Paint *Good* Pictures[;] no one will buy them[.] I think it is very sad and such a Pity the sort of thing that takes Now—

38

cheap—of course that comes First—then Comes the Picture[,] if You Can Call it so —(I often dont)—The colours are daubed on in great smears and dashes. The drawing has gone . . . at a distance it looks like something, but close You Cant see anything[.] Now *I hate Pictures* that dont look right *close*—Sometimes the Colour of them is good—Powerful—and Strong[,] but—so was Millais and with all else it ought to be added in More and More—do I grow to think Millais wonderful—to me—there is no question He is greatest[.] People quarrel with Me because I think Him greater than Watts—but is it conceited to say[?]—*I know He is*—and Watts himself says so also[.] Ah if I could Paint like Millais—then then You'd see a *Proud Person indeed.*"

33   ALS: 13 August 1896, 39, Frognal, Hampstead, N.W. to John Ruskin. Envelope and eight pages. Pen sketch of a girl with tambourine at head of third page.
       Greenaway includes a sketch of the painting she has been doing of a girl playing a tambourine—"which Johnny calls the Salvation Army." She then digresses on flowers and art: "I've got a liking to put Flower branches along the top of things and dont seem to mind if You dont see where they come from, and yet want it quite *correct* in its way of growing and the shape of its flowers and leaves [—] isn't

that strange [?] —Yet somehow isn't that *Art*[?]—it's so difficult to define it—I should not mind much about defining it—if only I could do it well."

34*   St. John's Wort. Ten pencil sketches, one pencil and watercolor sketch, 145 x 115 mm overall.

35   ALS: 9 May 1899, 39, Frognal, Hampstead, N.W. to John Ruskin. Envelope and eight pages. Pen sketch of a young woman sitting on a hillside at head of first page. S., p. 241.
       She tells of intending to paint a group of girls in a wedding procession, which she has been thinking of for some time. She admires the portraits done by Sir Joshua Reynolds that she saw at the National Gallery. She describes being introduced to Princess Louise while visiting the Home Art Industries exhibition at the Royal Albert Hall. She humorously relates how, when she curtsied to the Princess, her purse burst open and the money fell to the floor. She speaks of the differences between using oil and water to paint colors: "The Oil Portraits are going on. I Find it so difficult [—] Curiously the Most difficult Part to get the Colours to represent the Colours I see—they are so different in water Colour—they Produce such different Colour—If I Could do it I would like it—but I rush off to My Flowers—Spring daffodils and Primroses[,] Blackthorns and Whitethorns[.]

62

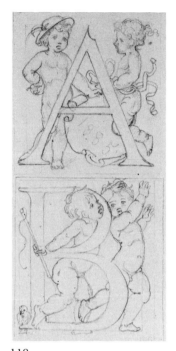

113

36   ALS: 24 May 1896, Centre Cliff Hotel, Southwold, to John Ruskin. Envelope and eight pages, including pen sketches of a font, a figure, a bridge, and two of angels.

She describes what she has been seeing while visiting Southwold churches with Dorothy Stanley: "Such a beautiful church like a Small Cathedral [—] There are beautiful carved Angels all along the Roof inside with Golden wings and coloured dresses [—] so nice and such a beautiful carved oak Screen with old Paintings of the Apostles on the lower Part[.] there is a curious figure Stands up in the church—called a Jack in Armour—and a Jack smite the clock—They Pull a rope then He strikes on a Sort of Gong every time the clergymen and choristers enter the church. I have never seen one before . . . We went to see a lovely old church . . . at a Place called Blythburgh[;] it reminded Me Somehow of Winchester —The Floor was red and Pale Yellow bricks and the roof all Painted and such beautiful Flying Angels with their wings outspread [a sketch here] beautiful—and a queer little Painted Man—who rang a bell when the clergyman was to come in[,] but he had[,] I believe[,] been Part of a clock—not like the Jack smite the clock . . . I see there is a tomb of an old British King called Anna, so I suppose it is his chapel . . . built in 14 something[.] The old seats had Funny little Figures on

the ends of them[,] all different[,] and the Font [a drawing here of one of the figures] so curious [a drawing here of the font] with two stone tools [—] one for the clergyman to kneel on[,] one for the God-mother. There were lots of remains of old Brasses on the Floor—¶I like the churches being beautiful . . ." She also speaks of the "Bright Coloured Bathing Machines[,] Red and Green—Green and white—Pink and green[,] like Toy Houses" along one of the beaches.

37*   View of church with cemetery. Pencil (sketchbook page), 78 x 123 mm.

38*   Bathing machine. Pencil (sketchbook page), 126 x 180 mm.

39   ALS: 26 [and 27] January 1898, 39, Frognal, Hampstead, N.W. to John Ruskin. Envelope and eight pages. Pen sketch of a girl watching some ducks with a windmill in the distance at head of first page. S., p. 229.

She is borrowing from Ruskin some of the drawings she had given him over the years as gifts; she says she is glad he won't mind them going to an exhibition at the Fine Art Society. She nominates the Ophelia painting [by Millais] as the greatest of modern times and also comments on how the public is now appreciating the work of both Millais and

58

63

59

65

Leighton. Complaining of her technical shortcomings, she proceeds to explain her working methods: "I will never begin a lot of things together again—because then you cant do new ideas or try different ways of work. And I always could only do one thing at once—I live in the one thing and think about it and it's like a real thing or Place For the time[.] even now—the Moment I'm doing a new drawing[,] The Morning rushes by—I'm so happy[,] so interested—I only Feel the tiredness when I cant go on because it is too late—or too dark."

40 ALS: 3 March 1897, 39, Frognal, Hampstead, N.W. to John Ruskin. Envelope and eight pages. S., pp. 215-216.

Greenaway thanks him for lending a few of the drawings she had previously given him, so that they could be shown in the Victoria Exhibition. She relates more about the adventures of Rover, and also a story told by her model. She speaks retrospectively of her drawing techniques: "I see Now where their arms are too thin or too Fat. For one thing[,] in Pencil drawings You cant alter Much or You destroy the Freshness of the drawings—in the book ones of course I could always alter and I used to make a study too. So they were more correct[,] but they generally lose a little in action—and a First Impression look."

JOHN RUSKIN

41* "Procession of children with flowers For the new year 1888." Pencil and watercolor, 117 x 276 mm; signed "KG."

42* "A happy new year to you JR [John Ruskin] from KG 1900;" group of young girls with flowers. Pencil and watercolor, 120 x 215 mm.

43 John Ruskin. *The art of England.* Lectures given in Oxford, by ... during his second tenure of the Slade Professorship. Orpington, George Allen, 1884.

26 cm. Dark green cloth with remains of paper label. Includes, as Lecture IV, "Fairy Land, Mrs. Allingham and Kate Greenaway."

44 John Ruskin, ed. *Dame Wiggins of Lee, and her wonderful cats:* A humorous tale written principally by a lady of ninety. Edited, with original verses, by ... and with new illustrations by Kate Greenaway. Orpington, George Allen, 1885.

19 cm. Brown cloth with gold pictorial stamping, cream endpapers. Greenaway illustrations on pages three, four, eight, nine. Inscribed to Frances Hooper from the collection of Delia White Vail.

45 ALS: no date [*ca.* Dec. 1885], "Tuesday," Witley, Surrey to Joanie Severn. Four pages.

She is thankful that Ruskin is feeling better. Then she comments on the illustra-

156 b

156 c

158

156 a

61

2

1

9

10

51

63

103

102

132

7

8

42

66

135

120

24

CINDERELLA.

Then Her Godmother said to her go into
the Garden and bring me in the
Largest Pumpkin you can find
So Cinderella went out and found
a very large Pumpkin which she
brought to her Fairy Godmother —

47

20

99

FIRST ARRIVALS

It is a Party; do you know
And there they sit, all in a row,
Waiting till the others come
To begin to have some fun.

Hark! the Bell rings sharp and clear,
Other little friends appear;
And no longer all alone
They begin to feel at Home.

To them a little hard is fate
Yet better early than too late
Fancy getting there Forlorn,
With the tea and cake all gone.

Wonder what they'll have for tea;
Hope the Jam is strawberry.
Wonder what the dance and game;
Feel so very glad they came.

Very Happy may you be,
May you much enjoy your tea.

108

137

98

Procession of Children with Flowers

For the Portfolio 1888 K.G.

41

71

145

143

17

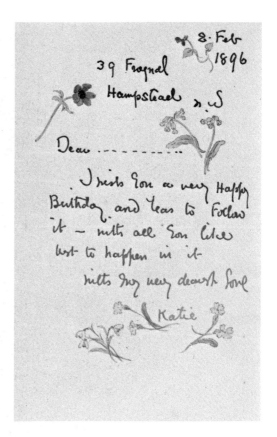

8. Feb
1896

39 Fragnal
Hampstead n.w

Dear ....

I wish You a very Happy
Birthday and Years to Follow
it — with all You like
best to happen in it

with my very dearest love

Katie

Professor Ruskin

56

74

60

144

This is intended for the tree of Knowledge the
people running to pick the fruit. the horses in the
distance.

This is intended for Pandora about to open the box
A Raven is holding the motto shorlords and right shroud, and
greeting —

69

77

ALMANACK FOR 1892

134

70

tions in *Dame Wiggins of Lee:* "It seems a Pity the Dame Wiggins wont be Coloured[,] but he can bring one out Later on Coloured—that is one thing[.] I have sent the Marigold Garden and will send the Alphabet as soon as I get home."

46   ALS: 30 March 1895, 39, Frognal, Hampstead, N.W. to John Ruskin. Eight pages. Full-length pen portrait of a girl on seventh page. S., p. 165.
She speaks of visiting the du Mauriers and of admiring Mr. du Maurier's drawings for *Punch.* She describes of her present work: "I am doing Cinderella Carrying in the Pumpkin to her Fairy Godmother—you dont see the Godmother—I have put a row of Scarlet Beans as a background—I am going to grow a Row in the Garden on purpose." She writes admiringly of two of Giorgione's paintings at the "Venetian Gallery" and of Elgood's drawings of gardens at the "Fine Art," and then complains, "I wish I could paint better." She wonders that she likes nothing having to do with the tropics: "I never can somehow like a palm tree in a Landscape—while I love pines."

47*   "Cindrella [sic] Then her godmother said to her, go into the garden and bring me the largest pumpkin you can find..." Pencil and watercolor, 133 x 80 mm.

48   ALS: no date [ca. Fall 1884], "Tuesday,"

11, Pemberton Gardens, Holloway, N. to Joanie Severn. Four pages.
Her tone is somewhat despairing with regard to Ruskin's health after reading a review of his latest lecture, and she asks Mrs. Severn to do what she can to prevail upon him "to come up to London with you and leave these Dreadful Lectures." She continues: "It is dreadful[.] I do hope he May be prevented giving any More Lectures now—People will not forget it and He will be so sorry after[,] when he can see clearly again...I got the World [London newspaper] yesterday[;] it is very terrible—I feel afraid to send it for fear it make him worse. You may see your way to telling him part of it and persuading [him] to come back with you and see Sir W. Gull...He sent Me word some days ago—he was having Grim Fight with the Vivisectionists—little did I think what it meant." Then, she promises to send little Violet a letter to "set her mind at rest." She is continuing to send Ruskin cheerful letters, and wishes that Dr. Adams or "they *would* have tried to do something."

49   ALS: 30 July 1890, 50, Frognal, Hampstead, N.W. to Joanie Severn. Four pages.
Concerned over Ruskin's ever getting well, Greenaway writes in some anguish: "Yes, indeed I care. I'm *so* glad to have it—*so* glad to know he thinks of Me—tell

78

71

him—with My very dearest love—that it Makes Me proud[,] Happy[,] glad—all things to know that he remembers Me— and that I'm deeply grateful And think of Him so much indeed[.] So always, He seems so a part of my life—I should feel very strange if I had not Him to think of. tell Him I thank him deeply for all things ... I'm very sorry about those delusions—still it is Much so Much [better] that he is quiet, but I should like that he could have No painful thoughts ... it seems he will never be able to work again to finish The Praeterita or anything else— though I'd far rather it is unfinished for ever than written at times when he doesnt know—really what he says."

50   ALS: 7 August 1894, 39, Frognal, Hampstead, N.W. to John Ruskin. Two pages. This letter was torn in half and later repaired.

This is a letter of parting after a visit with Ruskin. "Then what shall I call you now? ¶ I was *so* sorry to leave you—I am so sorry to have left. I feel too Mournful to write to day, yet long to say just a few words to tell you what great Happiness, it has been to see you once more—and talk to you—I *am* so glad I have seen you, though as the beautiful Hills drifted farther and farther away, it was sad—that is the worst of it. it is so beautiful to Come—so terribly sad to go—Yet How I rejoice—there is Yet You—

¶ I will write again very soon[.] I shall feel less mournful then." In subsequent letters to Ruskin the salutation is a brief "Dear   "

51* ALS: 14 [and 21] August 1894, 39, Frognal, Hampstead, N.W. to John Ruskin. Envelope, watercolor and four pages. Pen sketch of a woman in Greek dress on third page, and one of wheat sheaves on fourth.

She describes seeing a little girl with pigeons near the British Museum when last visiting the glass exhibit. She comments about the colors of the various glass objects and about the draperies which she saw on statues in the Museum. She describes girls haying. On a separate piece of paper is a brown ink and watercolor drawing of a wild rose. About this she writes: "Will you like the little wild Rose a little—though it has not serrations enough to its leaves[?]". She promises to send him more "flower letters" in the future.

52* ALS: 31 October 1895, 39, Frognal, Hampstead, N.W. to John Ruskin. Four pages, including pen sketches.

This is a rather effusive letter following a recent visit with Ruskin at Coniston. At the head is a sketch of a dog, labelled "he," and a cat, labelled "she," the latter wiping its eyes with a handkerchief. There is much about Rover, and three

75

73

sketches of him jumping about are included on page three. She begins: "*No opening the Study door this Morning—No looking in and seeing You there—No meeting You out with Bramble [Ruskin's dog]—No anything except being Far off and feeling very Miserable—to know it is so—I Hope You feel a little Sorry too—a little Sorry—because I feel it is Months and Months, before I see Your dear—dear—Face again[.] It was worse leaving You this time than last—because You were so Much More your old Self—and you were Kind and Gentle to Me—then I thanked you in My Heart Dear—so—so much . . . I am very low today—but it will be better in a few days when I get over it—The Coming is such Joy—the going Such Pain—Dear—*"

53* ALS: 12 January 1898, 39, Frognal, Hampstead, N.W. to John Ruskin. Envelope and eight pages. Pen sketch of a child looking at trees in a valley at head of first page, and one of wrapped-up Rover on page six. S., pp. 228, 237.

She describes her intense enjoyment of the Millais paintings at the "R.A.," which also had an exhibition of Elgood's gardens that she liked very much. She states her forebodings about the Fine Art exhibition, since paintings have not been selling well; in that regard, she com-

plains of ignorant critics and the transience of taste. She also describes Rover's skin disease.

54* ALS: 1 June 1898, 39, Frognal, Hampstead, N. W. to John Ruskin. Envelope and eight pages. Pen sketch of flowers at head of first page and one of Rover and swans on page five.

She quotes several lines of Burns' "My love is like a red red rose." Her description of Rover and his friends the swans is quite detailed: "Dear Rover still swim[mi]ng up and down the Highgate Ponds accompanied by the two Swans. it seems curious For two swans to be Friends with a Black Dog. [Here she illustrates the scene.] This is the way they Follow his Course every Morning[,] only I have Put them too Near."

55* Kate Greenaway. . . . . *Almanack for 1893.* [London], George Routledge & Sons, Limited, [1892].

10 cm. Cream glazed pictorial boards, blue-green endpapers. Presentation copy, with original watercolor inscribed "John Ruskin from Kate Greenaway 1892" on half-title page.

56* ALS: 8 February 1896, 39, Frognal, Hampstead, N.W. to John Ruskin. Envelope and one page. Pencil and watercolor drawings of flowers decorate the envelope and stationery.

76

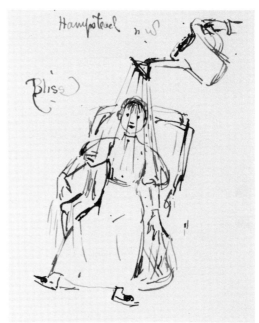

74

"Dear—I wish You a very Happy Birthday and Year to Follow it—with all You like best to happen in it[.] With My very dearest Love   Katie."

57*   ALS: "Christmas Eve" [1895], 39, Frognal, Hampstead, N.W. to John Ruskin. Envelope (16 x 20 cm) and five pages. Ink and watercolor sketches of holly and mistletoe on first page, of house in the snow on page two, and of street lamps on page three. Floral watercolor sketch on envelope.

   Wishing she could say rather than write her Christmas greetings to him, she nevertheless writes, and includes with the letter a six-quatrain poem by Tennyson, "Ring out wild bells," on a separate sheet of paper.

58   ALS: 2 November 1896, 39, Frognal, Hampstead, N.W. to Violet Dickinson. Four pages, including pen sketches. S., pp. 222-223.

   Answering Dickinson's request for information about Ruskin and commenting upon some of his critics, Greenaway writes: "of the way people talk against Him in Venice— I Hope You will try a little Not to quite believe it all. For believe Me it is sure Not to be all true and even if He has been very inaccurate[,] the world owes Him so Much—that one May well and justly—(I think)—Forget His Faults. ¶The world *is* very ungrateful like all

Nature is—and takes all the good it can get and then Flings the Giver of it away. That is our way—and it is a Cruel one—and there's another reason also, a reason that once I used Not to believe in—but I do Now—and that is that so many of the second rate Authors and Artists seem to have a Most bitter jealousy of the great ones—it is very curious to Me—but they do—they love to Find a Fault . . . We ought to be—so grateful to them instead For what they Make the world for us . . . I know in Mr. Ruskin's case—He is too ready to believe all he hears, but I think it Should be forgiven—that the beautiful things He tells You—and the New life of Art you enter into—Compensates. ¶Never shall I Forget what I felt in reading Fors Claveriga For the First Time[,] and it was the First book of His I had ever read. I longed For each evening to come that I Might lose Myself in that New Wonderful World." She also refers to a small painting of a panel of angels and at the head of the first page includes a pen sketch a little angel near a cottage. A pen sketch of herself at a pulpit appears on page four.

59   ALS: 8 June 1900, 39, Frognal, Hampstead, N.W. to Joanie Severn. Envelope and four pages. S., p. x.

81

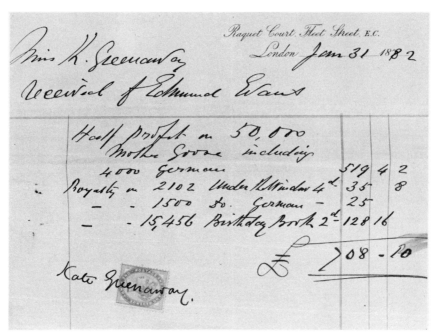

80

This letter concerns the disposal of her letters written to Ruskin over the years, and of his to her. ''In the later letters I think there is Nothing that I should object to any one reading—in the early ones Nothing I should Mind you reading[,] but there Might be things in some one would feel [''better'' crossed out] Perhaps better Not Published— ¶I dont know if any of My early letters still exist—I do not know if He kept them. I remember You telling Me You had destroyed some that You thought [''were'' crossed out] I would rather were destroyed[.] ¶I have a great Many letters of his—one for Nearly Every day For Three Years[,] but they are all of the time of My early letters before his great illness since—He has never written —as You will remember. I should like to have any letters in the life[,] if one is written[,] that were thought desirable— ¶I am not sure the later ones of Mine are Much in a literary way, but He did say some of the earlier ones ought to exist as long as the Most beautiful of my drawings should —because they also were beautiful—I tell You this because You know How great was the [''Friendship'' crossed out] affection between us that You will not think it conciet [sic] I Feel so honoured by it. that I Can only Feel honoured For ¶ My Name to ever to appear Near His.''

FREDERICK LOCKER-LAMPSON AND FAMILY

60* F. Locker-Lampson. Watercolor, oval, 120 x 105 mm. S., facing p. 86.

61 Frederick Locker. *London lyrics.* London, [Chiswick Press], 1881.
    23.5 cm. Gold-stamped vellum, white endpapers. Signed black-and-white tailpiece illustration by Kate Greenaway, a mounted proof. Black-and-white frontispiece illustration by Randolph Caldecott, in two states, one a mounted proof.

62* ''Beneath a summer tree, Her maiden reverie Has a charm;'' young lady seated. Pen and brown ink, 101 x 76 mm; signed ''KG,'' dated 1881.
    Gift to Frederick Locker, illustrating a line in the poem ''To my grandmother'' from his *London lyrics,* 1881.

63a* Maud Locker-Lampson. Watercolor, 98 x 134 mm; signed ''Kate Greenaway 1883.''
    In pencil on reverse: ''F. Locker   Miss KG gave me this.''

63b* Oliver Locker-Lampson. Watercolor, 98 x 134mm, signed ''Kate Greenaway 1883.''
    In pencil on reverse: ''Miss K.G. gave me this   F. Locker-L.''

82

89

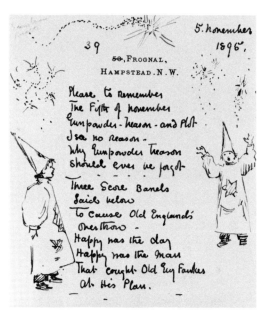

91

64 ALS: no date [ca. Christmas 1885], 50, Frognal, Hampstead, N.W. to Mr. [Frederick] Locker. Four pages.

Wishes that her Christmas drawing were better done so that at least part of Christmas would please him. She describes the festive air about Hampstead this time of year and adds at the end of the letter that she wishes Christmas were past since she does not like it either. About Christmas cards she writes: "I have not seen any good Christmas Cards this year—nothing new or of any interest—and I think all the Colour Prints very bad—common looking—People say trade is begin[nin]g to shew signs of getting better."

65* Two children with primrose balls. Pencil and watercolor, 68 x 105 mm; signed "KG."

In pencil at bottom: "FL [Frederick Locker] from KG."

66* ALS: no date, "Thursday," to Mr. [Frederick] Locker. Two pages (text in pencil). Pencil and watercolor drawing of a girl crying amid discarded toys at head of first page.

She requests that he come see her since he has been in London "all three days" and hasn't done so.

67 ALS: "Christmas" 1887, 50, Frognal, Hampstead, N.W. to Mr. [Frederick] Locker. Two pages. Pencil and watercolor drawing of two children, one seated, with yellow flower balls at head of first page.

She expects that he is happy that his son Godfrey is home for the holiday. She is sending Godfrey's bookplate and says: "I am afraid all the Heraldic part is very dreadful[,] but if it is too bad—perhaps you can get some one who does know and *can* do it—to touch it up[.]"

68* Heraldic bookplate for Godfrey Locker-Lampson. Relief print, 90 x 68 mm; signed "KG."

69* Designs for Frederick Locker bookplate. Four pencil sketches, each 92 x 71 mm.

70* Kate Greenaway. ...Almanack for 1893. [London], George Routledge & Sons, [1892].

10 cm. Cream glazed pictorial boards, blue-green endpapers. Presentation copy, with original watercolor on half-title page, inscribed "Frederick Locker-Lampson From Kate Greenaway 1892."

RANDOLPH CALDECOTT

71* Caricature of three children. Ink sketch in the Greenaway manner by Randolph Caldecott, 67 x 104 mm, [1878?]. S., p. 69.

92

96

72   ALS: 23 October 1885, 50, Frognal, Hampstead, N.W. to Joanie Severn. Three pages. She sends the drawings by Caldecott, commenting: "Do look at the Man looking through his eye glass at the smoke Coming from his boots, and then the Cabbage leaf Pie, and the Barber Cutting the Wedding Cake, and aren't the Covers fine[?]—the blue Stockings—but they are all so Clever. So very Clever and Funny."

VIOLET DICKINSON

73*   ALS Fragment: 6 August [1861], "Friday Morning," 39, Frognal, Hampstead, N.W. to Violet Dickinson. Pages one and two. Pen sketch of a tall and a short woman, labelled "They were by Fate divided," at head of first page.
     She speaks of green paper in the bedroom and how to achieve the correct color. She complains of the hot weather.

74*   AL Fragment: 8 July 1896, 39, Frognal, Hampstead, N.W. to Violet Dickinson. Pages one and two, including pen sketch at head of first page. For part of the missing portion, see S., pp. 190-192.
     This has no salutation, only a drawing of a woman with the contents of a watering can being poured out on her head, titled "Bliss." She complains of insects and the heat.

75*   ALS: 10 December 1896, 39, Frognal, Hampstead, N.W. to Violet Dickinson. Four pages, including pen sketches. S., p. 193. She mentions her visit to Violet's and "the giddy whirl" of Violet's friends. She complains of a cold, speaks of a visit from Mr. Ponsonby, and talks of Leighton's drawings. On the first page she has drawn a "Solitary Hermit," labelling his "Solitary Candle" and "Solitary Cup of Tea" as well. At the bottom of the page, after "Dear What I shall come too —," is a sketch of "the Far off World."

LADY MARIA PONSONBY

76*   ALS: 8 September 1895, 39, Frognal, Hampstead, N.W. to Lady Maria Ponsonby. Envelope and six pages, including pen sketch.
     She comments on the improper dress at the beach when she was last at Cromer and wishes that Lady Maria could have walked with her "Along the sands at 11 o'clock one Morning—the odd thing to Me is—How they get the Courage to leave their Homes like it—also at Cromer—the Propriety I have been used to seems thrown to the winds—but one easily gets Hardened I find—I hardly knew where to look at first—in a few days I was quite used to it—and looked on I fear in Placid Calm—a whole Family like this Young Man." Following this on page four is an amusing drawing of beachwear.

84

94

77 ALS: 19 October 1896, 39, Frognal, Hampstead, N.W. to Lady Maria Ponsonby. Four pages.

She speaks of Rover being covered with mud. She mourns the loss of Mr. du Maurier, who is buried in Hampstead. She writes about her visit to Stoke Court, where Lady Dorothy and Miss Nevill were also visiting, and continues: "it was very interesting seeing Grays Summer House and the Churchyard and his Tomb, and they have such Nice Gardens and a Fountain[.]" She also mentions that an exhibition of English humorous art is to open at the Fine Art Society on the next Saturday.

ARLINGTON HOUSE

78* Young ladies and children with garlands of flowers, calligraphic "Guest Book" (left) and "Arlington Manor" (right). Two watercolors, each 268 x 199 mm, for double title page; both signed "KG 1898."

These works are here reproduced, less calligraphy, on the endpapers. Arlington Manor, Newbury, Berkshire, was the country home of Sir Francis Henry Jeune (later Baron St. Helier).

79 ALS: "New Years day" 1897, 39, Frognal, Hampstead, N.W. to John Ruskin. Envelope and eight pages.

She describes a play called "Freezing a Mother in Law or a Frightful Frost"—"it was not very probable"—that was presented at Lady Jeune's on New Year's Eve, and gives a list of the guests at the party. She tells him also that she is finishing some drawings for the Institute.

PUBLISHED WORKS

PUBLISHING: REWARDS
AND FRUSTRATIONS

80* DOC: 31 January 1882. Receipt from Edmund Evans, Raquet Court, Fleet Street, E.C., London. One page. Signed by Kate Greenaway.

"Half profit on 50,000 Mother Goose including 4000 German...Royalty on 2102 Under the Window...1500...German...15,456 Birthday Book..." Total: 708 pounds, 10 pence.

81 Kate Greenaway. *Am Fenster.* In Bildern und Versen von... Der deutsche Text von Kathe Freiligrath-Kroeker. Munich, Theodor Stroefer, [1880].

24 cm. Dark green glazed pictorial boards, blue endpapers. German translation of *Under the window.*

82 ALS: 22 November 1880 from Austin Dobson, 13, Grange Park, Ealing, W. Two pages, with a two-line postscript. S., p. 85.

He thanks her for the gift of the *Birthday book* and then extols her great talent: "And how lucky the little people are to

95

get such pictures! I cant help thinking that I should have been a better man if I had had such pleasant playbooks in my unartistic childhood. You have a most definite and special walk, and I hope you wont let any one persuade you out of it."

83   ALS: 9 August 1880, 11, Pemberton Gardens, Holloway, N. to Austin Dobson. Four pages.
        "I will Try and Carry out your wishes as to Subject—but it will have to be a very Small drawing—I really had No time to undertake it at all. Only I was very pleased to be able to oblige Mr. Loftie—as to price[,] that is rather difficult for me to fix until I have made the drawing, but I know it would be 4 or 5 Guineas and it Might have to be More. It depends on the time it takes. I have had to Make it a rule to keep drawings Now, because they do Not pay Me unless I do so, but I do sometimes sell the Originals for the same price over again[.]"

84   ALS: 9 October 1882, from Austin Dobson, Board of Trade, S.W. Three pages.
        Dobson sends her an exemplar of his verse "Home beauty" [published in the *Magazine of art* in 1883] and writes: "Will you not consent to fill the space round them with a few little figures such as you drew for Godfrey—in *outline, not coloured?* The Editor of the *Magazine of*

Art has no doubt, he ritt me, that they shall be glad to have them, and, of course, *pay* for them well...only dont as Mr. Locker said 'fush' yourself over it or trouble yourself about original figures; it is your ordinary figures I want."

85   ALS: 10 October 1882, 11, Pemberton Gardens, Holloway, N. to Austin Dobson. Four pages, with a short postscript in pencil.
        She agrees to do the drawings for his verse, and then states her reservations about the firm which publishes the *Magazine of art:* "They used my drawings ever so many times over for different things and sold them after for illustrations to advertisements. I objected and they said it was not Intentional on their part and it should not be repeated[,] but I still Saw them after that, so I would Not do any drawing for them any more unless I retain the Copyright—and they only used it for the purpose it was originally done for. ¶It would Not pay Me to make the drawing under 10 pounds, and then they would also have to return Me the drawing—I doubt if they would Care to Give so Much as that, but I fancy the St Nicholas people would. Ive promised often to do them Something, and have never had time..."

86   ALS: 18 October 1882, from Austin Dob-

111

105

son, Porth-y-Felin, 75, Eaton Rise, Ealing, W. Four pages.

He reports that the editors of the *Magazine of art* agree to her terms (as stated in her letter of 10 October 1882). After stating the request of the editors, he gives her leave to decline the job: "What they want (I quote the Editor's words) 'is some "MOTHER GOOSE" in monochrome and more or less *in outline*.' ¶I think I know you well enough to believe that you will quite frankly decline, if you have any desire to do so. *And pray do not think of me at all*. I only wrote the verses to please you. The rest was an afterthought—and like most of my afterthoughts—very quickly acted upon." He says he would be glad "to write some verses for you to illustrate [for *St. Nicholas* magazine]—and, I think, *in America*, they will be *almost* as pleased to get my verses as your drawing."

87   ALS: 19 October 1882, Witley, [Surrey] to Austin Dobson. Four pages.
"I shall like very much doing the drawing only they must knock off the clause about its quality[.] Im sure to do it as well as I can, because I never pass what I know to be bad work for my own sake—but if I do it, they must have it—or it dont matter though after all—because plenty of others would with your verses."

88   ALS: 18 November 1882, 11, Pemberton Gardens, Holloway, N. to Austin Dobson. Three pages.
"You must repress that Editor. it is Quite Impossible for the drawing to be Made for a long time yet, however the Sketch is done—So if you will Not Mind the trouble of coming, I shall be Most glad to see you...You will see[,] I am sure[,] when I explain to You how it is that I am obliged to get these things done at once. Talking is so much better than writing[.]"

89*   ALS: 2 February 1884, 11, Pemberton Gardens, Holloway, N. to Joanie Severn. Envelope and three pages. Pencil sketch of "child-wind" and the moon over city at the end. S., p. 124.
About some verses that Mrs. Severn evidently had been sending her to include in a publication, she says that one or two "are quite new to me and would be exactly what Id like to put in," but some are "a little too much about children—children I find like to know about other things—or what other children did—but not about children in an abstract sort of way—that belongs to older people." Then she remembers the poems she liked best when she was a child: "How Horatius Kept the Bridge... The Wreck of the Hesperus...the Pied Piper...the Rope Walk...I find something to like in most things..."

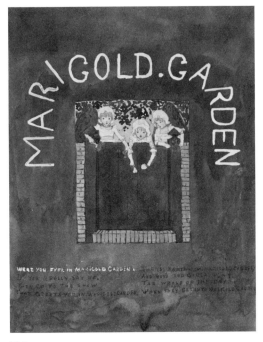

106

110

90 ALS: 5 November 1887, 50, Frognal, Hampstead, N.W. to Mrs. W. J. Loftie. Four pages.

> She discusses the pros and cons of illustrated book covers. She agrees on the good effect of the printed cover for *Under the window*, but continues: "I'm absolutely Stupid over covers though, and never do good ones—My own taste is for plain Covers[,] Leather or cloth—then coming to everything inside the book, but there is a great deal in the use of a thing, and Mr. Anderson May like to have the picture on the Covers. I know, it does attract because Mr. Evans has often told Me that the shilling books sell ever so much better if they have a picture on the cover."

91 ALS: 5 and 7 November 1895, 39, Frognal, Hampstead, N.W. to John Ruskin. Envelope and eight pages. Pen sketches of Guy Fawkes figures and fireworks on first page, and of moon over the city on third.

> She begins with an illustrated poem, "Please to remember the Fifth of November," and then describes the festivities of Guy Fawkes Day. She tells him that she is sending a copy of Alcott's *Old fashioned girl.* She discusses some of the poems that she has been reading lately and comments favorably on Swinburne. Then on page six she writes: "The dancing little Girls are going off to

America to day—then I have another Page to do—and all the while I want to amuse Myself—to do Girls with Roses— Girls with May trees." The drawing she refers to here is described on page four of her 1 November 1895 letter to Ruskin: "all little Boys, and Girls, at a Party— dancing and—taking their tea, with Cakes—and standing shy with their Fans, and the little boys Feeling they Have got to ask the little Girls to dance with them and they dont know How to, quite." On page six of that letter is a sketch of one of the dancing girls with a fan in hand.

92* Three girls with fans. Pen-and-ink, 93 x 71 mm, for illustration in "Off for dancing school," *Ladies home journal,* March 1896; signed "KG."

> Matted with number 129.

93 ALS: 6 February 1899, 39, Frognal, Hampstead, N.W. to Wilfred Evans. Two pages.

> She speaks of her works, probably meaning their copyright, being sold to others for their uses: "it would do Me a great deal of harm to have them sold For small sums and used For any thing[.] ¶ Of course if You choose to Put them in the hands of Some other Publisher (not selling them) that is another thing and later on they Might be worth more than they are at Present—For the taste lies another way,

88

109

but that would Pass—I should certainly object to them being sold[.]"

BEATING THE BOUNDS

94* "Ready for the march;" beadle and muster of nine schoolboys with willow wands. Pencil sketch, 115 x 177 mm, for illustration in Thomas Hughes, "Beating the bounds," *St. Nicholas*[.] *Scribner's illustrated magazine for girls and boys*, April 1879.

95* "Ready for the march;" muster of ten schoolboys with willow wands. Ink and watercolor, 114 x 185 mm, for illustration in Thomas Hughes, "Beating the bounds," *St. Nicholas*[.] *Scribner's illustrated magazine for girls and boys*, April 1879.

96* "The beadle leads the procession;" beadle in cocked hat, gold-laced coat, and silver-headed staff. Ink and watercolor, 112 x 92 mm, for illustration in Thomas Hughes, "Beating the bounds," *St. Nicholas*[.] *Scribner's illustrated magazine for girls and boys*, April 1879; signed "KG."

97 *St. Nicholas*[.] *Scribner's illustrated magazine for girls and boys*. New York, Scribner & Co.; London, Sampson, Low, Marsten & Co.; vol. 6, no. 6, April 1879.
     35.5 cm. Pictorial wrappers. Includes four black-and-white illustrations by Kate Greenaway for "Beating the bounds" by Thomas Hughes, pages 389-395, and one by her for "The little

big woman and the big little girl" by M.M. D., page 383.

THE LANGUAGE OF FLOWERS

98* Title-page layout (without text) with lilies, cherubs, and ribbon. Brown ink and watercolor, 117 x 112 mm, for *Language of flowers;* signed "KG."

99* Cherubs carrying a basket of roses. Brown ink and watercolor, 83 x 108 mm, for *Language of flowers*, verso of title page.

100 Kate Greenaway. *Language of flowers* illustrated by ... Printed in colours by Edmund Evans. London, George Routledge and Sons, [1884].
     15 cm. Green glazed pictorial boards, with cream background, bright yellow endpapers.

101* Rosebuds. Brown ink and watercolor, 43 x 32 mm, for *Language of flowers*.

102* Pot of carnations. Brown ink and watercolor, 63 x 37 mm, for *Language of flowers*.

103* Nosegay of lilies. Brown ink and watercolor, 84 x 77 mm, for *Language of flowers*.

104 ALS: 9 November 1884, 11, Pemberton Gardens, Holloway, N. to Joanie Severn. Envelope and two pages. S., p. 128.
     She tells her she is sending her a copy of *Language of flowers*, which Ruskin thinks very bad and about which she writes: "I am very disgusted Myself— *only* I *dont* feel *I am* so much to blame—

118

115

as the Printers—who have literally blotted every picture out[.]"

MARIGOLD GARDEN

105* Young girl. Pencil sketch, 185 x 133 mm, for *Marigold garden,* cover.

106* "Marigold garden" and three girls at garden gate. Cover layout sketch in pencil and watercolor, 235 x 180 mm, for *Marigold garden.*

107* "First arrivals;" three children on settee. Set of five woodblocks (key block and one each for colors pink, red, yellow and green) for *Marigold garden.*

108* "First arrivals;" three children on settee, fruit garland, and text (in pencil). Brown ink and watercolor, 202 x 152 mm, for *Marigold garden;* signed "KG."

109* "Mammas and babies;" six young girls with dolls. Ink and watercolor, 70 x 145 mm, for *Marigold garden;* signed "KG."

110* "When you and I grow up;" two seated children looking out to sea, text (in pencil), and St. John's Wort. Brown ink and watercolor, 203 x 152 mm, for *Marigold garden;* signed "KG."

111* "Blue shoes;" two young girls. Brown ink and watercolor, 107 x 126 mm, for *Marigold garden;* signed "KG."

112 Kate Greenaway. *Marigold garden.* Pictures and rhymes by ... Printed in colours by Edmund Evans. London, New York, George Routledge and Sons, [1885].

28 cm. Green glazed pictorial boards, green endpapers. Presentation copy with original pen sketch, inscribed "Amy Hirshall from Kate Greenaway 1899" on front flyleaf. Originally included a letter from Kate Greenaway to Mrs. Hirshall, dated 25 July 1899.

ENGLISH SPELLING-BOOK

113* Letters A and B with putti. Pencil studies for alphabet, 12.8 x 6.2 mm; upper study dated 1885, lower signed "KG."

114 William Mavor. *The English spelling-book* accompanied by a progressive series of easy and familiar lessons by ... Illustrated by Kate Greenaway. Engraved and printed by Edmund Evans. London, New York, George Routledge and Sons, 1885.

18 cm. Gray pictorial boards, printed in orange and black, white endpapers.

115* Young woman and child. Engraved wood (display?) block, 12.5 x 8 mm, matching the Greenaway illustration on the cover of *The English spelling-book* by William Mavor; "KG" signature reproduced.

Formerly in the collection of Edmund Evans.

116* Girl in field with torn frock. Brown ink, 100 x 100 mm, for *The English spelling-book* by William Mavor.

90

116

117   Kate Greenaway. ...*Almanack for 1895.*
      [London], George Routledge & Sons,
      Limited, [1894].
      10 cm. Cream glazed pictorial boards,
      dark blue endpapers.

118* Seated mother with young child and book.
      Brown ink, 127 x 127 mm, for *The English
      spelling-book* by William Mavor; signed
      "KG."

119   Kate Greenaway. ...*Alphabet.* London,
      New York, George Routledge & Sons, [*ca.*
      1885].
      7 cm. Yellow glazed pictorial boards,
      yellow-green endpapers.

      BOOK OF GAMES

120* "Battledore & shuttlecock;" three girls
      playing in garden. Ink and watercolor, 112
      x 115 mm, for *Kate Greenaway's book of
      games;* signed "KG."
      The watercolor shows a fading of green
      pigment. Greenaway commented about
      this problem in correspondence (see
      numbers 122 and 126).

121   Kate Greenaway. ...*Book of games.* Lon-
      don, Glasgow, Manchester, New York,
      George Routledge & Sons, [1889].
      23.5 cm. Blue pictorial cloth, stamped in
      gold, black, red and yellow, yellow end-
      papers. Green glazed pictorial wrapper
      pasted on front endpaper.

122   ALS: 21 February 1891, 50, Frognal,
      Hampstead, N.W. to Joanie Severn. Four
      pages.
      She fears Ruskin did not like the flower
      drawings very much. Speaking of the
      success of the exhibition, she writes that
      the Fine Art Society's people "did see the
      little Copper Plate and longed to have it
      for the PV Card." [This probably refers to
      a copperplate that Ruskin did of "Miss
      Primrose," a girl with yellow ribbons,
      discussed in Greenaway's letter to him of
      1 March 1898.] She then comments on
      the difficulty of getting the correct shade
      of green: "the colours were too green—I
      could not somehow get the colour quite
      right[.] I expect Mine has faded to an
      ungettable colour but I will try again if
      you like[,] on a bright day[.] To day is too
      dark for anything[.]"

123   ALS: 12 October 1898, 39, Frognal, Hamp-
      stead, N.W. to Joanie Severn. Four pages.
      She complains of being tired after her
      journeys and sends her love to Ruskin.
      Also she laments that the paper of the
      drawings she did for Ruskin "seems to
      have changed Colour where it was ex-
      posed to the light[.] My Brother says it
      must be something in the Paper—For
      they were securely Fastened up in the
      Frame. I only took them out to Pack them
      up to send them."

125

124

124* "Puss in the corner;" five girls in an orchard. Ink and watercolor, 115 x 152 mm, for *Kate Greenaway's book of games*; signed "KG."

125* "Frog in the middle;" group of children dancing and chanting. Ink and watercolor, 101 x 140 mm, for *Kate Greenaway's book of games*; signed "KG."

126* "Touch wood;" five children outdoors. Brown ink and watercolor, 102 x 155 mm, for *Kate Greenaway's book of games*; signed "KG."
    The green color at the upper edge has been protected by an earlier mat.

127* "Hunt the slipper;" group of children seated in a circle. Brown ink and watercolor, 111 x 165 mm, for *Kate Greenaway's book of games*; signed "KG."

128* Tulip. Ink and watercolor, 93 x 51 mm, for *Kate Greenaway's book of games*.

129* Buttercup. Brown ink and watercolor, 67 x 27 mm, for *Kate Greenaway's book of games*.
    Matted with number 92.

130* Kite. Brown ink and watercolor, 68 x 68 mm, for *Kate Greenaway's book of games*.

ALMANACKS

131* Kate Greenaway. *Almanack for 1883.* London, New York, George Routledge and Sons, [1882].

A collection of copies showing cloth and paper binding variants, the suite housed in a special presentation box by Jean Gunner. Box in half natural Irish linen, covered in blue and beige printed paper, with each book separately housed in a recess with tabbed shelf, protected by polyester film window.

132* Kate Greenaway. *Almanack for 1887 by* ... [London], George Routledge & Sons, [1886].
    8 x 10.5 cm. Cream glazed pictorial boards, blue-green endpapers. Presentation copy, with original watercolor on half-title page, inscribed "Ruth Anderson From Kate Greenaway 1891."

133 ALS: Christmas 1891, 50, Frognal, Hampstead, N.W. to Mr. Frederick Locker. Three pages.
    She compliments him on a recent portrait of himself and then writes: "I send You my little Almanack, though I daresay You Have already seen it[.] There is Not Much Variety in them Now, is there, but Nothing ever seems Possible for the Price in the way of change—either in getting up or Cover—so on they go in the old way—which I think a Mistake[.]"

134* Kate Greenaway. *...Almanack for 1892.* [London], George Routledge & Sons, Limited, [1891].
    10 cm. Cream leatherette, stamped in

127

gold and green, dark blue endpapers. Presentation copy, with original watercolor on half-title page, inscribed "Mrs. Arthur Severn From Kate Greenaway 1891."

135* Children at a stile. Brown ink and watercolor, 101 x 100 mm, for "Autumn" in *Kate Greenaway's almanack for 1892:* signed "KG."

136 Four watercolors, each 111 x 57 mm, for *Kate Greenaway's almanack for 1892:* each signed "KG."

  a* "March:" woman losing her hat to the wind.

  b* "April:" woman shielding herself from the rain.

  c* "May:" woman with a Maypole.

  d* "January:" woman in winter costume.

137* Two children in window, caption panel below, with flower garland at bottom. Ink and watercolor, 104 x 72 mm, for "January" in *Kate Greenaway's almanack for 1888:* signed "KG."

138* Mother with young child in a window, caption panel below, with flower garland at bottom. Ink and watercolor, 104 x 72 mm, for "February" in *Kate Greenaway's almanack for 1888:* signed "KG."

139 ALS: 25 February 1896, 39, Frognal, Hampstead, N.W. to John Ruskin. Envelope and eight pages. Pen sketch of a young lady on seventh page, and one of a woman's head on eighth.

She mentions that she is reading the second volume of "Lady Mary Wortley Montague." She states her dislike of the Aubrey Beardsley drawings and discusses her feelings about art and its place in her life. Included are two sketches: one full length of a young lady, the other a study of a woman's head with a cherry background. She writes further: "Mr. Dent [J. M. Dent & Co.] is to be the New Publisher of the books. I think they will be decidedly improved[.] The Almanack is to be done again this Year. They would like another New book also—but I do Not know if there will be time for that. They will all have Nice New Covers—be generally improved."

140 AL Fragment: 16 August 1896, 39, Frognal, Hampstead, N.W. to Violet Dickinson. Two pages. Pen sketch of a woman's head looking toward sailboats at head of first page.

She discusses Violet's vacation and laments that she hasn't visited the cottage this year. Her opinion of the 1897 *Almanack* is: "nice Printed on rougher Paper, but I think it too thick and I don't (Curiously) Care for the Cover Much.—It isn't New enough . . . It will be tiresome if this Man won't let me arrange it More—For it is a Thing I do Know . . ."

141 ALS Fragment: 18 August 1896, 39,

129

101

Frognal, Hampstead, N.W. to Violet Dickinson. Two pages. Pen sketches of a girl in a chair and of a garden at head of first page.

She discusses buying some red roses to serve as models for painting, says that she does not have Violet's new address, and that she has a card for the funeral of Sir John Millais. She comments about Wilfred Evans and the arrangements for the 1897 *Almanack:* "He is going to write to Mr. Dent—we are going to try to get the Cover altered—it is tiresome[.] of course[,] there is not a Free choice because of expense[;] the binding has to cost very little[,] still we should do better I think than that—If I ever do another book, I shall design the whole thing[—] cover and all[—]then they must take or leave it—Possibly they would leave it."

142   ALS: 7 November 1899, 39, Frognal, Hampstead, N.W. to John Ruskin. Envelope and eight pages. Pen sketches of a young woman holding a spray of flowers against a landscape background at head of first page, of Rover looking out the window on sixth page, and of a model on the eighth. S., pp. 245-246.

She laments that Guy Fawkes Day was so quiet and that there are no "good childrens books about just now ... The Rage For Copying Mine seems over." She then discusses children's tastes and her own when she was a child: "I think they often like Grown up Books ... at any rate I

did—From the Kenny Meadows Pictures to Shakespeare I learnt all the Plays when I was Very Young indeed—It is Curious How Much Pictures Can, tell You[—]like the Plays without words[.] I suppose I asked a good deal about them and was Told—and read little bits anyhow—I never remember the time—when I didn't Know what each Play was about—They were My Sunday Evening's Amusement—and another book called the Illuminated Magazine that had all Sorts of things in it. Some I specially liked called "The Recreations of Mr. Zigzag the Elder"[—]Perhaps You knew the Magazine and them. They were accounts of the Old London Churches and Old Places of Interest[:] the Lollards Tower[,] St. Johns Gate[,] St. Bartholomews Church—Now I believe these were in a book Called the Family Magazine—I believe one of our three Cherished large Volumes has that Name, the other two The Illuminated[.] How Much Prettier those old Illustrations are than the Modern engraved Photograph[.] I hate the Modern book and Magazine Illustration. But[—]there is a But—the Illustrations of Hugh Thompson and Anning Bell—Also Byam Shaw[—]are quite beautiful—and quite different—." She describes having been to an exhibition at the Fine Art Society where she saw Remington's landscapes.

94

128

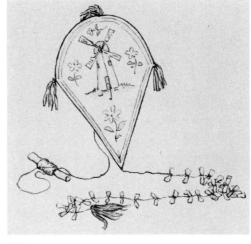

130

LARGE WATERCOLORS

143* Surrey cottage scene with children carrying flower balls. Watercolor, 252 x 354 mm; signed "KG."

144* Mother and two young girls sitting before a window. Watercolor, 278 x 220 mm; signed "KG."

145* Surrey cottage scene with mother and children. Watercolor, 239 x 393 mm.

146* Children picking flowers before a Surrey cottage. Watercolor, 224 x 319 mm; signed "K. Greenaway." S., facing p. 198.

147* Woman and two young girls before a wall and brick houses. Watercolor, 265 x 316 mm; signed "KG."

148* Woman and two young girls under a flowering tree. Watercolor, 231 x 270 mm; signed "K. Greenaway."

149* Mother and two young children looking out to sea. Watercolor, 184 x 253 mm; signed "K. Greenaway."
    This work is sometimes called "The sailor's wife."

150* Invitation to private view of Kate Greenaway's exhibition of watercolors at the Fine Art Society, 7 February 1891. Colored wood engraving, 125 x 175 mm.
    Illustration for the verse "The butterfly" in *Little Ann.*

151 ALS: 3 July 1891, 50, Frognal, Hampstead, N.W. to Joanie Severn. Four pages.

She complains about the Fine Art Society's exhibition of February 1891: "If ever you want to have a Moment to spare[,] Never undertake to have an exhibition of Pictures all to Yourself—bear that in Mind—I've never had such a driving time of work—and with my other duties—really I'm Never free."

152 Two receipts of sale from the 1891 exhibition at the Fine Art Society.

DOC: Handwritten receipt on ledger-style lined paper, titled "Sales of drawings by Miss Kate Greenaway." Four pages, 32 x 20 cm.

DOC: Receipt on official "Fine Art Society" lined paper, listing the drawings by Miss Greenaway sold since the close of the exhibition of 1891. One page, 26 x 21 cm.

153 ALS: 29 December 1893, 50, Frognal, Hampstead, N.W. to Gerald Ponsonby. Three pages. S., pp. 182-183.

This concerns the frustrating hours that Greenaway endured in preparing for the January 1894 exhibition of her works at the Fine Art Society. "I Believe the Exhibition is finally settled *at last*[—]drawings to be sent in on the 15th and Private View to take Place on the 20th—*And it is nice weather to get on in.* Black night Here the last three days[.] I think the Fine Art, *Mr. Huish of course*[,] changed the date about Nine times—First they couldnt then they could—First the Small

136 a

136 b

Room then the big one. *He* suggested Palms to fill up the Corners—Think of my poor little lot of works Floating about in that big Room—I wrote a beautiful letter suggesting that a considerable outlay in Palms seemed to me inevitable—But the letter was not allowed to be sent[.] My Brother considered it *Flippant* and un-business like—I thought this Rather Hard—as I had abstained from Remarking that a few Apple trees or Roses might be More in accordance with the Sentiment of my drawings—than Plants of an Oriental Character. However, I'm going to have the Small Room."

154* Invitation to private view of Kate Greenaway's exhibition of watercolours at the Fine Art Society, 19 February 1898. Colored wood engraving, 110 x 135 mm.
    Illustration for frontispiece in *Kate Greenaway's almanack for 1895.*

155 *'Catalogue of a collection of watercolour drawings by Miss Kate Greenaway, R.I.* exhibited at the Fine Art Society's... February 1898.' [N.p., n.p., n.d.].
    21 cm. Paper covers, ten pages. The catalogue proper (pages three to eight) is heavily annotated. Manuscript note on front wrapper: "Priced Catalogue. Not to be taken away."

CARDS

156
  a* Portrait of a young girl with a wreath of flowers. Circular watercolor, 54 mm diameter, for card; signed "KG."

  b* Portrait of a young boy with cap. Circular watercolor, 54 mm diameter, for card; signed "KG."

  c* Portrait of a young girl with bonnet. Circular watercolor, 54 mm diameter, for card; signed "KG."

157 Two Marcus Ward & Co. greeting cards, each 95 x 95 mm; "KG" signature reproduced.
    For watercolor originals see number 156.

158* Young girl in bonnet, with birds and goldenrod. Ink and watercolor, circular border in pencil, 60 mm diameter, for card.
    In pencil at bottom: "to FL [Frederick Locker] from KG."

159 Uncut sheet of four greeting cards with verses, 290 x 220 mm overall; "KG" signature reproduced.
    For watercolor original of "Golden Rod" see number 158. Note pin holes for aid in registration.

160 Two greeting cards with verses, printed by Charles Goodall and Sons, mounted on thick card stock, gilt bevelled edges, each 110 x 80 mm; "KG" and "Kate Greenaway" signatures in facsimile. On

136 c

136 d

verso: "the 'Kate Greenaway' Series No. 501. Goodall Trade Mare [sic]."
One card signed "F.L.-L." [Frederick Locker-Lampson].

161 Four New Year and Christmas greeting cards, printed by Charles Goodall and Sons, mounted on thick card stock, gilt bevelled edges, oblong, two cards 88 x 181 mm, one 76 x 185 mm: "KG" and "Kate Greenaway" signatures in facsimile. On verso: "the 'Kate Greenaway' Series No. 504. Goodall Trade Mare [sic]."
One card signed "F.L.-L." [Frederick Locker-Lampson].

162 Four reward-of-merit cards with gold borders, two cards 65 x 50 mm, two 50 x 65 mm.
Unsigned reproductions of four different illustrations by Kate Greenaway, each of three children in red coats.

163* Doll's greatcoat, brown felt with gilt buttons. 23 cm.
Similar to that worn by the young coachman with crop in hand pictured on a Marcus Ward & Co. greeting card with "KG" signature reproduced, shown here with the coat.

164 Metal button, marked on back "T.W. & W.," "H M," and "Paris Breveté," 18 mm diameter.
After the illustration in *Under the window* for the verse "'Shall I sing,' says the lark," shown with a trade card reproducing the same design in an advertisement for Osborne & Co.'s Crockery Warehouse, West Lynn.

165 Metal button, 31 mm diameter.
After the illustration of the trumpeter in *Under the window* for the verse "Pipe thee high and pipe thee low."

138

150

149

147

126

164

163

148

146

99

SUMMARY REGISTER OF THE FRANCES HOOPER
KATE GREENAWAY COLLECTION

ORIGINAL ARTWORKS

WATERCOLORS

Thirty-three drawings for published illustrations, including
- For *Marigold garden*
  - Cover layout sketch
  - Half-title illustration
  - "Blue shoes"
  - "First arrivals"
  - "When you and I grow up"
  - "Willy and his sister"
  - "Mammas and babies"
- For *Book of games*
  - "Puss in the corner"
  - "Touch wood"
  - "Battledore & shuttlecock"
  - "Hunt the slipper"
  - "Frog in the middle"
- For *Language of flowers*
  - Title page
  - Cherubs carrying a basket of roses
  - Woman and two children receiving alms
- For her almanacks
  - 1887 "March"
  - 1888 "January"
  - "February"
  - 1891 title page
  - "December"
  - 1892 "Autumn"
  - "January"
  - "March"
  - "April"
  - "May"
- For *Little Ann*
  - The field daisy
- For "Beating the bounds"
  - "Ready for the march"
  - "The beadle leads the procession."

Set of three children's heads for cards.

Two tailpieces.

Four portraits, including
  Frederick Locker-Lampson
  Maud Locker-Lampson
  Oliver Locker-Lampson.

Twelve sketches and studies, including
  Two for illustrated verses (unpublished)
  Procession presented to Ruskin, at one time in the possession of Vita Sackville-West.

Fourteen drawings not identified as published, including two processions presented to Ruskin.

Seven large landscapes and scenes, including
  Three Surrey cottage scenes
  "The sailor's wife."

DRAWINGS AND SKETCHES

Seventeen pen drawings, including
  For *The English spelling-book*
    Girl with a torn frock
    Seated mother with a young child and a book
    Child leaning against a fence in moonlight
    Two children on a fence looking at the moon
    Toddler sitting on a stool with bowl and spoon
    Child in nightcap with a loaf of bread
    Two boys consoling a playmate in tears.

Seventy-three pencil sketches, including layouts, mostly for *Marigold garden*, some for almanacks and *Language of flowers*, some not used.

Three small envelopes decorated with watercolor sketches (topiary, flowers and birds), one addressed "Oswald. Dickinson. Esq.," two to Violet Dickinson.

Crayon layout for an almanack, not used.

Four pencil drawings in morocco-backed case, including one for *Fors clavigera*.

Two pencil sketches for bookplate of Violet Dickinson.

Layout sketch for bookplate of Sarah, possibly Sarah Nickson, not used.

Three sketches, authenticity questionable.

Pen sketch by Randolph Caldecott in the manner of Kate Greenaway.

COLLECTED ITEMS

Six sketchbooks, some with watercolors, including one with pencil studies of an alphabet, one of plans for books and drawings, and one from Coniston.

Volume of "Original drawings... for The Christmas Box" containing layout designs and suggestions of contents for a proposed publication, with autograph covering letter to Edmund Evans.

Red morocco Arlington Manor guestbook in slipcase with double title-page illustration in watercolor and pen by Kate Greenaway.

Two volumes of "Original drawings by Miss Kate Greenaway" containing 107 watercolor, pen-and-ink, and pencil drawings. Include drawings for illustrations and tailpieces published in books and magazines.

Volume of "Original drawings by Kate Greenaway" containing mostly pencil drawings, sketches and layouts. Includes material for bookplates, cards and magazines. Bookplate of Frederick Locker on inside front cover.

Volume of spurious material with "Original drawings and manuscript—Kate Greenaway" on spine.

PRINTS AND REPRODUCTIONS

Intaglio (display?) woodblock of cover illustration for *The English spelling-book.*

Three suites of relief woodblocks for illustrations in *Marigold garden,* each suite containing one key block and either four or five color blocks
"First arrivals"
"Willy and his sister"
"In an apple tree."

Two engraved prints (one colored) of "Miss Primrose."

Two leaves of color proofs for *The queen of the pirate isle.*

Four proofs of bookplates, one each for Frederick Locker, Hannah Jane Locker-Lampson, Oliver Stillingfleet Locker-Lampson and Vera Evelyn Samuel.

Two proofs of tailpiece for *London lyrics.*

Three full-page illustrations from *Illustrated London news.*

Various illustrated book wrappers and envelopes, pages from magazines and books (some uncut).

Eight bookplates.

Three slipcases and one bound volume containing cards, menus, memorials, calendars, and other illustrated items.

Various cards and other illustrated items, including unmounted and uncut illustrations for cards, some without letterpress, invitations to Greenaway exhibitions, trade cards and reward-of-merit cards.

APPLIED DESIGN

Doll's leghorn hat from the late nineteenth century, in the Greenaway mode.

Doll's coat from the Greenaway period, after one of her designs.

Eight metal buttons with designs after Greenaway illustrations.

Recent fabric with design after Greenaway alphabet illustrations, made into apron.

Sample of wallpaper after a Greenaway design.

Various modern notecards, cards, stickers, bookplates, etc., with facsimile reproductions of Greenaway illustrations.

BOOKS AND ARTICLES

BY KATE GREENAWAY (Listed alphabetically by substantive title, the almanacks grouped together in one chronological arrangement)

A apple pie. London, New York, George Routledge and Sons, [1886].

A apple pie. London, New York, Frederick Warne & Co., [n.d.].

A apple pie. An old fashioned alphabet book. [New York, Merrimack Publishing Co., n.d.].
    Two copies; variant printings.

Almanack for 1883. London, New York, George Routledge and Sons, [1882].
    Seven copies, including presentation copy with original Greenaway drawing; variant bindings, one unbound, untrimmed and incomplete.

Almanach de...pour 1883. Paris, Librairie Hachette et Cie, [1882].

Almanack for 1884. London, New York, George Routledge and Sons, [1883].
    Six copies, one signed by Greenaway; variant bindings.

Almanack for 1885. London, New York, George Routledge and Sons, [1884].
    Six copies; variant bindings.

Almanack for 1886. London, New York, George Routledge & Sons, [1885].
    Five copies, including presentation copy with original Greenaway drawing; variant bindings.

Almanach de...pour 1886. Paris, Librairie Hachette et Cie, [1885].

Almanack for 1887 by... [London], George Routledge & Sons, [1886].
    Four copies, including a presentation copy with original Greenaway drawing; variant bindings.

Almanach de...pour 1887. [Paris], Librairie Hachette et Cie, [1886].

Almanack for 1888. [London], George Routledge & Sons, [1887].
    Three copies, including two presentation copies, one with original Greenaway drawing; variant bindings.

Almanach de...1888. [Paris], Hachette et Cie, [1887].

Almanack for 1889. London, Glasgow, New York, George Routledge and Sons, [1888].
    Three copies, including two presentation copies, one with original Greenaway drawing; variant bindings.

Almanach de...1889. Paris, Librairie Hachette et Cie, [1888].

Almanack for 1890. [London], George Routledge & Sons, [1889].
    Three copies, including a presentation copy with original Greenaway drawing; variant bindings.

Almanach de...1890. [Paris], Librairie Hachette et Cie, [1889].

Almanack for 1891. [London], George Routledge & Sons, Limited, [1890].
    Four copies, including a presentation copy with original Greenaway drawing; variant bindings.

Almanach de...pour 1891. Paris, Librairie Hachette et Cie, [1890].

...Almanack for 1892. [London], George Routledge & Sons, Limited, [1891].
Three copies, including two presentation copies with original Greenaway drawings; variant bindings.

Almanach de...pour 1892. Paris, Librairie Hachette et Cie, [1891].

...Almanack for 1893. [London], George Routledge & Sons, [1892].
Four copies, including two presentation copies with original Greenaway drawings; variant bindings.

Almanach de...pour 1893. Paris, Librairie Hachette et Cie, [1892].

...Almanack for 1894. [London], George Routledge & Sons, Limited, [1893].
Three copies; variant bindings.

...Almanack for 1895. [London], George Routledge & Sons, Limited, [1894].
Five copies, including a presentation copy; one unbound and incomplete.

Almanach de...pour 1895. Paris, Librairie Hachette et Cie, [1894].

Almanack for 1924. London, New York, Frederick Warne & Co., Ltd., [1923].
Illustrations from *Almanack for 1883* with text for 1924.

Almanack for 1925 by... [London], Frederick Warne & Co., Ltd., [1924?].
Two copies. Illustrations from *Almanack for 1887* with text for 1925.

...Almanack for 1927. [London], Frederick Warne & Co., Ltd., [1926].
Illustrations from *Almanack for 1891* with text for 1927.

Almanack for 1928. [London], Frederick Warne & Co., [1927].
Illustrations from *Almanack for 1894* with text for 1928.

Almanack for 1883 (–1894, 1897).
Boxed set of first editions for the years 1883, 1884 (two variant bindings), 1885, 1886, 1887, 1888, 1889, 1890, 1891 (English text with the cover for the French edition), 1892, 1893, 1894, 1897; variant bindings.

Alphabet. London, New York, George Routledge & Sons, [1885?].
Four copies; variant bindings.

...Alphabet. London, New York, Frederick Warne & Co., [n.d.].

...Alphabet. [New York, Merrimack Publishing Corp., n.d.].

Am Fenster... Die deutsche text von Kathe Freiligrath-Kroeker. Munich, Theodor Stroefer, [1880].

...Birthday book for children... London, George Routledge and Sons, [1881].
Four copies, including two presentation copies; variant bindings.

...Birthday book for children. London, New York, Frederick Warne & Co., [n.d.].
Four copies; variant bindings.

...Book of games. London, Glasgow, Manchester and New York, George Routledge & Sons, [1889].
Two copies; variant bindings.

Kate Greenaway pictures from originals presented by her to John Ruskin and other personal friends (hitherto unpublished). With an appreciation by H. M. Cundall. London, New York, Frederick Warne and Co., 1921.
Three copies.

Language of flowers. London, George Routledge and Sons, [1884].
Seven copies; variant bindings.

Language of flowers. London, New York, Frederick Warne & Co., Ltd., [n.d.].

Language of flowers. New York, Avenel Books [n.d.].

La lanterne magique par J. Levoisin. Avec les dessins de... Paris, Librairie Hachette et Cie, [n.d.].
French translation of *Under the window.*

Little men and women from the pages of Kate Greenaway. New York, F.A.R. Gallery, [1946].

Marigold garden. London, New York, George Routledge and Sons, [1885].
Four copies, including a presentation copy with original pen sketch.

Marigold garden. London, New York, Frederick Warne & Co., [n.d.].
Five copies; variant printings.

Mother Goose or the old nursery rhymes[.] Illustrated by... London and New York, George Routledge and Sons, [1881].
Two copies, one including watercolor copies of illustrations on half-title and title-pages.

Mother Goose or the old nursery rhymes[.] Illustrated by... London, New York, Frederick Warne and Co., [n.d.].
Ten copies; variant bindings, variant printings.

Mother Goose or the old nursery rhymes[.] Illustrated by... [New York, Merrimack Publishing Co., n.d.].

My coloring book. New York, Merrimack, [n.d.].

Under the window. London, New York, George Routledge & Sons, [1878].
Four copies, including one with two original watercolors; variant bindings, variant printings.

Under the window. New York, McLoughlin Bros., [1880?].

Under the window. London, New York, Frederick

Warne & Co., [n.d.].
Three copies; variant bindings, variant printings.

BY OTHERS, ILLUSTRATED BY KATE GREENAWAY

Browning, Robert. *The pied piper of Hamelin...* With 35 illustrations by... London, Glasgow, New York, George Routledge and Sons, [1883].
Two copies, including presentation copy; variant printings, including first issue of first edition.

Browning, Robert. *The pied piper of Hamelin.* London, New York, Frederick Warne and Co., [n.d.].
Two copies, variant printings.

Browning, Robert. *The pied piper of Hamelin...* New York, Merrimack Publishing Corporation, [n.d.].

Campbell, Gertrude Elizabeth (Blood). *Topo, a tale about English children in Italy...* With 44 pen-and-ink illustrations by... London, Marcus Ward & Co., 1878.
Includes three original pencil sketches signed by Greenaway.

Cresswell, Beatrix F. *The royal progress of King Pepito...* illustrated by... London, Brighton, Society for Promoting Christian Knowledge; New York, E. & J. B. Young & Co.; [1889].
Two copies, variant bindings.

Ellice, Robert, ed. *Songs for the nursery...* With illustrations by Kate Greenaway, Miss Bennett, Robert Barnes, etc. London, W. Mack, [1884].

Foster, Myles Birket. *A day in a child's life.* Illustrated by... London, New York, George Routledge and Sons, [1881].

Haile, Ellen. *The two gray girls and their opposite neighbors.* New York, London, Paris, Cassell & Co., Ltd., [1880].

Harte, Bret. *The queen of the pirate isle.* Illustrated by... London, Chatto and Windus, [1886].

Jeune, Margaret Dyne (Symons). *My school days in Paris.* London, Griffith and Farran, 1871.

Locker, Frederick. *London lyrics.* London, [Chiswick Press], 1881.
First issue of first edition, with both original and altered frontispiece plates by Randolph Caldecott.

Mavor, William Fordyce. *The English spelling-book...* Illustrated by... London, New York, George Routledge and Sons, 1885.
Two copies.

The quiver of love, a collection of valentines, ancient & modern. With illustrations in colors from drawings by Walter Crane and K. Greenaway. London, Belfast, Marcus Ward, 1876.

Routledge's Christmas number [1882]. London, New York, George Routledge & Sons, 1882.

Ruskin, John, ed. *Dame Wiggins of Lee, and her seven wonderful cats.* Orpington, George Allen, 1885.

Ruskin, John. *Fors clavigera.* Orpington, George Allen, 1883-1884.
Letters 91st through 96th, September 1883—Christmas 1884. Two copies each of letters 91st, 93rd and 95th.

Russell, Mary Annette (Beauchamp). *The April baby's book of tunes...* London, Macmillan and Co.; New York, the Macmillan Co.; 1900.

St. Nicholas[.] Scribner's illustrated magazine for girls and boys, vol. 6, no. 6, April 1879.

[Selous, Henry Courtney.] *The children of the parsonage...* with illustrations by... London, Griffith and Farran, 1874.

Taylor, Jane and Ann Taylor. *Little Ann and other poems* by... Illustrated by... London, New York, George Routledge & Sons, [1883].
Five copies, including two presentation copies, one with signed original watercolor.

Toy Land, Trot's journey, and other poems and stories. Illustrated by... New York, R. Worthington, [1879].

Weatherly, Frederick Edward, ed. *The illustrated children's birthday-book...* With illustrations by Kate Crauford, Kate Greenaway, Robert Barnes, Mrs. Staples, Miss Bennett, Miss Thomas, etc. London, W. Mack [1882].
Two copies; variant bindings.

BY OR ILLUSTRATED BY ASSOCIATES OF KATE GREENAWAY

Birrell, Augustine. *Frederick Locker-Lampson, a character sketch...* New York, Charles Scribner's Sons, 1920.

Bloomfield, Robert. *The horkey...* With illustrations by George Cruikshank. London, Macmillan and Co., 1882.

Dobson, Austin. *De libris, prose & verse.* London, Macmillan and Co., Ltd., 1908.

Doyle, Richard. *Manners and customs of ye Englyshe...* [London], Bradbury & Evans, [1849].
Inscribed to Kate Greenaway from Frederick Locker with caricature of Locker and Greenaway.

Evans, Edmund. *The illuminated Scripture text book.* London, Frederick Warne & Co.; New York, Scribner, Welford, and Armstrong; [1872?].

Evans, Edmund. *The reminiscences of...* edited and introduced by Ruari McLean. Oxford, Clarendon Press, [1967].

Frank, Ernst. *16 Duettinen aus "Am Fenster" in Bildern and Versen von Kate Greenaway...Op. 14.* Leipzig, Fr. Kistner, [1881?].

Ruskin, John. *The art of England.* Orpington, George Allen, 1884.

Ruskin, John. *Lectures on art...* Orpington, George Allen, 1887.

> Inscribed to Kate Greenaway from John Ruskin.

Ruskin, John. *Modern painters II...* Orpington, George Allen, 1883. Two volumes.

Ruskin, John. *Praeterita.* Orpington, George Allen, 1886. Two volumes.

Ruskin, John. *The seven lamps of architecture* ... London, Smith, Elder and Co., 1849.

> Includes ALS from Ruskin.

Swinburne, Algernon Charles. *A letter by...on learning that Kate Greenaway had died.* [Introduction by John S. Mayfield.] [Jacksonville, Florida], John S. Mayfield, 1944.

> Three copies; variant coloring in title-page vignette.

RELATED AND REFERENCE WORKS

Brewer, Frances J., comp. *The John S. Newberry Gift Collection of Kate Greenaway presented to the Detroit Public Library.* Detroit, Friends of the Detroit Public Library, 1959.

Durer, Albrecht. *The construction of Roman letters.* Cambridge, Dunster House [Bruce Rogers], 1924.

Engen, Rodney K. *Kate Greenaway.* London, Academy Editions; New York, Harmony Books; [1976].

Ernest, Edward, ed. *The Kate Greenaway treasury.* Introduction by Ruth Hill Viguers... Cleveland, New York, World Publishing Co., [1967].

> Two copies.

France, Anatole. *Girls and boys, scenes from the country and the town...* New York, Duffield & Co., 1917.

Johnson, Diana. *Fantastic illustration and design in Britain, 1850-1930.* Providence, Museum of Art, Rhode Island School of Design, [1979].

King, Arthur. *The house of Warne, one hundred years of publishing.* London, New York, Frederick Warne & Co., Ltd., [1965].

Moore, Anne Carrol. *A century of Kate Greenaway.* New York, London, Frederick Warne & Company, Inc., [1946].

> Two copies.

Pierpont Morgan Library. *Early children's books and their illustration.* New York, The Pierpont Morgan Library; Boston, David R. Godine; [1975].

Salzmann, Christian Gotthilf. *Elements of morality, for the use of children...* London, printed by J. Crowder, for J. Johnson, 1791. Three volumes.

Spielmann, Marion Harry and G. S. Layard. *Kate Greenaway...* London, Adam and Charles Black, 1905.

Two copies, Numbers 10 and 20 of the limited edition, each signed by John Greenaway and including an original sketch by Kate Greenaway.

Spielmann, Marion Harry. *Kate Greenaway, sixteen examples in colour of the artist's work...* London, A. & C. Black, 1911.

Stevenson, Robert Louis. *A child's garden of verses...* New York, Oxford University Press, 1947.

Thompson, Susan Ruth, comp. *Kate Greenaway, a catalogue of the Kate Greenaway Collection, Rare Book Room, Detroit Public Library.* Detroit, Wayne State University Press, 1977.

Waugh, Ida. *Holly berries* with original illustrations by... [New York, Merrimack Publishing Corporation, n.d.].

GREENAWAY RECORDS AND PAPERS

MANUSCRIPT

Autobiographical journal, text in pencil, with sketches. One volume, softbound, *ca.* 110 pp., 22.5 x 18 cm.

CORRESPONDENCE

Most of Kate Greenaway's letters in the Collection were written from one of three addresses: 11, Pemberton Gardens, Holloway, N., London; 50, Frognal, Hampstead, N.W.; or 39, Frognal, Hampstead, N.W. Some others she posted from places where she regularly spent her holidays, such as Witley, Surrey.

To Violet Dickinson, 1896-1898: 17 letters, 8vo, *ca.* 15.5 x 10 cm.; 33 letter fragments, various sizes.

To Austin Dobson, 1880-1883 and "New Years Eve" (1885 or after): ten letters, 8vo, *ca.* 15.5 x 10 cm.

From Austin Dobson, 1874-1897: 14 letters, 8vo, *ca.* 15.5 x 10 cm; five letters, note cards, 9 x 12 cm.

From Mrs. Austin Dobson, 1874: one letter, 8vo, *ca.* 15.5 x 10 cm.

To Edmund Evans, 1890: one letter, 8vo, *ca.* 15.5 x 10 cm. In a bound volume entitled "Original drawings by Kate Greenaway for 'The Christmas Box' with autograph letter," pasted on the recto and verso sides of the seventh leaf.

To Miss Lily Evans, 1882-1891: five letters, 8vo. *ca.* 15.5 x 10 cm.

From John Greenaway, 1920: one letter, 8vo, *ca.* 15.5 x 10 cm.

To Mr. or Mrs. Locker (Locker-Lampson): 18 letters, one note, most *ca.* 15.5 x 10 cm.

To Rev. W. J. Loftie, 1880: one letter, 8vo, *ca.* 15.5 x 10 cm.

To Hon. Gerald Ponsonby, 1893 and "Last Day of May—Dreadful" (*ca.* 1895): two letters, 8vo, *ca.* 15.5 x 10 cm.

To Lady Maria Ponsonby, 1893-1901: 19 letters, 8vo, *ca.* 15.5 x 10 cm.

> All of these were written from 39, Frognal, Hampstead, N.W.

To John Ruskin, 1885-1900: 334 letters, 8vo, *ca.* 15.5 x 10 cm.; 6 postcards.

> Of these letters, 67 (written from 2 Sept. 1890 to 21 July 1891, and from 12 March 1894 to 17 July 1895) are on stationery bordered in black. The others are on either blue or white paper.

To Mrs. Arthur (Joanie) Severn, 1883-1901: 236 letters, 8vo, *ca.* 15.5 x 10 cm.; 6 postcards.

Miscellaneous, 1879-1899: 12 letters; one postcard; one autographed photo-postcard.

> The correspondents include: Miss Mary Anderson, Miss Downing, Edmund Evans, Wilfred Evans, Mrs. Hirshall(?), Lady Jeune, Mrs. W. J. Loftie, Miss Mordora(?), Lady Dorothy Nevill, Miss Prance, Lily Severn, Mrs. Norman Shaw, Miss Shaw, Mr. S. Van de Velee, and Victoria, Crown Princess of Germany (photo-postcard).

RECEIPTS

From Edmund Evans, 1880-1897: 70 documents, 24 x 16 cm.

For sales of drawings at and since the 1891 exhibition at the Fine Art Society, London: two documents, 32 x 20 cm. (four pp.), 26 x 21 cm. (one p.).

For sales of drawings at the 1894 exhibition at the Fine Art Society, London: one document, four pp., 32 x 20 cm.

OTHER

Autographs: five separate sheets, one a calling card with an embossed photo of the artist.

Miscellaneous materials pertaining to exhibitions of Greenaway's drawings at the 1891 and 1894 exhibitions at the Fine Art Society, London:

Published catalogues of watercolor exhibits by Greenaway at the Fine Art Society, London: January 1874, one volume, paper wrappers, 12 pp., 21 x 14 cm., annotated. February 1898, one volume, paper wrappers, ten pp., 21 x 14 cm., annotated; two copies.

Photographic portraits of Kate Greenaway: one head-and-shoulders, one half-length.

HOOPER RECORDS AND PAPERS

Correspondence with dealers concerning Kate Greenaway items, including receipts.

Correspondence with other collectors, public and private, concerning Kate Greenaway.

Typescript lists of other Kate Greenaway collections.

Notes on items in the Collection, including information on provenance.

Partial register of the Collection, particularly the letters, prepared by Laurence Gomme (index cards).

Annotated sale catalogues listing Greenaway-related items, many now in the Collection.

Working manuscripts of lecture on Kate Greenaway given by Frances Hooper on 11 April 1972 at the Woman's Athletic Club of Chicago.

Two photographs of Frances Hooper with dogs.

Text set in 10 and 8 point Bookman phototype and printed offset on Hunt-watermarked Curtis No. 2 paper by Davis & Warde, Inc., Pittsburgh

Direct color separations by Pittsburgh Atlas Photoengraving Co., Pittsburgh

Color and halftone printing by Davis & Warde, Inc.

Black-and-white photography by Alan Cherin Studios, Pittsburgh

Bound by Penn State Bookbinding Co., Pittsburgh

Designed by Rob Roy Kelly, assisted by Henry M. Yocco and John Sotirakis